THE KNOWLEDGE MANAGEMENT TOOLKIT

ISBN 0-13-009224-X

Box	Step
1	Analyze the Existing Infrastructure
2	Align Knowledge Management and Business Strategy
3	Design the Knowledge Management Infrastructure
4	Audit Existing Knowledge Assets and Systems
5	Design the Knowledge Management Team
6	Create the Knowledge Management Blueprint
7	Develop the Knowledge Management System
8	Deploy, Using the Results-driven Incremental Methodology
9	Manage Change, Culture and Reward Stuctures
10	Evaluate Performance, Measure ROI, and Incrementally Refine the KMS

PHASE 1: INFRASTRUCTURE EVALUATION

PHASE 2: KM SYSTEM ANALYSIS, DESIGN AND DEVELOPMENT

PHASE 3: DEPLOYMENT

PHASE 4: EVALUATION

THE KNOWLEDGE MANAGEMENT TOOLKIT

ORCHESTRATING IT, STRATEGY, AND KNOWLEDGE PLATFORMS

SECOND EDITION

AMRIT TIWANA

PRENTICE HALL PTR
UPPER SADDLE RIVER, NJ 07458
WWW.PHPTR.COM

Library of Congress Cataloging-in-Publication Data

Tiwana, Amrit, —
    The knowledge management toolkit: orchestrating IT, strategy, and knowledge platforms/Amrit Tiwana.—2nd ed.
        p.   cm.
    Includes bibliographical references and index.
    ISBN 0-13-009224-X
    1. Knowledge management.   I. Title.
    HD30.2.T59 2002
    658.4'038--dc21

                                                    2002025298

Editorial/production supervision: *Kerry Reardon*
Composition and interior design: *Laurel Road Publishing Services*
Cover design director: *Jerry Votta*
Cover designer: *Anthony Gemmellaro*
Art director: *Gail Cocker-Bogusz*
Manufacturing manager: *Alexis Heydt-Long*
Manufacturing buyer: *Maura Zaldivar*
Acquisitions editor: *Victoria Jones*
Editorial assistant: *Michelle Vincenti*
Marketing manager: *Debby VanDijk*
Project coordinator: *Anne R. Garcia*

© 2002, 2000 Pearson Education, Inc.
Publishing as Prentice Hall PTR
Upper Saddle River, NJ 07458

Prentice Hall books are widely used by corporations and government agencies for training, marketing, and resale.

For information regarding corporate and government bulk discounts please contact:
Corporate and Government Sales (800) 382-3419 or corpsales@pearsontechgroup.com

Printed in the United States of America

ISBN 0-13-009224-X

Text printed in the United States

11th Printing   February 2008
Pearson Education LTD.
Pearson Education Australia PTY, Limited
Pearson Education Singapore, Pte. Ltd.
Pearson Education North Asia Ltd.
Pearson Education Canada, Ltd.
Pearson Educación de Mexico, S.A. de C.V.
Pearson Education–Japan
Pearson Education Malaysia, Pte. Ltd.

Credits for Chapter-Opening Quotes
Chapter 3: Simon, H.A. (1988). "Managing in an information-rich world." In Y.K. Sketty and V.M. Buehler (eds.), *Competing Through Productivity and Quality.* Cambridge, MA: Productivity Press. **Chapter 5:** Foreword by Arthur C. Clarke, "Intelligent Software Agents" by Richard Murch, Tony Johnson, Prentice Hall (1998). **Chapter 6:** "What Life Means to Einstein: An Interview by George Sylvester Viereck," for the October 26, 1929 issue of *The Saturday Evening Post.*
Chapter 8: "The Speaker's Electronic Reference Collection," AApex Software, 1994.
Chapter 9: Rita Mae Brown. **Chapter 11:** From THE ART OF WAR by Sun Tzu, translated by Samuel B. Griffith. Translation copyright ©1963 by Oxford University Press, Inc. Used by permission of Oxford University Press, Inc. **Chapter 12:** As quoted by Richard Murch and Tony Johnson in "Intelligent Software Agents: Prentice Hall (1998).
Chapter14: L. Lodish, "Vaguely Right Approach to Sales Force Automation," *Harvard Business Review,* 52, 119–124 (1979).

To Sherry

BRIEF CONTENTS

CONTENTS

PART I   THE RUBBER MEETS THE ROAD

PART II   THE ROAD AHEAD: IMPLEMENTING KNOWLEDGE MANAGEMENT

CHAPTER 4   THE 10-STEP KNOWLEDGE MANAGEMENT ROAD MAP   67

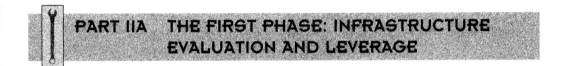

PART IIA   THE FIRST PHASE: INFRASTRUCTURE EVALUATION AND LEVERAGE

PART IIB   THE SECOND PHASE: KM SYSTEM ANALYSIS, DESIGN, AND DEVELOPMENT

PART IIC THE THIRD PHASE: DEPLOYMENT

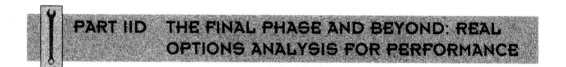

PART IID   THE FINAL PHASE AND BEYOND: REAL OPTIONS ANALYSIS FOR PERFORMANCE

PART III SIDE ROADS: APPENDICES (On the CD-ROM)

PREFACE

Real knowledge is to know the extent of one's ignorance
—Confucius

The Knowledge Management Toolkit provides a strategic road map for implementing knowledge management (KM) in your company. This book rests on two assumptions. First, that there is no silver bullet. Second, the value of a business's knowledge is determined by its masterful application.

FEATURES IN THIS EDITION

Following the popularity of the first edition, this edition has an entirely rewritten chapter on strategy; real-options analyses have been added for KM evaluation; the notion of knowledge platforms is pervasively emphasized; the role of digital peer-to-peer networks is discussed; several new cases have been added; and the distinction between knowledge integration and transfer runs deep. Several other features of this edition are noteworthy. For starters, all figures are made electronically available on the CD-ROM. In addition, the entire appendix, including the entire KM assessment kit, is now digitized on the CD-ROM. The entire bibliography is also provided in electronic form.

How to Use This Book

In spite of the hyperlinked, web-like world we live in, I highly recommend that you go against that notion and read this book in a linear fashion: Begin with Chapter 1 and continue through Chapter 4. Once you reach Chapter 4, if you have a strong reason to jump to any other chapter, do so. Chapters 5 through 14 make the most sense if you read them *after* you've read Chapter 4. The reason for this recommendation is simple: Each of Chapters 5 through 14 represent one step of the 10-step road map introduced in Chapter 4. The 10-step road map appears at the beginning of each of Chapters 5 through 14, with details of the current step

---

[a]The *silver bullet* is a term rooted in folklore of the American Civil War. It supposedly emerged from the practice of encouraging a patient who was to undergo field surgery to bite down hard on a lead bullet "to divert the mind from pain and screaming" (*American Slang*, Harper and Row: New York, 1986).

highlighted in the respective chapters. Every chapter except Chapter 1 ends with a "lessons learned" section that summarizes the key points covered in that chapter. This might be useful as a checklist when this book is not gathering dust on your bookshelf.

Many of the software tools mentioned in the book are included on the companion CD-ROM. Most, though not all, tools on the CD-ROM have feature restrictions of some type. They are not here to give you entire software suites to help you cut down the expense of building a KM system or to charge you an extra ten dollars for a CD-ROM that cost only twenty cents to produce. These tools are here because I believe that they add value and help you make sense by seeing the technologies that we talk about in the pages that follow.

HOW THIS BOOK IS ORGANIZED

Table P–1 summarizes the organization of this book. An additional table in Chapter 4 (Table 4–1) leads you through the individual phases and steps of the KM road map. The techniques described in this book need not always be applied across the organization; they can be applied at the level of communities, business units, or departments.

Table P-1 How This Book Is Organized

Chapter	What Is Covered
PART I: INTRODUCTION	
Chapter 1	Introduction, KM's value proposition.
Chapter 2	Imperatives for KM, its need, potential business benefits of KM.
Chapter 3	How to make the transition from IM to KM, topologies of knowledge, differences between IT tools and KM tools, why KM is difficult to implement.
PART II: THE ROAD AHEAD	
Chapter 4	The 10-step roadmap for implementing KM in your company.
PART IIA: LEVERAGING YOUR EXISTING INFRASTRUCTURE	
Chapter 5	How to build a knowledge platform based on your existing IT infrastructure.
Chapter 6	How to align business strategy and KM in *your* company.

Table P-1 How This Book Is Organized (cont.)

Chapter	What is covered
PART IIB: THE SECOND PHASE: KM SYSTEM ANALYSIS, DESIGN, AND DEVELOPMENT	
Chapter 7	How to lay the infrastructural foundations of your company's knowledge platform, choose the collaborative platform, the seven layers of the KM architecture.
Chapter 8	Audit, analyze, and identify existing knowledge assets in your company.
Chapter 9	How to design a right-sized and well-balanced KM team.
Chapter 10	How to create a KM blueprint customized for your company and robust enough to be "future-proof."
Chapter 11	How to develop the KM system, understand how it can be integrated with existing technology standards.
PART IIC: DEPLOYMENT	
Chapter 12	How to deploy the system using the results-driven incrementalism (RDI) methodology, select pilot projects, maximize payoffs, and avoid common pitfalls.
Chapter 13	Understand the reward structures, cultural change, and leadership needed for making KM successful; in your company, decide whether you need a CKO or equivalent manager.
PART IID: REAL-OPTIONS EVALUATION	
Chapter 14	Decide which metric(s) to use for KM in your company—real-option analyses, balanced scorecards, quality function deployment, Tobin's q—and how to use it, arrive at lean metrics that help you calculate ROI on your KM project.
PART III: SIDE ROADS: APPENDICES	
Appendix A	The KM assessment kit and CD-ROM forms.
Appendix B	Alternative schemes for structuring the front end.
Appendix C	Software tools.

ASSUMPTIONS ABOUT YOUR COMPANY

There are certain assumptions that I make about you as a reader of this book. I would hope that most, if not all, of these are true if this book (which is written with these assumptions about you as a reader in mind) is to help you and your company with implementing knowledge management.

WHAT THIS BOOK IS NOT ABOUT

Let me first explain what this book is not about and what it is that distinguishes this book's approach. This book is:

- *Not about trends*: Forget trends and forecasts about how businesses are disintermediated, organic, flattened, and T-shaped. This book is not about trends. Predictions, as all research, weather forecasts, and stock markets suggest, is rarely an accurate predictor of the future. What you'll learn in this book will probably still apply when organizations supposedly become X-shaped, intermediated, or inorganic. Rather than being a trend in itself, this book will help you benefit from those trends.

- *Not about new vocabulary:* This book is not out to invent new buzzwords. Buzzwords come and go; KM is here to stay.

- *Not about the silver bullet*: This book is not the silver bullet for KM and does not claim to be one. It is not about trademarked methodologies that promise the world but scarcely deliver a village.

- *Not about analogies*: Analogies can sometimes be helpful but can also be very misleading. Analogies are an effective way of communicating strategies, but a *very* hazardous way of analyzing them. Remember that the road map is not a "shrink-wrapped" methodology. Nowhere in the following pages will you find a discussion about how KM is like ecology, bungee jumping, war, or making love. The same holds true of the cases discussed in this book. Cases are instances of strategies, not strategies themselves.

- *Not about* my *opinion*: Opinions can be wrong. This book is built on lessons learned from years of cumulative research spanning several countries and hundreds of companies, big and small, in diverse industries. Wherever there is an opinion, I'll tell you it's an opinion, and that opinion is not necessarily a fact.

Think of this book as a conversation between you and me. I would love to hear your comments, suggestions, questions, criticisms, and reactions. Feel free to e-mail me at Amrit_Tiwana@bus.emory.edu.

Amrit Tiwana
Atlanta

ACKNOWLEDGMENTS

Robert Dubin pointed out as early as 1976 (*Theory Building in Applied Areas*, Rand McNally: Chicago, 17–26) that there is probably a five- to ten-year period before a theoretical model becomes *fashionable* in the real world. I owe much intellectual debt to Ikujiro Nonaka, Karl Weick, Tom Davenport, Robert Grant, Bob Buckman, Peter Drucker, Michael Zack, Andrew Inkpen, Wanda Orlikowski, Marco Iansiti, Karl Weick, and James Brian Quinn, who have long influenced my own thinking. It is on the shoulders of these giants that this book stands.

Among the many people in the industry I wish to thank for their support are: Elaine Viscosi at Intranetics, Inc. for permission to use a sample intranet deployment (described as Urban Motors in Chapter 9); Ed Yourdon of The Cutter Group; Chuck Sieloff of Hewlett-Packard; Johanna Rothman of Rothman Consulting; Joni Schlender of Plumtree Corporation; Steve Shattuck of Alpha Microsystems; Jean Heminway of Xerox Corporation; Susan Hanley at AMS Inc; Michael Davis of OSIS; Ray Edwards of Lighthouse Consulting; Joni Schlender of Plumtree Software; Harry Collier of Infornotics, England; Jim Eup of Powerway; Mark Turner of the Natural Language Processing Lab at Thomson; Gordon Podolski of Nortel; Jeff Barton of Texas Instruments, for his insightful analysis of this book; Glenn Shimkus of Platinum Technology, Inc.; Rick Dove of ParadigmShift International; Thomas Davenport of Accenture and Babson College; Phil Armour; Mark Montgomery of GWIN; Fanuel Dewever of Newcom, Belgium; Steve Singer of CIO; Gord Podolski of Nortel Networks; Bettina Jetter of MindJet LLC,; Simon Tussler of the Boston Consulting Group; Phil Armour; and others whom I have inadvertently left out.

Foremost, I would like to thank Ashley Bush, who has served as a rare and inimitable intellectual sounding board for the ideas that follow.

I would also like to acknowledge the invaluable support that I have received from my colleagues and friends, including my mentors, Eph McLean and Bala Ramesh, and Mark Keil, Daniel Robey, Arun Rai, Maryam Alavi, Anandhi Bharadwaj, and Vijay Vaishnavi, from whom I have learned more than I can articulate. Thanks are also due to my associates, Smiley and Sharky, without whose help this book would have been a more formidable task. For posterity's sake, this book was written on a Macintosh.

Built on the shoulders of the giants in information systems research, this book is my humble attempt at proving that there is more relevance in the cumulative body of research that comes out of the ivory towers than we usually get credit for.

This book would have been an impossible task without the enthusiasm of my editor, Victoria Jones; my original editor, Miles Williams; and my initial contact at Prentice Hall PTR, Mark Taub. The quality of this book also owes a lot to my technical reviewers, including Corinne Gregory of Data Dimensions, Chuck Fay of FileNet Corporation, and to my anonymous reviewers. The credit for the readability of this book goes largely to my development editor, Mary Lou Nohr, whose insights, arguments, and suggestions helped me see the forest when all I could see were the trees. The credit for the aesthetics and elegant design goes largely to Kerry Reardon.

Most importantly, I would thank my family, for without them this book would have been nothing but a glimmer of an idea, if even that.

ABOUT THE AUTHOR

 AMRIT TIWANA is an assistant professor of Decision and Information Analysis at the Goizueta Business School at Emory University in Atlanta. Dr. Tiwana's consulting and research specializes in helping large businesses strategically deploy digital knowledge management platforms to support innovation-intensive teams. His research has appeared in several journals including *Communications of the ACM, American Programmer, Decision Support Systems, IEEE Internet Computing, Information Systems Journal, Journal of Knowledge Management,* and several international conferences. His work has been translated into French, Chinese, German, Spanish, and Portuguese. Dr. Tiwana holds a Ph.D. in management information systems from the Robinson College of Business at Georgia State University. He is a member of *IEEE, ACM,* and *Academy of Management.*

PART I
THE RUBBER
MEETS THE ROAD

CHAPTER 1
INTRODUCTION

IN THIS CHAPTER

✔ Define knowledge management (KM).

✔ Evaluate KM's value proposition.

✔ Define what KM is not.

✔ Understand whether your company is ready for KM.

AS WE GAIN MORE KNOWLEDGE, WE DO NOT BECOME CERTAIN,
WE BECOME CERTAIN OF MORE.
—AYN RAND

Data. At first we had too little. We asked for more and we got it. Now we have more than we want. Data led to information, but what we were looking for in the first place was knowledge.

As an increasing number of companies now realize that knowledge is their key asset, they want to turn to managing this asset to deliver business results. But where and how do you begin? What is KM's value proposition? What types of companies can actually begin KM? Is it a technology problem or a management problem? What happens to the millions that your company has invested in information technology (IT) if it is replaced by yet another hyped "fix-it-all" technology? Can you build upon existing IT investments? What kinds of people, skills, and organizational structures are necessary to pull it off? How can KM be aligned with your business's strategy? Is there an architecture that you can use? How can you deploy KM in your own company? Are there any business metrics for it? How can you maximize the payoff? Can your small business without deep pockets afford it? How do you know whether your business is ready for it? These are some of the questions that this book will help you answer.

KNOWLEDGE MANAGEMENT: IN SEARCH OF ALCHEMY

KM might be "hot" as of today, but successful managers have always realized its value. Long before terms such as *expert systems, core competencies, best practices, learning organizations*, and *corporate memory* were in vogue, successful businesses knew that their key assets were not its buildings, its market share or its products, but lay in the heads of its people.[1]

KNOWLEDGE AND MANAGEMENT

Forty percent of the U.S. economy is directly attributable to the creation of intellectual capital.[2] As a result, over 10 percent of the gross domestic product (GDP) in the developed countries is being reinvested in knowledge development.[3]

So, what is knowledge? Knowledge is a fluid mix of framed experience, values, contextual information, expert insight, and intuition that provides an environment and framework for evaluating and incorporating new experiences and information. It originates in individual minds but is often embedded in organizational routines, processes, practices, systems, software, and norms.[4]

KM enables the creation, distribution, and exploitation of knowledge to create and retain greater value from core business competencies.[5] KM addresses business problems particular to your business—whether it is creating and delivering innovative products or services; managing and enhancing relationships with customers, partners, and suppliers;[6] or improving work processes. The primary goal of KM in a business context is to facilitate opportunistic application of fragmented knowledge through integration.

5

KNOWLEDGE MANAGEMENT'S VALUE PROPOSITION

The ability of companies to exploit their intangible assets is far more decisive than their ability to exploit their physical assets.[7] As markets shift, uncertainty dominates, technologies proliferate, competitors multiply, and products and services become obsolete rapidly, successful companies are characterized by their ability to create new knowledge consistently,[8] quickly disseminate it, and embody it in their new products and services.[9] The road to harnessing their expertise comes with few shortcuts. Why now? There are eight reasons for this:

1. *Knowledge integration is the engine of economic prosperity.* Knowledge is rapidly displacing capital, monetary prowess, natural resources, and labor as the quintessential economic resource.[10] With shortening product and service life cycles, knowledge integration—internally, and across customer and supplier networks—undergrids companies' ability to ask the right questions. The scarcity of innovative knowledge increases the rewards for turning tacit knowledge into market offerings.[11] Because there can be winners only if there are losers, the better a business gets at this, the higher are its odds of success.[12]

2. *Unpredictable markets necessitate "organized abandonment."* The next critical piece of critical information could take any form—an evolving social trend affecting customer preferences, a new management practice, a nascent technology, or a political or economic development in a remote manufacturing location.[13] KM lets you proactively improvise products,[14,a] get out of projects and product lines that can drag your business down, and get into others that maximize growth potential as radical market shifts threaten to put your business in the wrong place, at the wrong time, or with the wrong product.[b]

3. *KM lets you lead change so that change does not lead you.* Even conventional retailers such as Wal-Mart consider their competence in logistics management—a knowledge-intensive activity—to be their primary driver of business success. By rapidly exploiting and applying fragmented internal and external knowledge, a business can reliably detect emerging windows of opportunity before competitors.[15]

4. *Cross-industry amalgamation is breeding complexity.* Complexity, uncertainty, and ambiguity are the hallmarks of today's production and business systems, irrespective of the nature of business or type of industry. Knowledge management has allowed the likes of Bay Networks, Dell, and Cisco to turn this complexity to their advantage.[16]

5. *Those who forget the past are condemned to repeat it.* Without a way of capturing and integrating past experience, any development process can quickly dissolve into chaos.[17] KM helps leverage past experience by making knowledge about past projects, initiatives, failures, and successes readily accessible. It also enables knowledge-intensive collaboration across individuals, teams, and communities of specialists.

---

[a]Improvisation can also be viewed as a process.

[b]National Semiconductor, an excellent example, closed down its division Cyrix Corporation, the well-known manufacturer of low-end Intel-clone microprocessors in 1999, when it realized that it was pulling the entire company down as it tried to withstand price-based assaults from mighty Intel that had pockets deeper than those of National.

6. *A bridge is needed across the Atlantic.* Not only competitors but suppliers, business partners, and internal offices are increasingly globally distributed. Keeping pace with developing threats or opportunities in other countries is a tedious, time-consuming, and difficult process that KM facilitates.

7. *Tacit knowledge is mobile.* The most valuable knowledge, skills, and competencies in your business reside tacitly between the ears of your employees. As easily as these elements accompany employees home every night, they can also be lured into a competitor's corner office. Tacit knowledge can rarely be fully articulated, yet it can be easily manifested through application, integration, and collaboration.[18] Although KM cannot disembody this knowledge from these processes, it can maximize its productive application for both leading and adapting to turbulent business environments.[19]

8. *Knowledge application requires "water-cooler" and "coffee-machine"* [20] *cultures; IT barely supports sharing.* KM requires an informal culture of sharing that information systems do not inherently support.[21] Knowledge, as artificial intelligence research ironically reminds us, is not about machines but about culture.[22]

KM Platform versus KM System

While the KM system refers to the technology component of what facilitates integration, application, and management of knowledge, a KM platform includes the KM system infrastructure, knowledge management strategy, cultural facets of knowledge work, design of incentive schemes, and measurement and evaluation mechanisms in place. A KM system is therefore a subset of the KM platform.

KM is not compulsory, but neither is survival. The capacity to integrate and apply distributed knowledge to create agility, responsiveness, and adaptivity is now, more then ever, the *only* competitive differentiator. No business—big or small, old or new—can afford to under-invest in building the capacity to harness this last scarce resource.

Recognizing the Writing on the Wall

The recognition that the value of complex products resides not in the factories and buildings used for fabrication but in the minds of people who create them has been pronounced in the business world well before Thorstein Veblen wrote about it in *The Engineers and the Price System.*

Figure 1-1 shows the darling tools of managers as they evolved from the 1950s to the 2000s. Some of these died much-anticipated deaths as fads, and some live till this day. Notably, one consistent and pervasive thread runs through all these—leveraging knowledge, experience, intellectual assets, and their management. And this consistent thread has led businesses to what we now call *knowledge management.*

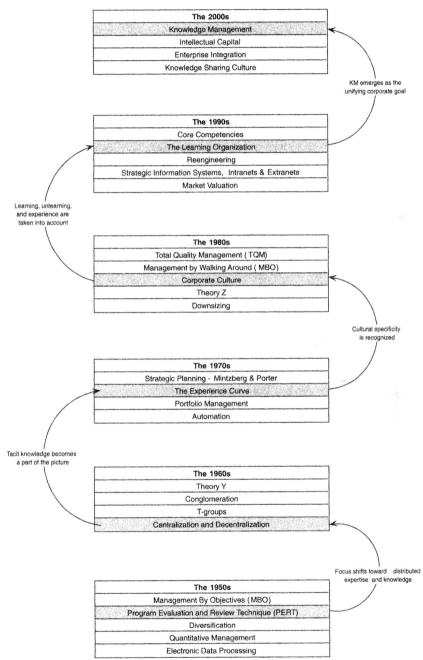

Figure 1-1   Managers' tools through the decades: Knowledge management has been coming since the 1950s.

Under the Magnifying Glass

KM is much more than just technology—a focus that will be evident throughout the rest of this book. Competing on knowledge requires solid grounding in business strategy. Only then can your company effectively prioritize its investments in KM and leave competitors biting the dust off shrinking margins, shorter product development times,[23] and fickle customers.[24]

Who Should Be Pursuing Knowledge Management?

Two types of companies should be pursuing KM. The first type is one that has realized the need to keep up with its competitors and remain a legitimate player in a disruptive marketplace.[25] The second type is one step ahead: It already has the core knowledge necessary. This company realizes that what is innovative knowledge today will be commonplace, core knowledge tomorrow. Such companies are struggling with their ability to keep ahead, not just viably compete.

What Knowledge Management Is Not About

To cleanse you of vendor sales pitches, you must be clear about what KM is *not*.

- *KM is not knowledge engineering.* KM is a business problem and falls in the domain of information systems and management, not in computer science. KM needs to meld information systems *and people* in ways that information management never has.

- *KM is about process, not just digital networks.* Management of knowledge has to encompass and improve business processes.[26,c] Technology is only an enabler that can rarely produce the same results in two different organizations.

- *KM is not about building a smarter intranet.* A KM system can use your company's intranet as its front end, but one should never be mistaken for the other. The "just-add-water" approach traditionally used with packaged intranets collapses face down when used for KM.

- *KM is not about a one-time investment.* KM, like any other future-oriented investment, requires consistent attention and continued evaluation, even after it begins to deliver results.

- *KM is not about enterprise-wide "infobahns."* Although enterprise integration helps, the primary focus of KM is on helping the *right* people *apply* the *right* knowledge at the *right* time.

---

[c]Unlike business process reengineering, KM is about supporting critical processes such as business decisions with the *right* knowledge at the right time.

WHAT THIS BOOK IS ABOUT

This book seeks to bridge the gap between KM theory and practice. It shows you how you can implement both a KM strategy and a KM system in *your* company. It helps you ask the right questions—not attempting to give you generic answers to unasked generic questions. It provides you with practical guidance on linking KM to business strategy, rather than falling into a philosophical or technical quicksand. A 10-step road map, each step of which is illustrated with real-life examples, guides you through the process of *actually* implementing KM in your company.

WHY NOT THE "M" WORD?

The following chapters provide a road map that I will refrain from calling a methodology. The term *methodology* connotes a process that can be carried out in almost the same way in just about any company and still deliver the same results. Methodologies are generalized treatments created for generalized problems. They do not come bundled with an intimate knowledge of *your* company's history, culture, experience, goals, realities, or problems. Every phase, and in turn, step on this road map will help you develop a KM strategy in the context of *your* own company. By focusing on the right questions, you can arrive at answers that are right for your situation.

THE 10-STEP ROAD MAP HELPS YOU...

This book walks you through a road map with four phases involving ten different steps that will help you leverage your company's existing infrastructure; design, develop, and deploy a KM system that is aligned with your business strategy on top of existing infrastructural capabilities; undertake cultural and organizational changes that can make KM succeed in your company; and show you ways to evaluate its effectiveness.

Identify Knowledge Critical to Your Business

This book helps you understand how KM contributes to your company's competitiveness. It guides you through the process of identifying knowledge that is critical to your own business processes and helps you identify opportunities for exploiting this knowledge. KM, however important, is not for every company: This book will help you determine whether your company is ready for KM.

Align Business Strategy and Knowledge Management

Business vision operates at a high level of abstraction, and systems development needs low-level details and specifications. This book helps you raise KM system design to the level of business strategy and pull strategy down to the level of systems design—without undermining either. Deliberate strategic alignment is more likely to deliver solid business results than is a pepper-sprinkling approach.

Analyze Existing Knowledge in Your Company

You must begin with knowledge that already exists in your company in various forms. This book will describe the process of assembling an appropriate knowledge audit team, the actual steps involved in the audit process, and methods for analyzing implications of those results on the system's design.

Building on, Not Discarding Existing IT Investments

The value of supporting KM with technology comes from leveraging existing IT investments. This book shows you how you can build further on these infrastructural pieces, identifying which components can be used *as is* and which need further development.

Focus on Processes and Tacit, Not Just Explicit, Knowledge

Tacit knowledge is the most important type of knowledge that exists in your company and one that is least supported by IT. This book helps you incorporate support for tacit knowledge sharing and integration, rather than repeat the same old mistake of ignoring it, as information systems design has done to this point.

Design a Future-Proof, Adaptable Knowledge Management Platform

This book describes the seven-layer KM platform architecture and guides you through the process of customizing it specifically for your own company through a series of diagnostic iterations. It also assists you to analyze the appropriate choice of collaborative platform, based on your project's strategic leanings and past investments.[27,28] This book further helps you "future-proof" this blueprint so that it is immune to technological changes down the road.

Build and Deploy a Results-Driven Knowledge Management System

This book shows you how to use the results-driven incrementalism (RDI) methodology so that each increment in your system is based on the previous increment's results. In other words, the entire system is driven by business results, avoiding common pitfalls—both cultural and technical—that such a system is vulnerable to. It also helps you analyze the process of selecting pilot deployments before the system is introduced on an organization-wide scale.

Implement Leadership and Reward Structures Needed to Make Knowledge Management Work

This book will help you determine the type of knowledge-sharing culture, leadership, and KM-friendly reward structure that is needed to make KM work in your company. Through several examples of companies that have been very successful, even with moderate technology, and those that have failed, notwithstanding the best technology, the book illustrates the criteria that might work in your own company.

Evaluate Initiatives Using Real Options Analyses

A common myth is that KM returns on investment (ROIs) cannot be calculated. This book shows you that both the long-term and in the short-term benefits of KM can be accurately calculated through real options. It also shows how inputs for option spaces can be easily tracked and how a balanced portfolio of KM initiatives can be maintained to mitigate unanticipated risks.

Learn from War Stories

And yes, this book does include war stories from managers who have struggled with the concept of KM—some have become KM legends, and some still need this book. There are high-profile pioneers, and there are market leaders who fell victims to disruptive innovations. Such war stories and results from early adopters are interesting examples but dangerous strategies, for reasons that will soon be described.

GENERAL WARNING: "MANAGERIAL INSTINCT NOT INCLUDED"

The 10-step road map provides you with a tool, a mechanism, an enabler to which you need to add the most important ingredient: your instinct. This includes intimate knowledge of your own company, its existing culture, its strategic focus, and its unique problems. Through every step on this road map, you'll find the answers to developing both KM strategy and a strategically aligned KM system by asking the right questions. Every step is illustrated with examples of both successes and failures.

These are not examples to follow blindly but examples to help you comprehend the intricacies of the KM design process. You will find recommendations for design. You must take these recommendations and judge their fit to your own company. This book serves you as a toolkit, but no one else but your own team can use this toolkit to develop a KM solution that works in *your* company. Implementing KM sounds easier than it actually is, but don't let this keep your company from starting now. There might never be a second chance.

Let us begin by taking a closer look at how knowledge and KM at some companies alchemize ordinary resources into consistently innovative formulas for market success.

CHAPTER 2
THE KNOWLEDGE EDGE

IN THIS CHAPTER

✔ See how knowledge contributes to market valuation and corporate prosperity.

✔ Understand why knowledge can deliver a sustainable competitive advantage and increasing returns.

✔ Pinpoint the key drivers of KM.

✔ Realize how KM helps avoid reinvention, loss of know-how, and repetition of mistakes.

✔ Understand how KM can help companies deal with complex expectations, intricate processes, fleeting opportunities, deregulation, globalization, the need for predictive anticipation, and product-service convergence.

A LITTLE KNOWLEDGE THAT ACTS IS WORTH INFINITELY MORE THAN
MUCH KNOWLEDGE THAT IS IDLE.
—KAHLIL GIBRAN

When engineers at Ford Motor Company[1] looked back at their record-breaking best seller, the Ford Taurus, no one in the entire company could really place his or her finger on the reason why the car had become such a runaway success. PalmPilot, the nifty little personal digital assistant (PDA) made by 3COM,[a] became an instant best seller as soon as it was introduced, gained a market share of several million and growing, and a huge following of loyal and die-hard fans that beats even that of the original Apple Macintosh (and, since, the iMac). Two major companies, Texas Instruments and Sharp Electronics Corp.,[2] released more feature-rich, more powerful, and faster PDAs, competing hard on prices, features, and value for the consumer's dollar. The Texas Instruments Avigo, a PalmPilot look-alike, had all features of the PalmPilot plus some more, cost one-third as much, and came with more software and an infrared wireless data link to connect to laptops.

With all those features, better prices, and arguably better value for money, the Avigo still could not stand up against the PalmPilot. If it was not price, features, or value for the money, what is the basis of competition between these products?

Consider Apple Computer, for example. The company has consistently managed to produce innovations in the computing industry, yet its market success is, at best, moderate. In 1999, Apple introduced the Cube computer—a one-foot PC that was years ahead of its time. Much like the Apple Newton that inspired the PalmPilot, the Cube was a marvel of engineering but a commercial disaster. Clearly, having innovative capacity and being able to apply that knowledge to generate commercial success are not necessarily correlated.

MAKING SENSE OF NONSENSE

A harried glance at the Fortune 500 list reveals that many companies that rank low sometimes exceed the market valuation of the Fortune 10. The likes of Intel, Amgen, Monsanto, Dow Chemical, and AOL easily surpass asset-intensive companies such as Chrysler and General Motors. What accounts for these abnormal differences?

If you take a closer look at how the value of a company is determined, you will notice another measure called *market valuation*. In simple terms, this represents *the* measure of value that the investors and the markets associate with a company. It is only when you take these figures into account that you realize that the prosperity level of a firm is not what it seems to be on the surface. These companies, even with assets running into tens or hundreds of billions, are less well off than they might seem at a first glance.

At first, these observations seem quite contradictory and out of the ordinary. But consider the businesses of these companies: Microsoft makes operating systems such as Windows; Intel makes microprocessors that run Windows PCs; Merck and Pfizer produce innovative drugs; Coke has enough loyal fans (like this author) who refuse to drink Pepsi; Lucent invented the

---

[a]The PalmPilot was originally manufactured by US Robotics and later acquired by 3COM. In late 1999, Palm devices owned 70 percent of the hand-held computing device market share.

transistor and now produces, among other things, semiconductor chips; Citigroup operates in the financial markets; and Citibank is a major issuer of credit cards. These are all companies with "real" assets such as buildings, manufacturing facilities, equipment, and offices far lesser in value than their market valuation. Even the few odd ones here have something in common with the rest: they are capital-intensive but not capital-centric anymore. Wal-Mart, for example, is not viewed as a discount store by investors and not valued on the basis of what is on its shelves. Its strong suit is impeccable, real-time logistics.

One common theme brings together all these companies and their very different reasons for being successful. Companies such as Microsoft, Intel, AMD, Cyrix, AOL, Coca-Cola, eBay, eFax, and Yahoo! share something that cannot be shown on the balance sheets. Their intangibles:

- Brand recognition
- Industry-driving vision
- Patents and breakthroughs
- Customer loyalty and its reach
- Innovative business ideas
- Anticipated future products
- Past achievements
- Groundbreaking strategies

Whether it is the creation of a new retail channel for books through the Web (Amazon.com) the creation of a graphical Web browser (Netscape), a discontinuous technological breakthrough, or owning the entire market share for PC operating systems and perceivably future operating systems (Microsoft), an achievement that might *now* seem very doable and feasible—it is the fact that they did it first and they did it almost right when it was the least expected that counts. These companies are driven by and valued for their knowledge, not their capital assets.

WALT DISNEY COMPANY AND MICKEY MOUSE

The Walt Disney Company has seen the value of intangible assets since the early 1970s. In 1978, the film *Star Wars* generated $25 million from its box office receipts and a whopping $22 million from the sales of *Star Wars* logo merchandise. In 1979, the retail value of goods using characters owned by Walt Disney was estimated to be over $3 billion. Walt Disney happens to be a few of the luckier companies that have actually converted their intangible assets into dollar profits. Consistently. Recent successes have only increased the company's income from such royalties, even though the figures are not officially available.

These are business that threaten to destroy existing businesses by competing in unanticipated ways or by creating entirely new markets. Their likes have the potential to replace your business, if not eliminate your entire market.

INTELLECTUAL CAPITAL

Companies with high levels of market valuation are often companies with high levels of intangible assets, often referred to as their *intellectual capital*. Intellectual capital might be any asset that cannot be measured but is used by a company to its advantage. Knowledge, collective expertise, good will, brand value, and patents fail to show up on conventional accounting documents. No wonder very few companies with the highest levels of intellectual and intangible knowledge assets make it to the upper echelons of the *Fortune* sales-based rankings.

Skilled people and their competencies, market positions, good will, recognition, achievements, patents, contacts, support, collaborators, leadership, "sticky" customer bases, and reputation are some of those key intangible assets that are hard to put a dollar figure on, yet they represent most of the market value that companies have. Even some intangible assets, such as reputation, can do little to sustain your business if you are Atlanta's most reputable travel agent who still cannot match Priceline.com's price *and* service—in other words, value. In the end, the only competitive edge that sustains is knowledge. KM provides you the "window" to see opportunity coming and act upon it by applying knowledge that is otherwise idle.

KNOWLEDGE, MARKET VALUE, AND PROSPERITY

As businesses shift from an asset-centric environment to a knowledge-centric environment, traditional value measures become increasingly fallible. When Netscape Corporation (later acquired by America Online) went public a few years back, the market valued this $17-million company at $3 billion at the end of the very first day of trading. Although the average company on Wall Street has a market/book value ratio of 3, Netscape's opening day trade ratio was a monstrous 175. The market did not value the company on the basis of its buildings and computers but on the basis of its knowledge assets: its invention of the Web browser, innovative projects, patented technology, and employee-founder Marc Andeersen (who invented the Web browser and went to work for America Online since its acquisition of Netscape in 1998).

Market value also matters to startups or growing small companies. Borrowing capital for expansion into the rapidly opening international markets is not usually easy because the *typical* company cannot always offer compelling assurances to venture capitalists and external financiers. In a knowledge-based economy, this security is the value of its intangible assets and their perceived future value—these carry more weight than last year's balance sheet or income statement. Market valuation is a pervasive though risky determinant of its future potential and explains why companies such as Apple[b] and Netscape ever got financed in the first place.

THE FATE OF INNOVATIVE NONEXPLOITERS

As the legend goes in the Silicon Valley, it's not the innovators but the exploiters who make the billions. Apple Computer, Inc. was born in its most successful form by a momentary knowledge link (evoked as a realization) established by Steve Jobs, its co-founder, when he was viewing a demonstration of a crude version of the embryonic idea of a GUI (graphical user interface) at Xerox Palo Alto Research Center (PARC) in the early 1980s. Jobs asked himself the right question: How could he use this immature technology to change the future of computing? The GUI—a driver of Apple's stellar success—is now the de facto interface in contemporary computer operating systems, ironically including Windows.

Apple figured out its GUI from PARC, Microsoft exploited the Apple operating system to create Windows. Xerox created the computer mouse that is produced by hundreds of companies other than Xerox. Sony, which is often wrongly credited with the invention of the VCR, exploited Ampex's 1950s innovation of video recording and the semiconductors industry is built around Bell Labs' Nobel Prize-winning invention of the transistor.

The saddest example of an innovative nonexploiter is perhaps Xerox, whose PARC created the fundamental set of technologies upon which today's computer industry is built. Xerox was the greatest innovator of its time but a pathetic exploiter of its own knowledge. Xerox still makes photocopiers.

The Back of the Envelope at Ford Motor Company

Ford manufactures a broad range of cars and trucks targeted at various consumer segments. A study done at Stanford University reveals how knowledge utilized in the conceptual design stage of a typical Ford car drives between 70 and 90 percent of its final life-cycle cost.[3] Even though design accounts for only 5 percent of the final cost of a typical car, it influences 70 percent or more of the vehicle's final cost. Similarly, material (as shown in Figure 2-1) constitutes 50 percent of the final cost of a typical car, but its influence on the final cost is only about 20 percent.

Most conceptual design and decision making are done with canonical tools and "low-technology media," such as *paper and pencil on the back of an envelope,*[c] because of their flexibility and agility. Even with seemingly labor- and raw material-intensive products, Ford's major cost drivers are its decisions in the design process. By perfecting the design process, Ford can ensure that the price tags on its cars remain competitive. In companies such as Ford—

---

[b]The three-part PBS <www.pbs.org> documentary, "Triumph of the Nerds," provides an interesting story about Apple's financing, as told by the original venture capitalist. This series was later followed by another three-part series by Robert Cringley, "Nerds 2.0," which provides a historical account of the emergence of the Internet-centric computing business models that have driven several successful multibillion-dollar startups.

[c]These are exact quotes from the Stanford presentation report.

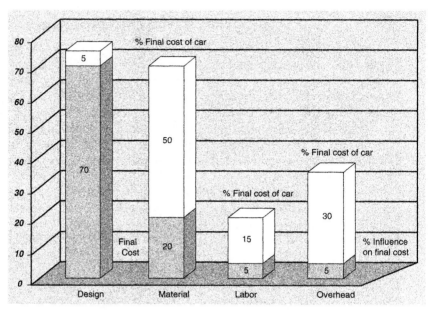

Figure 2-1 Seventy percent of Ford's costs are driven by decisions made in the conceptual design stage, even though this process accounts for only 5 percent of the actual cost of its typical car.

which we have always taken for granted in the conventional economy—there lies the potential for effectively leveraging past experience and process knowledge to generate a sustainable advantage that can keep them far ahead of their pack.

THE DRIVERS OF KNOWLEDGE MANAGEMENT

Knowledge has been the staple source of competitive advantage of some classic companies (such as Coke) for hundreds of years—not exactly a new concept.[4] Turbulently changing environments, rapidly evolving technologies, and a different breed of knowledge workers create the demand for an entirely new organizational structure that is process-oriented, team-based, and brain-rich but asset-poor. Except for rare cases of intangible assets (such as Coke's formula) that do not grow if shared, knowledge grows in value if it is appropriately shared. Table 2-1 highlights the key drivers that make KM a compelling case for businesses. Several, if not all, will probably apply to your business, irrespective of your industry.

Table 2-1 The Drivers, Problem Symptoms, and Solutions That Create a Strong Value Proposition of Knowledge Management

Driver	Problem Symptoms	Threat and KM Solutions	Notes and Exemplars
Knowledge-centric drivers			
Knowledge recognition failure	Companies don't know what they already know	Reinvention Failure to apply existing knowledge	A major British chemicals company was developing a process that had gone through several iterations in its pilot tests a few years ago. As the company scaled up this process to its full production level, a flaw in the seemingly perfect solution showed up: A sludge deposit was produced at the bottom of the process tank. The company attempted to salvage its development and invested in further research, hoping to eliminate this problem. A junior team member decided to investigate existing British patents, just in case some other company had already encountered a similar problem. Licensing the process, they thought, might be cheaper than developing it from scratch. The patent office searched through all its patents and found a patented solution that was owned by the very same company. Sometimes, trend data holds valuable embedded knowledge that businesses fail to leverage because they are simply unaware of them. The "poster child": Wal-Mart used data mining technology to gain critical sales-related knowledge of how beer and diapers sold together on Friday nights and used it—the knowledge, not the information technology—for better inventory management. Wal-Mart's example, although deceptively close, is not that of market research but that of knowledge application.
Rapid knowledge dissemination and application	Employees can't find critical existing knowledge in time Lessons are learned but not shared No knowledge is gained from failures; failures are soon forgotten Expertise is not shared	Inconsistent performance across locations Expertise localization Repeated failures Inability to apply what is known[5] Competitors innovate at a faster rate[6]	Failed approaches and decisions often provide equally useful insights into what not to do. Without learning from failures and their analyses, workers pursuing current projects might unknowingly repeat past mistakes. Lacking easy access mechanisms, people often tend to use the incomplete information they already possess, with the result that designs are generated without the benefit of existing expertise.[7]

Table 2-1 The Drivers, Problem Symptoms, and Solutions That Create a Strong Value Proposition of Knowledge Management (cont.)

Driver	Problem Symptoms	Threat and KM Solutions	Notes and Exemplars
Tacit knowledge walk-outs	Employee departure causes loss of key clients, suppliers, best practices, and even revenue[8] Departure of some employees reduces collective firm-wide competence	Critical tacit knowledge is closely held by a few key individuals; capabilities can be moved to competitors KM provides processes to retain tacit knowledge through informal methods and pointers	The banking industry provides an outrageous example of how knowledge that walks out of your company's door can become an instant threat: 60 of the 140 analysts working for ING Baring left the bank and reappeared in the trading room of its competitor, Deutsche Morgan Granfell. Soon, Barings Bank collapsed.
Knowledge hoarding	Individual employees closely guard knowledge and insights; fear of job security exists Collaboration is only namesake	Arguments flare over turf, not approaches Collaborative knowledge sharing needs strong motivators	Hoarding is a human tendency[9] that can be overcome only by providing an irresistible incentive to share. In classic management theory, this problem has often been addressed as agency-agent conflict, where a manager tries to maximize his or her gain, even if it is opposed to maximizing that of the company. The only solution is to tie the two together. In other words, give incentives that are too attractive to be ignored! In most Western countries, these incentives equal financial rewards; in other countries, such as Japan and India, they primarily hinge on recognition. Arthur Andersen (AA), a management consulting firm, has successfully implemented this strategy by making an employee's contribution to the internal knowledge repository an essential evaluation criteria for promotion.
Unlearning	Assumptions, rules of thumb, heuristics, and processes associated with business processes are unreliable or outdated	Unlearning is not systematically incorporated; knowledge is not revalidated Old practices, methods, and processes continue to be inappropriately applied	When American Airlines realized that it was making more money selling ticket reservation and routing information through its SABRE reservation system, it had to stop thinking like an airline. It needed to stop believing that its business was focused on selling airline tickets and flying its own planes. It needed to focus on itself as an information broker, not as an airline. Realizations such as this that allow companies to realign their strategic focus do not come easy and are often too easy to miss. KM can help identify such shifts, encourage systemic unlearning by monitoring internal and external data, and sift out trends that deserve immediate attention.

Table 2-1 The Drivers, Problem Symptoms, and Solutions That Create a Strong Value Proposition of Knowledge Management (cont.)

Driver	Problem Symptoms	Threat and KM Solutions	Notes and Exemplars
Technology drivers			
Technology provides temporary advantage	Technological innovation and adoption fails to sustain competitive advantage Technology-driven advantages are soon copied.	Technology acts as an entry precursor and core capability leveler, not a sustainable competitive differentiator KM provides a robust differentiator	In the long run, technology, laws, patents, and market share fail; nothing provides an advantage more than temporarily. Technology provided Citibank only a temporary competitive advantage when it first introduced the Automatic Teller Machine (ATM). Duplicating pieces of differentiating technology might be expensive but are not impossible. Before long, any technology that provides a competitive advantage to one business becomes a staple component of the services and products offered by any firm engaged in that business. Citibank lost its advantage when other banks started providing ATM services, and ATMs were no longer considered an added value but rather an expected value. Similarly, Microsoft's Hotmail service popularized e-mail systems that allowed users to check their e-mail through a conventional Web browser. Soon copied, the Web-based interface is now a norm for most Internet service providers. What was originally an innovative technology application soon became a basic expectation in the consumer market.
Compressed product and process life cycles	Market information, service, and physical product life cycles have significantly shortened, compressing the available window for recouping development expenses. Frequent changes in the software, communication protocols, and computing hardware and software.	Complex and often irreversible design decisions need to be made quickly and accurately; KM can provide facilitate this KM develops process competence, resulting in time-to-market and cost reduction	

21

Table 2-1 The Drivers, Problem Symptoms, and Solutions That Create a Strong Value Proposition of Knowledge Management (cont.)

Driver	Problem Symptoms	Threat and KM Solutions	Notes and Exemplars
Strategic alignment	Information technology is confused with information and CRM technology with customer knowledge Business and IT strategy are not "on the same page"	Business needs and strategy must not drive technology investments Customer knowledge and relationship building needs must drive customer interaction and relationship management technology choices	Even though there is no publicized KM agenda within Microsoft, it has been essentially managing knowledge all along. The critical difference between Xerox's legendary PARC and Microsoft is that PARC created a lot of knowledge but Microsoft (and Apple) actually applied it to make the difference, create new markets, and generate economic value. In the technology industry, companies that have prospered are not the companies that invented new technology but those that applied it. Microsoft is perhaps a good example of a company that had first relied on good marketing, then on its market share, and now on its innovative knowledge—mostly external. The customer base it built for its Windows operating system was probably its strongest asset when it decided to compete seriously in the Web browser market. Microsoft, a latecomer to the Internet market, came to the sweeping realization that the Internet was going to change everything, including its own product markets. Its strategy took a U-turn in 1995 and began focusing on the Internet (every software product that Microsoft made in 1999 worked with the Internet in some manner). Microsoft's reputation and strong skills base, coupled with its cash flow, provided it with all it needed to compete in the car retail business (www.carpoint.com), then the travel business (www.expedia.com), and more recently, in the toy business, as well. Besides a strong brand recognition, the company leveraged its existing collective skills to plan for the future. When Microsoft began delving into the toy market in late 1998 with its Actimates series of electronic toys (including Barney and Arthur), it brought together its competitive advantage from manifold sources within Microsoft: marketing abilities, software capabilities, hardware skills, and its brand value.

Table 2-1 The Drivers, Problem Symptoms, and Solutions That Create a Strong Value Proposition of Knowledge Management (cont.)

Driver	Problem Symptoms	Threat and KM Solutions	Notes and Exemplars
Structural drivers			
Functional convergence	Complex dependencies among and between different functional areas necessitate inputs and cooperation from different divisions to accomplish joint objectives[10] Diverse expertise must be integrated to innovate Brainstorming, strategy planning, competitive response, and proactive positioning need collaboration, often across multiple functional areas, departments, and companies with differing notions, values, and beliefs Employees work in parallel to complete assignments spanning traditional boundaries and functional areas. Complex products require melding of knowledge from diverse disciplinary perspectives	Team members lack understanding of the critical process factors for areas other than their own KM facilitates seamless integration of business divisions and collaborative firms KM encourages conversation and discussion that precede collaboration and effective sharing of knowledge Cultural enablers facilitate cooperation across design, engineering, packaging, manufacturing, and marketing that is critical for innovation	In addition to the traditional functional barriers that exist between marketing, design, purchasing, and manufacturing that can be observed in most industrial organizations, the diversity of the expertise needed for complex projects creates serious barriers for commonly accepted, agreed-upon, shared understanding

Table 2-1 The Drivers, Problem Symptoms, and Solutions That Create a Strong Value Proposition of Knowledge Management (cont.)

Driver	Problem Symptoms	Threat and KM Solutions	Notes and Exemplars
Convergence of products and services	Products and services are increasingly bundled Blurred boundaries between products/services	Perceived market value of products might vary, depending on how the bundling is done KM provides a continually refined, process-focused reference point for future bundling decisions	Hal Rosenbluth, CEO of Rosenbluth Travel, a $1.3 billion* global travel management company, was quoted in *Sloan Management Review* as saying that his company was not in the travel business but in the information business. Its biggest competitive advantage was to have understood and applied its knowledge and intuition of how deregulation would change its business. Rosenbluth's forefathers, who started his business generations back, understood this, as well, when they realized and believed that they were not in the business of selling ship passages to people who wanted to cross the Atlantic but were in the business of getting entire clans of people successfully settled in then-emerging America. Howard Schultz, the president of Starbucks (this author's favorite caffeine overdose spot!) still believes that he is in the "romance-theatrics and community" business and not in the coffee business! Silly as it might sound, these companies have succeeded beyond a trace of doubt, simply because they realized the process knowledge focus (e.g., knowing what the romance or change-the-world business means and doing what it takes to bring substance to that seemingly esoteric perception) and worked hard to keep it in continuous or long view.** Steve Jobs (the founder of Apple) never considered himself in the computer business but rather in the "change-the-world-business."

Table 2-1 The Drivers, Problem Symptoms, and Solutions That Create a Strong Value Proposition of Knowledge Management (cont.)

Driver	Problem Symptoms	Threat and KM Solutions	Notes and Exemplars
Temporary organizational structures	Ad hoc project-centered team structures bringing together the best of talent and expertise Expertise gained during development of a product or service is not readily available to subsequent project teams Skills developed during the collaboration process *lost and redistributed†*	Knowledge integration across business units helps in reducing process complexity Relationship building based on customer knowledge reduces logistical complexity in interacting with your business	In the development of complex products and services, it is a *sine qua non* to draw needed expertise from a variety of functional areas, such as technical design, engineering, packaging, manufacturing, and marketing. It requires melding of knowledge from diverse disciplinary and personal skills-based perspectives where creative cooperation is critical for innovation. Expertise and skills that are needed for a project might be distributed both within and outside the responsible company; therefore, people from different companies often come together to work together to bring in the entire skill set that a product or service might demand. In a project-oriented, team-based organizational structure, skills developed during the collaboration process might be lost after the team is broken up and redistributed among other newly formed teams. When such a team is disbanded, the process knowledge acquired by the team and needed for tasks such as product modification, service development, or maintenance is lost for future use. [11] The rapid growth in many skills markets and the shortage of highly specialized skills are critical factors contributing to the severe shortage of qualified personnel and high turnover, especially in high technology and areas of fringe specialization.
Deregulation and globalization	Virtual collaboration and global remote teaming occurs among highly distributed teams and partnering firms	Intensified competition from deregulated marketplaces can lead to the loss of competitiveness without appropriate partnering	Businesses that once were organized along geographic lines now are reorienting themselves according to markets, products, and processes. Companies such as Lotus, Verifone, and Microsoft are using this phenomenon to their advantage by shifting "mental labor" intensive software development and coding to their programmers in India and Russia, who do a good job at one-tenth the wage that a programmer would demand in Redmond, while retaining design and strategic planning at their base offices.

25

Table 2-1 The Drivers, Problem Symptoms, and Solutions That Create a Strong Value Proposition of Knowledge Management (cont.)

Driver	Problem Symptoms	Threat and KM Solutions	Notes and Exemplars
			Buckman is a multinational chemicals company that invents, develops, and manufactures specialty chemicals for industrial and agricultural uses. The 1,200-employee company is based in Memphis, Tennessee with offices and representatives in 82 countries. A company such as Buckman, with offices in over 80 countries, is understandably faced with barriers of time, culture, language, and distance. The company realized that empowering its employees to truly satisfy customer needs required both a customer knowledge-sharing environment and easy access to customer information. The KM program in the company is targeted at helping its employees get all the knowledge they need to help do business with and satisfy the needs of its customers more effectively.
			Hewlett-Packard , with over 100,000 employees generating over $35 billion in revenues, operates in 110 countries. The solution to its increasingly complex problem of fragmentation of skills and knowledge was addressed by a management team at HP when they formed a unit called the *Product Process Organization* (PPO) within HP. This division is an internal consulting group that leverages best practices in new product development processes among the company's highly decentralized and autonomous operating businesses. The PPO serves as an internal consulting group and draws its employees from a diverse, cross-functional pool.
Process focused drivers			
Expensive, repeated mistakes and reinvention of solutions	Businesses are disconcerted by reinventing solutions and repeating mistakes because they could not identify or transfer best practices and experiential knowledge across locations or projects	Knowledge is neither being effectively retained nor shared KM support can help your business realize what it already knows	American companies annually spend between $2 billion and $100 billion by repeating exactly the same mistakes.[12] Learning from the past is how things should work, but they rarely do. Organizations have been disconnected by reinventing solutions and repeating mistakes because they could not identify or transfer best practices and experiential knowledge from one location to another or from one project to another. When such knowledge—both explicit and tacit—is not retained, a potentially

Table 2-1 The Drivers, Problem Symptoms, and Solutions That Create a Strong Value Proposition of Knowledge Management

Driver	Problem Symptoms	Threat and KM Solutions	Notes and Exemplars
	Businesses incur unnecessary expense to relearn the same lessons		competitive knowledge asset has been squandered, and the company incurs unnecessary expense to relearn the same lessons.
Proactive opportunity-seeking behavior	Inability to integrate external knowledge with internal expertise Inability to recognize the forces that will shape your future markets	KM provides an opportunity to anticipate such change, realize that it's coming, and lead it. KM, by integrating otherwise-dispersed knowledge, lets you apply your company's collective knowledge to turn business turbulence into opportunity	The ability to integrate external knowledge with internal expertise can provide companies with the capability proactively to anticipate changing markets and respond ahead of time. The ability to anticipate and react proactively to market trends is a critical capability required of any company because these forces will shape your business's markets. It is sometimes too easy for even the best companies to miss a beat here and fall far behind. Microsoft, for example, did not anticipate the explosive rise of Internet and soon found that Netscape, a seemingly insignificant startup company, had entered a market niche and secured a dominant position.
Responsiveness	As competitors become increasingly responsive to customer needs, companies must match the effort, using the right application of knowledge within the proper structures and processes Responsiveness that exceeds that of competitors is key to differentiation.	The ability to proactively anticipate and respond to market trends Use aggregated knowledge to control complex, multi-participant business processes	Wal-Mart is a frequently cited example of a company that has put the just-in-time (JIT) inventory management system to good use. Wal-Mart is in the same line of business as many other competitors, such as Kmart and Target stores. Wal-Mart is the only retailer that comes on the Fortune 10 list because it delivers value to the customers not just through better products but also through exemplary logistics based on knowledge gained from its sales data—and applied to make the difference. The Swedish company Asea Brown Boveri (ABB) [13] is a global company that makes and markets electrical power generation and transmission equipment, high-speed trains, automation and robotics, and control systems. The company has over 200,000 employees that are led by only 250 senior managers. When formed by the merger of the Swedish ASEA and the Swiss firm Brown Boveri in 1987, one of the key strategies was to move power from the center to its operating companies. The head office staff was reduced from 6,000 to a total of 150 people with a matrix management structure worldwide. Several layers of middle management

Table 2-1 The Drivers, Problem Symptoms, and Solutions That Create a Strong Value Proposition of Knowledge Management (cont.)

Driver	Problem Symptoms	Threat and KM Solutions	Notes and Exemplars
			were stripped out, and directors from the central headquarters were moved into regional coordinating companies. The company was split into 1,400 smaller companies and around 5,000 profit centers, functioning as closely as possible to independent companies. At the same time, a new group-coordinating arrangement was introduced where everyone in the company had a country manager and a business sector manager, and about 65 global managers ran the eight business sectors.
Economic drivers Increasing returns	Physical assets—both production-oriented and technological—lose value as they are used.	Sustainability of knowledge-based competitive advantage comes from knowing more about the same things than your competitors Customer knowledge generates superordinary returns to scale—creating a self-reinforcing cycle Multiple users can simultaneously benefit from knowledge assets and increase its value as they add to, adapt, enhance, enrich, and validate it. A bulk of the fixed cost in knowledge-intensive products and services usually lies in their creation, rather than in manufacturing or distribution. Once such knowledge-intensive products have been created, their initial development cost can be spread across mounting volumes.	When you give a book (a physical asset) away or sell it, you lose it.[14] You cannot sell it again. Conversely, you can sell the same knowledge again and again. Similarly, you can use the same knowledge again and again. This is what economists call the *law of increasing returns*: The more you use it, the more value it provides— thereby creating a self-reinforcing cycle. Very unlike the economist's finite resources, such as land, capital, and labor, knowledge and intellectual capital are infinite resources that can generate increasing returns through their systematic use and application. Advantage lies in knowing more about the same things than your competitors.‡ Around 1988, Octicon, the Danish manufacturer of hearing aids, had seen its market share and profitability decline as competitors introduced more advanced and cheaper products. When Lars Kolind became CEO in 1990, he set out to create an environment that would promote the flow of knowledge and encourage entrepreneurial behavior because he realized that technological innovation and time to market would be critical success factors. Organizational charts, offices, job descriptions, and formal roles were abandoned, and company employees were expected to choose their own projects and work in fast-moving, cross-functional teams.

Table 2-1 The Drivers, Problem Symptoms, and Solutions That Create a Strong Value Proposition of Knowledge Management (cont.)

Driver	Problem Symptoms	Threat and KM Solutions	Notes and Exemplars
			Did all this help? One might be inclined to think it did, because these changes produced dramatic results: Return on equity climbed from the low single digits in the late 1980s to over 27 percent in the 1990s as Octicon developed and rapidly commercialized innovative products such as its digital hearing aid.

*. This figure was current as of 1990, when this quote was made. The company is worth a lot more now.

**. See also: Swanson, E.B., and Ramiller, N.C. "The Organizing Vision in Information Systems Innovation," *Organization Science* (8:5), 1997, pp. 458 and Fransman, M. "Information, Knowledge, Vision, and Theories of the Firm," In *Technology, Organization, and Competitiveness*, G. Dosi, D. Teece and J. Chytry (eds.), Oxford University Press, London, 1998, pp. 147-191.

†. The use of the term team liquidity is widely reported in research literature; the consequences of such liquidity are discussed further in our paper, Ramesh, B., and Tiwana, A. "Supporting Collaborative Process Knowledge Management in New Product Development Teams," *Decision Support Systems* (27:1-2), 1999, pp. 213-235.

‡. Lincoln Re, the insurance company also illustrates this point. See Zack, Michael H, Developing a Knowledge Strategy, *California Management Review*, vol. 41, no. 3, Spring (1999), pp. 125-145.

CREATING THE KNOWLEDGE EDGE

Companies must constantly look for ways in which they can keep their *knowledge spiral*[15] steadily moving upward. Any competitive advantage that is not based on knowledge can be, at most, temporary. Achieving the upward trend largely depends on a company's ability to create new knowledge. It might mean using R&D to create new products by using existing knowledge in a new way, or it might mean gaining new knowledge about customers. Customer loyalty programs, such as the many frequent flyer airline clubs or frequent shopper cards given away by grocery stores, provide valuable insight into the spending habits of major target customer groups. KM can help companies accelerate the knowledge spiral and, in effect, accelerate both creation and application of new knowledge.

KNOWLEDGE INTEGRATION AT PFIZER

In the pharmaceutical industry, for example, companies are using information technology to transform their raw and untapped data resources into competitive tools to provide customers with critical information and value-added services. Pfizer Inc., a $10-billion firm based in New York, has launched a massive sales-force automation program that enables its 2,700 sales representatives to customize their sales pitches, using readily accessible information about any specific drug while providing doctors with accurate details of dosage, side effects, and treatment regulations.

Several other companies have tried their hand at managing their knowledge and competencies to compete effectively in a cutthroat marketplace. Taking a closer look at some of the more successful KM efforts (see Chapter 6) will provide us with a good starting point to dig deeper into the strategic and design aspects of a business-driven KM strategy and a well-designed KM system. For now, we preview some of those ideas.

ELIMINATING THE WRONG TRADEOFFS

Although the concept of knowledge has been around since Adam and Eve, its business significance has been recognized on a large scale relatively recently. Although discussing this subject at a philosophical level will further develop it at a more conceptual level, your business probably can't be run at a philosophical or conceptual level. Companies desperately trying to implement a KM system often stray from the business strategy perspective to either a technologically obsessed strategy or a deeply philosophical perspective, neither of which bears fruit in the real world. As a result, the focus of their plan is either too constricted, often to the advantage of the product vendor trying to help them build a KM strategy, or too broad to be implementable. In an ideal world, we would like to have an all-encompassing and theoretically perfect implementation; in the real world, we end up making choices and tradeoffs. Making the wrong tradeoffs could potentially kill not just the KM initiative but also your company.

BEWARE OF RELABELED CANS OF WORMS

Managing the knowledge assets of a capitalist company is a relatively new and undeveloped area, although research in adjacent areas, such as corporate memory systems, organizational learning, and rationale capture, has been going on for decades. The emergence of KM has opened up a new can of worms, and as we try to cluster them in a smaller number of cans (organizational, technical, managerial, strategic etc.), vendors seem to be pointing only to the original big can. This is no different from the kind of problem that was rampant in 1970 when two of the founders of the information systems field (IS) wrote about similar problems in EDP.[16] As companies such as Monsanto, Microsoft, and Skandia have started talking more about KM, companies with products from all related areas, such as data warehousing, Intranets, discussion list tools, and object-oriented database systems, have been involved in a relabeling frenzy, touting their products as the ultimate KM solutions. The fact is, however, that there is no one single, canned approach to managing knowledge. What you need is a good understanding of your business and a convincing business case; only then can you even think of beginning a KM initiative.

THE FOGGY ROAD AHEAD

In many service industries, the ability to identify best practices and spread them across a dispersed network of operations or locations is a key driver of added value. Such a strategy can create powerful brands that are continually refreshed as knowledge about, for example, how to serve customers better, travels across the network. This often results in a commonly encountered dilemma: It may be all but impossible to tell whether value has been created by the brand or by knowledge. How much does McDonald's brand depend on, for example, network-wide knowledge of how best to cook french fries?

X MILLION SOLD: DEVELOPING AND TRANSFERRING BEST PRACTICES

McDonald's, for example, gets comparable outlets to work together to benchmark performance, set aspirations, and make product mix and service decisions. These peer groups are supported by a real-time information system that transmits sales to headquarters hourly. The system enables corporate headquarters to keep a tight grip on the valuable knowledge that links its outlets.

However, McDonald's is based on a model in which the corporation defines rigid standards, not only for its products but also for the processes that deliver them. The company's squabbles with franchisees over its 1999 introduction of the *Arch Deluxe* product and the 29¢ Wednesday hamburger promotion illustrate the degree to which this formula can conflict with entrepreneurship. There are indications that McDonald's may devolve more decision making to franchisees and seek to learn more from them, particularly about new business development.

LESSONS LEARNED

Knowledge is the key differentiator of companies that have learned to survive and thrive. Intangible assets derived from processes based on the application of knowledge are the key determinants of market valuation of companies—old and new, big and small. To summarize these relationships, the following are a few key points about how knowledge gives today's companies the edge to compete successfully:

- *Market valuation is largely based on intangible assets.* Market valuation refers to the value that investors and stock markets place on your company. In companies that have learned to leverage their intangible assets well, this value might be several times more than their capital assets.

- *Technology itself is a blunt competitive edge. Long live knowledge!* Companies have unsuccessfully tried to differentiate themselves solely through the use of innovative technology. Technology, unfortunately, is too easy to copy. Even if you have patent protection for your new technology, it can be copied by global competitors in countries where domestic patent laws are difficult to enforce or your patent will provide you only a temporary competitive advantage for 17 years (the life of a U.S. patent). Knowledge, unlike technology that can be copied or market share that can be threatened by price cutting, provides a hard to imitate edge.

- *KM has compelling drivers that make it a strong business case.* We discussed several points that make a compelling case for KM when you need corporate support and funding to initiate it.

- *Knowledge, unlike any physical asset, delivers increasing returns.* Physical assets—both production-oriented and technological—lose value as they are used. Knowledge, however, increases in value.

- *KM helps avoid unnecessary work duplication, expensive reinvention, and repeated mistakes.* Almost any experienced manager has encountered these woes. Effective KM can provide channels for smart knowledge integration and application.

- *KM can save your company from "knowledge walkouts."* When an experienced employee leaves your company, he or she might take away intricate tacit knowledge on which your business depends. KM provides an opportunity to mitigate the effects of such walkouts.

- *KM can compress delivery schedules and help you deliver ahead of time.* Where companies try to differentiate themselves through fast delivery, KM can serve two purposes: Through process competence development,[17] it can help your company deliver in the shortest possible time frame, and through reuse of existing knowledge,[18] it can do so at a fraction of the cost of starting with a "blank sheet."

- *KM can make your company a proactive anticipator.* Gandhi once commented, "We must become the change we want to see." The problem with today's business environment is that change occurs so fast that companies barely have a chance to realize that change is occurring until it's too late. Applying knowledge, as opposed to letting it sit idle, lets you proactively anticipate change and strategically react to it. KM provides an opportunity to anticipate such change, realize that it's coming, and lead it.

- *KM mutually reinforces corporate agility.* KM has a two-way relationship with organizational agility. The ability of companies to react comes from their knowledge, and this agility reinforces their ability to apply such knowledge.

In the next chapter, we see how this data→ information → knowledge transformation (and a corresponding shift from data management [DM]→ information management [IM] → knowledge management [KM]) takes place and the enabling conditions plus technology that make it happen. We also take a look at some companies that have been very successful at this transformation and some that have unexpectedly failed. We will also look at the corporate determinants of technology choice.

Chapter 3
The Origins
of Knowledge

IN THIS CHAPTER

✔ Differentiate between knowledge, information, and data.

✔ Understand the lingo of KM concepts.

✔ Understand conversion processes underlying the data management (DM) → information management (IM) → KM
transformation.

✔ Apply criteria that determine whether
your company is ready for KM.

✔ Use a framework to retrofit KM to IT
infrastructure.

WHAT INFORMATION CONSUMES IS RATHER OBVIOUS: IT CONSUMES
THE ATTENTION OF ITS RECIPIENTS. HENCE, A WEALTH OF INFORMATION CREATES A
POVERTY OF ATTENTION, AND A NEED TO ALLOCATE THAT ATTENTION EFFICIENTLY
AMONG THE OVERABUNDANCE OF INFORMATION SOURCES THAT MIGHT CONSUME IT.
—HERBERT SIMON

Numerous debates have been raised in company boardrooms, industry consortia, conferences, and academia on the true meaning of knowledge. Because this author does not intend to contribute any further to this debate, this book will take a more conservative approach and attempt to build on an understanding of what knowledge means to different firms and people. First, though, we must pin down the definitions of data and information, which normally precede knowledge. Without this background, we cannot reach consensus on what we are trying to manage in the context of KM.

Before you can understand and apply the 10-step KM road map introduced in the next chapter, you must clearly appreciate the distinction between DM, IM, and KM, relate KM to organizational learning; describe processes used to convert data and information into knowledge; describe knowledge flows; and categorize various types and components of knowledge. This understanding is essential because it is too easy to mix up these categories and end up trying to solve a nontechnology problem with an expensive piece of technology, or vice versa.

This chapter will use the *knowledge leveragability* framework to explain various stages of knowledge on a knowledge map. This discussion will provide you with the basis to make an initial judgment about your company's readiness for KM. With all the lip service given to KM, very few companies have been able to do it successfully. The few that have, have demonstrated enviable gains in both profitability and competitiveness. The ones that have failed have left us with lessons that are used in this chapter to describe problems, hurdles, and challenges in implementing KM.

FROM DATA TO INFORMATION TO KNOWLEDGE

Let us begin with where we want to go—knowledge—then look at its predecessors: information and data.

KNOWLEDGE

Many of us have an intuitive feel for what knowledge means. Let us survey formal definitions of knowledge.

Webster's dictionary gives the following description:

> **knowledge**: 1. applies to facts or ideas acquired by study, investigation, observation, or experience 2. rich in the knowledge of human nature 3. **learning** applies to knowledge acquired especially through formal, often advanced, schooling 4. a book that demonstrates vast learning.

The first definition implies that knowledge extends beyond information. It has something to do with facts and ideas that have been acquired mostly through experience and includes formal and informal learning.[a]

---

[a]Formal and informal learning could be through past experience, failures, and successes, both within and outside your own company.

Roget's Thesaurus provides a set of synonyms for knowledge:

Knowledge.—**N.** cognizance, cognition, cognoscence; acquaintance, experience, ken, privity, insight, familiarity; comprehension, apprehension; recognition; appreciation; judgment; intuition; conscience; consciousness; perception, precognition.

The synonyms give a better description of Webster's highly constricted definition above. The inclusion of *intuition, recognition, ken, art, perception*, and *precognition* define knowledge in a more complete manner. Knowledge is deeper, richer, and more expansive than information.

For consensus, let us stick with Davenport and Prusak's definition of knowledge, which best captures both its valuable and almost impossible-to-manage characteristics:

Knowledge is a fluid mix of framed experience, values, contextual information, expert insight and grounded intuition that provides an environment and framework for evaluating and incorporating new experiences and information. It originates and is applied in the minds of knowers. In organizations, it often becomes embedded not only in documents or repositories but also in organizational routines, processes, practices, and norms.[1]

Simply put, knowledge is actionable information. *Actionable* refers to the notion of relevant and being available in the right place at the right time, in the right context, and in the right way so that anyone (not just the producer) can bring it to bear on decisions being made every minute. Knowledge is the key resource in intelligent decision making,[2] forecasting,[3] design,[4] planning,[5] diagnosis, analysis, evaluation, and intuitive judgment. It is formed in and shared between individual and collective minds. It does not grow out of databases but evolves with experience, successes, failures, and learning over time.

Information versus Knowledge

The key link between knowledge and information is probably best expressed in the commonly accepted idea that knowledge in the business context is nothing but *actionable information*. Knowledge allows for making predictions, casual associations, or predictive decisions about what to do—unlike information, which simply gives us the facts.

Knowledge is not clear, crisp, or simple. Instead, it's muddy,[6,7] intuitive, hard to communicate, and difficult to express in words and illustrations, and a good chunk of it is *not* stored in databases but in the minds of people who work in your organization. It lies in connections, conversations between people, experience-based intuition, and people's ability to compare situations, problems, and solutions. Only a minuscule portion of this tacit knowledge gets formalized in databases, books, manuals, documents, and presentations; the rest of it stays in the heads of people.

Knowledge is supported by both formal *and informal*[8] processes and structures for its acquisition, sharing, and utilization. Knowledge workers or employees broadly communicate and assimilate values, norms, procedures, and data, beginning with early socialization[9,10] (when they first fit into the organization and slowly become more willing to share) and proceeding through ongoing formal and informal group discussions and exchanges. Information, in contrast, is more devoid of such owner dependencies, as illustrated in the comparison shown in Table 3-1.

Data and information are essential, but it's the knowledge that can be applied, experience that comes into context, and skills that are used at that moment that make the difference between a good decision and a bad decision.

FROM DATA TO KNOWLEDGE

There has been an emerging shift in firms, beginning with a focus on data, much evident in the early interest in electronic data processing (EDP) and further refining into IM) and information systems (IS). As firms are beginning to get comfortable with both data and percolated data (i.e., information), the next challenge that comes into the picture is that of making sense of this overwhelming amount of information itself. Where does this process begin?

Table 3-1 Comparing Information and Knowledge

Information	Knowledge
Processed data	Actionable information
Simply gives us the facts	Allows making predictions, casual associations, or predictive decisions
Clear, crisp, structured, and simplistic	Muddy, fuzzy, partly unstructured
Easily expressed in written form	Intuitive, hard to communicate, and difficult to express in words and illustrations
Obtained by condensing, correcting, contextualizing, and calculating data	Lies in connections, conversations between people, experience-based intuition, and people's ability to compare situations, problems, and solutions
Devoid of owner dependencies	Depends on the owner
Handled well by information systems	Also needs informal channels
Key resource in making sense of large volumes of data	Key resource in intelligent decision making, forecasting, design, planning, diagnosis, and intuitively judging
Evolves from data; formalized in databases, books, manuals, and documents	Formed in and shared among collective minds; evolves with experience, successes, failures, and learning over time
Formalized, captured, and explicated; can easily be packaged into a reusable form	Often emerges in minds of people through their experiences

AN EXAMPLE: TAKING A FLIGHT

Let me give a simple example of typical decision-making "content," wherein the boundaries between knowledge and its predecessors are, at best, hazy. Suppose I am trying to take an urgent flight from Atlanta, Georgia to Shanghai, China. If I look up information in the time table shown on a travel agent's Web site, I move through the stages of data gathering to knowledge application in the following steps:

1. The Web site provides me a flight map, along with departure times for flights that currently have seats available. Assuming that there are no restrictions, such as visa controls that I might need for my trip to China, I must be able to read and interpret what shows up on the page to collect the necessary raw data effectively.

2. I know that the flight will stop over in London. The flight that leaves in an hour is a British Airways flight that stops over at Heathrow airport in London. The flight that leaves in another two hours is a Delta flight that stops over at Gatwick airport in London. Comparing the current time with the departure times, I have the necessary information.

3. I know however, from a previous trip to New Delhi via London, that flights originating in North America have to transfer passengers over to Gatwick airport for their connecting flights to the Asian continent. I also know that the bus ride from the Heathrow to Gatwick airports takes over an hour. So I realize that the plane that leaves first will not arrive before the one that leaves later. I applied what I knew from previous experience, made a judgment based on this knowledge, and took the later flight, which gave me enough time to pack and shave.

THE ORIGINS OF DATA

Every time you check out at a grocery store, each beep on the cash register adds yet another piece of data to the grocery store's database. The transaction records information from the Universal Product Code (UPC): what product you bought, at what time, and in what quantity. What it does not tell the grocery store is *why* you bought it—why that specific brand, why at that time, and why so much.

From the perspective of a firm, *data is a set of particular and objective facts about an event or simply structured records of a transaction*. The event might be the purchase of your favorite beer at the grocery store or a change in the stock price of the stock you might be betting your life's savings on. Without a larger context, such figures do not say anything meaningful. A transaction at a grocery store, for example, does not tell you whether the brand of beer you bought is selling more than the others today—in this store or nationwide—and whether it did so yesterday. Though raw data in itself has purpose, it might have little or no relevance.

There are firms and organizations whose very survival rests solely on their effectiveness and efficiency in handling and keeping this raw data. Their lifeblood is keeping records. The Internal Revenue Service (IRS), the Social Security Administration (SSA), and the U.S. Census Bureau are examples of organizations with strong *data cultures*.

When we talk about managing data, our judgment is mostly quantitative.[11] How much data can be processed in an hour, how much it costs to capture a transaction, how much capacity we have, and so on. Qualitative measures are considered secondary. These measures address issues such as the timely availability of data when we need it and whether the data we need is easily retrievable.

Illusions and Data

The quantity of data captured often gives firms an *illusion* of rigor and accuracy.[12,13] The often false belief that firms tend to stick with is that having collected a lot of data means that ensuing decisions will be good, accurate, objective, and rational. With the extent of technology in place in most businesses, collecting large volumes of data is rarely, if ever, a problem. In fact, a great deal of an effective executive's time is spent seeking out knowledge—not information. Data, in itself, possesses no inherent meaning. The more of it you have, the harder it gets to make sense of it.

Let's take a simple example. How many times do you think that you could manage your budget better? That is a frequent thought for many of us. Take two different approaches. In one approach, you know what your income is, and you have a rough idea of how much you've spent on major purchases, for example, over the past six months. You can then immediately make sense of where major chunks of your money are going and possibly take steps to control them. An alternative data-rich approach would be to take each and every gas, rent, utility, restaurant, and phone bill over the past six months and try to make sense out of all that information put together. You will probably be able to make more sense when you are dealing with a smaller amount of data, as in the first case.

Running even a small business often involves larger volumes of data than a typical family's household budget. As businesses grow, the amount of data that might have been gathered can become so overwhelming that they might end up in an insurmountable *data glut*. Data, although important to firms, has little use in itself unless converted into information. Data for the sake of being accurate and specific is useless if it is collected at the cost of generating information from it.

INFORMATION AND NOISE

Drucker describes *information as data endowed with relevance and purpose.* Information has its root in *inform*, which means something that changes or shapes the person who gets it. It is the recipient of this information who decides whether it is information or noise. If someone told you that Microsoft stock went up by two dollars, and in fact you do own some of it, that information shapes your idea of how well Microsoft is probably doing. However, if someone told you that the Belgian stock exchange took a downward plunge, it might have little meaning for you, who are sitting in the United States without a stake in the Belgian market, and you might consider that noise, rather than information. On the other hand, a manager in Belgium might find the same message very relevant and will not perceive it as noise. What qualifies as useful information in different situations is a subjective judgment.

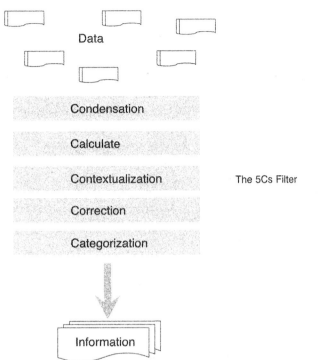

Figure 3-1 The five Cs filter that converts data to information.

Information moves around through electronic networks and social networks. The existence of the Internet today means that there is more relevant and irrelevant information around us than we have time to deal with. Davenport and Prusak[14] proposed a five-C filter for converting data to information, as applied to KM. Figure 3-1 further builds on that discussion.

Table 3-2 shows different ways in which meaning can be added to data to transform it into information.

The Data-Rich and Information-Poor Society

Look at your checkbook. How frequently do you update its balance register? If you're like most of us, you use the balance register quite frequently. But how frequently do you actually use it to *make changes* in your spending patterns. Rarely? This exactly is the problem with many organizations and businesses. They tend to collect a lot of data, hoping that it will give them that imaginary esoteric notion of the fountainhead of competitive advantage any firm yearns for.

The advantage that a firm gains is not from its data riches but from its knowledge riches. Management of knowledge, not data or information, is the primary driver of a firm's competitive edge.

Table 3-2 Different Ways of Creating Information by Adding Meaning to Data—The Five C's

Addition to Data	Result
Condensed	Data is summarized in more concise form, and unnecessary depth is eliminated.
Contextualized	We know why the data was collected.
Calculated	Analyzed data, similar to condensation of data.
Categorized	The unit of analysis is known
Corrected	Errors have been removed, missing "data holes" have been accounted for.

Source: Based on a discussion by Davenport, Thomas H., and Laurence Prusak, *Working Knowledge: How Organizations Manage What They Know*, Harvard Business School Press, Boston (1998).

THE BIG SLIP BETWEEN THE SWIPE AND THE REFRIGERATOR

At every swipe that each product at your local grocery goes through and before the product ends up in your refrigerator, there is a wealth of captured data. The UPC and the accompanying bar code scanner tell the store about the product, its date of manufacture, the time and date the sale was made, who sold it, how it was charged, etc. Although it's exciting to see how much data is captured in one swipe, the threat comes from that very ability: the collection of too much data all too easily. As firms overcome their inability to gather data by using pieces of technology, they often begin to overkill in the amounts of data and information that they capture. The result is that firms end up with overwhelming volumes of data—so overwhelming that they have a hard time figuring out just what to do with it.

Knowledge Integration Across Levels

Very often, when data is shared and distributed among people within a firm, it starts to become increasingly useful as some people perceive it as useful. Figure 3-2 illustrates that, as data, information, and knowledge held at the individual level interact in a team context, new knowledge is created at the team level. Similarly, as data held at the team level interacts with other teams' knowledge in a company's context, new knowledge is created at the organizational level. In this manner, increasingly valuable knowledge can be created at higher levels through integration.

The fundamental mistake that companies repeatedly make is that of equating information and knowledge. For example, bringing locally created knowledge into view from a specific department is only the first step toward making that knowledge useful elsewhere. A company may believe that making its sales figures for its personal digital assistant (PDA) available

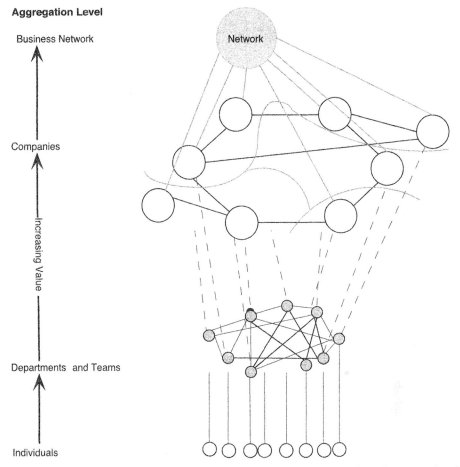

Figure 3-2   Integration of knowledge creates new knowledge at the subsequent levels.

to its engineering and product development department is covering a lot of ground in sharing knowledge, but that company would be, unfortunately, mistaken.

A good case in point is Hewlett-Packard (HP). HP pursued a strategy of making its best practices available throughout the company. Although HP was quite successful in identifying its best practices, it was not successful in moving them from one location to another.

When an intranet, for example, moves the knowledge without the practice, what actually gets moved is the *know-what* without the *know-how*. What do not move in this way are the warranting mechanisms and standards of judgment on which people distinguish the valid and the worthwhile from the useless pieces of "knowledge." Managing knowledge means adding or creating value by actively leveraging know-how, judgment, intuition, and experience resident within and outside the company. It involves delivering value to the customer by integrating knowledge in products, services, and processes.

CLASSIFYING KNOWLEDGE

Knowledge can be classified along four key dimensions: (1) type, (2) focus, (3) complexity, and (4) perishability over time, as shown in Figure 3-3.

Such knowledge can be tacit or explicit. As Figure 3-3 only partially illustrates, the complexity of knowledge is closely related to other dimensions. One way of looking at knowledge from a pragmatic viewpoint is to consider one key subdimension, category of complexity. We deal with this next.

CATEGORIES OF KNOWLEDGE

Knowledge can be classified into two broad categories: tacit and explicit. These are compared in Table 3-3.

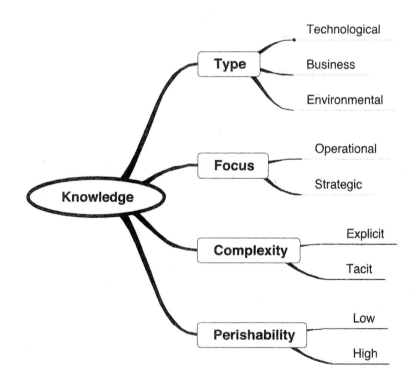

Figure 3-3   A map of some key facets of knowledge.

Table 3-3 Comparing Tacit and Explicit Knowledge

Characteristic	Tacit	Explicit
Nature	Personal, context-specific	Can be codified and explicated
Formalization	Difficult to formalize, record, encode, or articulate	Can be codified and transmitted in a systematic and formal language
Development process	Developed through a process of trial and error encountered in practice	Developed through explication of tacit understanding and interpretation of information
Location	Stored in the heads of people	Stored in documents, databases, Web pages, e-mails, charts, etc
Conversion processes	Converted to explicit through externalization that is often driven by metaphors and analogy	
IT support	Hard to manage, share, or support with IT	Well supported by existing IT
Medium needed	Needs a rich communication medium	Can be transferred through conventional electronic channels

- *Tacit knowledge* is personal, context-specific knowledge that is difficult to formalize, record, or articulate; it is stored in the heads of people. Tacit knowledge consists of various components, such as such as intuition, experience, ground truth, judgment, values, assumptions, beliefs, and intelligence. The tacit component of is mainly developed through a process of trial and error encountered in practice.

- *Explicit knowledge* is that component of knowledge that that can be codified and transmitted in a systematic and formal language: documents, databases, webs, e-mails, charts, etc.

COMPONENTS OF KNOWLEDGE

Intuition, ground truth, judgment, experience, values, assumptions, beliefs, and intelligence—a KM strategy and a KM system must support all of these components.

Truth

Projects and investments made in companies are often based on a set of assumptions: These assumptions might be about markets, customers, the business environment, consumer preferences, competition, etc. Often, the entire set of decisions that might have been made earlier might not hold in future situations because these assumptions might have changed.

Discovering, recording, and maintaining these assumptions and the *ability* to do a what-if analysis akin to a scenario analysis with spreadsheets is a critical component of a complete KM system. The problem, however, is that these assumptions are often deeply embedded in individuals from a specific functional area; they almost seem so natural and so basic that they never explicitly surface.[15]

Judgment

Very unlike information, which is facts; and data, which is factoids; knowledge has a component of judgment attached to it. Although a colorful and precise stock ticker and a real-time graph are excellent information tools for any stock broker, it means nothing if that broker can't act on or make a decision based on the data they provide. Unactionable information is *not* knowledge. However, if our stockbroker recognizes that he or she needs to sell like crazy when the trend chart looks like "this" or needs to hold when it looks like "that," he or she is making judgments based on the data provided. Judgment allows knowledge to rise above and beyond an opinion when it reexamines itself and refines every time it is applied and acted on.[b]

Experience

Knowledge is largely derived from experience and has a historical perspective. Being able to transfer knowledge implies that a part of experiential knowledge also gets transferred to the recipient. Experienced people are usually valued in a company (and are often paid more) because they possess this historical perspective from which they can view current situations and make connections—something that a typical newcomer does not have.[16]

RULES OF THUMB, HEURISTICS, AND TRICKS OF THE TRADE

As people's experience in their jobs increases, they begin to figure out *shortcut solutions* to problems that they have seen before. When they see a new situation, they match it to compare patterns that they are aware of. An experienced car driver, for example, recognizes that an excessive rattle in the car *could* mean a flat tire. Similarly, a computer technician can match a computer that fails to boot up with a pattern that he or she might have seen before, for example, a bad hard drive or failed power supply. With experience, these *scripts* guide our thinking and help us avoid useless tracks[c] that we might have followed earlier. Such *rules of thumb* or *heuristics* provide a single option out of a limited set of specific, often approximate approaches to solving a problem or analyzing a situation accurately, quickly, and efficiently. They play out as scripts. Our experience teaches us these scripts.

---

[b]A number of tools in IT's Pandora's box, including case-based reasoning (CBR) and machine learning systems, can be used to make these kinds of judgments very accurately and in real life. But these come only when the business case has been evaluated and the preceding data-cleansing stages have been accomplished perfectly.

[c]*Tracks*, in this context, refer to decision paths, or known problem-solving methods.

Beyond simplistic situations, it is the subconscious repertoire of scripts and rules of thumb that make experienced managers more valuable than new hires. Contrast this with information. Is there anything like this associated with information that flows through your company's information systems? Tacit knowledge, however complex to understand and manage, holds the promise for long-lasting impact if we can successfully tap into even a fraction of what is available.

Values, Assumptions, and Beliefs

Very often, business processes are based on a set of deeply ingrained but oblivious and unarticulated assumptions. Engineers might *assume* that anything that is behaving strangely has to have an underlying rationale. Managers often mistakenly might assume that their ordinate goal is to maximize their profit center's financial profits. Given that there is more information that is possibly relevant, we are *boundedly rational.* Herbert Simon has written a noteworthy retrospective commentary on this.[17]

Next come beliefs. Companies are often shaped by the beliefs of a few key people working there. The culture of having fun is ingrained in the work environments of Southwest Airlines and Starbucks; creating "insanely great" products (such as the iMac and the commercially unsuccessful Apple Cube) is the culture at Apple; and profits and market dominance are ingrained at Microsoft. These beliefs, values, and assumptions are ingrained in the very character of the firm, often by its founders.

Such values, assumptions, and beliefs are integral components of knowledge. And knowing, capturing, and sharing a component of knowledge can make all the difference between complete knowledge and incomplete, unactionable information. Not all beliefs can be "captured" explicitly. It is for this reason that you will see repeated emphasis on providing systemic pointers to people holding such components.

KNEE-DEEP IN THE REASONING AND ASSUMPTIONS MUDDY

Often, managers have some deeply held, extensively shared, often believed but rarely tested assumptions about the key decisions they make and the basis on which they make them. Like many other things in a dynamic environment that firms operate in, these assumptions can and often do change. When a major manufacturer of a PDA rethought the assumption that the size of the device needs to be no larger than the competitor's product, he gave a free hand to the design team. The design team looked at the most popular brand of shirts sold to the target-buyer market and measured the pocket sizes, resizing the product so that it comfortably slid into a typical shirt pocket. This meant reexamining the very assumption that the size of the device needed to mirror the competitor's. It meant rethinking the underlying criteria for the sizing decision. But it worked. The market share of the device grew substantially after a few of these retested assumptions were applied to the design decisions for the next version of the product.

Starfish Software (www.starfish.com), the developer of the Personal Information Utility (PIU), Sidekick for Windows, did something similar. A single successful product has allowed this company to thrive ever since the introduction of MS-DOS in the early 1980s. In a recent product revision, the company, which had been integrating an increasing number of features to keep up with competing products, rethought two basic assumptions. The first assumption was the need to compete with the feature-rich products in its market. The second assumption was to keep the newer releases of the product compatible with the older versions so that existing customers could easily upgrade. When Starfish asked its existing customers for suggestions, it realized that those assumptions were quite misplaced. So the company scrapped all but the basic functionality in the product that the users said they "never used" and gave them exactly what they asked for—a "light and fast" program. Even though the program has half the number of the features that competing products have, a loyal customer base, willing to pay for a product whose competitors were giving theirs away for almost free, only grew. And it grew exponentially.

Intelligence

When knowledge can be applied, acted on when and where needed, and brought to bear on present decisions, and when these lead to better performance or results, knowledge qualifies as intelligence. When it flows freely throughout a company, is exchanged, grows, and is validated,[d] it transforms an *informated*[18] company into an *intelligent enterprise*. The term *intelligent enterprise,* coined by James Brian Quinn, refers to organization-wide intelligence.[19]

EXTERNALIZATION BEFORE DIGITIZATION

Knowledge creation processes can be thought of as those activities that surround the conversion of subjective tacit knowledge (based on experience) to objective explicit knowledge, also called *externalization.* The problem with this process is that tacit knowledge based on experience is often difficult to articulate, formalize, and encode.

For example, when you drive on an interstate, you make a complex set of decisions based on traffic patterns, your position relative to other vehicles ahead of and behind you, traffic speed, local speed limits, etc. Using experience, you can often subconsciously make these decisions in split seconds without fatal errors. However, it would be extremely difficult if you were to codify this series of decision processes or transfer them to another person.

The process of externalization results in the conversion from a tacit, unarticulated form to an explicit form of representation, which is easier to move across communication networks, when compared with tacit forms that cannot be penned down in any

[d]*Validation* refers to the process of repeated confirmation stemming from ongoing applicability or rejection due to a lack of such applicability.

> readily explicated form. Externalization is often driven by metaphors and analogy. Seeing how a new project in your company is similar to another, unrelated project that your company undertook in the past is an example of such analogy.

INTEGRATION OF KNOWLEDGE SOURCES

So, what are the primary feeds to a KM system? From where does knowledge come into the system? A quick roundup of the sources from which knowledge comes is presented in Table 3-4.

Although the list in Table 3-4 is a partial one, it is clear that much of the knowledge can be explicated, put into systems, and reused. However, some critical pieces of tacit knowledge are extremely difficult, if not impossible, to externalize in such a manner.

Table 3-4 Sources of Knowledge That Feed a Knowledge Management System

Source	Explicit/Codificable	Tacit/Needs Explication
Employee knowledge, skills, and competencies	✔	✔
Experiential knowledge (both at an individual and group level)	✔	✔
Team-based collaborative skills		✔
Informal shared knowledge	✔	✔
Values		✔
Norms		✔
Beliefs	✔	✔
Task-based knowledge	✔	✔
Knowledge embedded in physical systems	✔	✔
Human capital		✔
Knowledge embedded in internal structures		✔
Knowledge embedded in external structures	✔	✔
Customer capital		✔
Experiences of the employee	✔	✔
Customer relationship management	✔	✔

THE THREE FUNDAMENTAL PROCESSES

Three basic processes of knowledge management, as will be elaborated in the next chapters, are:

1. *Knowledge acquisition.* The process of development and creation of insights, skills, and relationships. An experienced stock broker who can see the trend line on a computer monitor and tell which way the market is headed is an example of intuition or acquired knowledge. It is this type of knowledge on which IT components surrounding this process need to focus. Data capture tools with filtering abilities, intelligent databases, keyboard scanners, note-capture tools, and electronic whiteboards are examples of information technology components that can support knowledge acquisition (Figure 3-4).

2. *Knowledge sharing.* Disseminating and making available what is already known. An expert system that helps a novice technical support person answer tech support calls at the help desks of Microsoft is a good example of knowledge that is being shared with that person.

3. *Knowledge utilization.* Here, learning is integrated into the organization. Whatever is broadly available throughout the company can be generalized and applied, at least in part, to new situations. The example of the guy at Microsoft is a perfect case of this: Sharing and utilization are taking place simultaneously.

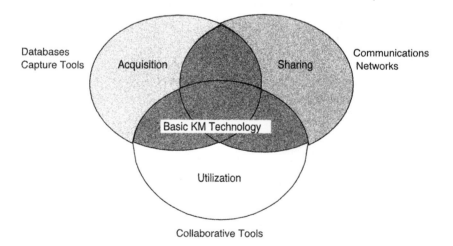

Figure 3-4 The basic elements of KM and typical technology tools that can be used to support each stage.

LEVELS OF PROFESSIONAL KNOWLEDGE

A company's knowledge can be viewed at four levels.[20] Not all these stages stand to benefit from a KM system. The four levels of professional intellect, in the decreasing order of importance, (Figure 3-5) are:

1. *Know-what.* This level represents cognitive knowledge. This is an essential but insufficient basis for competing. An analogy would be the kind of detailed knowledge that a recent college graduate might have. The new graduate might know what should be done but might not have ever have done it in real life.

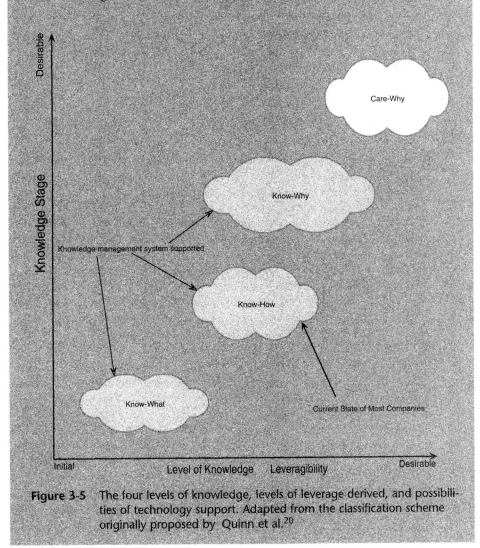

Figure 3-5   The four levels of knowledge, levels of leverage derived, and possibilities of technology support. Adapted from the classification scheme originally proposed by Quinn et al.[20]

2. *Know-how:* Know-how represents the ability to translate bookish (know-what) knowledge into real-world results. Most companies are at this level of understanding, where they can use known rules and apply them well. Professional know-how is developed most rapidly through repeated exposure to real-world, complex problems. Any networking or knowledge support system that intends to move workers from this level to the next must enable extensive exposure to problem solving.

Marketing departments, for example, know that advertising during the Super Bowl is expensive but that the payoffs are huge. This is a general rule that can be applied very well by a marketer. Being able to compete beyond these rules, which *might* be common knowledge, requires a shift from a know-how, information-oriented environment to know-why, that is, knowledge orientation. Professional know-how is developed most rapidly through repeated exposure to real-world, complex problems. Any networking or knowledge support system that intends to move workers from this level to the know-why level must enable extensive exposure to problem solving. But the knowledge economy demands more than just the ability to follow rules.

To be able to move knowledge workers from the know-how level, a KM system must support extensive discussion and conversation so that the participants and employees get a feel for the problems, rather than simply applying well-known rules that have worked in most situations. Conversation is stressed in meetings and brainstorming sessions, but an alarmingly small number of firms support the same types of conversations in systems intending to leverage their corporate knowledge.

3. *Know-why:* A system's understanding represents the know-why aspect of knowledge. Being able to compete beyond rules that *might* be common knowledge requires a shift from an information-oriented (know-how) environment to knowledge orientation (know-why). It's the deep knowledge of the complex slush of cause-and-effect relationships that underlie an employee's range of responsibilities. This knowledge enables individuals to move a step above know-how and create extraordinary leverage by using knowledge, bringing in the ability to deal with unknown interactions and unseen situations. Examples include a stock broker who intuitively knows just when to sell and buy or a baseball player who knows the perfect moment to hit.

Most companies are at one stage below this level of understanding—the know-how stage—where they can use known rules and apply them well. But the knowledge economy demands more than just that ability. To be able to move knowledge workers from the know-how level, a KM system must support extensive discussion and conversation so that the participants and employees get a feel for the problems, rather than simply applying well-known rules that have worked in most situations. Conversation is stressed in meetings and brainstorming sessions, but an alarmingly small number of firms support the same types of conversations in systems intending to leverage their corporate knowledge. Perhaps we have bought into the concept of expert systems and conventional decision support systems a little too much. Value creation from knowledge is enhanced if experimentation in the course of problem solving increases know-why and if incentive structures stimulate care-why, rather than focusing solely on know-how.

4. *Care-why.* Care-why represents self-motivated creativity that exists in a company. This happens to be the only level that cannot be supported by a KM system. Care-why explains why highly motivated, creative, and energetic groups and companies outperform larger corporations with more money and resources. This level of knowledge exists in a company's culture, and after we have done all we can to provide technology support for the other three levels, we must give this one our best shot, because technology is of little or no help at this level.

Perhaps we have bought into the concept of expert systems and conventional decision support systems a little too much. Value creation from knowledge is enhanced if experimentation in the course of problem solving increases know-why and if incentive structures stimulate care-why, rather than focusing solely on know-how.

The Collaborative Nature of Knowledge

One characteristic that distinguishes a firm's knowledge from its information assets is the foundation on which knowledge is primarily built. Collaborative problem solving, conversations, and teamwork generate a significant proportion of the knowledge assets that exist within a firm.

In today's dynamic environments and industries, even the knowledge about the process of doing things is incomplete at the outset and develops over time, through various kinds of learning. These processes consist of a series of interdependent solutions, each of which adds something to what a firm knows. As a demonstration of this, Marco Iansiti has published a detailed analysis of how Netscape built earlier versions of its Web browser.[e,21]

Knowledge involved in deliberation on alternative decisions that could have been made is typically lost in the process once the job is done. Knowledge utilization is inherently a collaborative process, and neither within-firm nor cross-firm utilization and transfer of knowledge can succeed without effectively supporting collaboration. This focus on collaboration is perhaps one of the primary distinguishing factors that differentiates knowledge support systems from information systems. A simple question such as, Has anyone seen something like this before? can perhaps generate an amazingly rich array of responses, all but one of which will soon be forgotten once the problem is solved. Fortunately, this happens to be one of the easiest avenues for capturing knowledge electronically, as illustrated in Figure 3-6.

Retrofitting Knowledge to Information Technology

Knowledge must be treated as a driver for technology choice, not vice versa. Table 3-5 shows how technology can be fitted to knowledge that it is meant to support.

---

[e]Netscape was bought out by America Online in 1998 for approximately $4 billion in a three-way arrangement between Netscape, America Online, and Sun Microsystems.

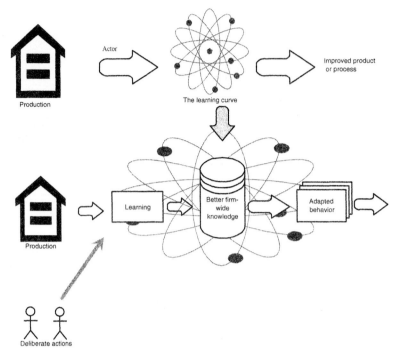

Figure 3-6   Key differences between the concepts of a learning company and a knowledge-leveraging company.

Table 3-5 Retrofitting knowledge to the choice and implementation of IT and IT support functions

Aspect	Asset and Outcome	Technology as a Secondary Asset-Based Choice
What is managed?	Knowledge Knowledge creation Knowledge reuse Knowledge integration	Hardware Software Communications network
Why manage it?	Provide historical basis for decisions Enable sound decisions Increase decision accuracy and choice efficiency	Implement reliable and high-quality hardware, software, and communication systems

Table 3-5 Retrofitting knowledge to the choice and implementation of IT and IT support functions (cont.)

Aspect	Asset and Outcome	Technology as a Secondary Asset-Based Choice
How do we manage it?	Integrated, cross-functional approach Include the entire extended enterprise, i.e., suppliers, consumers, consultants, vendors, and buyers	Integrate existing systems Control costs Make processes more efficient Learn from mistakes Reuse, not reinvent Inventorize*
Metrics and success criteria	Financial, tangible and intangible gains realized Impact on performance Impact on competitiveness Timeliness Benchmark performance	A working KM system A well-used KM system A growing KM system Users increasingly contribute and demonstrate reciprocity.
Who manages it?	The CKO** or equivalent manager Individual organizational units using it	The CKO or equivalent managerial employee The information technology function Network service providers. Practice leaders

*Inventorize refers to the concept of taking knowledge into account and formally recording its existence.

**The CKO title can be a misleading role definer. Many companies are structured in ways that do not allow a CKO, per se, to oversee KM. Numerous companies have scrapped the CKO title and assigned the role to equivalent high-level managerial workers such as competence managers and practice area leaders.

TAMING THE TIGER'S TAIL

KM has not (until this book) lent itself to any existing clear-cut strategy or technique. The same initiatives that might succeed in one firm might fail miserably in another. Implementing an initiative for managing knowledge is inherently difficult for several reasons, most of which have to do with the way firms have been run—more or less successfully—in more traditional settings, past eras, and structures. There is no KM silver bullet. In this section, we examine inherent barriers to KM and ways around them.

KNOWLEDGE MANAGEMENT IS EXPENSIVE

One of the biggest barriers to implementing a KM initiative in a company is that of selling the idea to senior management and to end users. KM is often an expensive proposition; it's not just the expense of the technology infrastructure to enable it but also the expense involved in implementing cultural changes and revitalizing employee reward structures. If your KM strategy is improperly planned, there is no immediate tangible outcome that can be easily demonstrated, and this further raises skepticism among upper management controlling the budget.

Easy Ways to Invest in Expensive Paperweights

Firms that have experimented with technology as a primary enabler for managing knowledge have learned a painful lesson. Building a knowledge exchange mechanism with fancy pieces of technology does nothing to motivate employees to part with their valuable and sustenance-critical expertise. The actually feasible solution lies in an amiable synthesis of people with technology and cultural change with technological change. The catch phrase is "People first, technology next." It's the *building people to work around technology* mentality that leads many initiatives of this type down the road to failure.

KNOWLEDGE HOARDING IS HUMAN NATURE

"Build it and they will come" might be an idea that does apply to many other things in business, but not to KM. Knowledge workers often tend to use all knowledge that's easily accessible but do not always share all knowledge that they own. After all, one might argue that, if all the skills of a CEO could be captured in a decision support system, why would you need to keep a CEO who takes home $200,000 a year! This is where a new way of thinking—a new approach to rewarding employees on the basis of contribution to the firm's knowledge and not just performance—needs to be put into place.

COMPANIES THAT MANAGE KNOWLEDGE WELL

Throughout this book, we look at good examples from small and large companies. We close this section with a brief look at companies that have reaped significant financial and customer satisfaction gains by managing specialized internal knowledge. Even though these companies have not implemented full-fledged, organization-wide KM programs, the gains from highly circumscribed versions of such programs show that there is a *lot* to be gained.

- Price Waterhouse used Lotus Notes and formed a central group to identify, capture, and document best practices throughout the company.
- Collaborative work was significantly improved.

- Information flows throughout the firm became frictionless.
- Price Waterhouse measures the return on its investments in terms of the gain in revenue generated through the use of such a system.
- Kaiser Permanente has leveraged its best practices extensively. In one case, the company implemented an open-access program a year earlier than expected just because it transferred best practices from one location to another across regions within the United States. The success of a best practice at one location makes it easier to sell its value to senior management at another location.
- Texas Instruments was low on its customer satisfaction rankings in 1992 because of the company's unusual failure to deliver semiconductors on time. TI's worldwide wafer fabrication team adopted and transferred best practices internally across several locations, effectively creating additional wafer fabrication capacity that would have needed a $500 million investment in a new fabrication plant. Besides saving half a billion dollars in additional investments, this knowledge-sharing initiative pulled the company up from the bottom to the top position on its industry's customer satisfaction rankings.

BUSINESS AND KNOWLEDGE

The firm, taken for granted in the conventional economy, appears to have a doubtful future in the knowledge economy. Well-established firms that were probably doing very well innovating and leading their industries have gradually begun to fade out. Examples abound. Netscape Corporation, which literally created the Web browser market, was bought out by America Online. CompuServe, one of the oldest online service companies that had flourished even before the mass advent of the Internet, was bought out by AOL. Many factors have convinced organizations facing a highly unpredictable business environment of the value of managing their primary, or rather, only competitive assets—their knowledge and their ability to learn faster than their competitors. Some of those factors are:

- Diminishing competitive power of leading firms
- Global competitive demands faced by companies
- Ever-changing business scenarios
- Everyday examples of failures and bankruptcies among companies that once led their markets

How Companies Learn to Learn

Although knowledge is thought of as the property of individuals, a great deal of knowledge is both produced and held collectively.[22] Such knowledge is produced when people in a company work together in tightly knit groups or communities of practice. Even though the employees and the knowledge they carry around in their heads is beginning to play the most significant part in the success of companies, it's unfortunate that companies fail to recognize this early enough.

Knowledge-Friendly Companies

Knowledge-friendly companies are those that realize that their knowledge can be the only asset from which they can hope to draw a long-term competitive advantage. Technology by itself, owing to its relative ease of replicability, has failed to provide this advantage. Core competencies are more than just know-what. They go beyond the typical form of explicit knowledge, such as a manual or a cookbook approach, and depend on the singular ability to put the know-what into action. And that is what distinguishes it from information. Having detailed information of yesterday's sales in your store located in Richmond, Virginia is information. Putting it into action, knowing what to do with it, interpreting it, and acting on it is where the challenge lies. Three factors that distinguish such companies from others.[23]

1. *Leveraged core competencies:* Companies such as Canon make significant investments in developing knowledge in the key areas of core competence (there are eight such areas, in the case of Canon). This investment has paid off in the long term: Canon attributes 30 of its very successful products to this ability. Companies that have a KM mindset use their well-developed core competencies as the launch pad for their new product and service offerings. This means that these companies are willing and able to make the commitment toward both identification and management of knowledge around the key areas in which their core competencies lie. At the heart of any successful KM project lies the focus on knowing what the firm needs first to prioritize. As intuitive and commonsensical it might seem, companies miss this point over and over. It's only after you get beyond this point that you can even think of building a KM system. Starting the other way around—fitting people to the latest technology that you want to introduce in your company—is predestined for failure.

2. *Continuous improvement of the value-added chain:* Wal-Mart is a great example of a company that continuously experiments with an eye on improvement. The company conducts ongoing experiments in its stores throughout the country. Wal-Mart is often discussed as the poster child example of a successful just-in-time (JIT) inventory management implementation in business schools. Wal-Mart, realizing that the value of information flows between its suppliers and stores, thought to leverage it. It effectively leveraged information to create knowledge, adding context and meaning to the numbers

generated by its checkout counter cash registers. The captured data is automatically converted into well-summarized information that is further converted into knowledge of its safe-stock levels for each product in its multitudes of product lines. The summary automatically informs and authorizes the supplier to replenish stocks in each of its stores. This entire process reflects an attitude that supports constant learning and addition to Wal-Mart's existing knowledge.

3. *Ability to revitalize fundamentally*: Another characteristic that distinguishes a company that is ready for KM is the ability to revitalize itself fundamentally. This might mean dropping old ways of doing things altogether or challenging the fundamental ways in which the company does business. Motorola is a classic example. The company simply drops entire product lines and enters new lines when the markets seem to be making fundamental shifts. This flexibility is perhaps the primary reason for Motorola's enviable success in the cellular telephone market. Companies that actually want to apply knowledge that they gain should be ready to accept such fundamental shifts that the knowledge might demand.

KNOWLEDGE-SHARING COMPANIES

Knowledge is one the few resources that demonstrates increasing returns to scale: The more you share it, the more it grows. In 1997, Netscape saw a rapid decline in its share of the Internet browser market as Microsoft's Internet Explorer gained market share at the expense of Netscape Communicator and Navigator browser products. In March 1998, Netscape made the source code of its browser products available at no cost and under licensing provisions almost free to anyone who cared to download it from Netscape's Web site (www.netscape.com). The company apparently gave away knowledge that cost millions of dollars to generate—an asset that any company would conceivably guard with its life.

Now, why in the world would Netscape do this? First, by making its products widely available, accepted, and used, it hoped to secure the market share of a complementary product—its own Web server software. Second, it hoped that millions of software developers would adopt, adapt, and enhance its products.

The software industry is not an exception. Our second example comes from the pharmaceuticals industry, one that, like the software industry, is highly knowledge intensive in nature. Incyte Pharmaceuticals, which achieved a market capitalization of over $600 million in under six years, followed a similar strategy by licensing its gene-sequencing knowledge nonexclusively to large pharmaceutical companies. This initiative helped it gain access to knowledge assets of its partners and created a standard platform for the provision of all genome data that becomes increasingly valuable as more and more companies begin to utilize it (see www.science.doe.gov/ober/). Table 3-6 presents some reasons and frequently encountered impediments for sharing knowledge.

Table 3-6 Sharing Knowledge: Reasons and Impediments

Enablers	Impediments
High levels of trust	Fear and suspicion
Rewards for sharing	Unintentionally rewarded for hoarding
Team-based collaborative work	Individual effort without recognition and reward
Aligned mission, vision and values, and strategy	Individual accountability and reward
Joint team-wide accountability and reward	Functional focus
Process focus	Lack of alignment
Focus on customer satisfaction	Not-invented-here syndrome
Open to outside ideas	Too busy to share
Eye on competition	Internal competition
Collaborative and cross-functional work	Incompatible IT
Need to share	Compartmentalization of functional groups
Localized decision making	Centralized top-down decision making
Group accountability and rewards	Employee-owner interest conflict

IS YOUR COMPANY READY FOR KNOWLEDGE MANAGEMENT?

We've looked in depth at knowledge and its value to business. We've looked superficially at companies that employ KM to their advantage (in Chapter 6, we will look in depth at other companies that have successfully institutionalized KM). Now it's time to look at your company.

A number of facilitating factors are required imperatives for any KM effort to succeed. You will notice that most successful adopters share many of these underlying facilitators that indicate their readiness for KM.

- *The scanning imperative*: This is the first facilitator for successful KM. Three simple questions can help you determine whether such a scanning imperative exists in your own company.

1. Does your company truly understand the environment in which it functions?
2. Does it gather information about practices and conditions outside the organization?
3. Is there awareness about how your company's internal operations compare with those of your competitor?

- *Shared perception of performance gaps*: Is there a shared and relatively well-agreed-on perception of how things are in your company and how they actually need to be? Maybe your customer response times are too long. Maybe the quality of your services is below the mark. There needs to be a fairly high degree of consensus on issues relating to performance gaps. Only then can you begin addressing the issues of primary concern and make an effort toward reducing those performance discontinuities and closely associated knowledge gaps. Recognizing these gaps also means that you can initially focus KM on addressing issues where the benefits could be most compelling.

- *Metrics*: There should be a considerable focus on how things are measured. Is everything measured solely on the basis of financial outcomes? If so, you need to incorporate a better set of metrics that also measures knowledge assets. And that is the hardest part. Without an explicitly recognized set of measures, how can you attribute any part of improved performance to your company's knowledge?

A major consulting firm measures the value it gains from its KM system by the number of additional consulting contracts completed and signed that result directly from what already exists in its portfolio of past projects. Even though there might be no perfect measure, there needs to be *some* way of measuring knowledge assets and the gains the company realizes by leveraging them (Chapter 14 addresses this issue in detail).

- *Corporate culture*: KM is *at least* as much about a company's culture as it is about the underlying technology. No technology, by itself, can take care of the often-ignored cultural part. Examples abound of companies that failed to realize any benefits from their KM systems just because the culture was not just right. You need to realize the significance of nurturing a conducive corporate culture before you begin to attempt leveraging knowledge. It exists, for the most part, in the heads of your employees. Figuratively speaking, technology can lead the horse to the water but cannot make him drink it.

A sharing culture in which problems, errors, omissions, successes, and disasters are shared and not penalized or hidden is mandatory. You must accept debate and conflict as ways of solving problems. In Chapter 7, where we discuss the design of the technology infrastructure, you will see how different computer-based tools can be used to resolve conflict and debate by calling on past knowledge. But such tools will be of no help if debates and conflict are discouraged and failures hidden. Chapter 13 takes on this issue.

- *Knowledge champions*: Unlike what most prior management ideas suggest, having just one champion for KM might just not cut it. New ideas and methods suggested by employees at all levels have to make it into the design. Because of the highly cross-functional nature of corporate knowledge, you need champions from different functional areas. Champions can define the vision, but everyone else in the company needs to support, agree on, refine, or even challenge it. Without this support, your company might be better off sticking to its old ways and avoid the bother of trying to implement a system that no one will *really* use.

Knowledge activists serve as catalysts of knowledge creation and as the *connectors* of present initiatives with those in the future. Present initiatives represent projects being pursued in the organization at any given point; future initiatives refer to projects that follow either directly or indirectly from those present efforts. The underlying element of a KM system is a supporting infrastructure of both IT applications, as well as organizational measures that facilitate creation, capture, reuse, maintenance, and transfer of knowledge.

- *Strategic alignment:* Like any information technology strategy, knowledge strategy needs to be closely tied to the company's business strategy. If the company's primary goal is to sell low-cost products, KM strategy must be aligned to support that goal. If the ultimate goal is customer satisfaction, the knowledge strategy needs to have a comparable and endorsing focus. A misalignment implies that your company is still missing a crucial facilitator to support knowledge use, application, and reuse.

- *Begin with what you know:* Before your company decides to become something new, evaluate what you are now. Without full awareness of what assumptions your company runs on now, you cannot gauge what needs to be done and where you need to begin. Rather than creating "new knowledge" in an attempt to breathe new life into your company's competitiveness, accept your current data and information assets and start by leveraging those first.

Finally, use the toolkit in Appendix A to assess your company's readiness for KM.

LESSONS LEARNED

Knowledge is best defined as actionable information—deeper, richer, and more expansive. Actionable implies that it is available when and where it is needed to make the right decisions and in the right context. It is valid information endowed with meaning, context, and purpose that brings it to bear habitually on decisions. Management of knowledge, not data or information, is, therefore, the primary driver of a firm's competitive advantage.

- *There are two primary types of knowledge.* Tacit knowledge is knowledge in the minds of employees that cannot be easily codified or explicated (therefore hard to manage or support with technology), and explicit knowledge is knowledge that can be stored and transferred, for example, electronically. Using the process of externalization, subjective tacit knowledge based on experience is converted into objective explicit knowledge. Tacit and explicit knowledge can further be organized as strategic and operational, multilocational and centralized, migratory, and situated. These include components such as experience, ground truth, judgment, heuristics, values, assumptions, and beliefs.

- *Experiential knowledge is stored as scripts.* Knowledge is largely derived from experience. Being able to transfer knowledge implies that a part of experiential knowledge—scripts, intuition, rules of thumb, heuristics, and methods—gets transferred to the recipient, as well.

- *Knowledge is essentially collaborative and falters with a data-hoarding mentality.* New knowledge is created, in part, through the collaborative processes that employees pursue as a part of their work. The threat to such enabling collaboration comes from the "more is better" data-hoarding mentality inherited from data processing and data management eras.

- *The five Cs:* Data is converted to information through condensation, contextualization, correction, categorization, and correction.

- *Managing knowledge is essential.* KM can help your company deal with market pressures; avoid the infinite, expensive loop of work duplication and precinct reinvention; and deal with the threat of job mobility of employees holding critical parts of your firm's tacit knowledge drivers.

- *Managing knowledge effectively can produce enviable results:* KM holds many promises for increased efficiency of processes and proactively responsive corporate capabilities.

- *Beyond know-how, toward care-why:* Professional intellect can be thought of as a moving scale that begins with know-what and proceeds through know-how and know-why to care-why. The first three stages are well supported by a KM system. First bring your company to the know-why stage using technology and cultural enablers. Most companies are still at a know-how-driven stage.

- *Intranets and extranets can be a starting point for building a KM system:* An intranet is not a KM system but can be built on further to create the most suitable front end for one. A KM system has a different content focus, has higher performance demands, uses a narrow base, and productizes knowledge.

- *Success of a KM system depends on reciprocity.* KM depends on knowledge sharing, reciprocity, and a supporting culture. Reciprocity drives people's willingness to share knowledge, and such reciprocity can be introduced only through appropriate reward systems and corporate culture change.

- *Is your company ready for KM?* Companies that have successfully deployed KM share seven characteristics that can help you decide whether your company is ready for it.

With this background, let us proceed to the 10-step KM methodology that provides a road map for planning, developing, aligning, and successfully implementing both a KM system and incremental KM strategy in your company.

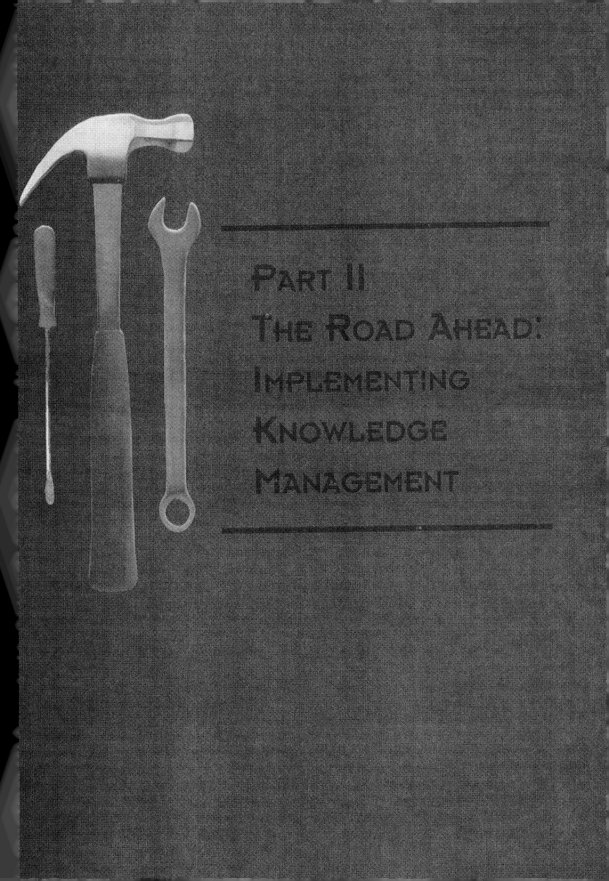

PART II
THE ROAD AHEAD:
IMPLEMENTING
KNOWLEDGE
MANAGEMENT

CHAPTER 4
THE 10-STEP KNOWLEDGE MANAGEMENT ROAD MAP

IN THIS CHAPTER

✔ Understand the 10-step KM road map and how it applies to *your* company.

✔ Understand the four phases constituting these 10 steps: infrastructural evaluation; KM system analysis, design and development; deployment; and evaluation.

✔ Understand where each step takes you.

✔ Articulate a clear link between KM and business strategy.

✔ Learn how to prioritize KM support for processes to maximize business impact.

✔ Understand the key steps involved in knowledge auditing, knowledge mapping, strategic grounding, deployment methodology, teaming, changing management, and return-on-investment (ROI) metrics formulation.

✔ Use real-options analysis to guide your KM investments.

THEY COPIED ALL THAT THEY COULD FOLLOW BUT THEY COULD NOT COPY MY MIND, AND I LEFT 'EM SWEATING AND STEALING AND A YEAR AND HALF BEHIND.
—RUDYARD KIPLING

Knowledge management is a complex activity that cannot deliver business impact without a concrete plan. This chapter introduces that plan: The 10-step KM road map that will guide you through strategizing, designing, developing, and implementing a KM initiative—with *your* company in mind. Recall, this is a road map, not a methodology with a deceptive look of a cookie-cutter formulation. Even if your competitors get to it, they cannot apply it because knowledge is protected by context as copy-protected software is protected by encryption.

This strengthening idiosyncrasy of knowledge also has a negative implication for you: You cannot easily copy a competitor's KM strategy. Examples from your industry's leaders can be useful for understanding KM, but they cannot show you the right way to do it. For these reasons, your KM system and KM strategy will have to be unique to your company. What follows in the next four sections of this book is an explication of the road map for developing an idiosyncratic knowledge strategy.

THE 10-STEP KNOWLEDGE MANAGEMENT ROAD MAP

Each of the next 10 chapters that follow will describe one each of the 10 steps in the KM road map. These steps and their sequence are described in Figure 4-1.

To grasp the bigger picture, look at the four phases that the 10 steps of the road map comprise:

1. Infrastructural evaluation
2. KM system analysis, design, and development
3. System deployment
4. ROI and performance evaluation

These four phases are described in Parts II, III, IV, and V of this book. Table 4-1 describes how each of these steps is logically arranged in these chapters.

PHASE 1: INFRASTRUCTURAL EVALUATION

The first phase of the 10-step technique involves two steps. In the first step, you analyze your existing infrastructure, then identify concrete steps that you can take to leverage and build on your KM platform. In the second step, you perform a strategic analysis to link KM objectives and business strategy.

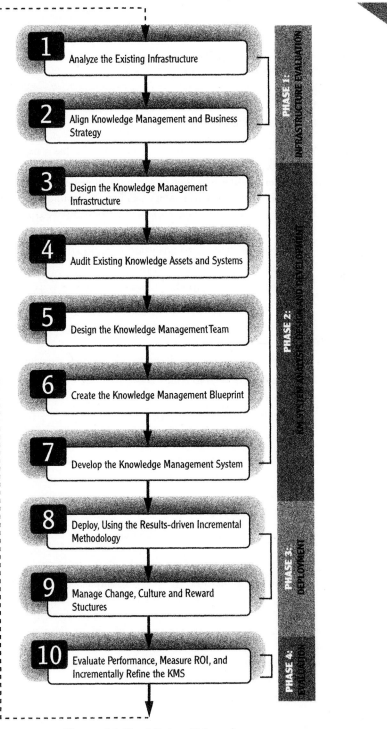

Figure 4-1 The 10-step KM road map.

Table 4-1 Organization of Chapters Describing The Four Phases
            of The 10-Step KM Roadmap

Part	Chapter	Step
PHASE 1: INFRASTRUCTURAL EVALUATION		
II	5	Step 1: Analyzing existing infrastructure
	6	Step 2: Aligning KM and business strategy
PHASE 2: KM SYSTEM ANALYSIS, DESIGN, AND DEVELOPMENT		
III	7	Step 3: Designing the KM architecture, and integrating existing infrastructure
	8	Step 4: Auditing and analyzing existing knowledge
	9	Step 5: Designing the KM team
	10	Step 6: Creating the KM blueprint
	11	Step 7: Developing the KM system
PHASE 3: DEPLOYMENT		
IV	12	Step 8: Deploying with results-driven incrementalism (RDI) methodology
	13	Step 9: Leadership issues
PHASE 4: METRICS FOR PERFORMANCE EVALUATION		
V	14	Step 10: Real-options analysis of returns and performance

STEP 1: ANALYSIS OF EXISTING INFRASTRUCTURE

In this first step, you gain an understanding of various components that constitute the KM strategy and technology framework. By analyzing and accounting for what is already in place in your company, you can identify critical gaps in the existing infrastructure. Consequently, you will be able to build on what already exists. Instead of *telling* you what components to build on, I will guide you through the process of making those decisions specifically in the context of your company. Although leveraging existing infrastructure is the logically, scientifically, rationally, theoretically, common-sensically, and financially right approach, it also stands a better chance of generating stronger management support for your KM project because of the perception that you are not completely abandoning the "old" existing investments.

STEP 2: ALIGNING KNOWLEDGE MANAGEMENT AND BUSINESS STRATEGY

Business strategy is usually at a high level. Developing systems is always at a low level: Specifications and features are needed, not abstractions or visions. The second step in the 10-step road map allows you to make the connection between these two: Raise KM platform design to the level of business strategy and pull strategy down to the level of systems design. As a part of the process of creating this alignment between KM and business strategy, Chapter 6 describes what you must do.

PHASE 2: KNOWLEDGE MANAGEMENT SYSTEM ANALYSIS, DESIGN, AND DEVELOPMENT

The second phase of KM implementation involves analysis, design, and development of the KM system. The five steps that constitute this phase are:

1. KM architecture design and component selection
2. Knowledge audit and analysis
3. KM team design
4. Creation of a KM blueprint tailored for your organization
5. The actual systems development process

Let us briefly examine each of these steps and understand the key tasks that need to be accomplished at each step.

STEP 3: KNOWLEDGE MANAGEMENT ARCHITECTURE AND DESIGN

As the third step toward deploying KM, you must select the infrastructural components that constitute the KM system architecture. KM systems use a seven-layer architecture, and the technology required to build each layer is readily available. Integrating these components to create the KM system model requires thinking in terms of an *infostructure,* rather than an infrastructure. Your first big choice is the collaborative platform. We will reason through the choice of the preferred collaborative platform to decide whether the Web or a proprietary platform is better suited for your company. You will also identify and understand components of the collaborative intelligence layer: artificial intelligence, data warehouses, genetic algorithms, neural networks, expert reasoning systems, rule bases, and case-based reasoning. You will also examine how newer developments, such as peer-to-peer platforms, hold promise for corporate KM.

Step 4: Knowledge Audit and Analysis

A KM project must begin with what your company already knows. In the fourth step, you audit and analyze knowledge, but first you must understand why a knowledge audit is needed. Then you assemble an audit team representing various organizational units, as described in Chapter 8. This team performs a preliminary assessment of knowledge assets within your company to identify those that are both critical and weak.

Step 5: Designing the Knowledge Management Team

In the fifth step on the KM road map, you form the KM team that will design, build, implement, and deploy your company's KM system. To design an effective KM team, you must identify key stakeholders both within and outside your company; identify sources of expertise that are needed to design, build, and deploy the system successfully while balancing the technical and managerial requirements. We examine the issues of correctly sizing the KM team, managing diverse and often divergent stakeholder expectations, and using techniques for both identifying critical failure points in such teams.

Step 6: Creating the Knowledge Management System Blueprint

The KM team identified in Step 5 builds on a KM blueprint that provides a plan for building and incrementally improving a KM system. As you work toward designing a KM architecture, you must understand its seven layers specifically in the context of *your* company and determine how each of these can be optimized for performance and scalability, as well as high levels of interoperability. You will also see how to position and *scope* the KM system to a feasible level where benefits exceed costs. Finally, you will see ways to *future-proof* the KM system so that it does not "run out of gas" when the next wave of fancy technology hits the market. This step integrates work from all preceding steps so that it culminates in a strategically oriented KM system design.

Step 7: Developing the Knowledge Management System

Once you have created a blueprint for your KM system (Step 6), the next step is that of actually putting together a working system. We will tackle the issues of integrating a system across different layers to build a coherent and stable KM platform.

PHASE 3: DEPLOYMENT

The third phase in the 10-step road map involves the process of deploying the KM system that you built in the preceding stages. This phase involves two steps:

1. Deployment of the system with a *results-driven incremental* technique, more commonly known as the RDI methodology. This step also involves the selection and implementation of a pilot project to precede the introduction of a full-fledged KM system.

2. Cultural change, revised reward structures, and the choice of using (or not using) a CKO to make KM produce results. This is perhaps the most important complementary step that is critical to the acceptance of a KM system in any company.

   Let us take a brief look at these two steps.

STEP 8: PILOT TESTING AND DEPLOYMENT USING RDI METHODOLOGY

A large-scale project such as a typical KM system must take into account the *actual* needs of its users. Although a cross-functional KM team can help uncover many of these needs, a pilot deployment is the ultimate reality check. In the eighth step on the KM road map, you must decide how you can select *cumulative* releases with the highest payoffs first. You will evaluate the need for a pilot project; if it is needed, select the right, nontrivial, and representative pilot project. You will also appreciate scope issues and ways to identify and isolate failure points. Finally, you will evaluate how to use the RDI methodology to deploy the system, using cumulative results-driven business releases.

STEP 9: LEADERSHIP AND REWARD STRUCTURES

The most erroneous assumption that many companies make is that the intrinsic value of an innovation such as a KM system will lead to its enthusiastic adoption and use. Knowledge sharing cannot be mandated: Your employees are not like troops, they are like volunteers. Encouraging use and gaining employee support requires new reward structures that motivate employees to use the system and contribute to its enthusiastic adoption. Above all, it requires enthusiastic leadership that sets an example to follow. Chapter 13 guides you through these leadership and incentive development issues.

PHASE 4: METRICS FOR EVALUATION

The last phase involves one step that most companies have been struggling with: measuring business value of KM. When pushed for hard data, managers have often resorted to ill-suited and easily misused approaches, such as cost-benefit analysis, net present value (NPV) evaluation, vague ROI measures, or, at best, Tobin's q. Chapter 14 describes the traps that companies are most vulnerable to and suggests ways to avoid them while devising a robust set of company-specific metrics for KM.

STEP 10: REAL-OPTIONS ANALYSIS FOR KNOWLEDGE MANAGEMENT

The tenth step—measuring ROI—must account for both financial and competitive impacts of KM on your business. This step guides you through the process of selecting an appropriate set of metrics and arriving at a lean but powerful composite. We will use the Nobel Prize-winning real-options approach for analysis. We will also evaluate many ways in which real-options data can be tracked. We also see how successful companies have approached metrics, what errors they have made in the past, and how you can learn from their mistakes.

Being able to measure returns serves two purposes: It arms you with hard data and dollar figures that you can use to prove the impact of effective KM, and it lets you refine KM design through subsequent iterations.

LESSONS LEARNED

The 10-step road map is built on years of cumulative research involving small and large companies in a variety of industries worldwide. It is a road map that—unlike a cookie cutter methodology—will help you build both a KM strategy and a KM system that is tailored to *your* company.

Part IIA
The First Phase:
Infrastructure
Evaluation and
Leverage

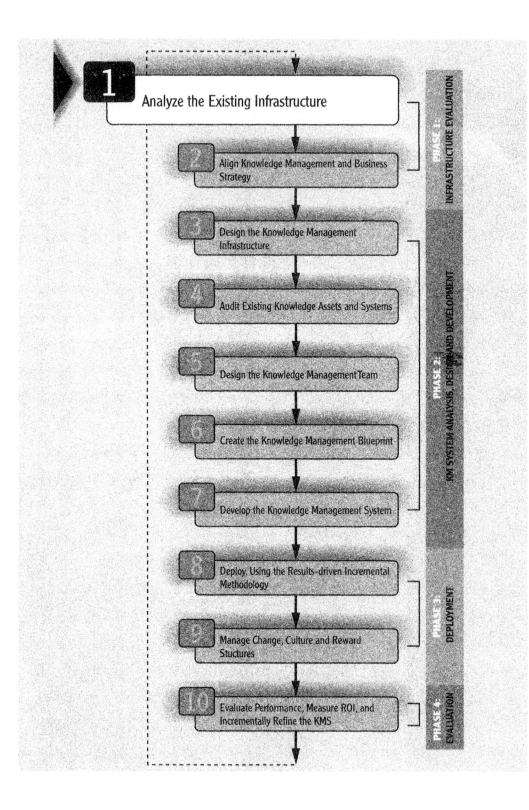

1 Analyze the Existing Infrastructure

2 Align Knowledge Management and Business Strategy

3 Design the Knowledge Management Infrastructure

4 Audit Existing Knowledge Assets and Systems

5 Design the Knowledge Management Team

6 Create the Knowledge Management Blueprint

7 Develop the Knowledge Management System

8 Deploy, Using the Results-driven Incremental Methodology

9 Manage Change, Culture and Reward Stuctures

10 Evaluate Performance, Measure ROI, and Incrementally Refine the KMS

PHASE 1: INFRASTRUCTURE EVALUATION

PHASE 2: KM SYSTEM ANALYSIS, DESIGN AND DEVELOPMENT

PHASE 3: DEPLOYMENT

PHASE 4: EVALUATION

CHAPTER 5
THE LEVERAGED INFRASTRUCTURE

IN THIS CHAPTER

✔ Comprehend the technology components of a KM platform.

✔ Analyze, leverage, and build on existing infrastructure.

✔ Deploy knowledge servers for enabling enterprise-wide integration of islands of digital sources.

✔ Perform a preliminary business needs analysis to evaluate relevant knowledge server choices.

✔ Identify the limitations of implemented tools and identify existing gaps in your company's existing infrastructure.

GREAT IDEAS OFTEN HAVE THREE STAGES OF REACTION—
FIRST, "IT'S CRAZY AND DON'T WASTE MY TIME."
SECOND, "IT'S POSSIBLE, BUT IT'S NOT WORTH DOING."
AND FINALLY, "I'VE ALWAYS SAID IT WAS A GOOD IDEA."
—ARTHUR C. CLARKE

The greatest difficulty lies not in persuading people to accept new ideas but in persuading them to abandon their old ones. What if the lofty promise of competitiveness cost your business the abandonment of your existing practices, your communication systems, your networks, and your infrastructural investments? Hard sell. Ignoring the economic theory of sunk costs, the hard fact is that you cannot afford to abandon what you have or, for the most part, you cannot afford to change substantially what is working for your company right now—just on the premise of a distant rainbow. KM initiatives that will gain management support to continue funding and keep risks low will have to build on existing systems.

We call this concept the *leveraged infrastructure*. You build your entire KM platform over and above the existing infrastructure; you put in parts and tools that integrate with what already exists. What works for Ford, Microsoft, and Monsanto need not work for your company. After all, losing a couple of hundred million dollars is only a small dent in Microsoft's budget. What about yours?

This chapter helps you through the analysis and evaluation of your company's existing infrastructure. By understanding components that constitute the KM technology framework, you can identify gaps in your present infrastructure. There is no perfect recipe for KM, and prescribing one is fraught with risk. The key lies in accurately identifying and fixing what will work as part of the KM platform and what will not. In the end, you must tie in what already exists and coherently integrate it.

LEVERAGING WHAT EXISTS

Technology's most valuable role in KM is broadening the reach and enhancing the speed of knowledge transfer. Technology plays three key roles in KM. First, it facilitates communication. Second, it provides the infrastructure for storing codified and explicated knowledge. Third, it assists with mapping dispersed bits and pieces of tacit and explicit knowledge to establish and maintain intricate interdependencies among them. Depending on whether your work processes rely more on tacit or explicit knowledge, two of these three facets will become more pronounced, as shown in Figure 5-1.

Remember that the formal notion of KM is relatively new but the concepts and facilitating technologies have existed for years. So bear in mind the following ideas when you are looking at what can be leveraged:

- *From the machine to the mind*: Innovation, generation of new ideas, and exploitation of a firm's intellectual prowess: These are keystones that a KM system needs to support.[1]

- *Collaborative synergy*: Successful KM is anchored to collaboration and collaborative success. If the KM system cannot support collaboration, knowledge sharing, learning, and continuous improvement, it's not worth the bother—it's destined to die for lack of use.

- *Real knowledge, not artificial intelligence*: A good KM system is not about capturing your smartest employee's knowledge in a knowledge base or expert system. Even though that was the original intent of the artificial intelligence community, the possibility of that has

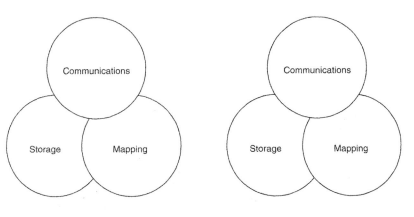

Figure 5-1   Different roles of IT become pronounced, depending on whether a knowledge platform is tacitly or explicitly knowledge-intensive.

now become a joke. While considering components to leverage, count out technology investments that focus solely on codification of tacit knowledge.

- *Conversation as a medium for thought*: A KM system lives and thrives on conversation. Free, unrestricted, and easy conversation must be supported. The medium itself should not be a stricture.

- *Sources and originators, not just information*: A good KM system must make it easy to find sources of know-how, not just know-how itself, to locate people and expertise, and to reuse what exists, either in a tangible form or in someone's head.

- *Decision support*: Decision-making quality and accuracy should be enhanced by the historical perspective that a KM system has to support.

- *Flexibility and scalability*: A well-designed KM system is not written in stone. It has and needs room to grow and change with the business that it supports. Such flexibility in design will ensure future leveragability.

- *Pragmatism, not perfection*: A KM system should focus on pragmatism. Begin with what you have, then incrementally improve it. Trying to get everything in place before you are ready to get on board will most likely cause you to miss the boat.[2] As many managers I've talked to will attest, beginning in the most likely place or with the most promising critical process is better than not beginning at all.

- *The user is king*: In concert with significant changes in both applications and technology architecture is greater awareness of user-defined requirements within this environment. A key success factor in a KM system is the ability of end users to define and control interaction with numerous sources of information and to decide how information is classified, organized, and prioritized to suit perceived business needs and strategy.[3] A good KM system is built around people.[4] Any proposed system must effectively recognize the primary mechanisms by which workers "work" and build technology solutions to leverage and facilitate these processes. People are not built to work around the way your system is designed.

- *Ease of use*: A KM system has to be easy to use. Leveraging our knowledge of "good" Web design can partially ensure that. The role model is the telephone. Really.

BEGIN WITH WHAT YOU HAVE

Instead of grappling with the notion of knowledge in the dark, it's better to begin with what you already have. At the same time, compiling expertise of each employee will give you a good feel for who knows what throughout the organization. When Mercer Management Consulting (www.mercermc.com) realized that it was growing too fast to continue relying on informal networks of its consultants, it created a repository that it calls its *Knowledge Bank*. In 1996, the company appointed a manager, Jacques Cesar, to lead the effort. Cesar's team started out to serve as a catalyst, communicator, and clearinghouse for knowledge that existed within the company's offices and practices in 25 different countries. Throughout 1996, the team interviewed all the firm's partners, collected documentation, reports, white papers, and other documents to construct a bigger picture of the company's existing and germinating intellectual assets.

In 1997, the Mercer launched its Knowledge Bank. This was a humble beginning in an information system that cataloged all existing documents that the company had worldwide and included a yellow pages type directory that listed the areas of expertise, past projects, and experience of each of the company's consultants.

LEVERAGING THE INTERNET

A fleeting glimpse of existing technology in most companies reveals a transformative addition—the Internet. It offers hope for true integration of the islands of information and knowledge that dot the organizational landscape.[5] We next discuss some of the characteristics that make the Internet an inevitable choice.

GLOBAL REACH

The Internet was intended to be free for all. All you really pay for is the monthly fee to get on the Internet. In the context of KM, the Internet's global reach has five key implications:

1. *A cost-effective global network backbone:* In reality, the Internet, albeit cheaper than an equivalent leased network, is still an expensive proposition in some respects. Companies pay for access to the Internet and the Web, partly in hard dollars and partly in soft dollars, including time lost by employees who get too caught up in surfing the Web!

2. *Ubiquity:* The value of the Internet primarily lies in its ability to connect users anyplace and anywhere, as long as they have access to the Web. You could be in Atlanta and log on to a company intranet in Bangkok, and vice versa. What would have once cost hundreds of thousands of dollars—connecting five offices in five countries—can now be done for a minuscule fraction of that cost with technologies such as virtual private networks (VPNs).

3. *Distributed connectivity:* Similarly, distributed resources and databases can be interconnected cost-effectively and reliably, using virtual networks tunneled within the Internet. Web browsers provide a ubiquitous interface that easily is customized to support multiple languages, regional preferences, and features across the enterprise, which might span national boundaries.

4. *Robust global data path:* The Internet is a robust global connection mechanism. Unlike a leased line that can bring the network down at any one point of failure, the Internet offers multiple paths for reliably moving time-sensitive data, even if networks fail at multiple points. The inherent nature of the Internet offers unprecedented redundancy and robustness. Peer-to-peer technologies hold great promise for knowledge platforms for this reason.[6]

5. *Open and global competitive intelligence:* The Internet makes it possible to reach other sites, such as competitor portals, as easily as your own. This open accessibility reduces the cost of having to keep up with what the competition is up to. In the context of KM, the Internet makes it viable and cost-effective to tap into readily available, continuously and invisibly importable external electronic information on competitive businesses.

THE SOUL OF THE NETWORK

Ignoring the soft costs for the time being, let's look at the hard costs, such as monthly access fees. Usually, this money goes to the Internet service provider (ISP), which charges you for connecting to an access point that lets you connect to the backbone networks. The U.S. portion of the Internet can be thought of as having three levels. At the bottom are local area networks (LANs); for example, campus networks. Usually, the local networks are connected to a regional or midlevel network. The midlevels connect to one or more backbones. A backbone is an overarching network to which multiple regional networks connect, and they generally do not serve any local networks or end users directly. The U.S. backbones connect to other backbone networks around the world. A few years ago, the primary backbone was the NSFNET. On April 30, 1995, the NSFNET ceased operation, and now traffic in the United States is carried on several privately operated backbones. The new "privatized Internet" in the United States is becoming less hierarchical and more interconnected. The separation between the backbone and regional network layers of the current structure is blurring as more regional companies are connected directly to one another through network access points (NAPs) and as traffic passes through a chain of regional networks without any backbone transport.

PLATFORM INDEPENDENCE

Data in the enterprise is often available in a multitude of incompatible and/or platform-dependent formats: Windows PCs, UNIX workstations, proprietary systems, Linux machines, Apple Macintosh systems, and Palm OS devices. Business information no longer comes from or resides in a single place; it is derived from disparate information streams—collaborative documents, Web pages, news feeds, e-mail, etc. At the same time as firms, enterprises, and knowledge workers are seeking integrated solutions to managing and using information resources, the emergence of intranet technology has presented enormous opportunities for information sharing and content delivery to enterprise workers and collaborative audiences. The platform-independent nature of the Internet makes feasible an integrated solution that can bring together data and documents across otherwise isolated computing islands. This integrative ability is attributable to the use of a common, relatively standardized Hypertext Markup Language (HTML) and the complementary Hypertext Transfer Protocol (HTTP). These provide that magical binding glue that we have always wished for.

THE KNOWLEDGE PLATFORM: A 10,000-FOOT VIEW

Many of the technologies that support the management of knowledge have been around for a long time.[7] The Internet has finally provided the ether to meld these.[8] In this section, we examine enabling technologies that make the KM technology framework possible. Following an analysis of these extant technologies, many of which might already be in place—albeit fragmented—in your own company, we can make judgments about what can be taken as is and what more needs to be added to leverage existing infrastructure.

Figure 5-2 shows the key components of a KM platform. You might recognize that many of the technologies and tools already exist in your own company. The implementation effort for the KM system will then bring together these and new pieces into a coherent system.[9,10] Each component is discussed in further detail in Chapter 7.

INTEGRATING TECHNOLOGY

A large set of technology components around which a KM system is built is often already in place. The key drivers of an effective KM system are the proper leverage and tight integration (e.g., using knowledge servers) of existing technology, tools, and information resources.

Knowledge Servers as Integrators

Although a significant volume of information is spread out across the enterprise and the intranet provides a medium for integrating it to some extent, new information generated every day adds to the chaos. The technology components that constitute a KM platform must be integrated into a seamless whole, so that the process of adding new content to the virtual repository is then as painless and efficient as possible. A knowledge server can be the basis for

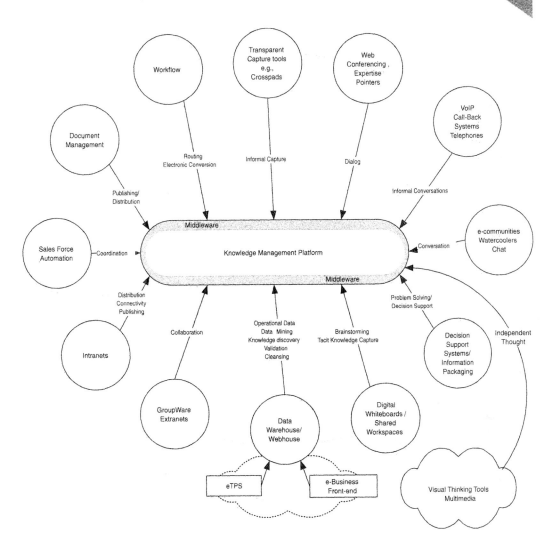

Figure 5-2   Key components of a KM platform.

such integration. It allows smooth integration across multiple enterprises that use the same knowledge server. Figure 5-3 shows how a knowledge server can connect islands of data in situations where the intranet is not expansive and new information is being generated at a high rate. A knowledge server relies on the Internet for creating an extensible architecture for unifying and organizing access to disparate corporate repositories and digitized data sources. Table 5-1 summarizes how such servers help in assembling a coherent enterprise-wide KM system from discrete combinations of technology components.

The knowledge server creates a reference to each new document that is similar to a card in a library card catalog. Each card captures key metadata, such as author, subject, and title, as

Table 5-1 How Knowledge Servers Integrate Explicit Knowledge Enterprise-Wide

Before	After
Cumbersome to integrate	Partly automated
Employees unaware of postings and documents	Personalized push channels provide periodic updates to users
Multiple versions of documents result in inconsistencies	Multiple versions minimized
Scope of content limited to application	Enterprise-wide scope

a standard set of properties and maintains a link to the original content, which the knowledge server indexes in a text-search engine. On the basis of the text index and the metadata properties captured for each card, the knowledge server automatically organizes cards in a hierarchy of administrator-defined categories that users can browse via a Web browser, typically on the intranet. Knowledge servers provide several business benefits as a direct result of the high level of integration that they make possible (see Table 5-2).

The strength of knowledge servers comes from their ability to integrate existing repositories without having to start from scratch. Furthermore, the KM team can then take existing explicit knowledge into account efficiently, allowing more time and resources to deal with the harder part of managing tacit knowledge. Furthermore, because knowledge servers do not have

Table 5-2 Business Needs and The Characteristics of Knowledge Servers That Meet Those Needs

Business Need	Technical Characteristics of Knowledge Servers
Adaptability	Plug-in modules provide support for new data formats and delivery mechanisms as they emerge. This provides unprecedented extensibility and adaptability.
Automated tracking	Intelligent agents and Web crawlers navigate through integrated internal repositories and external sources to inform users of new content as it becomes available. New content can either be delivered through push mechanisms or made available at personalized pull-based portals on the company intranet.
Determination of emergent structure within large volumes of new and often chaotic information.	Meta information provides automated content aggregation and electronically catalogs new information as it gets added to the system.
Extant content utilization	Because knowledge servers build upon existing repositories, they can take existing content into account and organize it to make it more amenable to browsing and searching.

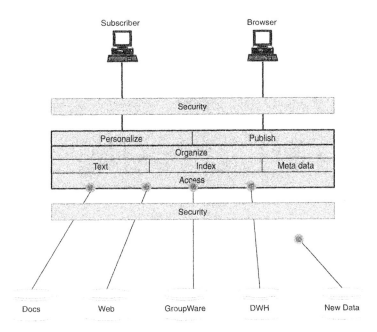

Figure 5-3   How a knowledge server leverages the existing infrastructure.

a systems administrator deciding what information everyone else needs, they overcome a frequently encountered barrier faced by information management tools by putting that choice in the hands of end users. Figure 5-3 shows the integrative concept behind a knowledge server.

KM IN THE SEMICONDUCTOR INDUSTRY: GASONICS INTERNATIONAL

GaSonics is a company operating in North America, Europe, Asia, and the Pacific Rim with annual revenues in the range of $120 million. GaSonics produces processing systems for fabrication of semiconductor wafers. Companies manufacturing electronic chips for use in electronic equipment use systems such as the ones that GaSonics produces.

GaSonics systems have for a long time enjoyed a reputation for high reliability and low systems downtime, when compared with industry averages. The company depends on its customers for feedback, and it extensively uses this feedback to improve both its existing systems and services. Faced with extremely low margins like other competitors operating in the industry, GaSonics realized that it needed to reduce operating costs and improve internal efficiencies. Because the whole process of designing and building wafer processing equipment is knowledge-intensive, GaSonics decided that the answer lay in streamlining its use of internal knowledge.

The Starting Point: Technical Publications

The technical publications department writes, typesets, updates, provides, and supports technical manuals, literature, and other information that supports GaSonics' products. The company found that its technical publications department was an increasingly major cost center for four reasons:

1. Because equipment sold by GaSonics was expensive, typically over $100,000 apiece, downtime costs for customers resulted in thousands of dollars lost every time the system went down. Hence, the technical publications department at GaSonics needed to provide an increasingly high number of customer-customized versions of their publications. This, in effect, is similar to mass customization.

2. Updates were frequently required.

3. Customers demanded electronic versions of product manuals.

4. The cost of archiving old documentation was increasing at an abnormal rate.

Table 5-3 GaSonics Goals and Objectives

Technical publications department goals	Business unit goals
Speed up delivery of technical documentation.	Reduce training and support costs.
Improve usability of documentation and application manuals.	Increase equipment uptime. Reduce training and support costs.
Improve content and currency of publications.	Increase equipment uptime. Increase service revenues. Reduce training and support costs. Improve customer service through better feedback mechanisms.
Link publications to other enterprise resources.	Improve customer service through better feedback mechanisms.
Make technical literature, documentation, and publications easily accessible.	Improve product and service offerings. Improve customer service through better feedback mechanisms.

GaSonics realized that its technical publications department was the most logical place to begin its KM initiative. Because the goals of the business unit and the technical publications department were highly congruent, improving one, the company hoped, would improve the other. Table 5-3 shows the two sets of objectives.

The Goal: Three Months to Target

GaSonics planned for a KM system that could be operational within three months. The challenges that came up included:

• The need to replace legacy data and paper-based information with consistent and accurate electronic data equivalents

• The ability of customers to customize product and service documentation electronically

- The need to integrate with other enterprise systems
- The need to justify of costs involved in doing the above

GaSonics reduced paper-related costs by 50 percent immediately. Besides this obvious financial benefit, the company reduced training costs, used technicians instead of engineers for providing support, and improved the quality of solutions provided by making maintenance efforts work right the first time more frequently that it had done in the past.

LESSONS LEARNED

We examined how, as the first step in the KM methodology, the existing infrastructure can be leveraged. You need to take several material steps to analyze and leverage existing infrastructure and enabling technology components. The key points to keep in mind while analyzing existing infrastructural components are summarized here.

- *Understand the role that your existing networks play in KM.* Begin with the technology and network infrastructure investments that you already have in place.

- *Integrate, build on, and leverage enterprise resources.* Technology's most valuable role in KM is broadening the reach and enhancing the speed of knowledge transfer. The key to successful KM lies in leveraging the existing infrastructure, primarily communications and storage capabilities that are already in place.

- *Look before you leap.* Understand the KM technological framework and its components. Examine your needs, determine the processes that most need KM support, and identify existing infrastructure can meet those needs.

- *Focus on pragmatism, not perfection.* Identify extant explicit knowledge; take stock of what information and knowledge already exists, beginning with explicit knowledge sources. Analyze and build on data mining, data warehousing, project management, and decision support system (DSS) tools that are already in place.

- *Remember the golden rule.* A good KM system is built around people. Don't try to force people into the KM system's mold.

- *Use knowledge servers to integrate the islands of information and create new knowledge.* Examine your business needs and determine the feasibility of a knowledge server as an enabler.

- *Plan for flexibility and scalability.* A well-designed KM system design must be flexible and scalable, and not written in stone. The Web-based approach holds the greatest promise for system scalability, flexibility, and longevity.

In the next chapter, we take a look at the second step in the 10-step KM road map and see how KM and business strategy can be aligned right from the start.

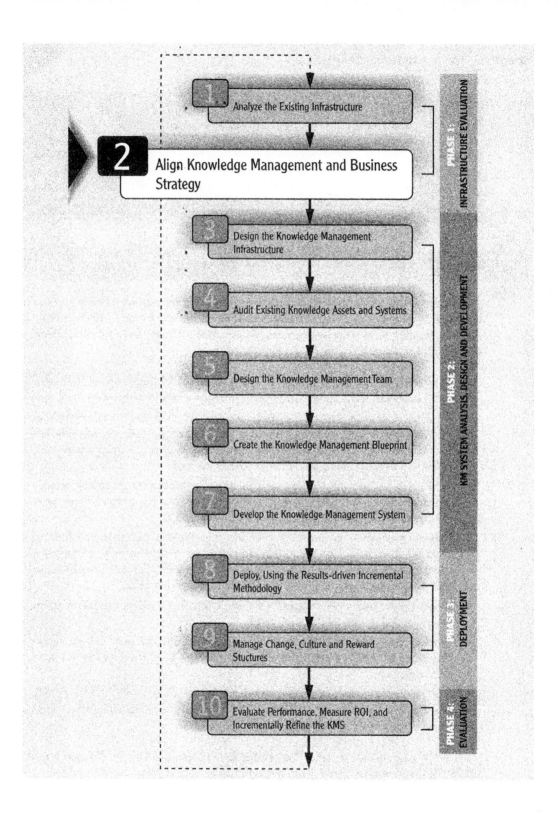

1. Analyze the Existing Infrastructure

2. Align Knowledge Management and Business Strategy

3. Design the Knowledge Management Infrastructure

4. Audit Existing Knowledge Assets and Systems

5. Design the Knowledge Management Team

6. Create the Knowledge Management Blueprint

7. Develop the Knowledge Management System

8. Deploy, Using the Results-driven Incremental Methodology

9. Manage Change, Culture and Reward Stuctures

10. Evaluate Performance, Measure ROI, and Incrementally Refine the KMS

PHASE 1:
INFRASTRUCTURE EVALUATION

PHASE 2:
KM SYSTEM ANALYSIS, DESIGN AND DEVELOPMENT

PHASE 3:
DEPLOYMENT

PHASE 4:
EVALUATION

CHAPTER 6

ALIGNING KNOWLEDGE MANAGEMENT AND BUSINESS STRATEGY

IN THIS CHAPTER

✔ Understand how alignment of KM and business begins with strategic visioning.

✔ Determine how knowledge integration and knowledge transfer involve high-level trade-offs.

✔ Develop KM into a buffer for uncertainty and internal, competitive, and industry-wide surprise.

✔ Analyze knowledge gaps using real-options analysis.

✔ Translate business strategy into an executable KM strategy and architecture.

✔ Identify the critical success factors for a KM initiative

✔ Mobilize initiatives to internally sell the initiative

IMAGINATION IS MORE IMPORTANT THAN KNOWLEDGE.
—ALBERT EINSTEIN

A clearly articulated link between KM and business strategy is the key predictor of its success. Obsession with information technology is a common trap. A symptom of companies that fall in this trap is that their KM initiatives focus on developing new IT applications for supporting digital capture, storage, retrieval, and distribution of an organization's explicit knowledge. Technology, unfortunately, still falls short of magic. The critical linkage between business and knowledge strategy, although much talked about, is often ignored in practice. Strategy is not executable if left at the abstract level. Effective KM requires a balanced mix of technology, cultural change, purposeful reward systems, and business focus that is in step with the company's business strategy.

In this chapter, we see how high-level business strategy can be translated into pragmatic goals for KM. We examine how knowledge maps can translate strategic vision into a supporting knowledge strategy.

STRATEGIC VISIONING

Companies are too often driven by strategic plans, not strategic visions. Strategic planning has not lived up to the irrational expectation of providing step-by-step instructions for managers to execute strategies. Strategic thinking cannot be done as strategic programming. Companies need to take a 180-degree turn and move from strategic programming to strategic thinking. Managers and businesses need to capture what they learn both from the soft insights and experiences and from hard market data, then synthesize that learning into a vision *worth pursuing*.

Such strategic orientation requires knowledge of the complex environment in which your company operates and comprehension of the complex processes that it undertakes. Managers must understand the general competitive conditions, the latent needs of customers, industry structures, new technology, and strengths of rival firms. Managers must think of KM investments as real-options investments. When they do so, they are investing in creating the conditions that are necessary for collaboration to ensue and novel business insights, ideas, and capabilities to emerge. They stimulate conversations that would otherwise never occur, create new lenses for old problems that might never have been used, and connect the views of experts and outsiders to generate fresh thinking. This requires you to think about three issues:

1. What is the industry context in which your business operates?
2. What is the level and nature of turbulence within it?
3. How profound is the uncertainty in your business?

The answers to these questions provide a useful starting point to think about the strategic choices that immediately follow.

KNOWLEDGE TRANSFER VERSUS INTEGRATION: THE STRATEGIC DICHOTOMY

Although the notion of organizational learning has elevated learning to a desirable outcome in most managers' minds, some business contexts demand action over learning. This dichotomy becomes clearer when we think of learning as knowledge transfer—for example, an individual teaching a colleague how to solve a specific problem. Knowledge transfer assumes certain conditions that do not necessarily always hold. Specifically, it assumes that:

1.   The two transacting individuals possess certain shared knowledge in order to effectively communicate

2.   Sufficient time is available to engage in such transfer

3.   Knowledge that is transferred remains valid by the time a transfer is completed.

Consider novel e-business projects in contrast, where each of these three assumptions is violated. Members often come from very different functional areas and share little in common; the short time frames for a project do not afford the luxury of teaching each the other's job; and the specialized technical or project-specific knowledge is volatile enough that it might no longer be valid by the time a transfer is completed. Even more importantly, individuals are reluctant to transfer their valuable skills because those skills form the very basis for their attractiveness to their employers. In such scenarios, knowledge integration becomes a viable alternative.

A strategy that emphasizes knowledge integration promotes synthesis of individually held knowledge at the project or task level while keeping cross-member learning down to a bare-minimum level. New knowledge, after all, is a consequence of the meeting, collaboration, and interaction of minds.[1]

Figure 6-1 compares knowledge transfer with knowledge integration. In summary, knowledge transfer refers to a general strategy of facilitating learning and exchange, whereas knowledge integration stresses rapid application of existing but disconnected knowledge. The level of uncertainty, needed variety, speed of response, and nature of turbulence in the business context can help determine which of these approaches best suits your KM initiative, as discussed next.

Knowledge assets are of little value if they cannot be mobilized rapidly. A common trap that KM initiatives fall into is that of adopting a knowledge transfer strategy when a knowledge integration approach is really needed. Careful analysis at this stage can ensure that your business does not turn into another case of the fox that starved to death with a ham tied to its back—a firm that had all the necessary expertise but simply could not apply it fast enough to respond when needed.

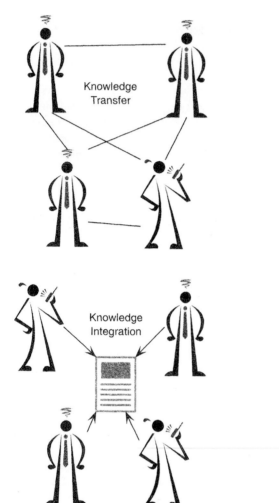

Figure 6-1 Knowledge transfer (top), compared with knowledge integration (bottom).

REAL OPTIONS UNDER UNCERTAINTY

With increasingly high uncertainty of markets, technologies, and customer desires, the right strategic bets have high payoffs far more quickly; the wrong ones can spell systemic catastrophe. Managers must explicitly consider the level of uncertainty their companies face to build flexibility and agility into their design. It is not merely a dichotomy between clarity of the future and absolute ambiguity. As Figure 6-2 shows, there is much in between.[2] Managers must recognize that they never face an all-or-nothing scenario. They rarely face a situation where nothing that they know is of value in determining the ways in which their product or service markets might evolve.

THE TRIGGER, THE TWITCH, AND THE EMERGENCE OF POLAROID

The success of well-known companies such as Microsoft, Starbucks, Palm, Southwest Airlines, and eBay comes from their ability to ask the right questions. This is nothing new; what is new is that only the recognition of KM makes this more likely. Polaroid, whose instant camera virtually created an entire market in itself, began with such a simple application of knowledge—knowledge that was soon converted into action, a product, and a very successful company. It all began one day in 1943 when Edwin Land's three-year-old daughter asked why she could not immediately see the picture that he had taken of her. Within an hour, Land conceived the camera that would take an industry by storm and transform then-small Polaroid into one of the most successful companies of our time. Land's vision was evoked by the synthesis of the insight evoked by his daughter's question and his extensive technical knowledge.

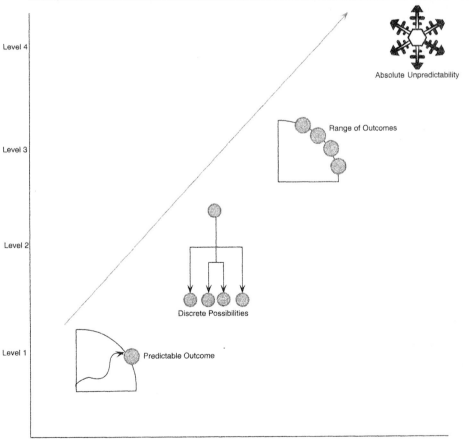

Figure 6-2   Levels of uncertainty.

Level 1

This is the lowest level of uncertainty, where the future of your company is fairly predictable. Strategic commitments in KM at this level are geared toward adaptation to external conditions. Traditional strategic analysis approaches are most applicable at this level. The strengths, weaknesses, opportunities, and threats (SWOT) framework has been the mainstay of business strategy for over 30 years. Such analysis involves an assessment of the company's strengths and weaknesses, relative to the opportunities and threats present in the environment in which your company operates. The objective is to sustain the company's strengths, mitigate its weaknesses, avoid threats, and grab opportunities. Traditional methods for strategic analysis might provide deep insight into strategic opportunities, but rarely do they provide foresight into rapidly emerging and disappearing opportunities. Moreover, because Porter's model operates at the industry level, it provides no guidance on how companies can compete *within* their industry.

Level 2

When a single predictable future cannot be visualized but several possible and likely outcomes are foreseeable, Level 2 uncertainty persists. Strategic commitments in KM at this level are geared toward ensuring that the most desirable of the few possible discrete outcomes are achieved. Managers must begin to think of such investments as creating options that allow their companies to change course to adapt to a different discrete goal if the market conditions demand.

Level 3

At this level of uncertainty, a range of possible outcomes exists. Specific outcomes are unpredictable beyond that general range. Strategic commitments in KM at this level are geared toward helping the company move in a general direction within the relatively fuzzy range of outcomes. At this level of uncertainty, ongoing experimentation is key. Pilot trials, test markets, and limited deployment experiments can provide useful insights before high-stakes commitments are made in either a KM system or strategy.

Level 4

At this level of uncertainty, no basis for forecasting the future exists, and little can be said about the ways in which a given market might evolve. Examples of such markets include the wireless Internet services markets in 2003, embedded RF tagging technologies in logistics in 2002, and Web standards in 1994. In retrospect, all of these markets might *appear* predictable. However, at the time these markets are shaping, predictability is not the norm. Strategic commitments in KM at this level are geared toward shaping rather than adapting both the business and the market in ways that help a company's offerings succeed in highly unpredictable markets.

Managers must resist the temptation to classify their lines of business as being level 1 or 4 and rely solely on their gut instincts. Thinking clearly about which of the four levels your business operates at, at various levels, is more likely to yield insights into meaningful ways to support knowledge development to support business development. At levels 3 and 4, it is also useful to consider historically similar patterns. In novel Internet-based businesses, for example, much can be learned from thinking of the radio (AM/FM wars), electricity markets (the AC/DC standards emergence), video cassette player standards (VHS and Beta), and even the railroads in the 1800s.

HOFFMAN-LAROCHE AND THE GOAL

Companies that want to leverage their knowledge assets must never lose sight of their context. They must approach KM with a focus on their core competencies and tie those in very tightly to the business strategy and vision. An integrative approach for identifying knowledge areas, specializations, and knowledge links has been successfully embraced by the pharmaceutical giant Hoffman-LaRoche. Success in the pharmaceutical industry depends on the speed of new product launches more than anything else. The faster a product is brought to market, the faster a company can recoup its development costs and generate higher profits. Hoffman-LaRoche calculated that every day gained in market availability represented a gain of $1 million.

THE RESPONSIVENESS QUADRAHEDRON: VARIETY AND SPEED

Next, consider the variety of responses that your business must deliver to compete successfully and the speed with which those responses must be delivered. Based on these considerations, projects, business units, or entire businesses can be classified into one of the four quadrants in Figure 6-3.[3]

In Quadrant 1, high levels of variety must be delivered without speed. The goal of a KM investment in this scenario is to generate structural flexibility. The means to accomplish this is the facilitation of knowledge transfer across functional silos. Because speed is not a key concern here, cross-functional knowledge sharing generates both variety and learning.

Next, consider Quadrant 2. Both variety and responsiveness are needed there. A KM strategy under these conditions must facilitate knowledge integration across functional silos. The goal is to minimize learning and maximize rapid application of existing but distributed knowledge.

In Quadrant 3, high responsiveness requirements and low variety mean that a KM initiative must nurture operational flexibility. This can be achieved if a KM system facilitates interfunctional knowledge integration. Although an approach that works in Quadrant 2 might work here, as well, lower levels of premium placed on variety of responses implies that such an approach would be an investment overkill, both financially and technologically.

The attractiveness of boundary-spanning knowledge integration dwindles in Quadrant 4, where the need for both responsiveness and variety is low. Few businesses fall into this category

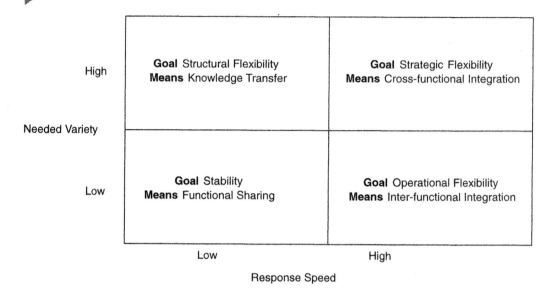

	Low	High
High	**Goal** Structural Flexibility **Means** Knowledge Transfer	**Goal** Strategic Flexibility **Means** Cross-functional Integration
Low	**Goal** Stability **Means** Functional Sharing	**Goal** Operational Flexibility **Means** Inter-functional Integration

Needed Variety

Response Speed

Figure 6-3   The responsiveness quadrahedron.

because few organizations operate in such stable environments. For those that do, the means to the goal of stability is sharing of knowledge within functional areas and among individuals from similar domains of expertise.

In the high responsiveness quadrants, speed of knowledge application is of essence. As products get complex, people from various functional areas get involved in a project. In the absence of a shared context, people coming from different backgrounds, with different values, beliefs, assumptions, and views are most likely to collide and immobilize the reaching of consensus or making of decisions.[1]

As pieces of knowledge begin to fit together, the most insightful part might come from the most unexpected source or employee.[4] Knowledge integration, which will soon be described as being closely supported by a personalization approach to KM, is well the preferred strategic choice in Quadrants 2 and 3.

COMMUNITY-CENTRIC SHARED CONTEXT BUILDING APPROACHES

IDEO, the industrial design firm, has some 300 professionals worldwide but operates a total of 10 offices (including four in the Palo Alto/San Francisco Bay area alone) so that no one office will have more than 50 people. Similarly, the Swedish software company WM-data employs 3,800 people but mandates that there be no more than 50 people in a single unit. Limiting the size of work groups is a commonly used, successful approach for creating shared context.

BUSINESS MODELS AND EXECUTABILITY

A business model can be thought of as a clearly articulated plan for adding economic value by applying knowledge to a set of resources to create a marketable product or service offering. Not all businesses use stable technologies for executing on stable business models. One or the other—or even both—can be new. Figure 6-4 illustrates the possible combinations.

Considering where your business falls on this grid can guide managers about the feasibility of knowledge transfer or integration approaches to KM. Businesses operating under existing business models use operational strategies, whereas those under new business models use transformational ones. Strategies are operational if companies face relatively low uncertainty and are focusing on playing an old game better than their competitors. Transformational strategies, on the other hand, require a company to give up the elusive notion of linearity. Instead, it must use incomplete information to make diligent decisions about investments, new ventures, collaborations, and product/market/technology choices.

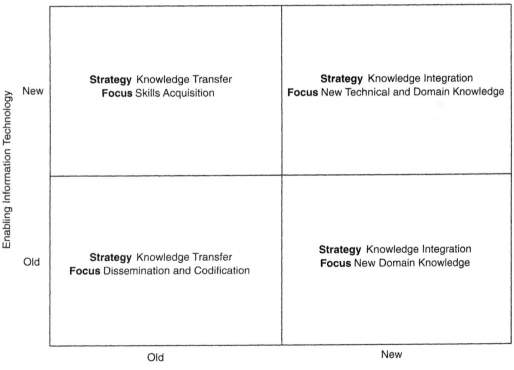

Figure 6-4   Permutations of business models and technology influence strategic choices.

Experimentation and iteration are imperative when facing transformational change. Unlike the highly linear operational strategies, transformational strategies are based on real options.

Consider a business that uses existing technology to implement an existing business model. In this case, an overarching knowledge transfer approach that focuses on dissemination of existing knowledge is most likely to serve best. When new technology is being used to drive an existing business model, knowledge transfer must focus on acquiring skills—specifically, technical ones. This choice is amplified when the underlying technology is also new.

As important as strategy is, the ability to execute is perhaps even more so. Often, a second-best strategy is preferable to the best one that a business is simply incapable of executing. When a firm lacks the necessary knowledge or expertise to execute its strategy of choice, KM must support the integration and application of complementary expertise that resides in its customers, partners, and suppliers. For example, Amazon.com, lacking deep knowledge of individual customers' preferences, uses their self-selected navigational behavior to customize offerings to each individual's tastes. Over time, the capacity of the system to distill high-level knowledge about customer preferences from low-level transactional data improves dramatically. The key then is to identify, attract, nurture, and motivate those that possess complementary knowledge. An effective KM strategy builds on this to generate reciprocal knowledge exchange or mutually valued benefits. As more of such bilateral knowledge flows occur, deep bonding with customers: (1) decommoditize commodity product and service offerings and (2) strengthen lock-ins.

WAL-MART AND SUPPLIER PROXIMITY

Companies that sell towels retailed by Wal-Mart do not own terry cloth weaving plants. Their business runs on the information and strategic knowledge pulled from their markets and retailers. That is their primary asset. All the manufacturing actually is done at mills in places such as Bangalore and Shanghai, to which production is outsourced.

Arkansas offers a perfect snapshot of this, where small companies that Wal-Mart buys from have based offices along the periphery of Wal-Mart's own buildings. Is it the case of being literally close to the customer? It's not being close to the customer, it's being close to the source of information—information that could suddenly become useful and turn into knowledge that any small company needs to keep its only customer happy.

CODIFICATION OR PERSONALIZATION?

Before we turn to mapping business strategy to KM, let us look at two expansive KM approaches: codification and personalization. There is no right or wrong approach—both are required in the right balance. The right balance is determined by your company's objectives in pursuing KM. For any KM initiative to be successful, both approaches must be present in the knowledge orientation of the firm but not with equal weight. If a company decides to use codification as its primary strategy, it should direct, for example, 80 percent of its efforts toward codification and the remaining 20 percent toward personalization. Table 6-1 compares these two focal choices.

As Table 6-1 illustrates, the personalization strategy is more focused on connecting knowledge workers through networks and is better suited to companies that face "one-off" problems that depend more on tacit knowledge and expertise than on codified knowledge. The codification strategy is more focused on technology that enables storage, indexing, retrieval, and reuse. This strategy is better suited to companies that repeatedly deal with sim-

Table 6-1 Comparison of Codification and Personalization KM Strategies

Business Strategy Question	Codification	Personalization
What type of business do you think your company is in?	Providing high-quality, reliable, fast, and cost-effective services.	Providing creative, rigorous and highly customized services and products.
How much old material, such as past project data, existing documents, and archived projects, do you reuse as a part of new projects?	You reuse portions of old documents to create new ones. You use existing products to create new ones. You know that you need not begin from scratch to deliver a new product or service.	Every problem has a high chance of being a "one-off" and unique problem. Although cumulative learning is involved, highly creative solutions are often called for.
What is the costing model used for your company's products and services?	Price-based competition.	Expertise-based pricing; high prices are not detrimental to your business; price-based competition barely (if at all) exists.
What are your firm's typical profit margins?	Very low profit margins; overall revenues need to be maximized to increase net profits.	Very high profit margins.
How best can you describe the role that IT plays in your company's work processes?	IT is a primary enabler; the objective is to connect people distributed across the enterprise with codified knowledge (such as reports, documentation, code, etc.) that is in some reusable form.	Storage and retrieval are not the primary applications of IT; IT is considered a great enabler for communications; applications such as e-mail and video conferencing are considered the most useful applications; conversation, socialization, and exchange of tacit knowledge are considered to be the primary uses of IT.

Table 6-1 Comparison of Codification and Personalization KM Strategies (cont.)

Business Strategy Question	Codification	Personalization
What is your reward structure like?	Employees are rewarded for using and contributing to databases such as Notes discussion databases.	Employees are rewarded for directly sharing their knowledge with colleagues and for assisting colleagues in other locations/offices with their problems.
How is knowledge exchanged and transferred?	Employees refer to a document or best practices database that stores, distributes, and collects codified knowledge.	Knowledge is transferred person to person; intrafirm networking is encouraged to enable sharing of tacit knowledge, insight, experience, and intuition.
Where do your company's economies of scale lie?	Economies of scale lie in the effective reuse of existing knowledge and experience and applying them to solve new problems and complete new projects.	Economies rest in the sum total of expertise available within the company; experts in various areas of specialization are considered indispensable.
What are your typical team structure demographics?	Large teams; most members are junior-level employees; a few project managers lead them.	Junior employees are not an inordinate proportion of a typical team's total membership.
What company's services do your company's services resemble?	Andersen Consulting, The Gartner Group, Delphi Consulting, ZDNET, Delta Airlines, and Oracle.	The Boston Consulting Group, McKinsey and Company, Rand Corporation.
What company's products do your company's products resemble?	Pizza Hut, Dell Computer, Gateway, Microsoft, SAP,* PeopleSoft, Baan, America Online, Bell South, Air Touch Cellular, Lotus, SAS Institute, IBM, Hewlett-Packard, Intranetics, and 3COM.	A custom car or bicycle manufacturer, Boeing, a contract research firm, and a private investigator.

The classification of KM strategies was first discussed in Hansen, M., N. Nohria and T. Tierney, *What's Your Strategy for Managing Knowledge?*, Harvard Business Review, March-April (1999), 106-116. This table further builds on it to provide diagnostic analysis.

*We have used enterprise resource planning (ERP) vendors in codification strategy examples because most of the software that is implemented is based on preprogrammed modules.

ilar problems and decisions. And remember, it's foolish to try using both approaches to the same degree. It is equally unsound to use only one. As one would suspect, the incentives needed to make either one work are very different. Focus on those incentives that help you get the primary strategy right.

CASE STUDY: BETTING ON THE RIGHT CHIPS AT TEXAS INSTRUMENTS

Texas Instruments (TI), the semiconductor firm that is credited with commercialization of the integrated circuit (also known as an *electronic chip*) began its KM initiatives centered on its technical literature and documentation. As one would expect, TI has overwhelming amounts of data relating to its semiconductor products. This data needs to be managed, updated, and effectively distributed. For example:[5]

- TI has about 3,100 data sheets relating to its semiconductor products. Each of these averages about 12 pages in length.
- TI produces and maintains about 50 user guides, each of which averages 250 pages.
- TI supports its products with 400 application notes, each of which is between 2 and 100 pages in length.
- TI maintains 14 gigabytes of SGML files and 12 gigabytes of metadata.
- TI revises about 90,000 pages of documentation every year.
- TI has about 100 technical writers, 5 illustrators, and 10 team leaders that collectively manage this process.

TI decided to change these work processes so that they would be better aligned with the ways in which documentation staff worked on these documents and technical literature. The focus was on creating content in a manner that allowed ease of *reuse* and enabled production of multiple outputs from a single input or data source. By tagging all content, TI hoped to be able to manage context, along with associated data. Jeff Barton of TI uses the notion of a fundamental shift to describe this process migration: from document thinking to object thinking.

To make this shift happen, the KM team actually converted all paper documents to an electronic form. The expense of the conversion process (which cost in the range of $12 per page) was justified on the basis of the following:

- *Cost containment:* Reusing portions of existing documents resulted in cost savings of up to 70 percent of the cost of new documents.
- *Value added:* By adding nontextual information to documents (such as code, models, executable files, and demo files), additional context was added to knowledge that was well explicated and codified.
- *Reduced labor cost:* It took fewer people to do the same job, so savings in employee compensation were a direct outcome.

The important lesson to take from this highly specialized initiative that primarily focused on managing already codified knowledge is that a good place to begin KM is with content that is already there. Creating metadata for that content is the next logical, though surprisingly expensive step.

KNOWLEDGE MAPS TO LINK KNOWLEDGE TO STRATEGY

Systematically mapping, categorizing, benchmarking, and applying knowledge with the help of a KM system can not only make such knowledge more accessible, but also prioritizes and focuses KM. Effective KM strategies using such "knowledge maps[7]" can help companies build a defensible competitive knowledge position—a long-term effort that requires foresight, hindsight, careful planning, alignment, and luck.

Let's examine the process, moving from a high level to the level of action, that you would use to create such knowledge maps.

STARTING AT THE TOP

Although execution of a KM initiative is important, its alignment with business strategy is critical. To articulate the strategy-knowledge link, a company must explicate its strategic intent, identify knowledge required to actually execute that strategic choice, and reveal its strategic knowledge gaps by comparing these with its actual knowledge assets. The strategic choices that your company makes regarding technology, markets, products, services, and processes have a direct impact on the knowledge, skills, and competencies that it needs to compete in its intended markets.[a] Later, we will translate the links into actionable goals. Such a linkage is illustrated in Figure 6-5.

Assessing your company's present knowledge position necessitates documenting its existing knowledge assets—the fourth step of the 10-step KM road map (Chapter 8).

For our initial *high-level* analysis, we can categorize knowledge into three classification "buckets":[6]

1. *Core knowledge*: Core knowledge is the basic level of knowledge required just to *play the game*. This is the type of knowledge that creates a barrier for entry of new companies. Because this level of knowledge is expected of all competitors, you must have it, even though it will provide your company with no advantage that distinguishes it from its competitors.
   - Let's take two examples: One from the consumer electronics (hard product) business and one from Internet programming (soft product). To enter the modem manufacturing market, a new company must have extensive knowledge of a suitable circuit design, all electronic parts that go into a modem, fabricating surface mount (SMD) chip boards, how to write operating system drivers for modems, and familiarity with computer telephony standards. Similarly, a company developing Web

---

[a]Zack further indicates that every strategic position is linked to some often-unique set of knowledge resources and capabilities.

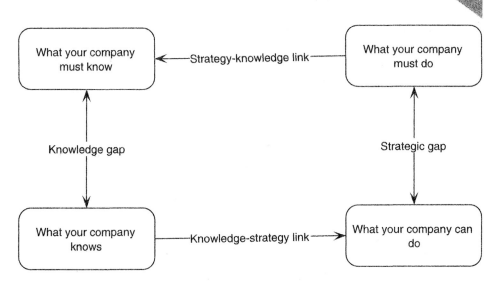

Figure 6-5   A high-level Zack framework-based strategic knowledge gap analysis.

sites for, florists, for example, needs server hosting capabilities, Internet program-ming skills, graphic design skills, clearly identified target markets, and necessary software. In either case, just about any competitor in those businesses is assumed to have this knowledge in order to compete in their respective markets; such essential knowledge, therefore, provides no advantage over other market players.

2. *Advanced knowledge*: Advanced knowledge is what makes your company *competitively viable*. Such knowledge allows your company to differentiate its product from that of a competitor, arguably through the application of superior knowledge in certain areas. Such knowledge allows your company to compete head-on with its competitors in the same market and for the same set of customers.

   • In the case of a company trying to compete in modem manufacturing markets, superior or user-friendly software or an additional capability in modems (such as warning online users of incoming telephone calls) represents such knowledge. In the case of a Web site development firm, such knowledge might be about inter-national flower markets and collaborative relationships in Dutch flower auctions that the company can use to improve Web sites delivered to its customers.

3. *Innovative knowledge*: Innovative knowledge allows a company to lead its entire indus-try to an extent that clearly differentiates it from competition. Michael Zack points out that innovative knowledge allows a company to change the rules of the game.

   • Patented technology is an applicable example of changing the rules. Innovative knowledge cannot always be protected by patents, as the lawsuit between Microsoft and Apple in the 1980s should serve to remind us. Apple sued Microsoft for copying the look and feel of its graphical user interface (GUI). The Supreme Court ruled that things such as look and feel cannot be patented; they can only be copyrighted. Microsoft won the case because it copied the look and feel but used entirely different code to create it in the first place.

CREATING A KNOWLEDGE MAP

Knowledge is not static.[7] What is innovative knowledge today will become the core knowledge of tomorrow. The key lies in staying consistently ahead of the competition. The knowledge map we'll create (see Figure 6-6) provides a snapshot of where your company is at any given time (such as today) relative to its competitors.

Here's how it works. Categorize each market player, including yourself, as an innovator, leader, capable competitor, straggler, or risky player. Next, identify your own business's strengths and weaknesses on various facets of knowledge to see where you lag behind or lead your competitors. Use that information accordingly to reposition either your knowledge or strategic business focus.

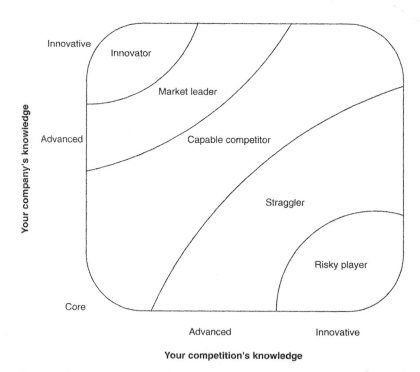

Figure 6-6   Creating a knowledge map to evaluate corporate knowledge.[8]

For example, if you are analyzing customer support knowledge in a competing company and realize that your competitor is an innovator and your own company is only a capable competitor, you can choose either to invest in catching or simply to compete in a different market segment.

ANALYZING KNOWLEDGE GAPS

The gap between what your company is doing and what it should be doing represents its strategic gap, as illustrated by Figure 6-5. Similarly, your company's knowledge gap is represented by what your company *should* (and possibly can) know and what it does know in order to support the competitive position that it has adopted. These two gaps must be aligned and must feed into each other to bridge existing gaps. Ignoring this comparison trivializes the idiosyncratic nature of strategic alignment.

KM strategy then must address how your company's knowledge gaps in identified critical processes are best bridged. In addition to balancing personalization and codification, you must then balance the level of exploration and exploitation at which you want your company to operate.

Exploration implies the intent of your company to develop knowledge that helps it create new niches for its products and services. This intent has profound implications for the design of both the KM strategy and system: Exploration alone cannot be supportively pursued or financially sustained for too long without having a negative impact on the company's bottom-line results.

Exploitation implies the intent to focus on deriving financial and productivity gains from knowledge that already exists, both inside and outside your company. Your company must simultaneously pursue exploitation (which results in short-term benefits) and exploration (which accumulates long-term benefits), varying the balance with strategic focus. In either case, integrate external knowledge into the KM strategy—only those companies that possess the best learning capability and absorptive capacity for external knowledge hold long-run viability.

Use knowledge to create value, that is, to innovate. Consider a variety of companies that have used their knowledge to create value: Wal-Mart in discount retailing, eMachines and Compaq in low-end computers, IKEA in home products retail, IDEO in product design, Barnes & Noble in book retail, Airtran in short-haul travel, Charles Schwab in investment management. These companies have not been so successful because they hired Web masters with long ponytails, were dynamic young startups, monopolized their markets, or had the latest technology. They were successful because they used their knowledge to innovate and create value.

Being an innovator on the knowledge map is of little help if you are not an exploiter. You must first be an exploiter (at least of your internal knowledge) before trying to be an explorer. The implications of this on KM system design are significant: Your KM system must support exploitation of available and accessible knowledge before it can begin supporting exploration.

Innovate or Imitate?

Intel has long enjoyed dominance in the microprocessor business that fuels growth in the personal computer industry. Even though cost-based competition has provided some of its competitors, notably AMD and Cyrix (a National Semiconductor division of which went out of business in May 1999 and was soon acquired by VIA Technologies of Taiwan), a short-term advantage, Intel chose to adopt an innovative rather than an imitative strategy. In choosing to do so, it introduced its line of low-cost Celeron (identical to its high-end processors, less the cache memory) processors, coupled with extensive price cutting. This forced Cyrix out of business because what it possessed was core knowledge. Cyrix's ability to reverse-engineer or emulate Intel processors, avoid the high costs of developing the Intel Pentium chip, further refine it, and sell it at a fraction of Intel equivalents (although consistently behind Intel's release schedules) allowed it to enjoy market dominance in the sub-$1,000 PC market for a few years. As Intel introduced its own line of low-end processors, Cyrix's market share began to dwindle, ultimately causing the company huge losses that forced it to exit the market.

AMD, which had originally adopted Cyrix's strategy of creating low-cost Pentium clones, finally moved from an imitative strategy to an innovative strategy. Rather than simply accept what its competitor, Intel, was doing and striving to do it better,[9] AMD made a departure with the introduction of its K6-3D-2 and K-7 series microprocessors that use a different but compatible architecture called *Super 7* (derived from the industry standard, Socket 7, that preceded Intel's introduction of the Slot 1 architecture). AMD was still surviving as a strong contender against Intel as of late 1999, primarily because it chose a proactive rather than a reactive competitive position[b]—it moved from being a capable competitor to an innovator. A noteworthy historical parallel in Intel's story is that the company had used a very similar *value subtraction* strategy for creating a low-end spin-off for its i486 series microprocessor about a decade earlier.

Adding Up the Numbers

To make sense of it all, look at Figure 6-7, which illustrates the linkages between a company's strategic context, KM strategy, and KM technology.

The competitive environment—a combination of technical opportunities, competitive threats, and regulatory controls—impacts both your company's strategic context (and in turn its products, services, markets, customers, and allocation of resources) and its KM strategy. KM technology (which includes the KM system) enables the realization of your company's chosen knowledge strategy. KM strategy in turn aligns KM technology design. It's your company's business strategy that drives its KM strategy and not the other way around. Similarly, KM technology choices enable its strategic context and are in turn influenced by it.

---

[b]Kim et al.[9] excellently characterize that companies spend too much time fixating on daily competitive moves, rather than creating growth opportunities through their knowledge.

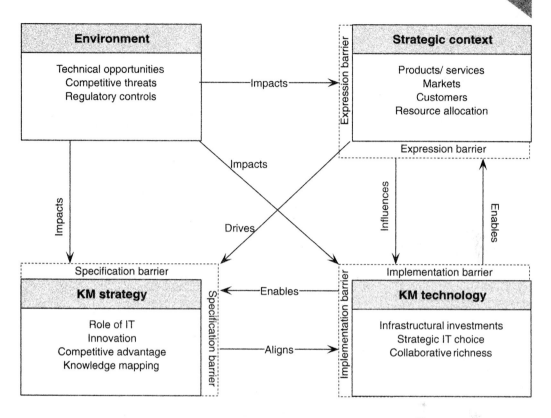

Figure 6-7   Aligning knowledge and business strategy.[10]

Strategic context has an *expression barrier* surrounding it. Your company breaches the barrier by articulating its business strategy, based on its vision and translated into actionable targets and goals. Knowledge strategy has a *specification barrier*—the need to specify critical knowledge that supports and refines your company's business strategy. This author would recommend using Michael Zack's knowledge mapping scheme to overcome the specification barrier that shields KM strategy. KM technology itself has an *implementation barrier* surrounding it. This barrier is primarily related to technology choice and design, and is rarely a hardy deterrent because it can often be copied easily by your competitors.

Summary

The process of creating a well-articulated link between business strategy and knowledge strategy is summarized in Figure 6-8.

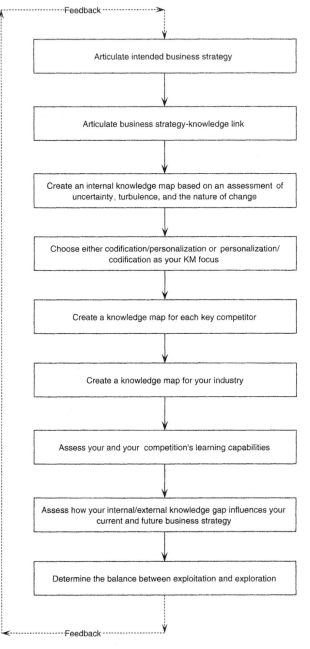

Figure 6-8   The process of articulating the link between business and knowledge strategies.

STRATEGIC IMPERATIVES FOR A SUCCESSFUL KNOWLEDGE MANAGEMENT SYSTEM

KM holds the potential to help your company not just to outcompete within given industry conditions but also to create fundamentally new and superior value that makes competitors *irrelevant.*[9] A core and quintessential tenet of any initiative that supports KM that is developed without the detection and correction of errors in "what we know" and how we learn becomes obsolete over a relatively short period of time.[1] The only thing that is likely to emerge from such a mechanism is bad and inaccurate decisions because the efforts aimed at managing knowledge are themselves based on faulty knowledge principles and ideas. As we begin to plan for managing knowledge in an organization, we must focus our undivided attention on a key set of attributes. These attributes have been extracted from studies of several exemplary KM project successes and abysmal failures in several U.S. and foreign companies.

SALEABILITY NECESSITATES DEMONSTRATION OF SHORT-TERM IMPACT

Continuing support for KM projects in the real world often depends on the demonstration of some tangible and short-term results. An approach some companies have adopted in the past is one where a very tangible productivity gain measure is used, along with proxy measures. The proxy measure guides the KM champions and the KM project, and the tangible measures demonstrate direct benefits to upper management. Showing benefits in a demonstrable form is a very tricky part of the job and often comes at a cost to the actual KM initiative itself.

Showing short-term benefits is akin to another more technical but badly executed activity—documentation of programming code. Although it is well documented that program documentation is essential, anyone who has spent even a little time behind a computer screen on a programming job knows that most documentation is done after the fact (and rarely captures the process that it originally intended to capture). Time spent writing this documentation is often time that could have been better used having your programmers move on to the next programming job.

MAKING THE CASE AT PLATINUM TECHNOLOGY

Platinum Technology Inc., based in Oakbrook Terrace, Illinois, is a company on the fast track. With close to $800 million in revenues in 1997 alone, Platinum has been on an acquisition warpath since 1994. Between 1994 and 1998, the company bought out 70 other companies. This series of acquisitions resulted in a 500-percent growth in its portfolio of product offerings. Platinum has almost 7,000 employees and has seen a sixfold growth in its sales force head count since 1995. These employees are distributed across Platinum's 120 offices worldwide.

Platinum realized early on that managing the company's knowledge assets were a critical enabler that would allow it to sustain this growth. With strong commitment from senior management, Platinum has been exploring the use of KM in the following areas of operation:

- Sales and marketing
- New product development
- Contracting and outsourcing
- Customer and partner interaction KM
- Consulting
- Education

In the sales and marketing division alone, an employee has a number of potential sources that can be tapped for information needed to make a sale or to pursue a prospective customer. These included:

- Over a hundred Lotus Notes databases
- Two custom-developed applications
- Thirty-five intranet sites
- Thousands of networked disk drives
- Printed documentation
- Discussion forums

The Problem

Platinum's marketing and sales department was faced not with information paucity but with information overload and redundancy. Even if an employee making a sales call could retrieve needed information, the employee would come across multiple versions of it in different locations. There was no telling what content was current and applicable. To overcome these challenges, Platinum's marketing and sales department took its first steps toward building a comprehensive KM system.

The System

The KM system that Platinum built was called *Jaguar*. Jaguar began with two components: an intranet-based system that contained detailed documents and information and Jaguar Direct, a machine-resident, bullet-style nugget information repository. The system was built on Documentum's EDMS software and E@asy software from WisdomWare (www.wisdomware.com) for capturing context and tacit forms of knowledge. The driving Web servers were based in the United States, Singapore, and Europe and were supplemented with fortnightly updated Notes databases replicated on 65 servers worldwide. Because the system was meant to support sales and marketing staff it, provided the following information:

- Platinum's products
- Current pricing
- Competitive information
- Enterprise-wide information, including that about other divisions of the company

- Worldwide sales calendars
- Information on Platinum's partners
- Details on mergers and acquisitions that were relevant to the company
- References to documents and manuals
- A subscription service that allows users to subscribe to content of interest

Development Stages

Platinum started at the point where it was easy to get a stable start: managing explicit knowledge. Only later did the company proceed to manage tacit forms of knowledge. The system made extensive use of icons to represent different types of content, and each content element had metadata attached to it. Easily recognizable icons were used to identify information that was newer than two weeks and information that had changed in the preceding seven days. As a KM team member put it, "We are a very visual society, so we made excessive use of icons. Ridiculous? Yes! But effective? Yes!"

Throughout the development process, the KM team asked the actual sales staff (the users) about what seemed to work and what did not. Based on their feedback, the system's developers promptly incorporated relevant suggestions and features. The company's knowledge champion says that over 50 percent of the enhancements came from end-user suggestions. As a result, about 40 percent of the company's sales force personnel use the system daily. With such an exceptionally high level of usage, Platinum found that banner advertisements within the site were the most effective way of making company-wide announcements.

At a later stage, the system introduced push content delivery. Users could select content areas that were of interest to them. As new content came in, users could either opt to receive it in an e-mail message or go to a personalized page on the site (akin to my.yahoo.com) and follow hyperlinks pointing them to new and relevant information as it became available. General updates were automatically sent every Sunday. The company hopes that by analyzing usage statistics on Jaguar, it can predict sales activity ahead of time. To ensure that content is relevant and up to date, e-mails are sent to contributors by the system one week before an expiration date (which is predetermined). If they do not review their contribution, it gets archived. Because the additional burden of validating and reviewing their own contributions was placed on employees, Platinum made sure that they were given extra time to spend on that task.[c]

The initial version of the system was implemented within four months of its initial approval. The system was so successful that it became the second most widely used application in the company, next only to e-mail.

Measurement

Lacking any other formal mechanisms for demonstrating a return on investment (ROI) for their KM investments, Platinum *demonstrated* the success of its system entirely in terms of financial benefits. Benefits quantified in terms of their effect on the company's bottom line are easier to sell to senior management. The KM team quantified benefits in the following terms:

- The system paid for itself in 1.5 months.
- The KM system resulted in cost savings of about $6 million in its very first year.
- Sales force productivity increased at that time by 6 percent.
- The system reduced international FedEx shipments by 15 percent (primarily resulting from the savings in not having to produce and distribute Lotus Notes and database CD-ROM updates to several dozen offices worldwide every few weeks).

The KM team further estimated that Jaguar saved an average sales and marketing person about two hours every week, created a *bottom-up pull* of knowledge and contributed to the competitive stand of the firm as a whole. Although the aforementioned benefits delivered a lot more value to the company, the KM team initially quantified these benefits only in terms of FedEx savings that resulted from the introduction of this system. By choosing such a metric, the KM team was able successful in demonstrating the tangible benefits (which exceeded the cost of the system) of the system (even though one might argue that they were pessimistically underestimated).

¹In line with our earlier observation that you cannot force employees to go out of their way to contribute their part to content maintenance without giving them the time leeway to do so.

ASSESSING FOCUS

The challenge of business and KM is to address the three-way strategic alignment between business, knowledge, and technology used to support the first two (see Figure 6-9). A company must consistently focus information technology and KM to support the primary business strategy.

Companies that are new to KM must address some "first" questions that often surface:

1. How can we turn the knowledge we have into something that adds value to the markets in which we operate?

2. What do we know or think we know about different aspects of our customers? Are we actually doing something with what we know about them?

3. How can we generate meaningful knowledge, rather than simply flooding our organization with indiscriminate information?

4. How can we create a knowledge-supportive organizational culture in which everybody is convinced of the contribution that knowledge can make to the success of the company?

5. Can we cut costs, reduce time to market, improve customer service, or increase margins by more effectively sharing knowledge and leveraging what we already know? Could such knowledge be applied to the activities of other divisions of our company, in other locations, and in foreign manufacturing sites? How can we ever transfer them and then make them work?

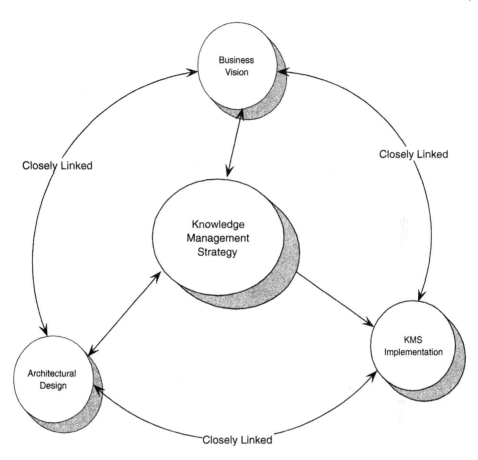

Figure 6-9   A recap on strategic alignment.

6. Are there any fundamental errors in what we think we know as a company? What will be the consequences of these errors? How can these be proactively fixed?

7. How can we manage our people, who will increasingly become knowledge workers or professionals, motivating them to generate knowledge and share it with their peers?

8. Which of these people actually play critical roles in developing and testing new knowledge and information that gets used here?

9. Are exciting ideas emerging within the company but failing to be commercialized? If these ideas are not reaching the market, what incentives, structures, or management processes seem to be blocking them? How can valuable knowledge that exists within the company be actually applied and benefited from?

10. Maybe our company has more money than ideas. Are there opportunities to form partnerships with companies that may be more in the flow of innovative ideas and knowledge? Given different cultures, how can this ever work?

11. Is the "not invented here" syndrome so strong that we are missing attractive business opportunities? Could knowledge-based collaboration (i.e., integration of external knowledge) with a wider range of innovative companies increase our value?

12. How does tacit knowledge—skills, intuitive abilities, employee experience—affect the generation and transfer of explicit forms of knowledge in our company?

The design of the KM architecture must be closely linked to the actual areas of expertise and competence that a business possesses. At the same time, it must address the fundamental question of how it adds value and agility to the business strategy at each stage of development. This necessitates the creation of a coherent blueprint that responds to the present and future needs of the company. This makes a long-term vision for a KM system an imperative, but it also has a prerequisite of a pragmatic, short-term orientation.

DETECTING LOST OPPORTUNITIES

While prioritizing the explication of knowledge, companies can easily fall into the trap of attempting to explicate knowledge that is not explicable and failing to explicate knowledge that should have been converted from tacit to explicit. Figure 6-10 shows the mistakes that companies often make in deciding on these tradeoffs.

The shaded gray box that represents appropriately leveraged knowledge in the figure indicates the correct positioning of a KM system and KM strategy. To give a fitting example, proponents of expert systems believed that it was possible to build a system that could replace human judgment. Although this might be possible in theory, it is too often far removed from reality. With unlimited time and money, very few things in this world are impossible. The question that opponents of expert systems have always posed is whether expert systems are worthwhile. KM takes a more cautionary position and does not propose that a system will solve your company's knowledge problems by itself. What will, however, is a system that serves as nothing but an enabler (in most cases) for knowledge sharing and links people, processes, culture, and values of the organization as a whole.

As Figure 6-10 illustrates, knowledge that could have been explicated, shared, distributed, and applied but that was never articulated represents a lost opportunity, due to the fail-

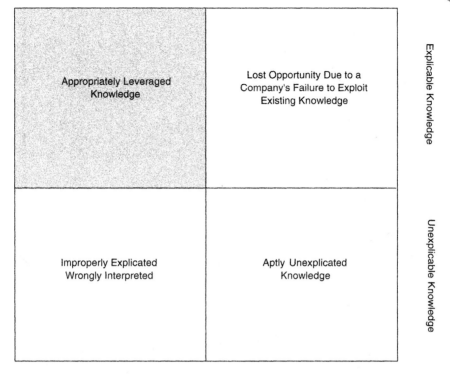

Explicated Knowledge   Knowledge Left Tacit

Figure 6-10   How businesses can be missing vital opportunities by adopting the wrong high-level KM strategy.

ure to leverage this asset. Expert systems often border the unsafe territory of to trying to articulate knowledge that cannot be explicated with the given resource constraints. Resource constraints that are the most deterministic in the process include time, people, and money. Knowledge workers have often seen management take the familiar "add more people" approach to salvage a failing project or effort. As one would expect, this does not work as well in a knowledge-centered work environment as it once did in a mechanistically industrial economy.

A future-oriented focus necessitates selection of a proper set of team players that will actually execute a KM initiative, as shown in Table 6-2 and discussed further in Chapter 9.

Table 6-2: Criteria for Selecting Key Players in the Implementation of a KM System

Core Capability	Business Skills Needed	Technical Skills Needed	Interpersonal Skills Needed	Focus Time Frame	Strategy Motivation	Structure Motivation	Technology Motivation	User Needs Fulfillment Motivation
CKO and team leaders	High	Medium	High	Present and Future	✓	✓		✓
Business systems analysis	High	Medium	Medium	Future	✓			
KM system architecture planning	Low	High	Medium	Future			✓	
Vendor selection	High	Medium	High	Present and future	✓	✓		
Monitoring	Medium	Medium	Low	Future	✓			
Technology implementation	Low	High	Low	Present			✓	

Based on an adaptation from I. Feeny and Wilcocks, Core IS Capabilities for Exploiting Information Technology, *Sloan Management Review*, Spring 1998, 9-21. The discussion has been extended to apply to KM systems and its underlying development processes.

CRITICAL SUCCESS FACTORS

Before we actually devise a blueprint for a KM system, we need to identify the bare essentials that must be supported in any successful KM system deployment. Before you unintentionally end up repeating some of the devastating mistakes that other companies have made in the past, let us probe the *key* lessons that successful KM projects have taught.

In a study of over two dozen companies that have successfully managed their knowledge assets, this author found a unique set of characteristics, values, and strategic leanings that distinguished these companies from those that had failed to leverage their knowledge or KM systems to create a sustainable competitive advantage within their industry.

1. *There is no silver bullet.* There is no silver bullet for KM. Despite what consultants eyeing your checkbook might say, all research suggests that there is *no one right way* to do it.

2. *A working definition of knowledge is needed.* Successful KM projects begin with a working definition of knowledge that is accepted unequivocally throughout the company. Executives have become skeptical toward new approaches to work that they have tried in the past—in most cases, approaches that promised a lot but delivered zilch. To avoid the déjà vu, you need to narrow down the scope of what you define as knowledge.

3. *Saleability requires value demonstration.* Selling KM to both managers and end users requires demonstration of at least some short-term impact. Some metrics, even if vague, are needed to gauge the effectiveness of KM. Failing this, your KM project risks being stifled in its early days.

4. *Tacit knowledge cannot be ignored.* Effective KM must include tacit knowledge right from the outset, even if the primary focus is on codification. Codification with no personalization is bound to fail. As explicated content and tacit knowledge pointers within a KM system grow, resource maps must be provided to help users navigate through them.[11,12]

5. *Focus on the future, not the past.* KM projects that succeed have an eye on the future and not the past or present. Information management handles the present, and data archives document the past.

6. *Respect confidentiality.* Effective systems for KM respect the confidentiality of users by allowing them to choose not to identify themselves. Although anonymity goes contrary to the idea of linking contributions to their originators, this balance is necessary.

7. *Secure management support.* Ongoing management support is needed for both the knowledge strategy and the KM system.

CASE STUDY: KNOWLEDGE MANAGEMENT AT ROLLS ROYCE

Rolls Royce was founded in 1906. In addition to making expensive cars, Rolls Royce is also a market leader in the long-haul aircraft engines market. As of 1999, Rolls Royce was serving about 300 commercial airlines where its competitive stance was the total cost of ownership.

The Problem

The problem with Rolls Royce was that everything that was done to maintain engines was time-sensitive. However, 20 million pages of paper documenting a variety of aspects of aircraft engine parts (see Table 6-3) were produced by the company.

Table 6-3 Sources of Documentation for Various Aircraft Engine Parts at Rolls Royce

Aircraft engine part number	Critical sources of knowledge
Trent 700	Engine maintenance manuals
Trent 800	Illustrated catalogs of parts
RB 211–524	Supply diagrams
RB 211–535	Service bulletins
Tay	Time limits manuals
IAE V2500-A1A5	Standard practices
IAE V2500-D5	Overhaul manuals
	Maintenance manuals

Each engine model had over 20 variants. Each variant needed to be serviced differently. About a hundred airlines with which Rolls Royce had active relationships were based in other countries. Despite several gigabytes of data in the company's mainframes, it was often difficult to get to the right piece of information in time. The consequences were not limited to just productivity and the financial health of the company but also linked to safety of the aircraft with which company employees worked.

Problem Scope

Rolls Royce decided to scope the problem down to the critical issues that had immediate paybacks for the firm. They decided that the key players to be considered would be limited to:

- Airlines
- Airframe manufacturers
- Engine and engine part manufacturers
- Component manufacturers

It was also decided that the scope of the initial KM project would be restricted to enabling different levels of reuse: mechanisms that would allow workers to find, use, reuse, and reintegrate knowledge related to servicing long-haul commercial engines.

Such scoping is essential to place reasonable limits on the expectations from a KM system. Scoping helps firms figure out whether the targets of their KM investments are the ones that need immediate attention, in terms of both business sense and strategic urgency.

Knowledge Management Project Goals

Rolls Royce was very good at laying out realistic and achievable goals up front. The initial set of goals specified for the KM system were classified in two broad categories:

- *Customer-oriented goals:* These were goals that would accrue benefits for the customer.
1. Reducing equipment downtime for maintenance
2. Doing it right the first time
3. Improving maintenance quality
4. Improving maintenance scheduling
5. Reducing data handling, as well as access and search costs.

- *Internal goals:* These were the benefits in terms of improved internal efficiency that were expected from the Rolls Royce KM system. The KM team hoped that the new system would help the company in the following ways.
1. Improve customer data access across multiple platforms
2. Deliver applications that require little or no training
3. Reduce publishing costs, ensure security, and comply with air traffic standards

Measurement

Lacking any other mechanisms for measurement, Rolls Royce measured its ROI using surrogate financial measures. Most of these figures were translated into dollar figures:

- Paper costs savings of $3 million
- Customer productivity savings of $1 million
- Five percent improvement in maintenance time
- Unmeasured savings in data processing costs

Of all the technical features and development path options mentioned in Chapters 7 and 11, this system resembled an improved version of an intranet. It had a user-specific table of contents, a customizable interface, and the ability to add annotations; it provided dynamic updates and delivered automatic notifications. Content authoring in this system (called *Enigma*) was done with SGML and a primitive Microsoft Word interface, rather than a Web browser.

LESSONS LEARNED

To summarize the main point raised in this chapter: KM and business strategy must drive each other. Creativity without strategy is called *art*, creativity with strategy is called *good design*. Translate this link to draw two sets of implications: those for business strategy, change management, and reward structures, and those for the design features that a KM system must support. When you are devising this critical link and using it as a basis for your KM system, keep in mind these points.

- *An effective KM strategy begins with a vision.* Knowledge drives strategy, and strategy drives KM. Effective KM must begin with a strategic vision and a clear definition of what knowledge is critical for your company.

- *Shift from strategic programming to strategic planning.* Managers and businesses need to capture what they learn from both the soft insights and experiences, as well as from hard data on the markets, then synthesize that learning into a vision of the direction that the business *should* pursue. This is informed by the context, turbulence, and uncertainty associated with a business.

- *Data extrapolation is a fallible predictor.* Don't assume linear relationships and look for patterns in data. Data is often random and is a poor means for predicting future opportunities and conditions.

- *Create internal, competitive, and industry-wide knowledge maps to give you a reality check.* These maps will help you figure out which areas of knowledge are empty, slightly lacking, or weak beyond hope. Accordingly, orient your KM system to strengthen strategic-gap knowledge in those areas in which your company will compete.

- *Focus on one but don't choose between codification and personalization.* Codification and personalization are two "equally right" KM strategies: Strike a balance between the two while focusing primarily on one.

- *Balance exploitation and exploration.* Both must be supported, but one without the other can be a death blow.

- *Determine the right diagnostic questions to ask:* Knowing the right answers to the wrong questions will not serve your KM project.

- *Mobilize initiatives to help you "sell" your KM project internally:* Even after all the noise about the "long view," most companies still look for short-term results. Balancing tangible short-term gains with long-term gains is the only way you can sell the project to your end users and top management. Your company's sudden introduction of a KM system to the surprise of end users is like an 800,000-ton aircraft carrier trying to make a sudden U-turn in the high seas.

The elegance of the techniques described in this chapter lies in their ability to take something as high-level as your company's vision and, through a series of clear, iterative steps, translate it into low-level strategic steps and KM system functionalities/features.

Having identified the key characteristics that are needed in a KM system for it to be aligned successfully with your business strategy, we have made it through the second step on our 10-step road map. Let us now examine and understand the third step in the next chapter: infrastructural components of the KM architecture that can allow you to realize the system to support this strategic link.

Part IIB
The Second
Phase: KM
System Analysis,
Design, and
Development

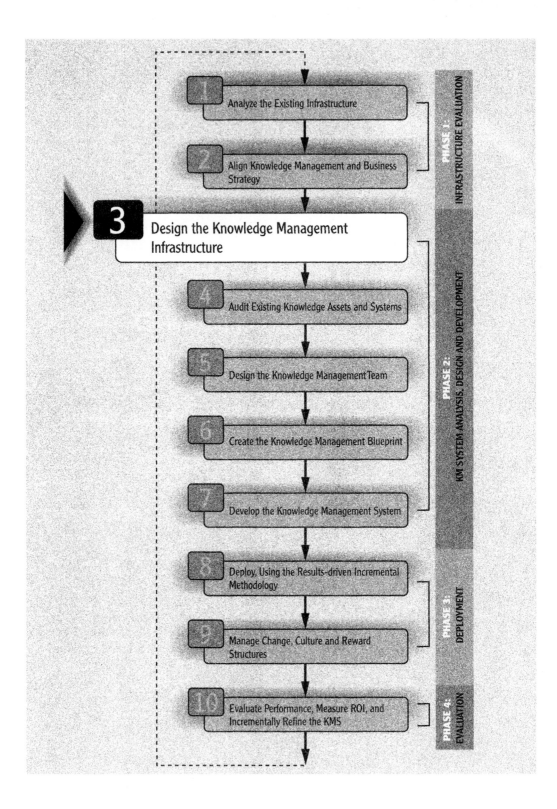

1 Analyze the Existing Infrastructure

2 Align Knowledge Management and Business Strategy

3 Design the Knowledge Management Infrastructure

4 Audit Existing Knowledge Assets and Systems

5 Design the Knowledge Management Team

6 Create the Knowledge Management Blueprint

7 Develop the Knowledge Management System

8 Deploy, Using the Results-driven Incremental Methodology

9 Manage Change, Culture and Reward Structures

10 Evaluate Performance, Measure ROI, and Incrementally Refine the KMS

PHASE 1: INFRASTRUCTURE EVALUATION

PHASE 2: KM SYSTEM ANALYSIS, DESIGN AND DEVELOPMENT

PHASE 3: DEPLOYMENT

PHASE 4: EVALUATION

CHAPTER 7
THE KNOWLEDGE
MANAGEMENT PLATFORM

KNOWLEDGE IS THE SMALL PART OF IGNORANCE THAT WE ARRANGE AND CLASSIFY.
—AMBROSE BIERCE

A little knowledge that is applied in making one critical decision is of much more value than gigabytes of data that are not being used.[1] With our eye on knowledge application, in this chapter, we implement Step 3 of the 10-step road map by way of the seven-layer KM architecture and its underlying infrastructural elements. We begin to look at technological pieces that make up the layer and analyze various components to transform existing infrastructure into one that supports KM. Our discussion of the seven-layer architecture spans more than one chapter: You'll become familiar with the illustration in the next few chapters.

The first layer in the architecture is the interface between the user and the system. We examine the elements and components to manage this portal best. We identify various knowledge sources to integrate into the KM system; this subject leads us to the third layer, where knowledge sources are used. Hence, we defer discussion of the access and authentication layer.

The third layer, the collaborative layer, prescribes the architectural elements of data storage, and we discuss implementation of its components: artificial intelligence, data warehousing, genetic algorithms, etc. We discuss methods for searching and retrieving information from this layer.

We then examine how the application layer helps integrate fragmented knowledge in various contexts. Technological pieces that make up each layer will be described, focusing on those that are less used or oblivious. I will discuss various components that help develop existing infrastructure into requisite *infostructure* that is required for effective KM. We will take your company into consideration and try to identify and understand components of the collaborative intelligence layer, including artificial intelligence, data warehouses, genetic algorithms, neural networks, expert reasoning systems, rule bases, and case-based reasoning. This chapter will describe techniques that you can use to optimize knowledge-object molecularity. It will help you identify the right mix of components for searching, indexing, and retrieval, and to create knowledge domain, form, type, product/service, time and location tags, and attributes. Finally, we will retrofit the aforementioned information technology components on Nonaka's SECI model—a technique that you can then use to validate the comprehensiveness of your own KM system's component set.

TECHNOLOGY COMPONENTS OF THE KNOWLEDGE MANAGEMENT ARCHITECTURE

Before we delve into actually using the seven-layer architecture for developing a KM system, we examine the technology pieces that constitute the seven layers. The seven layers of the KM system architecture that we use in the following chapters to help you build your KM system are illustrated in Figure 7-1.

KNOWLEDGE MANAGEMENT PROCESSES AND TECHNOLOGY ENABLERS

Select your technology components with the objectives clearly defined beforehand. Table 7-1 provides a technology selection map[2] that can help guide the technology selection process while keeping the actual need in focus. The processes that a KM system should support are listed in Table 7-1.

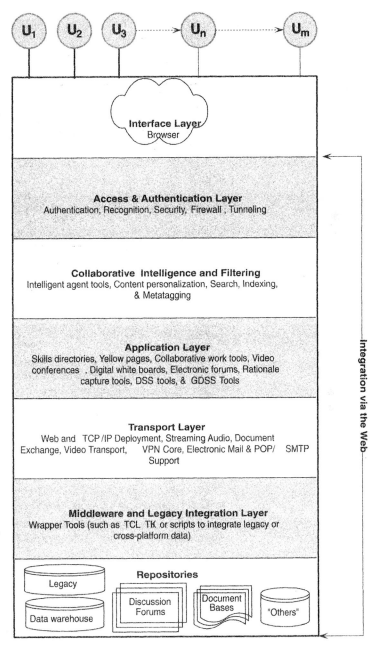

Figure 7-1   The seven layers of the KM system architecture. A KM system interfaces with its users U_1 through U_n (and offers scalability to handle even more users, as denoted by U_m) at the interface layer.

CASE IN POINT: BRITISH PETROLEUM

Communications technology does provide for transfer and exchange of structured and formalized knowledge; it also provides an outlet for knowledge that cannot or has not yet been structured but can be immediately applied. British Petroleum (BP) provides a picture-perfect example of the usefulness of video conferencing. BP experts in Italy used it to fix a problem in an oil rig in Latin America. Flying in experts would have taken days, but video conferencing allowed them to look at the problematic site remotely and fix the problem. Even though video conferencing cannot capture structured knowledge or distribute it, it facilitates the real-time transfer of contextual information—in this case, the condition of the oil rig—to enable application of distributed skills that exist in an organization. The video clip that might appear to be a simple piece of information to one person could be turned into applicable knowledge by specialists who can add context, experience, and interpretation to it.

Table 7-1 Knowledge Processes and Technology Enablers

Objective	Technology Enablers
Find knowledge	Knowledge bases in consulting firms; search and retrieval tools that scan both formal and informal sources of knowledge; employee skills yellow pages.
Create new knowledge	Capture collaborative decision-making processes; decision support system DSS tools; rationale capture tools; Notes databases; decision repositories; externalization tools.
Package and assemble knowledge	Customized publishing tools; information refinery tools; push technology; customized discussion groups.
Apply knowledge	Search, retrieval, and storage tools to help organize and classify both formal and informal knowledge.
Reuse and revalidate knowledge	Customer support knowledge bases; consulting firm discussion databases; past project record databases, and communities of practice.

As companies and work groups work their way, in sequence or in parallel, through one or more of the processes listed in Table 7-1, inputs are transformed into knowledge that is applied to create new products and services.

THE TELEPHONE AS A ROLE MODEL FOR KM SYSTEM DESIGN

When thinking of a KM platform, remember a device that is as common as a coffee pot and more useful than a PalmPilot—the telephone. The telephone represents the best set of characteristics that one could wish for in a system that supports knowledge flow effectively. As you speak into the telephone, you can convey context, meaning, attitude, and tone, along with information and data. Any successful KM system will have to possess the characteristics and communication richness of a telephone; because it is embedded in the organization, its use is almost transparent, rarely formal, natural, and hesitation free. The telephone provides us with a laundry list of basic characteristics that any system supporting knowledge must possess:

- The system should be well accepted in the community that will actually use it, not just the community that creates it.
- The system should allow and support rich communication.
- Context, meaning opinions, tone, and biases, should have a way to move through the system.
- The users should not feel as though they are using something they would not use if given a choice.
- The system should support informal communication and multiple ways of expressing ideas, thoughts, and communication.
- The system should be transparent to the user.
- The system should support the informal local *slang* used by its users. This is an imperative to prevent the system from decaying into a formality that no one actually cares to use—but still uses it because it is mandated.

THE SEVEN-LAYER KNOWLEDGE MANAGEMENT SYSTEM ARCHITECTURE

Let us gain a passing acquaintance with the seven-layer KM system architecture before we examine infrastructural components that comprise it. Figure 7-1 shows the seven layers in the KM system architecture.

FOUNDATION FOR THE INTERFACE LAYER

The interface layer is the topmost layer in the KM system architecture. This is, for the most part, the only layer with which end users directly interact. The effectiveness of this layer is a dominant determinant of the usability of a KM system. Let us first examine the requirements for the collaborative platform on which such a layer must be based.

SELECTION CRITERIA FOR THE COLLABORATIVE PLATFORM

For effective collaboration across the enterprise and the smooth sharing of structured knowledge, the collaborative KM platform must satisfy the following set of basic needs.[3]

1. *Efficient protocols*: The network protocols used should not clog up bandwidth of the network and should allow secure and fast sharing of content across far-flung locations, including mobile clients and traveling machines.

2. *Portable operation*: Companies often have various platforms and operating system environments in use by different departments. The collaborative platform must be able to operate in a portable manner across all these platforms.[a]

3. *Consistent and easy-to-use client interfaces*: Do not assume that users are technology experts; many of them might come from nontechnical domains, departments, and backgrounds.

4. *Scalability*: As the number of users grows, the collaborative platform should be able to scale up without degradation in performance.

5. *Legacy integration*: A large chunk of operational data in more seasoned (been around forever) companies often lies in mainframe databases. Therefore, the collaborative platform that you decide to use must be able to integrate this data into the final interface.[b]

6. *Security*: As an enterprise becomes increasingly distributed, security becomes an important aspect of design.

7. *Flexibility and customizability:* The lack of the end user's ability to filter out irrelevant content is perhaps the root cause for the information overload that most companies are facing. The choice of platform should allow for a reasonable degree of customization and flexibility in terms of what the user sees and needs to see.

THE WEB OR PROPRIETARY PLATFORMS?

In the past, firms tended to rely on external repositories of knowledge, such as market intelligence databases, for bringing in new knowledge with which they made decisions. However, with the increased penetration of digital work using personal computers, work done by

---

[a]The Web, with the use of the HTTP protocol, remains unbeaten in this respect. The browser is the most suitable universal client through which end users can run applications and access repositories without having to switch familiar platforms or operating environments.

[b]The Web-based intranet is again the best choice for this. A wide array of tools and scripting languages, such as TCL/TK, are available to accomplish integration. They can create *wrappers* that allow data from legacy systems to be accessed from Web browsers, irrespective of their platforms. Although legacy integration is important, it is also essential that a collaborative knowledge-sharing platform integrate well with existing systems and applications. The Web, again, beats most proprietary standards in this regard.

employees is already in a form ready for electronic manipulation. Companies are, therefore, creating internal repositories of knowledge bases of market knowledge, customer relationship management knowledge, profile knowledge, product development traceability knowledge, and collaborative knowledge repositories.

Although it is easier for raw inputs such as spreadsheets, meeting notes, design documents, etc., to be converted into a storage-friendly format, another problem arises: Companies have not been able to standardize on specific platforms and operating systems in a perfect manner. Some employees work on UNIX machines, some on Macintoshes, some on Linux platforms, and most others use Windows systems as their primary work environments. Some companies also use incompatible networks across organizational units. Although proprietary solutions might require less up-front development time because of their more comprehensive out-of-the-box attributes and have capabilities such as replication, security, controls, and development tools tightly integrated with them, the Web-based intranet might require a higher investment in the development stages (see Table 7-2). Increasingly high levels of integration of multimedia capabilities into Web browsers, along with guaranteed backward compatibility, allows easier representation of informal content than is possible using proprietary platforms.[3]

The Art of Packaging Knowledge

Filtering, editing, searching, and organizing pieces of knowledge, collectively called *packaging,* are essential though frequently overlooked components of successful KM. Packaging knowledge ensures that what is sieved proves useful, provides value, encourages application of that knowledge to address actual business issues, and figures into critical decisions. Search tools need to integrate knowledge latently existing in a company's transaction databases, data warehouses, discussion databases, documents, informal media, and, most importantly, in people's minds. Although plumbing the last source is not an easy or direct job, yellow pages and skills directories provide that capability to a moderate extent.

To capitalize on the wealth of intelligence available in an organization, knowledge must be packaged in such a way that it's insightful, relevant, and useful. Knowledge is generally shared with employee groups in teams with differing priorities, skill sets, training, functional responsibilities, and backgrounds; therefore, knowledge packaging efforts require several rounds of review and revision.

Ask selected end users to evaluate the material and provide ideas for how to improve its content, value, quality, and style so that it increases the perceived credibility and value of such content. The time required to do this does not come out of thin air. Allow employees the time to package knowledge for further use.

To make content useful, include:

1. *Identification*: Identify general domains of knowledge applicable to your company or business unit.

2. *Segmenting*: Identify segments and target users, and classify them into broad groups. Identify a small number of mutually exclusive groups.

Table 7-2 Comparison of Key Characteristics of Proprietary and the Web Protocol–based intranets as Primary Knowledge-Sharing Platforms

Characteristic	Proprietary	TCP/IP Intranets	Comments
Architecture	Proprietary	Open/evolving	The World Wide Web (www.w3.org) consortium is placing an increased focus on developing the Web as a powerful collaborative platform.
Security	High	Low by default	Security can be enhanced with a variety of security tools.
Authentication	Strong	Strong	Back doors and holes in open standards-based systems make them more vulnerable to compromise.
Direct (initial) cost	Moderate to high	Low	Development costs can be high for intranets if extensive custom programming work is involved.
Development cost	High	Low	Existing Web development skills can be leveraged for intranets.
Technological maturity	High	Low	Web protocols are still evolving.
Employee training costs	High	Low	Employees are often familiar with the Internet and the Web browser interface.
Initial investment	High	Low	This is indicative only of the up-front costs.
Legacy integration	Low	High	*Wrappers* can be written to allow access of legacy data through a Web browser.
Cross-platform integration	Low	High	Hypertext Transfer Protocol (HTTP) acts as the universal protocol that brings together content across all platforms that might be in use in your company.
Deployment time	Fast	Slower	
Out-of-the-box solution	Yes	No/sometimes	Software vendors can customize generic intranets for quicker deployment.

3. *Mass customization:* Mass customize content to suit each audience. Let the audiences further tailor the content targeted toward them through collaborative filtering mechanisms and choice-enabling software.

4. *Format:* Select appropriate format. Use indexes, groupings, site maps, mind maps, and tables of contents for easy navigation.

5. *Tests:* Don't assume that your end users want what you think they want. Test and refine the steps described above and seek user feedback as a positive indicator of perceived usefulness and improvement.

Knowledge Delivery *Weltanschuung*

The design philosophy—*Weltanschuung*[c]—of your KM system dictates how actionable information or knowledge is delivered.

The first choice is the method of delivery—when users want the knowledge (the pull approach) or when you want them to have it (the push approach). You can make both options available to every user without adding much complexity to the system itself—the push system can simply deliver the final content from the pull-based system.

Be aware that how information is filtered can be an issue of the push system: Filters may not be consistent with users' needs, so ask them what categories of filtering they want. Some filtering tools use intelligent agents to learn from each user's habits; users may consider this a violation of privacy. It's even possible, if the system is not powerful enough, that the filter may filter out wrong, possibly critically needed content. For example, a user who reads reports about a competitor's products will begin receiving more competitive intelligence reports. The problem begins, however, when he starts receiving job postings after having checked Steve Job's official title once.

Another decision is how much information should be delivered: all or selected parts. *Selective* delivery of content is the only way push mechanisms can be effectively used to push content through a KM system.

You may also consider when to deliver knowledge: when needed ("just in time") or when created or acquired ("just in case"). A middle path is not an option, but anecdotal evidence (for example, a customer study by Lotus) suggests that just-in-time delivery is more valuable than just-in-case. Certainly, just-in-case systems have their problems: Information, not knowledge, is delivered; users become inured to the flow or irrelevant information and simply ignore it; users pursue interesting threads not applicable or useful to their work.

COLLABORATIVE INTELLIGENCE AND FILTERING LAYER

Effectiveness of KM platforms is dependent not only on technical ability and reliability, that is, the infrastructure, but also on conversational robustness. This has been referred to as infostructure.4 This predetermines the extent to which the system provides a language structure and

---

[c]*Weltanschuung,* a German term for "world view," or "philosophy," has no close equivalent in English. This term has been in favor, especially with management researchers, who have been critical of how logical positivist epistemologists construe the reality of organization science as being completely free of human judgment.

DELIVERY OPTIONS

Push vs. Pull
- Pull system: A pull system requires a user to actively seek information.
  1. *User choice*: Users proactively seek knowledge as and when they need it
  2. *No distraction*: Pull systems do not distract users with unwanted updates but require user initiative. Users actually need to *go and get* what they need to know.

- Push systems: Distribute and deliver knowledge to their audience, after filtering it through highly customized filters.
  1. *Noticeability*: Push systems deliver information to users' desktops or electronic mail accounts and are more likely to get noticed.
  2. *Ease of use*: Within a work group, there might be some that might actually prefer receiving push, rather than have to deal with the effort of going and looking for the pieces of information that they might need to complete their task

All vs. Some
- All-inclusive: Unlike a filtering approach, all-inclusive systems deliver content in its entirety.
  1. *Suited for information management, not KM*: Volume, as Davenport and Prusak describe it, is data's friend. A few decades back when the focus of technology was electronic data processing, it was this lack of data volume that companies were trying to address. The problem today is the excess of information.
  2. *Data slam*: The onslaught of meaningless pieces of data, often called *data slam*, that attack and clog corporate Intranet sites and databases not only mucks up internal databases, it can also dangerously slow down management decision making by making systems slow, unwieldy and difficult to navigate.

- Selective: Selective delivery takes a minimalist approach. Selective delivery of content is the only way push delivery can be used effectively to push content through a KM system.
  1. *Useful, contextually applicable pieces*: Selective delivery mechanisms specifically extract useful and contextually applicable pieces from an enormous volume of processed data and information. Too many databases, too many documents, too many categories prevent users from efficiently finding information that they need.
  2. *Specifically analyzed information, contextual knowledge, and business intelligence*: Instead of dumping entire content of articles and reports into the system, it limits on-line content to abstracts, and directs interested readers to the original sources and authors for more information. Instead of a flood of data, decision makers need.

- Tradeoffs: One might argue that this might cause some critical piece of information—that could have helped—not to reach the consumer or knowledge

> worker requiring it. But that is a tradeoff. Not having something reach the user
> is better than having too much reach him. In the latter case, little or nothing will
> actually be used.
>
> **Just-in-time vs. Just-in-case**
> JIT: Lotus has been studying its customers and has found that knowledge is more
> valuable when it is delivered at the moment its needed—"just in time"—rather than
> being available at all times, just in case it might be needed.
>   JIC: Just-in-case systems devaluate knowledge as users become used to receiving
> information (this is not knowledge due to possible lack of action-ability) that is not
> relevant to their immediate work or task in hand. They may ignore the messages or
> spend time following threads that are interesting but not applicable or useful to them
> in their work.

resources that people use to make sense of events taking place within the network. The infrastructure underlying the intelligence and filtering layer supports the transition from infrastructure to infostructure. The aspect of taking infostructure into consideration along with the infrastructure is a crucial determinant of whether users will actually appreciate your system in preference over other sources and use it; the lack of this is the killer antidote for any KM system.

To avoid the "philosopher's trap" and accomplish nothing, use clear models or building blocks that define key concepts and provide direction for analysis, action, and—most importantl—results. The focus, at least in the beginning, needs to be on solutions that can find, summarize, interpret, and analyze large volumes of data and information efficiently and effectively. Table 7-3 exemplifies sources and types of feeds that a marketing KM system needs.[5]

INFRASTRUCTURAL ELEMENTS OF COLLABORATIVE INTELLIGENCE

To understand which of these technologies fit with your own KM system and how they can be integrated, it is essential to understand their role in the context of KM.

Table 7-3 Sources and Feeds for a Marketing KM

Source	Examples
Customer knowledge processes	• Feedback from customers.
	• Knowledge of new product development projects in customer companies.
	•. Potential needs of customers; possibly new needs.
	• Level of customer dissatisfaction.

Table 7-3 Sources and Feeds for a Marketing KM (cont.)

Source	Examples
Marketing—research/development connections	• The level to which the market data is used by your company's development teams. • The level to which marketing departments actually use insights provided by the development staff. • The extent to which your new service/product development efforts jointly involve ideas from both these parties. • Evaluation of one party's products (e.g., marketing plan evaluation by development staff), and vice versa.
Competitor knowledge processes	• How well are competitor information sources (e.g. online bookstores that allow buyers to compare prices for their selections with their competitor's prices in real time) integrated within your internal information systems? • Is the analysis of competitor information systematic and thorough throughout the development process for new services and products? • Do you use customer evaluations of your competitors' products as a benchmark for your own products or services? • Do you regularly examine the IT support that your competitors use?
Market performance	• How does your product perform in comparison with other competing products? • How do customers rate your service in comparison with your competitor's services? 1. In terms of quality. 2. In terms of value. • How well are information sources about the product markets in general integrated with your planning and development support systems with your intranet?
Technology change	• What is the rate of obsolesce of your product/service /methodology? • Is your market's underlying technology rapidly evolving or mature? How does this figure into your decisions? How do you know it is even looked at when key decisions are made? • Are sources of this information linked to the information systems used within your company? How well?

The Artificiality of Artificial Intelligence

Although KM is a fairly recent term, companies have been trying to capture and manipulate knowledge with computers since the 1970s. Artificial intelligence promised a lot but delivered little. What was once a crying concern among socialists and humanists is now a joke. Although some spin-offs of artificial intelligence have, indeed, been truly useful—expert systems, case-based reasoning systems, neural networks, and intelligent agents—their application domains are pretty narrow. The dream of the intelligent machine that would replace the human brain is long dead. However, that endeavor has left us with some technologies that have penetrated businesses for good.

Expert systems have been particularly strongly affected victims of excessive hype and overly high expectations. MIT media lab professor Marvin Minsky predicted in 1970 that:

> In from three to eight years we will have a machine with the general intelligence of an average human being. It will be able to read Shakespeare, grease a car, play office politics, tell a joke, have a fight. At that point this machine will begin to educate itself, and in a few months its intelligence will be at the level of a genius. After that, its power will be incalculable.[6]

Thirty-odd years later, expert systems have not lived up to those expectations. They have not revolutionized or rationalized the whole business environment, but they have left us with one profound understanding: Human knowledge is too complex to comprehend fully. It is with that caution that you need to approach the idea of a KM system and the KM initiative. It will not suddenly make your company the biggest money-maker in the industry. At best, it will help your company compete better and maybe contribute to its long-term survival. Let's restrain our hopes. Doing better than we hope to can only be a pleasant surprise.

Data Warehouses

Data representations, such as hypercube data models in multiple dimensions, help immensely in supporting decision making with concrete data from the past (a simple way of thinking about a hypercube model is as a system that lets you slice and dice existing data along various dimensions.)[7] A data warehouse is of little use unless the data is converted to meaningful information and applied when needed. Even if this data is used every time a relevant decision is made, it still represents only a fraction of the knowledge assets that the firm has and does not account for expertise that has not been explicated in databases and files. Although we do not want to get overly involved in discussing data warehouses, let us examine how a data warehouse falls into place in the scheme of things in a KM initiative. Many companies often have multiple databases existing throughout their hierarchies.

The key characteristics of a data warehouse and its relative fit are summarized in Table 7-4.

Genetic Algorithm Tools

Like neural networks, genetic algorithms are based on Charles Darwin's theory of natural selection—extended from animals to data. If you are trying to solve a problem or make a decision where standard rules of thumb fail to work or are impossible to use, trying genetic

Table 7-4 Characteristics and Relative Fit of a Data Warehouse in the KM Infrastructure

Characteristic	Level	Down Side
Response time	Low	Data might not be real time.
Scalability with growing needs	Medium	Depends on initial design optimization.
Flexibility of use	High	None.
Ease of use	High	Needs a good front end and interface for use.
Retrieval of data	Medium	The user needs to navigate through the interface and find the relevant data that helps make a decision.
Processing overhead	High	Not a relevant concern if the size is not too large.
Accuracy	High	Depends on the quality of data scrubbing. Accuracy is higher than the sources since "bad" data has been cleansed out.

algorithm-based solutions is a good choice. Very often, a genetic algorithm can simplify the amount of work required to solve a complex, decision-related problem, in comparison with techniques such as rule-based methods or case-based reasoning system. In essence, genetic algorithms enable a decision maker to say "I do not know how to build a good solution, but I will know it when I see it!"[7]

Table 7-5 summarizes the fit of genetic algorithm tools within the KM technological framework.

Neural Networks

A neural network is a networked computing architecture in which a number of processors are interconnected like the neurons in a human brain that can learn through trial and error. Much like genetic algorithms, neural networks have their roots in biology. A neural network can identify patterns within such data without the need for a specialist or expert. A basic neural network is illustrated in Figure 7-2. The top layer, called the *input layer,* receives data from external sources. The internal processing layer, which is hidden from the outside, is where all processing takes place. The lowest layer is the output layer, which transmits the outputs or guesses to the user. The internal layer has already learned from solving earlier problems and tries to apply those "lessons" to the new datasets that are fed into the neural network. In real applications, the neural networks are far more complex than the simple example described in Figure 7-2 and, in effect, more promising.

Although theories on which neural networks are built might suggest that such nets can deal with "dirty" data, reality is quite different. If you decide to use a neural network as a part of your explicative KM system, be prepared to spend a considerable amount of time training the neural network, cleaning up data, and preprocessing so that the neural net can better com-

Table 7-5 The Relative Fit of GA-Based Tools in the KM Technology Framework

Characteristic	Down Sides for KM
Medium to high accuracy of solutions	Limited and relatively specialized applications.
High response speed/fast problem solving	May deteriorate as the problem increases in complexity.
Limited scalability	Computing resources often fall short of a complex genetic algorithm-based solution.
High levels of "embeddability"	Tools based on genetic algorithms tend to be highly dependent on software and the nature of the problem. Although this specialization probably improves the performance of the tool, it also severely constrains its usability in other problem domains.
Development speed of typical solutions based on genetic algorithms is fairly high	Solutions tend to be fairly specialized and have a narrow application domain
Low to medium ease of use	A majority of popular commercial tools available are for specialized platforms that are typically not used in most business environments.

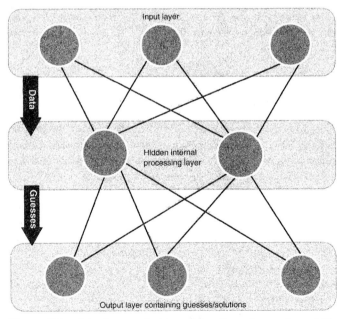

Figure 7-2   A basic neural network has three layers. In real-life applications, these nets grow immensely complex.

Table 7-6 Key Characteristics of Neural Networks and Their Fit in the KMS Architecture

Characteristic	Down Sides for KM Applications
High accuracy	Requires thorough training and preprocessing of data. Accuracy degrades as size and complexity increase beyond a certain level (depending on the type of problem being solved).
High response speed	Degrades as the net becomes increasingly complex.
High tolerance for "bad" data and noise contained within the input data	Requires preprocessing of data for the network to comprehend it. This requirement alone takes up a majority of the time spent building a neural network.
Mediocre flexibility	The neural network needs to be retrained with relevant data if it is to be used for a new application.
Low processing resource requirement	Requirements for processing power are lower than for most other types of data-based decision support systems.
Limited scalability	Data is needed; complexity of the problem might constrict scalability.
Limited need for domain experts or recorded expertise	Relevant data is needed. It also needs to be preprocessed.

prehend data that is fed to it. As problems become increasingly complex, the ability of neural networks to find proper solutions degrades.[8-11] The key characteristics are summarized in Table 7-6.

Expert Reasoning and Rule-Based Systems

The accounting profession has for decades accomplished tasks on the basis of rules ranging from simple to complex. A hypothetical example is what your tax accountant goes through when dealing with the IRS each April 15th: Regulations may specify that if a person's annual income is $120,000, the tax rate is 30 percent with a minimum deductible amount, and so forth. Similarly, engineering departments follow rules for design and development. However, problems in business that tend to involve higher levels of creativity and innovative off-the-block thinking might not seem to fit well into such problem solving and analysis schemes.

Rules can be represented in very simple terms after they have been broken down. A generic example is the following:

```
IF
      {some condition is met}
THEN
      {do this}
ELSE
   {do something else}
```

A more complex, nested version of this would be:

```
IF
      ({some condition is met}
AND
      {this condition is also met})
OR
      {this other condition is met}
THEN
      {do this}
ELSE
   (do something else)
```

After values are plugged in, a rule might be:

```
IF
      (retail price of PC is at least 25% lesser than a name brand
PC)

      AND
          (warranty period is the same)
      AND
          (processing power is at least 30% higher than the
      comparable name brand unit)
THEN
      (it will sell)
ELSE
      ((it will not sell)
   AND
   (the retail price or configuration will have to be readjusted)
```

Interpreting this rule is fairly straightforward. Assume that I am Xiao Wang, a generic computer parts importer who sells generic personal computers while competing against the more expensive name-brand machines that are sold in other stores. My pricing decisions are based on a model represented in a simple rule refined over time. The rule, as stated above, simply says that to be able to sell profitably, the prices of my generic, no-brand PCs need to be at least 25 percent lower and configurations 30 percent faster than comparable name-brand machines.

The value of rules becomes even more uncontestable once they are integrated into a larger grouping of tools that will constitute the technology enablers for your company's KM program. Although the examples above are unrealistically simple, actual rules tend to be far more complex and do very well once they are hard-coded into systems (by *hard-coded,* we do not mean unchangeably coded). Automated application of such embeddable rules frees your employees to spend their brainpower on knowledge tasks, such as socialization, that these techniques cannot address.

Although rule-based systems look neat, their application is rather restricted. They work well only when the following five conditions are simultaneously satisfied:

1. You know the variables in your problem.
2. You can express them quantitatively.
3. The relevant rule(s) applies to most of them.
4. These rules do not overlap.
5. The rules are rigorously validated.

Rule-based systems are diametric opposites of genetic algorithm systems. In genetic algorithms, you can specify universal conditions under which solutions are considered good, but you cannot apply expert knowledge on how to solve the problem. In rule-based systems, you can bring in expert knowledge, but you cannot specify any universal conditions that denote a good solution.

An example of such a situation is credit rating systems. In the rating of credit worthiness of a person, rules allow application of specific expert-elicited dictum, but no criteria can universally suggest whether the person is credit-worthy. Similarly for auto insurance, rule-

Table 7-7 Rule-Based Systems and Their Relative Fit in the KM Infrastructure

Characteristic	Down Sides of Using in a KM System
High dependence on domain experts and specialists	Extensive inputs from domain specialists are needed. Very often, expert knowledge is explicated only to a limited extent, because much of it is tacit. First cuts on elicitation of this knowledge range from poor to acceptable and rarely, ever rise, to the level of perfection.
Higher speed of development	Rule-based systems can be developed at a fast pace only if knowledge can be elicited from experts in a thorough manner. This often takes up the largest chunk of development time.
Low levels of scalability	As problems being addressed become complex or evolve over time, rule bases need to be refined. If rules change over time, experts often need to be brought in again to revalidate the rules in use.
Slow response speeds	If the datasets grow large, rules grow more intermingled and complicated. This can often pose a serious challenge to the computing power in use. As problems get complicated, a multitude of rules need to be matched, which again degrades the response speed.
Low to medium flexibility	Small bases are quite flexible, but as the problem becomes more complicated or involves new variables, the inflexibility of the system becomes an apparent disadvantage.

based systems can apply the universally accepted (for the insurance industry) and empirically validated rules that risks are higher among males who are single and under 25; however, no universal condition determines the risk of an applicant.

Rule-based systems can be expensive to develop because much of the development time and resources are spent eliciting knowledge from an expert. However, much of the knowledge is tacit, and as you would guess, not all of it is explicated (see Table 7-7).

Case-Based Reasoning

Case-based reasoning is a promising candidate for the KM infrastructure. This approach allows companies to take advantage of previous problems or cases and related attempts to solve them through analogies. Figure 7-3 illustrates in simple terms the inner workings of a case-based reasoning system.

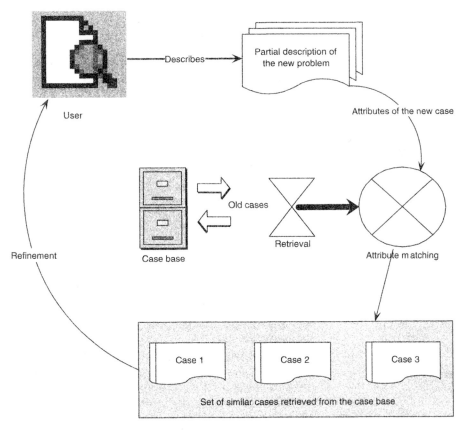

Figure 7-3 The basic idea behind case-based reasoning.

You, as the user, define a new problem that you are trying to solve on the basis of some attributes. Each attribute is assigned some weight, based on previous experience or existing knowledge. Based on these attributes, a search mechanism sifts through all cases in the case base. Cases that are closest matches to the case at hand are then retrieved. These cases can be used to refine the search further to retrieve even closer matches. Case-based reasoning also works very well with other decision-support technologies discussed earlier, allowing sufficient room for integration of case-based reasoning with several other components within a larger KM system. Case-based reasoning tools work especially well when the choice is between basing a decision on *some* data and no data at all. However new or however crude a case-based reasoning system is, it will always give *some* solution.

On the down side, a case-based reasoning system needs thorough initial planning. You must include all possible attributes that you might even remotely anticipate the need for later. If you add attributes later on, older cases that have those attributes will not show up in the search and retrieval process unless those attributes are explicitly added to old cases, as well.

Table 7-8 Characteristics of Case-Based Reasoning in KM

Characteristic	Down Side of Using Case-Based Reasoning in a KM System
High level of independence from specialists and domain experts	An expert must fine-tune the attribute matching and retrieval criteria.
High accuracy of solutions	Accuracy is not high to begin with. It improves as more cases are added to the case base.
Higher response times	As more cases are added to the case base, the performance of a case-based reasoning system can degrade. Attribute definition and indexing need substantial forethought to prevent serious problems due to growing case density.
High levels of scalability	Case-based reasoning systems offer a high level of scalability and lend themselves to work in distributed environments, such as across enterprise networks, rather easily. However, the attributes are not easily scalable, and all possible future attributes should be pre-defined at the outset, when possible.
Unaffected by noise	The retrieval cases will not be affected by the presence of "garbage" or noise in the input case attributes as long as the case base is populated with a sufficient number of cases.
Low ability to handle complexity	As the number of attributes increases, case-based reasoning begins to show weaknesses. First, all attributes in use now might not have been defined in older cases. Second, the interactions between multiple attributes cannot be judged accurately even if the case base is well populated with cases.

If you decide to build a new case-based reasoning system, it is often a wise idea to add new cases as they occur, rather than trying to add past cases through post hoc reconstruction (much like software documentation that does little good if written after the fact). Adding past cases can be a laborious and expensive process and is often the root cause of errors, if not done rigorously. Table 7-8 provides the characteristics that determine case-based reasoning's fit in your KM infrastructural decisions.

Companies have successfully applied case-based reasoning to tasks such as planning, scheduling, design, and legal deliberation. However, the best success stories of case-based reasoning lie in the areas of managing customer support knowledge at telephone help desks run by software companies. One can also envision the application of case-based reasoning to search for knowledge across a KM system. The logic would be as follows: "If Sam accessed sources A, M, and Z to solve a scheduling problem for our product in category S, then what knowledge sources would I need to access to solve a problem defined by attributes A1 and A2 in product category H?"

Putting It All Together

A critical differentiator among the tools discussed so far is the level of knowledge needed to use and apply a particular technology or tool successfully. Some tools require a high level of domain knowledge from the user, whereas others assume that the end user is a relatively passive observer in the process. The second dimension is the amount of time that is needed to find a solution with a KM tool in the specific business application domain of interest. The applications of these tools in a KM platform are summarized in Table 7-9.

Table 7-9 Applications of Various Intelligence Tools in a KM Platform

Tool	Applicability in a KM Platform
Case-based reasoning	The case-based reasoning (CBR) system searches a collection of previous cases, known as its *case base*, for past cases with attributes that match the current case. The user defines the problem to be solved, based on some attributes (each with varying degrees of importance, as indicated by their user-assigned weights). A search engine then searches through all the cases in the case base and retrieves those that match closely. As new cases are added, the CBR becomes increasingly powerful and accurate. Concepts are stored as real images, and the context of past decisions is satisfactorily retained. However, CBR requires the user to define all expected attributes in the initial stages of its development.
Data mining-based inference modeling	Data-mining tools analyze customer information embedded in vast amounts of operational data and facilitate knowledge-based market segmentation and customer profiling. These techniques have limited applicability for new customers.

Table 7-9 Applications of Various Intelligence Tools in a KM Platform (cont.)

Tool	Applicability in a KM Platform
Data Web-houses and warehouses	A data warehouse acts as a unifier of a multitude of isolated, distributed databases and aggregates, cleans, scrubs, and consolidates disparate data. Although data warehouses do not possess the ability to deliver real-time data, Web-enabled warehouses known as data *Web-houses* are moving in that direction. By aggregating data across multiple sources, they give decision makers the ability to run complex queries, slice and dice data, and most importantly, improve information quality and accuracy.
Document management systems	Document management systems make vast amounts of documents, such as product literature, electronic forms, specifications, and correspondence, easily accessible and adaptable through the Web. These systems often include workflow functionality that allows documents to be intelligently routed to select, relevant employees.
Fuzzy logic systems	In contrast, fuzzy logic systems, for example, need to be trained by domain specialists or experts—often too expensive or unfeasible. There might be experts available and accessible but their opinions might differ, or none of them might have comprehensive understanding of the problem. Even if you do get experts, they might have problems explicating their decision-making process in sufficient detail. Several companies have invested millions of dollars in expert systems, to little avail—simply because the experts were unable to state exactly what they knew and how they knew it.
Genetic algorithm	Genetic algorithms apply Darwin's survival of the fittest theory to computer programs and data. A genetic algorithm experiments with several new and novel problem solutions simultaneously. The programs and data sets that solve a problem survive (ranked high and retained for genetic refinement), and others are assigned a low rank and discarded. They are very effective in making decisions where the amount to data to be taken into account is very large and there are discontinuities in available data.
Collaborative filtering	Collaborative filtering automatically compares attributes of one set of customer data with other customers and provides ideas for personalization. This approach relies on an extensive base of similar customers. Collaborative filtering requires scalable personalization capabilities that can handle effective personalization as customer data volume grows. A good example of collaborative filtering that actually works can be found on Amazon.com's Web site, where the site recommends books based on past purchases by other customers with similar interests.

Neural networks	Neural networks are a networked computing architecture in which a number of processors are interconnected in a manner suggestive of the connections between neurons in a human brain and which can learn by a process of trial and error. They are especially useful when very limited inputs from domain experts exist or when you have the data but lack experts to make judgments about it.
Rule-based systems	Rule-based systems embed existing rules of thumb and heuristics in systems to facilitate fast and accurate decision making. However, five conditions must be met for them to work well: (1) you must know the variables in your problem/question, (2) you must be able to express them in hard, numerical terms (e.g., dollars), (3) the rule specified must cover most of these variables, (4) there is no overlap between rules, and (5) the rules must have been validated. These systems require continuous manual change, and conflict resolution between rules requires additional rule making.

The technological feasibility of each component can be guided by the comparison presented in Table 7-10.

Table 7-10 A Comparison of Intelligence Tools

Intelligence Tool	Response Time	Scalability	Flexibility	Ease of Use	Embeddability	Processing Overhead	Expert Dependence	Tolerance for "Dirty" Data	Implementation Speed	Tolerance for Complexity	Accuracy
Genetic algorithm	H	L	L	L	H	H	L	—	H	H	H
Neural networks	H	M	L	L	M	L	L	H	M	H	H
Fuzzy logic systems	H	L	M	H	M	H	H	H	H	M	M
Rule-based systems	X	L	M	H	H	M	H	L	H	M	H
Case-based reasoning	L	H	L	M	M	H	L	H	M	H	H

Legend: H = High; L = Low; M = Medium; X = Deteriorates as the number of active rules grows.

GRANULARITY IN KNOWLEDGE OBJECTS

Because a KM system is intended as a mechanism for securing corporate knowledge, it needs to be populated with knowledge objects. However, these knowledge objects can be specified at different levels of detail. For example, tasks in past projects can be recorded at different levels of detail. A key failure point in the design of a KM system is not deciding on the right level of detail at the start.

Let's take a look at a KM system in a diagnostic clinic.[12] The knowledge elements or objects can be represented at different levels of detail, as shown in Table 7-11.

Table 7-11 Levels of Increasing Granularity in a KM System Representing the System's Depth of Detail

Knowledge object	Example of Such an Object in a Clinical (Diagnostic) KM System
Knowledge domain	Internal medicine.
Knowledge region	Neurology.
Knowledge section	Brain diseases; tumors.
Knowledge segment	Diagnosis of brain tumors and cancerous growth.
Knowledge element	General diagnostic strategies.
Knowledge fragment	If the symptom reported by the patient is continual headaches, consider the possibility of a brain tumor.
Knowledge atom	Excessive and continual headaches is a symptom.

Too high a level of granularity will result in the loss of knowledge richness and context; too low a level will cause unnecessary drain on network, storage, and human resources, will raise the cost, and will reduce the value of the object.

Now, let us reframe this example using business data. Let us consider the use of a KM system to support customers who buy an AS/400 computer system that your company sells. Such a domain of knowledge could be represented as shown in Table 7-12.

The key lies in selecting the right level of molecularity of knowledge that will be stored in your KM system—the level that strikes an optimum balance between the two opposite extremes of too much detail and too little detail, both of which can render knowledge only marginally useful.

INFRASTRUCTURAL ELEMENTS FOR SEARCHING, INDEXING, AND RETRIEVING

Indexing and retrieval capabilities of a KM system determine the ease with which a user can find relevant knowledge on the system. Four types of navigation strategies can be deployed in varying combinations: metasearching, hierarchical searching, attribute searching, and content searching.

Table 7-12 Customer Support and Knowledge Levels: An Example

Knowledge Object	Example of Such an Object in a Business KM System
Knowledge domain	Customer support for home computers.
Knowledge region	Hardware.
Knowledge section	Memory diagnostics.
Knowledge segment	Diagnosis of memory-related problems using general diagnostic strategies.
Knowledge element	Memory diagnostic strategies based on symptoms; collect all symptoms and eliminate all possibilities until the only one left is a memory failure/hardware fault.
Knowledge fragment	If the symptom reported by the customer is system lockups and continual beeping, consider the possibility of a memory problem.
Knowledge atom	Frequent lockups; blue-screen-related beeping; failure to boot up are all symptoms.

Metasearching

Unlike the categories that follow, an approach based on metacategories allows the user to determine the focus of the search. This idea is conceptually similar to the purpose served by the *browse* functionality provided by the hierarchical search capability in a KM system. The main purpose of a metasearch function is to minimize the time spent in locating a general category for a piece of potential knowledge within a repository.

THE VALUE OF META INFORMATION

Without powerful search and retrieval tools that support meta information creation, a system will never go past the characteristic set of a traditional information system. Valuable, actionable information that is part of your underutilized intangible assets can be obtained through the tracking and assessment of knowledge production, manipulation, and processing. Defined as *meta information*, this information about information assists in defining, categorizing, and locating knowledge sources and resources. In essence, this function provides data about who is doing *what with what*. Meta information provides insight into information users, types of data and information being accessed, and where and which information repositories are being most frequently accessed.

Hierarchical Searching

If the user has successfully identified the broad categories, he or she can then continue to dig deeper into the repository without running the risk of going in a totally irrelevant or wrong direction. A hierarchical search strategy organizes knowledge items in a fixed hierarchy.

The user can follow or traverse links within such a structure to locate the right knowledge element efficiently and in a timely manner. The idea of using hyperlinks similar to those used in Web pages is a good example of such a navigation and search technique. This method is, therefore, apt for use in intranets because they support hyperlinking by default.

Attribute Searching

Searching by attributes uses a value input by the user. This attribute value is matched against closely related values attached to documents and pointers, such as skills databases. Those that closely match are returned as the final search results.

THE LIMITS OF ATTRIBUTE SEARCHING

Conventional attribute search mechanisms are of limited value in a KM system, for three reasons:

1. Excessive query matches: Search engines such as Yahoo! and AltaVista use simple keyword matching to find matches between target documents and keywords contained in a user's query, often returning hundreds, if not thousands, of irrelevant "hits." Due to the sheer simplicity of keyword matching (even with relevance rankings and Boolean AND/OR filtering), there is often the risk of finding information that is no longer valid. Date-based sorting provides little respite, because "new" information can also be invalid, stale, or outright wrong.

2. Breadth tradeoffs: Information retrieval tools, such as Verity and Fulcrum, provide relevancy rankings with query results. Although such tools mitigate the problem of excessive hits, they often limit their searches to certain data types.

3. Failure to understand meanings of words and exact context of use: The most severe limitation of search engines and information retrieval tools lies in their inability to understand the meanings of words that users intend to convey. For example, if the user asked a question with "blow" as a part of it, a conventional search engine is unable to determine whether the user meant an air current, flower blossoms, an explosion, an act of fleeing, bragging, an unexpected attack, or enlargement (all of which are defined as acceptable meanings of the word).

Content Searching

Content searching is the least efficient of the search strategies discussed here. The user enters an arbitrary search term, keyword, or text string. All items that match are returned with a relevance score. It is necessary that items with the highest scores (strongest match) are reported on the top of the results that are returned by such a search. (The metasearch technique is simply a more focused version of this technique that matches broad categories, rather than individual knowledge elements.) Score assignment is based on the frequency of matches within each knowledge element, such as a document or Web site.

Combining Search Strategies

To enable effective searching, use all or several of these search and retrieval strategies in parallel. Using a single search technique can pose severe limitations on the quality of the search. For example, attribute searching can work well only with textual knowledge items. However, this technique will not work too well for extracting informal knowledge items, such as sketches, audio files, video clips, or pointers to experts. However, the metasearch technique might serve that purpose well if the informal knowledge contents are properly tagged.

TAGGING KNOWLEDGE ELEMENTS WITH ATTRIBUTES

Because searching works primarily on the basis of textual string matching, it is important that content—both formal and informal—be tagged with a proper set of attributes. More advanced tools are available for pattern matching in drawings, photographs, etc., but these are not always a feasible option, for two reasons. First, these tools are still in their initial stages of development and work within highly specialized categories of informal data (rather than information or knowledge). Second, these tools are more expensive and complicated to implement, when compared with traditional, commercially available search tool solutions. Consequently, a company must define its own set of attributes to tag knowledge content with. Although many of these attributes can be common to a company and its partners, the need for such clear-cut definition cannot be overemphasized. A basic set of tagging attributes[13] is listed in Table 7-13; the attributes are described below.

Table 7-13 Tagging Attributes for Knowledge Content in a KM System

Attribute type	Tagging attribute
A	Activities
D	Domain
F	Form
T	Type
P	Products and Services
I	Time
L	Location

Tagging attributes are identified on the basis of extensive research on knowledge usage reported in Heijst, Spek, et al., *The Lessons Learned Cycle. in Information Technology for Knowledge Management.*, in U. Borghoff and R. Pareschi's *Information Technology for Knowledge Management*, Springer-Verlag, Berlin (1998), pp. 17-34.

Activities Attribute

The activities attribute refers to the organizational activities to which the given knowledge element is related. The values of this attribute must be defined up front, and individual values need not be mutually exclusive. This means that the same knowledge item could possibly fall under two or more activity categories. For example, a knowledge element related to burn-in testing of the computers that your company produces could fall under the following possible categories: testing, quality control, finishing, fault tolerance analysis, mean time between failures determination, etc.

Therefore, your company must have an explicit model of the activities and processes that are carried on during the course of "running the business." This might not be a perfect model to begin with. Begin with your best shot and incrementally improve the activity attribute value set.

Domain Attribute

The domain attribute tags the knowledge item to its subject matter. This attribute is the primary attribute that drives the metasearch process. Your company has most likely already identified the broad domains of expertise and skill areas that constitute it. Be wary of the trap of trying to define such domains at too micro a level. Domains need to be defined at an aggregate level.

Principles of knowledge engineering (a branch of computer science, not management information systems, that is often erroneously confused with KM) cannot be applied here because those are more concerned with modeling knowledge at the level of concepts and relations, which is too micro for our purpose here. If your company does not have such domains defined, you need to determine explicitly what your employees *think* their domains are and account for vocabulary mismatches to avoid overlapping domain names. This is a process best accomplished by trial and error; sequential application of guidelines of any sort will be of little or no avail.

Form Attribute

The form attribute defines the physical representation of the knowledge element. This attribute is tricky to define. You can begin with a basic set of values such as:

- Paper
- Electronic
- Formal (file, word document, spreadsheet, etc.)
- Informal (multimedia, sound, video tape, etc.)
- Collective
- Tacit or mental knowledge
- Pointer (to a person who has solved a problem of that nature before, etc.)

If information is available in other forms in your company, add them to this basic "starter" list. The pointer attribute value is similar to the concept of employee skills databases, where you might perform a search on "Web-database integration experts," and detailed contact information for all employees matching that attribute set will show up in the results. This is especially useful when your company's offices are geographically distributed or employee counts are high. For example, a search for a given attribute might help a consultant in Atlanta find a find a knowledgeable fellow consultant in the firm's Berlin office.

Type Attribute

The type attribute is more relevant to formalized knowledge that is captured in electronic or textual form, such as a document or a report. It specifies what type of a *document* that knowledge element is. Such values can be standardized across multiple companies, such as your company and its suppliers. Suggested starting values for this attribute, which can be later extended to account for tacit knowledge types, are:

* Procedure
* Guidelines
* Protocol
* Manual
* Reference
* Time line
* Worst practice report
* Best practice report
* Note
* Memo
* Failure report
* Success report
* Press release/report
* Competitive intelligence report

Beginning with these values, you can add other relevant types applicable to your company.

Products and Services Attribute

The products and services attribute specifies the product or service to which the knowledge element relates. This list should be kept specific and should not overlap. A consulting company, for example, might have, among others, the following attribute values:

* Strategic consulting
* Implementation consulting
* e-commerce consulting

Time Attribute

The time attribute is useful for timestamping events and knowledge elements. Timestamping is done automatically for files, but that timestamp marks the creation of that object, which might have a value different from the actual creation of that knowledge object. Consequently, creation or use of an explicated knowledge object must be specified. Not all knowledge objects can be assigned a value for this attribute so, assign a value to this attribute where possible. The time attribute can also be useful for narrowing retrieval processes.

Location Attribute

Use the location attribute to specify the location of pointers that track people within and outside the company. Not all knowledge elements will have a value assigned to this attribute, but it can be used to narrow searches by location. For example, a search procedure for an employee with certain skills could be restricted to Japan or, at a finer level, Tokyo. Be careful not to use too micro a level of classifications for this attribute tag. Make sure that the attribute usage and its values are actually significantly relevant. If the relevance or need for this attribute is moderate to low, you might save your company much time and money by simply dropping this off your list of attribute tags to be used.

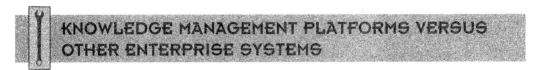

CIGNA AND KNOWLEDGE MANAGEMENT

At CIGNA Property & Casualty, a Philadelphia-based insurance company, the aim was to create an upward value spiral for know-how to be shared throughout the company. Information and knowledge contributed by employees is processed by "knowledge editors"—usually experienced underwriters—and distributed throughout the organization. CIGNA also uses KM to discover and maintain profitable niches and is using the skills and experience of people as building blocks for its success. CIGNA now recognizes that it is not the quantity of knowledge that is important; rather, the quality of that knowledge is the key determinant of profitable underwriting. Every company has a ton of information in its databases; the key to profitable underwriting isn't giving access to every bit of information, it's how you determine which information is relevant.

These attributes are summarized in Table 7-14.

KNOWLEDGE MANAGEMENT PLATFORMS VERSUS OTHER ENTERPRISE SYSTEMS

In this section, we will examine how a KM system differs from intranet, extranet, data warehouse, and GroupWare systems. We will also see how and which of these existing pieces of technology can harmonize with a KM system.

Table 7-14 Seven Attributes for Tagging Knowledge Objects

Tagging Attribute	Description
Activities	The activities attribute relates organizational activities to the given knowledge element. This attribute is defined in nonexclusive groupings, based on an explicit model of business processes and customer-related activities that occur in your business, and can be incrementally improved.
Domain	The domain attribute tags the knowledge item to its subject matter, broad domains of expertise, and skill areas.
Form	The form attribute specifies the physical representation (paper, electronic, multimedia, formal, informal, tacit, heuristic) of the knowledge element. Each knowledge element can have multiple, overlapping form attributes associated with it.
Type	The type attribute specifies the type of document in which a given knowledge element exists. For example, explicit type attributes include procedures, manuals, guidelines, time lines, best practices, memo, press releases, annual report, and competitive intelligence feeds.
Products/Services	This attribute specifies the specific, ideally nonoverlapping product or service to which the knowledge element relates.
Time	A timestamp that marks the creation of that object, which might have a value different from the actual creation of that knowledge. This attribute is useful for narrowing down the retrieval process when an approximate time block associated with it is known. Not every knowledge element can have a time attribute assigned to it.
Location	This attribute specifies the approximate physical or logical location of the knowledge element.

DIFFERENCES BETWEEN A KM SYSTEM AND A DATA WAREHOUSE

You might wonder what makes a KM system any different from a data warehouse. The key differentiators are as follows:

Types of Information Managed

A data warehouse focuses more on highly structured content, whereas a KM system needs to support both informal and formal (very unstructured, as well as highly structured) content and everything in between. A data warehouse does not and cannot support informal content, such as video content, audio recordings, scribbles, conversations, doodles on notepads, etc., that a KM system needs to be able to support. This implies that a data warehouse can be a part of a KM system only as a source of structured data that is input to the complex collaborative filtering mechanisms of the KM system.

Context

A data warehouse is arguably a resource of unquestionable value when you need to mine factual data. When such data is mined and interpreted, it provides value. But the need for interpretation is a fuzzy idea; data warehouses, by themselves, are devoid of context. Some products, such as Intraspect and Digital Knowledge Asset's SceneServer, allow some degree of context to be "wrapped" with the data that goes into a data warehouse; a KM system depends on much higher contextual focus than that typically provided by data warehouses.

Size

Because a data warehouse primarily focuses on clean, structured, and organized data, the size of a data warehouse is *always* large. Raw data, often in its native form, is stored here, so high storage capacity is a must. Unlike this, a KM system might have storage system sizes ranging from very small to extremely large. As support for multimedia content grows, storage needs skyrocket. However, a KM system never has raw data stored in it: Everything there is at least at the information stage of condensation, so size requirements for pure content (excluding multimedia) is often low.

Content Focus

The content focus of a KM system is on highly filtered information and on knowledge, whereas that of a data warehouse is on scrubbed, raw, clean, and organized data.

Performance

Because of the complex nature of retrievals and classification requests that a KM system must be able to handle, performance requirements and computing power needed for a KM system are much higher than those of a data warehouse. At the same time, if multimedia is digitally supported, processors need to be able to handle the additional processing burden of graphic renditions, as well. With multimedia-enhanced technology that has been around for a few years on personal computer platforms and with parallel processing capabilities of Pentium-class microprocessors, this is not a significant cost or technological feasibility concern.

Networks

A data warehouse does not need to be on a live network to function properly; however, this live network is imperative for a KM system that is trying to draw from resources available throughout the entire enterprise and beyond it—from the Internet and a collaborative, extended enterprise.

DIFFERENCES BETWEEN A KM SYSTEM, AN INTRANET, AND AN EXTRANET

An intranet certainly is a building block of a KM system that must never be confused for one. Intranets rely on firewalls to delineate TCP/IP-based communication networks with regular, hypertext, Web page-type content within organizational boundaries. The choice of the word *organizational* is probably incongruous here: A more descriptive and precise designation is *extended-*

enterprise-wide. Intranets often include the company's allies, partners, suppliers, and major customers, and allow knowledge exchange within this extended enterprise. Because an extranet can also be viewed as an extended version of an intranet, for this analysis, we will make no explicit distinction between the two. The key differences between an intranet and a KM system are as follows:

- Content Focus: Intranets focus on information delivery and publishing across the enterprise and the extended enterprise. However, KM systems focus more on actionable information—in other words, knowledge.

- Performance: Performance demands on KM systems are often higher than on basic intranets, in terms of both network bandwidth requirements and processing power demands. Although processing power is rarely the problem, network bandwidth often is.

- Broader Base: A typical intranet often has a broader base and a more open face to the outside world, such as the firm's major customers and partners. This is usually not the case with critical KM systems a company is using to gain a competitive edge and to leverage business processes across an extended enterprise and the firm's value chain.

RECIPROCITY IN KNOWLEDGE NETWORKS

A knowledge network is not limited by its reach and the extent to which it can be used to communicate but rather by the extent to which it supports reciprocity. The ability to support a multidirectional, complex mechanism for negotiation is required to enable this reciprocity. Users of a KM system will contribute only if they feel they are gaining something *valued by them* in reciprocation. This idea is very different from the primarily publishing-oriented model that intranets commonly seem to follow.

The notion of communities of practice stresses the need to limit, though not cut off, reciprocity to enable "legitimate peripheral participation." For example, employees should be allowed to "lurk" in electronic mailing lists and discussion groups. Technologies that understand this subtle difference and can parse how relationships between communities where reciprocity is cultivated differ from those within communities where reciprocity is inherent can actually help extend the reach between communities without disrupting the balance of reciprocity that exists within them.

DIFFERENCES BETWEEN A KM SYSTEM AND GROUPWARE

GroupWare products are often mistaken for KM systems. Because this is an area of significant misunderstanding and misdirected expenditure in companies, we look at this comparison very closely in Part III of this book. Our focus on the differentiation between GroupWare and KM systems is built around the following characteristics:

- Focus—function and content
- Archival versus generation functionality
- Internal versus external sources
- Relationship with knowledge generated from activities of the firm

Table 7-15 summarizes these differences.

Table 7-15 Systems Commonly Confused with Customer KM Platforms

System→	Intranet/Extranet	Data Warehouse	GroupWare
Type of content	Structured and semistructured	Highly structured, raw data	Semistructured, archival
Context	Fast, low-cost, mass-customized delivery throughout the enterprise	Source of aggregated, cleansed, structured, and context-devoid data	Collaborative work; largely internal
Size	Might grow over time	Always large	Might grow over time
Focus	Information delivery	Scrubbed, raw, clean, and organized data	Enables collaborative work through electronic channels
Performance	Varies	Computing resource-intensive	Not resource-intensive
Network dependence	Very high	Varies; high in data Web-houses	High
Scope	Intraorganizational (intranet) or interorganizational (extranet)	Internal	Largely intraorganizational, limitedly interorganizational

THE APPLICATION LAYER

Tools that enable integration of information across tacit (such as people) and explicit (such as databases, transaction-processing repositories,[14] and data warehouses) sources help create and share context (the process itself is called *contextualization*), and facilitate sense making. For example, brainstorming sessions, problem solving, idea generation, and strategy-planning meetings are usually highly interactive, involving multiple people, often from different locations, functional mixes, and operational bases.[15] Intranets and extranets provide paths for explicated knowledge; group support mechanisms and collaborative platforms provide paths for both explicated content and tacit context; and knowledge pointers provide directions to locations where actual tacit knowledge is situated. These tools constitute the application layer of the KM platform. Figure 7-4 shows the roles that various tools play as part of the larger KM platform.

The most visible components of this layer are discussed next.

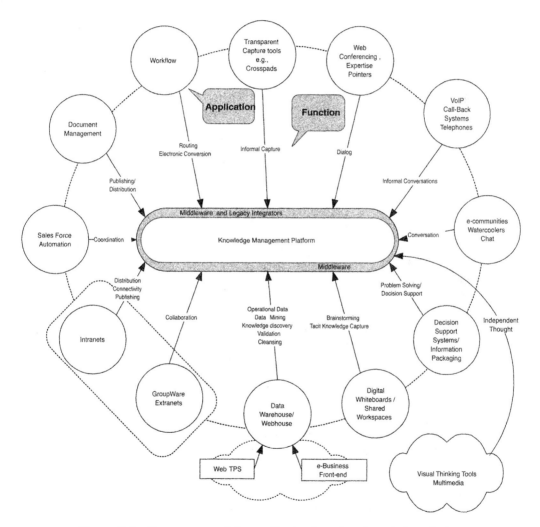

Figure 7-4   Components of the application layer in a knowledge platform.

Intranets and Extranets

Before the Internet entered the mainstream of computing, communication networks had to be either built or leased. Although building a dedicated communications link from one building to the next is not a very expensive proposition, building one from Atlanta to New York or Sacramento to Singapore surely is. Until the advent of the Internet as a public medium, the ability of larger companies to afford such networks provided them a temporary competitive advantage. Now, intranets allow the same networks to be constructed over the Internet. Virtual private networks (VPNs) allow secure, cost-effective, and unrestricted communication across regional and national boundaries. Although intranets have been in use for a while and many companies have used them effectively for improving information flow throughout their enterprise, the true value of the intranet as a tool for collaboration is yet to be realized. Similarly, extranets, which are farther reaching, more expansive, transorganizational versions of intranets, allow companies efficiently to tap into knowledge-based resources of partners and those of ally firms.

One of the most important aspects of information access is that of being able to view content of documents regardless of file format, operating system, or communications protocol. Intranets, owing to their consistent, platform-independent access formats, such as rich HTML, and a common, consistent protocol (HTTP), make this possible.

Context Sharing: Same Words, Another Language

Every effective effort targeted at managing knowledge needs some mechanism that allows open, supportive, critical, and reflective conversations between participants; this mechanism allows them to challenge, align, and establish a shared context. Without this context, the knowledge that flows within the company would be no different from its information flows along disjointed data points. We studied a company that was developing an add-on card that allowed personal digital assistants (PDAs) similar to the PalmPilot to receive messages over wireless paging networks. The people involved belonged not only to the company that was developing the product but also those outside it—the operating system developer, the company that wrote software drivers for the device, the marketing department that sold the product, and the company that provided the paging network services. To get these people to *talk* required a shared vision of what the product was to *supposed* be. Because the various people involved in the project came from different functional groups, different organizations, and different backgrounds, it was no surprise that they talked at different wavelengths. For such a team to be effective, it was essential to created a shared context.

POINTERS TO EXPERTISE

Besides their basic roles as publishing and information distribution platforms, intranets are the primary platform for the creation of *electronic yellow pages*. There is a limit on the knowledge that can be actually elicited from an individual with the necessary expertise. Beyond this fatigue point, pointers to the person who actually contributed that knowledge are needed to facilitate knowledge flow. Knowledge yellow pages and skills directories provide that link.

Yellow pages are simply a Web-searchable electronic version of skills lists, albeit with a lot more context added to them by past users. When a key resource person is needed or when a person with specific skill sets or expertise is required, keyword and attribute tag searching can pull up pointers with contact information about persons who qualify, both inside (such as employees in local and foreign offices) and outside the organization (such as consultants and researchers).

DOCUMENT MANAGEMENT

A lot of crucial information often exists primarily on paper. Companies try to convert this information into a more easily transferable and searchable electronic format by scanning these documents. This laudable effort should be pursued in moderation. It should not be the focus of a KM initiative, because this often sanitizes information of its context. Convert only those pieces of information that are needed. Simply cataloging information is often sufficient. Document management fosters the ability to develop a database of documents and classify them, automatically.

PROJECT MANAGEMENT TOOLS

Although the role of project management tools in the actual creation of knowledge is limited, these tools can provide a good basis for organizing and storing documents, records, notes, etc., coming out of a single project engagement. Project management tools often allow users to link the resources they use to the project management document, generate a variety of reports, and trace referenced hyperlinks. Such tools are quite novel, but they have a long way to go before they truly become useful in organizing knowledge. Another aspect of their relegation to the status of mere data sources comes from the inconsistent manner in which they are used. Many companies populate these tools in a postproject phase, leaving the accuracy of project history traceability open to questions.

VIDEO CONFERENCING AND MULTIMEDIA

Video conferencing enables people to exchange both full-motion video and audio across a distributed network. In a KM system, multimedia allows the system to capture informal content that would otherwise be lost forever. Multimedia content is classified as an information source because, by itself, it is devoid of context and needs interpretation. A multimedia clip of, for example, a moving machine part, when stored in an information repository, conveys a complex operation that would be complicated, time-consuming, and expensive to describe in explicated words. Multimedia, especially video content, bypasses limitations of language—an occasional barrier to knowledge sharing when you are working in transnational project teams. If a picture is worth a thousand words, a full-motion multimedia video clip is perhaps worth even more.

> ### P&G's MARKETING NET: HIGH-SPEED INTERNET MARKETING
>
> When it comes to the Web, Procter & Gamble is not counting on just Web-based retailing; e-Business is transforming internal processes, even in its traditional departments. To deploy collaborative knowledge sharing for improved decision making, P&G created Marketing Net, a Web-based digital library that lets marketing managers, sales groups, and executives view their proposed advertising copy, videos, and competitor's advertisements over the Internet without having to resort to shipping videotapes physically from office to office. Web-enabled knowledge sharing networks and brainstorming software tools allow teams distributed around the world to deliberate, debate, and refine their marketing material. The results: more widely shared tacit knowledge, 50 percent reduction in new concept development time, quicker business decisions, and reduced travel expenses.

Although video conferencing technology has existed for several years, most of the available solutions needed dedicated networks. Video conferencing requires high bandwidth on the network because each frame contains about as much data as an equivalent still picture file. Typically, 30 to 80 frames of video need to be delivered every second to deliver reasonable quality of video. Lackluster bandwidth availability prevents these frames from refreshing several times every second: The refresh rate can be slowed down so much that video content delivery might begin to resemble a series of independent, delayed static pictures following each other.

TRANSPARENT CAPTURE ENABLERS

Managers and project team members often take notes during meetings and brainstorming sessions. Whiteboards and legal pads, both of which now have electronic equivalents, are perhaps the most widely used nontechnical tools used in such sessions. A lot of information, ideas, possible directions, and approaches get thrown on the table in such meetings. When specific solutions are chosen, others are discarded. These discarded solutions are often valuable in other projects or helpful in revising strategies when changes in product target markets occur. Technologies such as the digital whiteboards allow such informal notes, including doodles, to

COLLABORATIVE KNOWLEDGE SHARING AT DOW CHEMICAL

Dow Chemical demonstrates how simple desktop collaborative tools can result in enviable paybacks without significant up-front investments. Dow Chemical Company realized by late 1996 that it was becoming increasingly difficult for its 40,000 employees to collaborate across its 115 locations in 37 countries. Traveling had been extensive until virtual teams began meeting by telephone. A presentation, plan, or other document would be put out on a machine running Windows NT Server (now Windows 2000), and each person in the conference would bring up the document at the desktop. The problem was that, as changes were made, each person would have to make them in his/her individual document, which left the door open to errors and inconsistencies.

The company then very successfully tried Microsoft NetMeeting conferencing software and made it available to its 28,000 desktop users at 250 sites around the world. Dow has enabled these virtual, globally distributed teams to exchange data, confer, share presentations, and collaborate on the same document at the same time, irrespective of their location. John Deere and Ford Motor Company have also had positive experiences with Web conferencing tools for encouraging and enabling knowledge exchange and sharing.

be captured electronically without affecting the way participants *ordinarily* go about their regular jobs. They can scan entire contents of a whiteboard and convert them into an electronic file that can then be distributed, posted, printed, exchanged, or e-mailed. Tools such as this are indispensable in moving a company from a structured, information-based focus to a formal and informal, knowledge-centric focus.

VIRTUAL SHARED SPACES

A critical component that promotes knowledge sharing, creation, and transfer but is missing in most information technology tools is the component that supports informal collaboration, discussion, and chat.[16] There must be a way to encourage *and enable* informal chat and conversations (even office gossip) that are a part of work life in most office settings. This has the following implications for KM system design:

- *Virtual meetings:* Web conferencing enables virtual meetings where users from different locations connect, conduct meetings, and share information as though everyone were in the same room. Participants can share applications, including program screens, presentation graphics, word processing, and spreadsheet software, and all meeting participants can see the same information in real time.

- *Document collaboration:* Web-based, real-time, distributed collaboration lets team members work together with many other participants on documents or information in real time or share an application running on a single computer with other people in a meeting. Everyone can view the information shared by the application, and any participant can take control of the shared application to edit or paste information in real time. This technology brings collaborative work to a new level that resembles two people working on a task on the same personal computer at a given time—the closest that you can come to working together physically.

- *Informal communication:* Because conversations can take place in natural voice and with electronic (visual) presence, informality, like that possible with a telephone, is possible to achieve. Participants can hang around, take part in discussions, argue, disagree, converse, and deliberate.

AMERICA ONLINE'S MOST WIDELY SHARED SECRET

For the believers of capitalism-free markets, the best proof of the value of real-time collaborative environments comes from America Online. If market acceptance is the litmus test for real-time collaboration, America Online has been passing it with flying colors for a long time, years before even Windows became mainstream. America Online had about 24 million customers in 2002. Even Microsoft's own online service could not compete with AOL for one simple reason—AOL had the best conversation tools built into its interface. Since AOL's inception, these have been called *chat rooms* and have been the favorite feature among AOL users and a primary reason for its continued success and popularity, despite the higher price that it charges for its services. In 2002, AOL had over 120 million registered users of its AOL Messenger and ICQ chat tools, who exchanged over a billion messages every day. Microsoft, embracing the value of real-time chat over the Internet, introduced a competing product, Microsoft Messenger (http://messenger.msn.com) in June 1999.

MIND MAPPING

Knowledge sharing can be synchronous or asynchronous. Software developers and programmers have used concept maps to organize logical, independent thought for several years. Mind maps, very similar to concept maps, can be used to organize individual or collective thought and represent it visually. Mind mapping can be an excellent knowledge creation and organizational tool, especially with the advent of excellent software supporting it. Some of these tools have most of the features of real-time collaboration software integrated in them and allow for collective deliberation over the Internet. A full version of the popular mind-mapping tool, Mind Man Personal, is included on this book's companion CD-ROM.

INTELLIGENT DECISION SUPPORT SYSTEMS

Decision support systems, case-based reasoning systems, and contextual information retrieval systems provide the needed historical base from past experience that help make both minor and major decisions fast and accurately. Data mining tools help extract trends and patterns from transactional repositories, such as data warehouses.

THE PROMISE OF PEER-TO-PEER KNOWLEDGE NETWORKS[17]

Peer-to-peer networking naturally extends to support KM because it closely mirrors face-to-face human communication. Peer-to-peer networking is defined as sharing of resources by *direct* exchange between individual systems in a digital network Each peer is connected directly to the Internet, and each peer can transact directly with other peers within its dataspace. Notwithstanding the impressive computational benefits of peer-to-peer computing, its social appeal as a technology that works like humans naturally do holds immense business potential. Its philosophy values adaptability and flexibility over structure and predictability to facilitate instantaneous formation of spontaneous, autonomous—even temporary—digital knowledge networks. The extension of the peer-to-peer model to KM applications is natural because of its ability spontaneously to facilitate rapid integration of previously unconnected expertise. This has important implications for realizing that simple parts could spontaneously aggregate into a powerful, collective brain.[18]

Knowledge and expertise existing in organizations generates more value when it is rapidly applied than when it is accumulated in systems and software. Application emphasizes integration over transfer of expertise. Integration implies application without the excessive delays and cost of transferring distributed expertise.

Networks of Friends and Their Friends

Any technology solution intended to harness the collective intelligence of dynamic networks of people must intrinsically value relationship, affinity, and interdependence that characterize human interactions. To do this, (1) it must rapidly get the right people involved and (2) enable them collectively to apply—not transfer—their expertise.

Sociologists have long recognized the potential of weak ties to spark innovation by bringing together expertise of whose existence individuals are unaware.[19] Members of a peer-to-peer network are connected through weak ties but can spontaneously convert them to temporary strong ties of direct exchange and coordination. By facilitating the digital equivalent of informal, hallway chat among individuals, peer-to-peer networks facilitate thought-flow—circulation of peers' know-how and tacit expertise, rather than just digitized content. Facilitating access to people and enabling new, instantaneous connections among them lays a foundation for creative social dialog.

Consider a simple example. If Alice asks Diane a specialized question and Diane does not know the answer, she can ask her friends, who can then ask their friends until an answer is found. Digital peer networks facilitate precisely such spontaneous linkages among friends of friends, albeit more instantaneously. Consider Figure 7-5. Alice (A) sends out a request for an expert's help with a specific best practice to immediate peers Bill (B), Charlie (C), Diane (D), and Ed (E). If none of them have the necessary knowledge, they *automatically* pass on Alice's trigger to their immediate peers, and so on until one of two things happens: (1) they run out of time (i.e., time exceeds a predetermined time-to-latency) or (2) one of the peers confirms having matching expertise. The matching process can use a combination of digital resources with each peer: a dynamic skills profile, history, and self-reported expertise to determine the best person to ask. If Kim (K) has the expertise, peer K sends a confirmation back to peer A, using the same route, informing peers on the way that a match was found. Alice can then *directly* access and leverage Kim's expertise, bypassing the rest of the network.

Affinity to Infinity

Individuals initially begin to share information, expertise, best practices, and content in peer networks because of the affinity that networks create. In business, professional interests and tasks create organization-spanning affinity. The opportunities for value creation and the likelihood of finding answers grow exponentially as such networks expand. Each additional member increases the potential value of the network manifold or, in economic terms, creates increasing returns.

Intricate webs of affiliations open multitudinous possibilities for collaborative knowledge integration in autonomous groups that can be spontaneously assembled and disassembled. Unless individuals know how to find and use human expertise, unstructured information, and

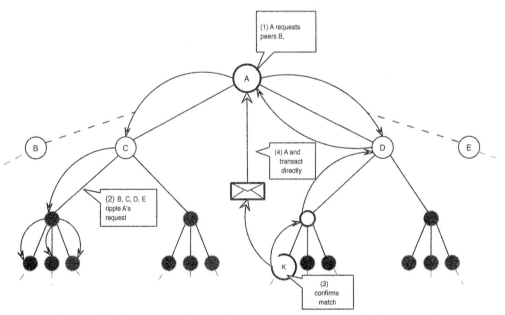

Figure 7-5   Knowledge integration in a peer-to-peer knowledge network.

codified knowledge, it will continue to remain enormously underutilized. By coupling individuals in and out of a smaller peer network, groups can opportunistically toggle from weakly tied groups needed to find knowledge to strongly tied groups needed to integrate it.[20] Seamless and ad hoc unification of expertise facilitates simultaneous distribution and integration of problem-solving efforts among employees, customers, and partners. As these individuals span many corporate boundaries, peer-to-peer networks equalize the simultaneous undersupply and oversupply of knowledge in pockets of collaborative communities.

Other Benefits of Peer-to-Peer Knowledge Platforms

Peer networking redresses three other issues that have long plagued KM technology: profile maintenance, bandwidth bottlenecks, and ubiquity. First, decentralization eliminates the overhead of maintaining resource and expertise profiles for individuals in corporate yellow pages. Second, knowledge sharing relies heavily on rich media, such as voice, video, and multimedia, to overcome the limitations of text to share tacit knowledge. Moderate gains in bandwidth usage can accrue enormous efficiency gains as use of rich media increases in direct peer transactions. Third, their explicit knowledge and profiles of mobile users can be redundantly replicated across nodes to ensure ubiquitous availability.

Technological Solutions for Motivational Issues

Notwithstanding these opportunities, human behavior—not technology—is the single most pronounced caveat. Unlike information sharing, knowledge sharing has a competitive dimension: The more valuable a nugget of knowledge is to an individual, the less likely he or she is to share it. After all, individuals' knowledge makes them valuable to organizations and projects them as experts to their peers. Given the choice, individuals will tend to receive more expertise and contribute little.

Understanding what motivates people to apply their expertise is key to avoiding the trap of building technology marvels that no one uses. First, users will contribute and share their insights only when they value their digital community. The community-building component reinforces not only the number but also the quality of interconnections among individuals. Mechanisms that openly track contributions discourage free riding. Second, shared context is essential to contribute meaningfully to collective tasks. Shared workspaces and contact lists can provide such context. Third, peer-to-peer environments must emphasize knowledge integration over acquisition or learning. The intent is not to teach peers how to do one's job. That is expensive, time-consuming, and threatening to individuals' ownership of expertise. Instead, it must be possible to bring several individuals' expertise to bear on solving a problem, typically through joint activity tools. Finally, such environments must provide reputation-building mechanisms to foster a pervasive thread of trust on which any community stands. Aggregating individual's contributions to the community and use of others' expertise over time provide future collaborators a historical perspective of an individual's value in past relationships. Reputations can be based on dynamic, ubiquitous user profiles that automatically update themselves as individuals interact in a peer-to-peer environment. Such mechanisms balance both contribution and use of distributed knowledge over time, allowing individuals to think long term but deliver in the short term.

RETROFITTING THE SECI MODEL

Now that you have a grasp on the technology and human components needed to implement a KM strategy in your company, let's see how they all fit into Nonaka's Socialization-Externalization-Combination-Internalization (SECI) Model.[21] Figure 7-6 illustrates this fit.

The interaction of knowledge at enterprise-wide (company) levels is indicated by C; at group or task team level by G; and at individual level by I. The corresponding technology enablers are exemplified in each quadrant. KM is done according to the SECI Model through a cycle of socialization, externalization, combination, and internalization of knowledge. Figure 7-6 illustrates how each of these phases is supported by technology that we discussed in this chapter. Note that some of the components overlap across phases of knowledge creation. This implies that the benefits of one technology element are manifested in multiple knowledge creation phases.

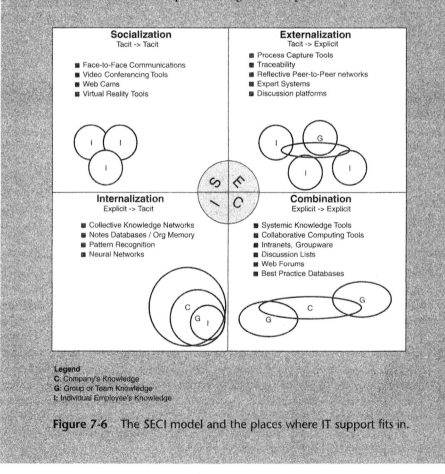

Figure 7-6 The SECI model and the places where IT support fits in.

LESSONS LEARNED

The critical aspect of building a KM platform is determining the best mix of available tools and integrating them into a coherent architecture. Keep in mind the lessons you've learned about these infrastructural components while determining this mix.

- *Choose IT components to find, create, assemble, and apply knowledge.* Because content comes from a variety of sources, both within and outside your company, the optimal choice of components must let you integrate and apply fragmented tacit and explicit knowledge in a cost-effective and timely manner.

- *Identify and understand components of the collaborative intelligence layer.* Artificial intelligence, data warehouses, genetic algorithms, neural networks, expert reasoning systems, rule bases, and case-based reasoning are some of the technologies that provide intelligence to the KM system. Understand how these tools and technologies work and when their use is appropriate.

- *Optimize knowledge object granularity.* Granularity of knowledge (represented in terms of knowledge objects or elements that are specified in descending order as knowledge domains, regions, sections, segments, elements, fragments, and atoms) objects refers to the level of detail in which they are stored in the KM system. Avoid overpopulating your company's knowledge repositories. At the same time, too little detail might make content useless or unactionable. The key lies in striking the right balance between too much and too little detail.

The business benefits of knowledge platforms are limited only by the imagination of application developers. The fourth step, auditing, which will be covered in the next chapter, takes into account the knowledge assets that exist within your company; let's figure out how you can *know what you know.*

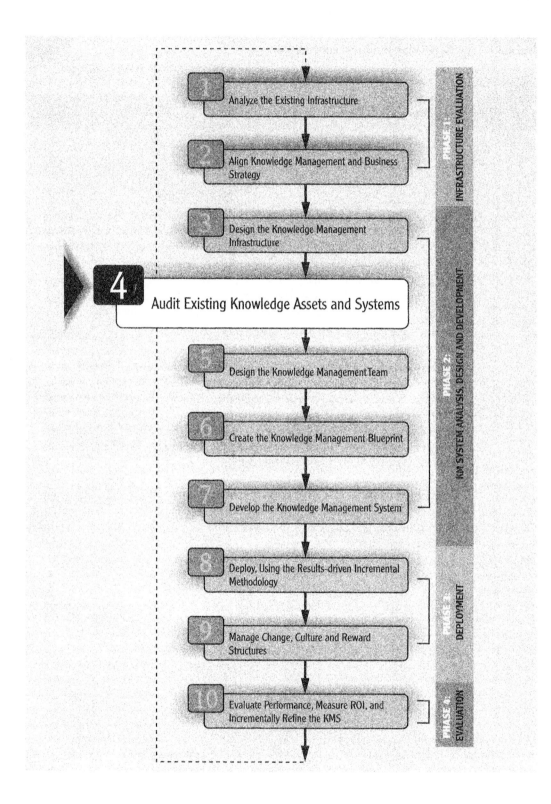

1 Analyze the Existing Infrastructure

2 Align Knowledge Management and Business Strategy

3 Design the Knowledge Management Infrastructure

4 Audit Existing Knowledge Assets and Systems

5 Design the Knowledge Management Team

6 Create the Knowledge Management Blueprint

7 Develop the Knowledge Management System

8 Deploy, Using the Results-driven Incremental Methodology

9 Manage Change, Culture and Reward Structures

10 Evaluate Performance, Measure ROI, and Incrementally Refine the KMS

PHASE 1: INFRASTRUCTURE EVALUATION

PHASE 2: KM SYSTEM ANALYSIS, DESIGN AND DEVELOPMENT

PHASE 3: DEPLOYMENT

PHASE 4: EVALUATION

CHAPTER 8

KNOWLEDGE AUDIT
AND ANALYSIS

IN THIS CHAPTER

✔ Understand the purpose of a knowledge audit.

✔ Use Bohn's *Stages of Knowledge Growth* to measure knowledge.

✔ Identify, evaluate, and rate critical process knowledge.

✔ Select an audit method.

✔ Form a preliminary knowledge audit team.

✔ Audit and analyze your company's existing knowledge.

✔ Identify your company's knowledge niches.

✔ Choose a strategic position for your KM system.

A GREAT DEAL OF INTELLIGENCE CAN BE INVESTED IN IGNORANCE
WHEN THE NEED FOR ILLUSION IS DEEP.
—SAUL BELLOW

Douglas Adam's *Hitchhiker's Guide to the Galaxy* (Ballantine Books, 1995) has a short conversation between the hitchhiker and his computer. The computer says, "I've checked it very thoroughly and that's quite definitely the answer. I think the problem, to be quite honest with you, is that you've never actually known what the problem is." Nothing sums up the current state of KM better than this conversation. Companies are realizing that managing their knowledge is the definite answer to *almost all* of their problems, but they do little to discover where exactly the problem lies.

With exactly that in mind, we will take a look at how we can define the exact problem and its roots. The knowledge audit and analysis process, the fourth step in the 10-step KM road map, is the key. You must begin KM by taking responsibility for and appraising what knowledge already exists. In this chapter, we discuss the purpose of a knowledge audit and see how a *Stages of Knowledge Growth* framework can be used to measure knowledge. We select an audit method to identify, evaluate, and rate critical process knowledge, using a preliminary knowledge audit team. We can then appropriately position and scope the KM initiative. Until you know what knowledge and knowledge processes surround your business, any KM effort is bound to go off course.

HINDSIGHT, INSIGHT, AND FORESIGHT

Experience is the greatest teacher of all. Just as actually receiving an electric shock best convinces anyone about the wisdom of not poking around electrical outlets, nothing teaches companies not to do things in certain ways better than having actually done them. In the KM audit, you must look at existing intangible assets, including rituals, processes, structure, communities, and people.[1] The goal is to invest in areas with the most potential for future strategic advantage.

WHY AUDIT KNOWLEDGE?

Knowledge of knowledge assets is a rich source of information about where the strengths of your company lie. It is invaluable when your company is:

- Devising a knowledge-based strategy
- Architecting a KM blueprint
- Planning to build a company-wide KM system
- Seeking to leverage what it already knows for market entry or exit
- Trying to figure a way out of corporate ebbing
- Striving to strengthen its own competitive weaknesses

- Facing competition from knowledge-intensive competitors that are far ahead on the learning curve

Figure 8-1 shows the basic steps involved in the audit process.

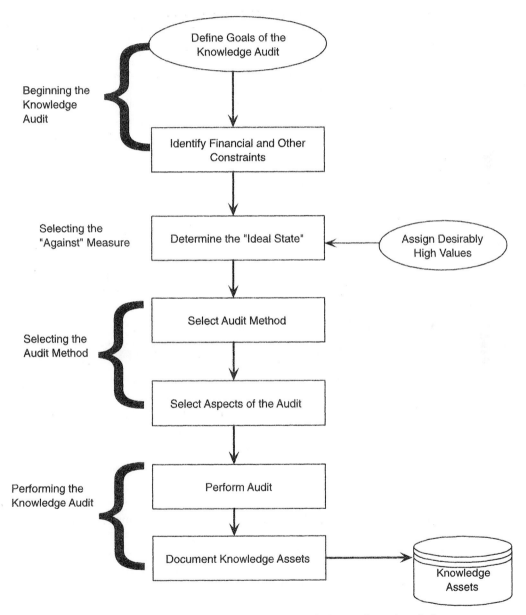

Figure 8-1   The series of steps involved in the knowledge audit and analysis process.

MEASURING KNOWLEDGE GROWTH

Very often, companies do not know where they stand in terms of the knowledge that they possess. Bohn's framework provides an excellent starting point for figuring out where you stand, relatively, in terms of your firm's knowledge. This framework applies to all types of knowledge-intensive industries, from consulting (production of services based on knowledge) to software (production of information products based on knowledge), to commodity production (physical goods), and publishing (services and production). In its most basic form, the growth of such knowledge in a firm can be described according to the stages illustrated in Table 8-1.

On these lines, as we move from the lowest stages of knowledge—stage 1 (or zero, discussed later)—toward the stages of perfect knowledge—stage 8—the way things are *normally* done in a company change. Take a look and compare how your company ranks along this scale. This should give you a fair idea of how strong the need for KM is in your firm. Table 8-2 shows where worker characteristics, suitability for automation, process types, and skill levels fall at each level along this continuum.

Integrating these two framework variations and applying that integration specifically to knowledge measurement, we get Table 8-3, which provides the final frame of reference against which you can measure the intellectual dimensions of the following:

Table 8-1 Bohn's Stages of Knowledge Growth

Stage	Name	Comment	Typical Form of Knowledge
1	Complete ignorance	—	Does not exist anywhere.
2	Awareness	Resembles pure art.	Primarily tacit.
3	Measure	It's pretechnological.	Primarily written.
4	Control of the mean	A scientific method is feasible.	Written and embodied in hardware.
5	Process capability	A local recipe exists	Hardware and operating manuals.
6	Process characterization	Tradeoffs to reduce costs are known.	Empirical equations (quantitative).
7	Know why	Takes on the form of science.	Procedures, methodologies, scientific formulas, and algorithms.
8	Complete knowledge	Nirvana.	Never happens; but you can always hope for it!

Table 8-2 Ranking Characteristics of Knowledge Work and Processes along Each Stage and the Effects of Each Stage on Them

Stage of Knowledge	1	2	3	4	5	6	7	8
Nature of production	Expertise based				Procedure based			
Role of workers	Everything			Problem solving		Learning and improving		
Location of knowledge	Tacit			Written and oral		In databases or software		
Nature of problem solving	Trial and error			Scientific method		Table lookup		
Natural organization type	Organic			Mechanistic		Learning		
Suitability for automation	None					High		
Ease of transfer	Low					High		
Feasible product variety	High			Low		High		
Quality control	Sorting			Statistical process control		Feed forward		

Because the distinction between adjacent stages in Bohn's stages is subtle, the breakdown of processes, as done in the table, is subject to minor debates. However, all classifications are within an approximate stage range.

- Your company's initial standing
- Your competitor's standing (you do not need inside financial information)
- Your company's progress along this scale
- Steps and directions to move your company up on this scale

You can use this framework precisely to map, evaluate, and compare the levels of knowledge existing in your company. The level of knowledge that a process has reached determines how a process could possibly be automated and controlled, and how the primary tasks of the knowledge workers and other aspects of KM can be planned to deliver maximum results. At the higher stages, knowledge can be used to make predictive inferences, as my "coffee" example describes in a following section. It can also make causal associations and prescriptive decisions that often tend to be tricky otherwise.

Table 8-3 Stages of Knowledge Growth: Where Does Your Company Stand?

Stage	Knowledge Stage	Knowledge Characteristic	Location of Knowledge	Work Processes	Learning Method
0	Total Ignorance	Cannot tell the good state from the bad	Undefined	Undefined	Undefined
1	Pure Art	Pure art	In the expert's head; so tacit that it cannot even be articulated.	Rely on trial and error.	Keep repeating processes. Hope for some pattern(s) to emerge.
2	Awareness	List of possibly relevant variables exists	In the expert's head (tacit); however, the expert can express it in words, diagrams, etc., although in a very limited way.	Experts can dictate conditions for processes to work well. Some degree of randomness still exists; start with methods that might have worked in earlier problems.	Experts, instead of all other people, keep repeating processes. Hope for some pattern(s) to emerge.
3	Measure	Pretechnological	You are able to decide which variables are more important by noting their correlation with desirable outputs.	Patterns begin to emerge; experts will, however, differ in their opinions on why successful processes were successful.	Same as above. You can be more creative and tweak processes to see changes.
4	Control of the mean	Scientific method feasible	Written and embodied in hardware/software to some extent.	Some parts of the knowledge underlying the process can be explicated, codified, and written down. However, a "recipe" is yet to emerge.	Keep good records of what was done, what happened, and the final outcomes.

Table 8-3 Stages of Knowledge Growth: Where Does Your Company Stand? (cont.)

Stage	Knowledge Stage	Knowledge Characteristic	Location of Knowledge	Work Processes	Learning Method
5	Process capability	Local repeatable recipe	A local recipe based on experience is developed; it often works, but not always; the notion of following a procedure to obtain desirable results begins to emerge. The recipe might or might not be formally written down in its entirety.	A semi-reliable recipe emerges. Some steps in the recipe might still be random or inconsistent. Work processes are tackled using this somewhat repeatable (partially explicated recipe).	Use the records kept in the preceding stages and determine statistic patterns that work.
6	Process characterization	Tradeoffs to reduce costs; a well-developed recipe along with a limited knowledge of how contingencies are to be handled now exists.	Knowledge is well documented in the recipe; a methodology is developed; it almost always works; applying the process is almost a mechanical task of applying the recipe.	Very mechanized; highly automated; uses a time-proven methodology.	Use the proven methodology; continuous application of the methodology (recipe) will allow weaknesses and problems in the recipe to emerge.
7	Know why	Science; automation is possible; a formal or informal quantitative model is developed.	Most of the relevant knowledge is documented; most of tacit knowledge is converted to explicit; almost all knowledge can be codified and built into computer software; strong knowledge of how contingencies can be dealt with now exists.	Codifed in computer software and process manuals.	More of the above; this is as good as it gets!

Table 8-3 Stages of Knowledge Growth: Where Does Your Company Stand? (cont.)

Stage	Knowledge Stage	Knowledge Characteristic	Location of Knowledge	Work Processes	Learning Method
8	Complete knowledge	Nirvana	Rarely possible.	No need for knowledge management or knowledge managers. Knowledge management becomes a natural part of the firm or group; it is done perfectly; unlikely to ever be achieved.	This stage might never be reached; you will never know when you are here; occasional variations resulting in the inability to apply processes from the preceding stage push it back to stage 7.

Based on Bohn, Roger E. Measuring and Managing Technological Knowledge, *Sloan Management Review*, vol. 36, Fall (1994), 61–73. Bohn provides an excellent discussion on measuring technological knowledge in this 1994 piece. My book extends this discussion to using it to measure knowledge in conventional knowledge or skill intensive processes.

ART TO SCIENCE

Progression of a company from one that is highly dependent on the tacit knowledge of a few individuals to one in which both explicit and tacit knowledge are shared and easily accessible can be best described as a progression from art (highly subjective and dependent on the doer's tacit knowledge) to science (repeatable and robust methodology capable of handling variations). At the higher stages, such as stages 6 and 7, a company gets a better handle on what should be done if the process has some unavoidable variation that is not documented. Most companies are at stage 2 or 3. To manage knowledge effectively, a company must progress to stage 5, 6, or 7. Stage 8, although desirable, has proved extremely difficult to reach.

MAKING COFFEE: A KNOWLEDGE-BASED EXAMPLE

Like many other overly caffeinated knowledge workers, this author nominates Starbucks Coffee as his favorite coffee shop.[a] The reason is that their coffee tastes almost the same in any of their locations throughout the United States. As Mrs. Field did for cookies, Burger King did for burgers, and Dunkin' Donuts did for doughnuts, Starbucks managed to perfect a recipe for making good coffee by perfecting a methodology for the coffee-brewing business. Each new employee learns it before he or she begins to work in the store. The result is consistently good, fresh, and strong coffee, the taste of which seems even more consistent than the coffee I make in my own coffeemaker at home. If we apply this scenario and retrofit it to the eight stages of knowledge growth, we could categorize it at either stage 6 or 7. In a metaphor for understanding the eight stages of process knowledge growth, let's see how the process of making coffee develops over different stages.

Stage Zero: Total Ignorance

You do not know the difference between good and bad coffee. Good coffee is the coffee that regular customers will like, and bad coffee is the type that will make those customers never return.

Stage 1: You Can Tell Good from Bad Coffee

You know when coffee is good, once you have tasted it. When you taste the same type of coffee again, you can compare it with the "good" (optimal value of "goodness") coffee you've had earlier.

Stage 2: You Have Created a List of Variables

You begin to figure out that the *goodness* of coffee (process output quality) is related to the following variables:

- Strength
- Temperature (not too hot and not cold) when delivered to the customer
- Bitterness, due to strength
- Viscosity (increases as coffee sits for a few hours)
- And some other taste variables that you cannot name

You also realize that there are certain background controls, such as:

- The amount of coffee added
- Temperature setting on the coffee percolator
- How long you let it sit after it percolates
- Weight of coffee/volume of water (coffee per cup)
- The order in which you added coffee and water (immaterial!)
- The fineness to which coffee beans were ground
- The elapsed time since coffee beans were roasted
- The elapsed time since coffee beans were ground (coffee beans oxygenate if exposed to air for a prolonged period of time)
- Other control variables

Stage 3: You Can Determine the Significance of Variables

At this stage, you can tell which variables in the list that you compiled above are important, marginally important, and unimportant.

You can now tell that:

- Too bitter = bad.
- Too "unbitter" = bad.
- "Unstrong" = bad.
- Too strong to drink = bad.
- Using beans ground yesterday morning and left exposed to air = bad.
- Coffee percolated more than 15 minutes ago = bad (the reason why Starbucks drains percolated but unsold coffee every 10 minutes).
- Hot coffee = good (Serving temperature 80–100 degrees).
- Unroasted coffee = bad.
- Coffee roasted > 24 hours ago = bad.
- Coffee ground < 2 hours ago = very good.
- Order of ingredients = immaterial.

Stage 4: You Can Now Measure Variables

As you move up the stages and progress to stage 4, you can now *measure:*

- The weight to coffee to be added
- The volume of water to be added
- Initial temperature settings on the percolator
- Percolation temperature
- Percolation time
- Post-percolation temperature
- Temperature at the time the coffee is served
- Elapsed time since coffee beans were roasted
- Elapsed time since coffee beans were ground

However, you cannot measure the more qualitative factors, such as bitterness or strength. This is a good example of how some factors can now be measured and have moved up to a higher stage; however, some processes are still at the lower stages. You might eventually find that these difficult-to-measure factors could be correlated with other factors that are measurable, such as the ratio of water to coffee grounds.

Stage 5: Repeatable Methodology or Recipe

You develop a recipe or methodology to make what is *typically* considered good coffee. You can now follow certain steps with a reasonable expectation that the resulting coffee will be acceptably good most of the time. You know the components of this recipe or methodology in terms of:

- Temperature settings
- Timing
- Length of time you can let coffee *set* after percolation
- Amount of ground coffee per cup of coffee

Stage 6: Repeatable Methodology + Localized Adaptability

Stage 6 is a slight improvement over stage 5. You can now adapt the recipe in a way that compensates for different types or flavors of coffee. You know that Colombian coffee need not be used in amounts measuring close to Italian Supreme or the Starbucks house brand. So you have a methodology and a limited degree of adaptability to compensate for variations within the time-proven recipe approach that you are using.

Stage 7: A Formal or Informal Model

You now have a formula approach to carrying out your process. You might have a specific formula saying that good coffee is made when $(0.56 \times$ weight of coffee $+ 0.12 \times$ volume of water$) = 1.414$, or something like that! The model need not be quantitative. It could be qualitative, partially empirical, or semiformal. But, at the very least, it specifies the approximate relationship between the significant variables.

In a similar vein, a consulting company might develop a model for strategic consulting analysis; a product designer might develop a model for product acceptance in typical markets, etc. Rarely does a business run as predictably and smoothly as employees in Starbucks make their coffee! But there are excellent examples that exhibit that rarity. Skandia and Monsanto are two such businesses.

Stage 8: Perfect Knowledge

This is the final frontier that we can never hope to reach, principally because we can never know when we are there. There might still be loopholes in processes that need plugging, there might be changes in the environment that need compensation, and so forth. And these relegate us to stage 7 or below, every time we think that we have reached stage 8. To come close to this stage, we need to be able to predict and compensate for the effect of disruptions and know what to measure in *advance*. This is why you need to build "unlearning" capabilities into your KM system. Despite all my love for coffee, a more accurate statement would be: Perfect coffee is something I have never had. If I ever did have it, I would never know. All I know is what good coffee tastes like! That about sums my coffee-based reasoning (not to be confused with CBR, case-based reasoning) for why we can never come up to stage 8 and stay there.

ANALYZING KNOWLEDGE IN LEGAL SERVICES: AN EXAMPLE

Legal services run the range described in Table 8-3. Preparing a simple will, for example, can be done with a $19.95 software program sold in most office supply stores in the United States. With your answers to specific questions, the program prepares a simple, legally acceptable will. This typifies legal service that has reached stage 7 in terms of its underlying process knowledge.

Preparing taxes with tax software, for people who have a single employer and no other sources of income, for example, can be done without the need for a tax accountant and with a $10 software program. This is another example of knowledge at stage 6 or 7, representative of a rather mechanical and highly automated procedure. The whole purpose of KM is to let us actually do things as simply, perfectly, accurately, and surely as we do our taxes by using software. Wishful thinking.

Consider taxes for people with multiple citizenships, taxes for people who might have changed state residency, or taxes for people with exceptionally high income. These still need an approach distant from an automated methodology. So these are at stage 3 and below.

KNOWLEDGE IN CRIMINAL LAW: AN EXAMPLE

Consider criminal law. Trial strategy, use of evidence, historical data, etc., that are involved in such cases are still at stage 3 or below. This profession requires experienced and skilled lawyers who need to use their tacit skills, experience, and judgment at each moment. People working on these tasks have skills and tacit knowledge they use to carry out the tasks, but they are rarely able to explain in sufficient detail how they do it.

However, some processes within these tasks can be pushed up to the higher stages. In criminal law, KM can be used to bring up profiles of past, similar cases to automate at least the argumentative defense that could be used in a court of law. Thus, certain processes can be moved up to the higher stages of knowledge.

THE KNOWLEDGE AUDIT TEAM

To perform knowledge audit and analysis, you need to select a multidisciplinary group of people truly representative of your company. Using IT staff is not an option, because they are likely to miss critical viewpoints and aspects in the final outcome. The audit team needs representatives from *at least* the following functional areas.

> ### KNOWLEDGE MANAGEMENT IN CONSULTING: AN EXAMPLE
>
> Strategic consulting companies such as McKinsey and the Boston Consulting Group (BCG) can and often do operate at stages 2 and 3. New consultants (often fresh MBAs) might be at stage zero, where they cannot even tell the difference between a good consulting project outcome and a bad one. As firms begin to proceduralize strategy projects and to execute them according to methodologies developed over time, these processes move to stages 5 and 6. BCG's well-known two-by-two grid describing cash cows, dogs, stars, and question marks is such an attempt to move from the lower pure-art stages to more procedural stages where divestiture decisions are reduced to two main variables: market share and rate of growth. However, BCG's recognition that there might be other variables that are also (probably) important indicates an awareness that some of their knowledge is at the lower stages, even though much of their analysis operates at higher stages of knowledge.

- *Corporate strategist:* Brings the big picture perspective into goal setting.
- *Senior management, visionary, or evangelist:* Aligns long-term KM vision with business strategy.
- *Human resource manager:* Brings an understanding of employee skills and skills distribution within the organization.
- *Marketer:* Provides a fair picture of actual market performance of the firm and the possible implications of its knowledge assets on the marketability of the firm's products and services at new price-service function points.
- *Information technologist:* Brings in knowledge, skills, and expertise for KM technology implementation. Also has intimate knowledge of existing infrastructure.
- *Knowledge analyst:* The middle role that integrates inputs from all other participants on the knowledge audit team in a consensual and unbiased manner. The analyst contributes a reasonably accurate market valuation of proprietary technology and processes, based on perspectives elicited from other team members. The analyst can be drawn from any functional area and must have a good understanding of both the business and business implications of each existing stream of knowledge assets.

Because the team is interdisciplinary, it is reasonable to expect some degree of discord and differences of opinion. However, as these differences are resolved, the different backgrounds of participants will turn out to be the biggest strength of the audit team.

PLANNING A KNOWLEDGE AUDIT

Once the knowledge audit team has been formed, members must agree on the motives and reasons for the audit. This is the hardest part and is often highly subjective and firm-specific. Once the rationale is explicitly written down, the team must identify the optimum level of performance and the highest, reasonably achievable levels of performance at which each component of the knowledge assets *should* operate. For example, the marketing department might say that it seeks to lower customer product return rates to 2 percent of all goods sold. Similarly, in a consulting company, the team might agree that it must be able to realize 98 percent customer retention or deliver all consulting deliverable within 60 days from the start of a project for all consulting projects and engagements under $20,000.

CONDUCTING THE KNOWLEDGE AUDIT

Building on the process model described in Figure 8-1, let us go through the actual audit and analysis. The knowledge audit consists of a sequence of six steps, as described below.

- *Define the goals.* The KM audit team agrees on the reasons for the audit, decides on the goals, and identifies the key financial, organizational, privacy-related, and strategic constraints that influence it. Define *specific* goals that both the audit process and KM are targeting.

- *Determine the ideal state.* Begin with a few key variables that are unequivocally considered critical and that can scope your KM project.

- *Select the audit method.* You will actually use a company-specific instantiation of the generic method to perform the audit.

- *Document existing knowledge assets.* This provides an internal benchmark to evaluate the impact of KM initiatives.

- *Track knowledge growth over time.* Progression from the initial stage (when the knowledge audit process is performed for the very first time) to later stages allows for easy comparison with the *ideal* state.

DEFINING THE GOALS

The first step in the knowledge audit process is to define the goals of the knowledge audit process and the constraints surrounding them. In a wishful-thinking corporate world, we would like to have all the resources that we want, but in reality, the situation is often very different. Goals need to be very specific because they provide the basis for many of the decisions that follow (see Figure 8-2).

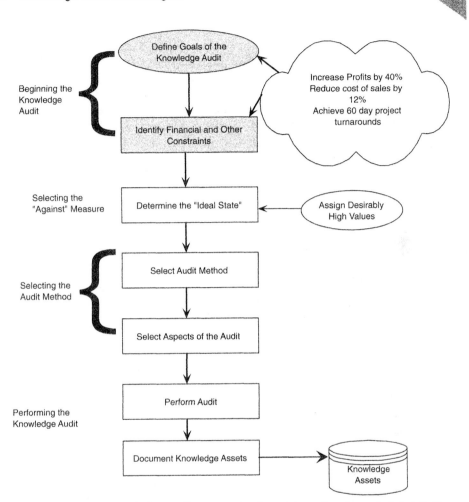

Figure 8-2   The knowledge audit process begins with goal and constraint definition.

Although organizing and managing the firm's knowledge in its entirety might be a worthy thought, the resources needed for that ambition might well be matched only by companies with *very* deep pockets. Besides, it's futile to begin on the KM road without knowing what brought you there in the first place. When you think about goals, think of specific ones, such as:

- We need to increase profits by 40 percent by next year.
- We need to reduce cost of sales by 12 percent before the end of the fiscal year.
- We want to improve customer retention by 4 percent within 18 months.
- We want to increase project turnaround speed by 14 days on the average over the next 3 years.

You can rarely be too specific in explicitly defining such goals. Without a very well-explicated goal, you can never be sure when to start and when to stop measuring. This means that you cannot have a reasonably safe idea whether the approach devised by your team is *really* working. Goals need not always be defined in terms of increased financial or performance measures.

A KM audit is *never* an all-or-nothing exercise. Taking a very comprehensive knowledge audit might seem like a long-term, expensive, and daunting task, and you often do better by breaking it up into more solvable and realizable, pruned-down pieces. This pruning is best done automatically, as is described next.

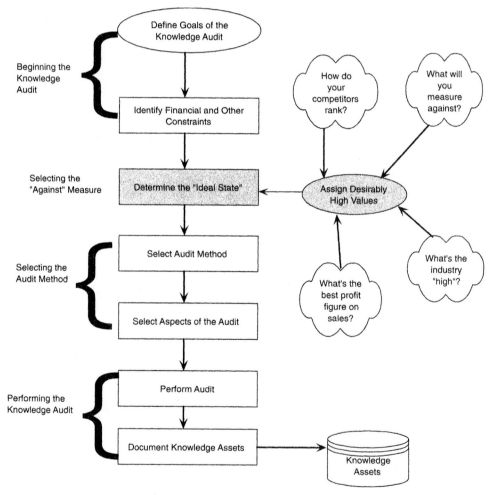

Figure 8-3   Determining the ideal state in a knowledge audit.

Constraint-Based Pruning

Automatic pruning refers to the next stage after goal identification, that is, constraint recognition. For example, if our big question is, How do we increase profits? knowing the constraints will help prune it down. If you know that you need to show an increase in profits within six months, you have taken yet another step in narrowing the focus of your efforts. You might also know that a division of your company, for example, HR consulting, is not making any money. You might also know that the senior management has put a hold on any new hires. You might also know that you have almost 90 percent of the customers in the market. Putting these together automatically prunes the goals and the original question. It now becomes, How do we increase profits within six months without hiring any new people or trying to get new customers?

DETERMINING THE IDEAL STATE

Determining what your company considers an *ideal state* is the second stage of the knowledge audit. In this stage, you and your knowledge audit team must reach a consensus on what you consider the best state that you could wish for and more reasonably reach, albeit with great difficulty. This is the best-case scenario against which you will judge your entire KM initiative later on (see Figure 8-3).

Knowledge of what the best value of your knowledge assets should be is essential to allow you to measure the results of your KM efforts against a relevant and stationary benchmark. As Figure 8-4 shows, an optimum target point is needed to measure performance in any given area. Optimums also allow for easy comparability of performance of multiple competitors and are especially useful for evaluating knowledge processes.

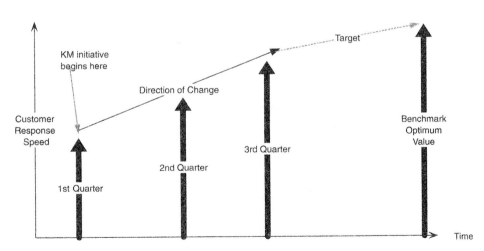

Figure 8-4   Optimum benchmark values help validate the effects of KM.

The first point in the figure, indicated by the first quarter in which the KM effort was initiated, indicates where the company began. The graph indicates customer response speed as a parameter, and the last value on the chart indicates the target value. This target value might be the company's self-set goal or a goal based on a competitor's performance. For example, you might decide that your company needs to beat its competitors by a 10 percent margin on this front. The graph then traces how your company is progressing on this front over (different) ensuing quarters.

Customer response speed illustrated here is only an example. KM systems usually start out to tackle much more complex and compound issues. However, because there is no acceptable unit for measuring knowledge on any front, it's best to measure all parameters in their original units and maybe devise a composite measure. (More specifics on measurement and metrics follow in Chapter 14). All these measures can help you assess the performance—good or bad—of your KM investments.

It's usually a good idea to assign high values to all these aspects. Process performance need not be compared with some arbitrary figure: It could be based on a function (such as 110 percent of the industry average) derived from industry averages, competitor figures, or market predictions. Lacking any such bases, you could always shoot for the *perfect figure,* such as no customer returns or 100 percent conversion of research outcomes to marketed products, etc. Though optimism is a good thing, be cautious of overly depending on such an approach: It can be far from realistic if perfect figures are used as a basis for comparison. Table 8-4 gives a few examples of such measures.

SELECTING THE AUDIT METHOD

The method you use for auditing your company's or group's knowledge determines the degree to which you will accurately gauge the current (pre-KM) state of that aspect or knowledge dimension (see Figure 8-5). This assessment is what helps you decide on the processes that need reinforcement and the processes that need capitalization.

For example, you might realize that there just isn't enough conversation and sharing of ideas going on in a specific department in your company. You might decide to augment this

Table 8-4 Measuring Knowledge Assets against Optimum Values

Knowledge Asset	Aspect	Current Firm Values	Optimum Values
Trademark	Value in dollars	$4 million	$25 million
Patents→products	% Converted	40%	90%
Know-how	IT architecture design; how many consultants actually know how to do it?	5 employees	40 employees
Repeat business	% of existing customer base	96%	100%

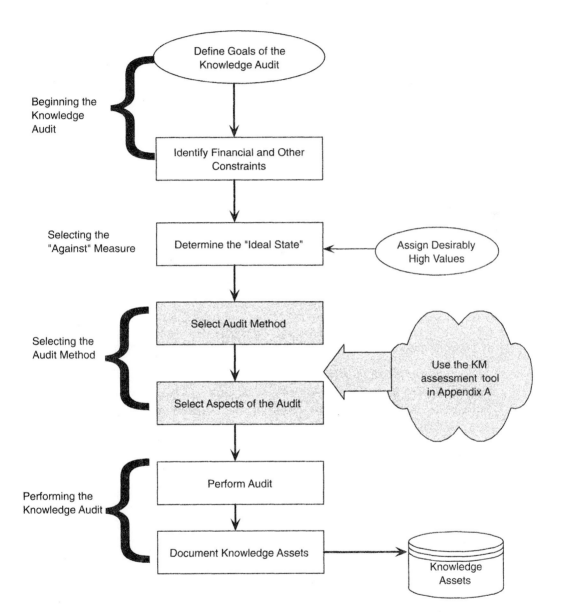

Figure 8-5   Selecting the audit method.

shortcoming with a Web-based message board and physical common space. In short, the choice of technologies (and accompanying cultural reinforcements) you focus on will largely be determined and influenced by this step in the knowledge audit process.

Perhaps the most useful resource at this stage will be the KM assessment tool provided on the CD-ROM accompanying this book (see Appendix A), which enables you to select the aspects that rank on the top of your company's list.[a]

The audit method that you decide to use must account for *at least* the following three critical intangible assets:

- Employee know-how
- Reputation (including goodwill or value attached to your brand)
- Organizational culture

Reputation and culture can be thought of as diffused tacit knowledge, so it follows that knowledge and know-how, in some form or another, account for the bulk of the value of the firm.[2] You must also determine the nature, strength, and sustainability of the current competitive advantage that the firm derives in terms of product and service delivery system features that it employs.[3,4,b] It helps to think in terms of the issues of protection, maintenance, enhancement, and leverage of these intangible assets.

Documenting Knowledge Assets

It is essential to document the knowledge-based assets that your company has in a consistent framework. The framework makes it easier to compare with previously measured values and with corresponding values for your competitors. Such a framework typically takes the form of the Capability Framework, described in Table 8-5.

Each unit of knowledge analysis and each diagnostic question can be answered in terms of Table 8-6, which allows you to measure "tacitness" of each knowledge element. The answer that closely matches the description identifies the stage of knowledge along the scale described in Table 8-3. The lower the value on this scale, the more important it might become to support that dimension of knowledge with a KM system, for example, to convert it into a form that can be more readily applied in a more explicit form.

---

[a]Customer surveys, interviews with clients, analyses of sales data and cost of sales, market reputation measures, analyses of competitor data, analyses of cash flows, analyses of knowledge flow bottlenecks, and focus groups can provide a lot more insight into the actual state of your company's knowledge assets than pure guesswork can. Market pull for your products and services, return on investments in IT and knowledge/discussion databases, employee skills, sharing of best practices across the enterprise, and core competencies are other feasible indicators.

[b]Many researchers have suggested that Michael Porter's well-respected and widely used models of strategic planning begin to fall apart when knowledge assets are taken into account.

Table 8-5 The Capability Framework for Positioning Knowledge-Related Assets

Regulatory Capability	Positional Capability
• Patents	• Path-dependent capabilities
• Trademarks	• Reputation
• Registered designs	• Value chain configuration
• Trade secrets	• Distribution networks
• Licenses	• Installed base
• Proprietary technology	• Customer base
• Methodologies	• Market share
• Databases	• Liquidity
	• Product reputation
	• Service reputation
	• Service product reputation

Functional Capability	Cultural Capability
• Lead times	• Tradition or corporate culture of being the best (Apple?)
• Accessibility of past knowledge	• Tradition of sharing
• Innovative capabilities	• The tradition of co-opetition
• Individual and team skills	• The tradition of risk sharing
• Distributor know-how	• Perception of quality standards
• Employee skills	• Ability of employees to work in teams
	• Capability to respond to market challenges
	• Innovation
	• Entrepreneurial and intrapreneurial drive in employees
	• Employee initiative and motivation

Based on an expanded adaptation from R. Hall and P. Andriani, Analyzing Intangible Resources and Managing Knowledge in a Supply Chain Context, *European Management Journal,* vol. 16, no. 6 (1998), pp. 685–697.

Table 8-6 Diagnostic Questions to Evaluate Each Unit of Knowledge Analysis on Bohn's Scale

Stage	Description/Diagnostic
0	We don't even know the good from the bad in terms of outcomes! (You probably don't need this book then; nothing is going to help!)
1	We have no knowledge; each time we have to make a decision, it is by trial and error.
2	We have only tacit knowledge which is in the form of personal knowledge held by person _____ and _____.
3	We have tacit knowledge; we have converted it into heuristics and rules of thumb;* they often work.
4	Knowledge (some) exists in explicated form, but no one really uses it.
5	Knowledge exists in explicated form. We use it but need tacit knowledge possessed by person _____ to be able to apply it in some circumstances; but unless things are really different from normal, we can do without the tacit component. Whenever we use this explicit knowledge, we validate it or contribute back to it.
6	Knowledge exists in explicated form. We use it but need tacit knowledge possessed by person _____ to be able to apply it well.
7	Tried and tested models now exist. We can simulate conditions; do what-if analysis in complex circumstances; modify behavior accordingly; it always works. Tacit content of the sum total of knowledge is very low. We validate existing knowledge whenever we use it. Our company has a strong "unlearning" capability. Our culture truly promotes knowledge sharing and synergy. We do not think that we have left any stone unturned in leveraging our company's knowledge. Employee walkouts do not hurt us in any significant way.
8	Difficult to characterize.

---

*For example, it is often, *but not always,* true that your car's battery is discharged if you left the headlights on for a few hours and now it does not start.

Once you go through this iteration, you can add it to a base starting value set, against which you will be able to compare developments and improvements over time after a KM program is implemented. Declining values will indicate a failure to improve processes, and climbing values indicate successful KM directions.

TRACKING KNOWLEDGE GROWTH OVER TIME

As you keep a score of these aspects surrounding knowledge, you can recognize changes over time by asking diagnostic questions (see Appendix A). Examples of such diagnostic questions include:

1. How is the *stock* of this knowledge resource increasing?
2. Is it increasing? If so, how do we know that it is?
3. How can we ensure that the stock (of knowledge) continues to increase?
4. Are we making the best use of this knowledge resource?
5. Do all employees recognize the value of this resource?
6. How durable is this knowledge asset? Will it decline over a period of time? How easily can others (competition) identify and copy this resource?
7. Can the competition easily nurture and grow this knowledge?
8. Is there any aspect that our competition has leveraged but we have not?
9. Can we imitate it? Need we?
10. Can this knowledge "walk out of the door"?
11. How is it changing *over time*?
12. Will our company need it after X (define X) years?

ANALYZING THE POPULATED CAPABILITY QUADRANTS

At the end of this audit process, you will have populated the Capability Framework (Table 8-5) with answers and ratings derived from diagnostic questions that you pose to your audit team. Some cells will have a lot of 1s and 2s (indicating highly tacit knowledge and a lack of explicated methodology that the entire firm can directly apply), whereas others will be populated with more 5s and 6s (indicating high capability maturity and the existence of a recipe).

An easy way to determine the quadrant that your own company's KM system needs to support might be to add the numbers in each of the four quadrants and analyze the ones with the weakest scores. However, you must avoid this easy way out, because it can be highly error prone. Because the number of diagnostics in each quadrant is not standardized and the significance of each question (as perceived by a number of stakeholders) will vary from one company to another, direct results cannot be calculated. However, these numbers (representing

Bohn's scores) will help your audit team decide and weigh each of these quadrants on a composite score basis. The populated cells of the framework can, therefore, help you determine the quadrants (representing four types of capabilities) that need the strengthening support of KM most and those that are already healthy.

CHOOSING YOUR COMPANY'S KNOWLEDGE NICHES

It is the sum total of the decisions made on the front lines that decide the future well-being of your company.[5,c] The knowledge audit provides a clearer picture of the K-spots, or the knowledge niches, on which a company must focus its KM efforts. Choosing these knowledge spots or areas of focus provides the best unbiased view of the technology investment needed to drive potent KM in your company.

STRATEGIC POSITIONING WITHIN THE TECHNOLOGY FRAMEWORK

Mapping knowledge in each of the areas that you chose in the earlier stages of the knowledge audit, as described in Figure 8-6, provides excellent insight into the way KM and business strategy can be kept in perfect synchronization. This insight can help in determining the strategic position and competitive advantage possessed by the firm in terms of the explicit and tacit knowledge contained within the firm—in people's heads, databases, resident experience, electronic discussions, and KM systems.

The results of the audit can then help you decide how you want to position KM to provide the maximum value while balancing competitive advantage possessed by your firm. Four positioning choices are described next.

THE FOUR POSITIONING CHOICES

Once you map each knowledge element or asset on the framework described in Figure 8-6, you can tell whether it is a strength or weakness. The shaded areas indicate a high competitive advantage—areas where your knowledge is already well managed but can possibly be improved. Similarly, the right cells in the matrix represent the two quadrants where KM holds the most promise for producing groundbreaking results. Knowledge that falls outside these shaded areas represents those areas where the support of a KM system and an effective KM strategy is most needed. Strategic positions A through D (see Figure 8-6) are described below.

---

[c]In business, as in war, front-line decisions can have critical impact on performance.

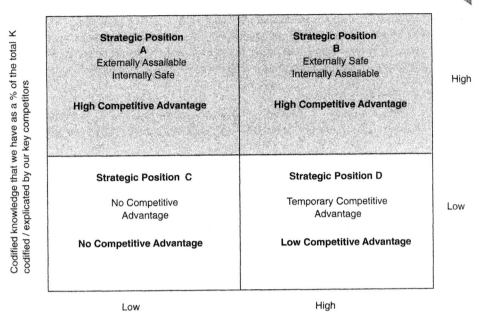

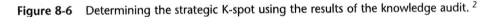

Tacit knowledge content as a % of the total knowledge that we have

Figure 8-6   Determining the strategic K-spot using the results of the knowledge audit. [2]

Strategic Position A

Strategic position A indicates that your company is internally safe but externally vulnerable on this front. The level of explicated knowledge is high, and tacit content is low. Your competitors do not have much more knowledge than you have available and ready to apply. This is perhaps the best-case scenario for KM.[6,d] Very few companies actually fall in this quadrant. We researched several companies that have had a fair degree of success in their KM efforts, and our initial findings indicate that companies that are actually pursuing KM effectively fall in Quadrant A.[7] However, in that quadrant, your company is externally vulnerable because almost all the knowledge you have is well explicated and codified. If your competitors manage to obtain any portion of this readily applicable and explicitly codified knowledge, they could use it to their advantage and against you in their own business. In such a case, your focus should be more on security measures, rather than KM.

Strategic Position B

Position B indicates that your company has managed to explicate *some* portion of its knowledge; however, this is a relatively small percentage of what your competitors have managed to explicate. In this position, tacit content of knowledge in your company is rather high.

---

[d]This holds especially true for companies that have a strong leaning toward codification.

This is an excellent scenario for an efficacious KM initiative and support, using a well-funded KM system. Technology can be a major, if not the only, savior for your firm's competitive advantage. Even though your company might be externally safe, a key employee leaving your company and joining a competitor might reverse the entire balance.

Strategic Position C

This position is a fundamentally weak position, where your company has no strategic advantage whatsoever. Probably a lot more issues besides KM need to be addressed.[8]

Strategic Position D

Most companies considering KM fall into this quadrant. These companies are presently successful but need to manage knowledge in such a manner that their temporary advantage is converted into a longer term, sustainable competitive advantage. These companies have much to gain from an investment in KM systems,[9] technology, and infrastructure. Such companies include consulting companies, where the founders of the firm have a bulk of the firm's total knowledge. In such cases, the tacit portion of knowledge is very high in relation to the portion that has been formalized, captured, and explicated (or externalized).

WHO ACTUALLY SEES THE ROAD AHEAD?

An outstanding example of a company that falls in this quadrant, often a topic of passionate debate both in business school classrooms and Web chatrooms, is Microsoft. Bill Gates, its founder, has provided the driving "bigger-picture" vision to the company since its inception. Microsoft has been trying both to distribute and to explicate *his* knowledge by bringing complementary and intellectually able stakeholders, such as Nathan Myvrhold, into the company and documenting decisions more excruciatingly than ever before. The same has reportedly been going on at lower levels throughout the company, as well.

Companies falling into strategic positions B and D are the best cases for KM.

LESSONS LEARNED

The knowledge audit process, the fourth step in the 10-step KM road map, begins with a clear understanding of its purpose, its short-term and long-term goals, and the identification of its constraints. Knowledge of knowledge assets is critical to the proper planning of a KM system and is a rich source of information about where the strengths of your company lie. Keep in mind the following points while auditing your company's knowledge assets.

- *Hindsight + insight = foresight.* Extrapolation from the past cannot, by itself, predict the future course of events, such as project success. However, if hindsight is combined with insight into past processes, the combination can provide a robust indicator for the future. Keep this in view when you are trying to decide on processes that are considered critical (which is a highly subjective judgment) by your company.

- *Apply the six-step knowledge audit process.* This includes the following: defining the goals, selecting the audit method, determining the ideal state, performing the knowledge audit, documenting existing knowledge assets, and determining your company's strategic position.

- *Think of coffee, processes, and KM together.* Notwithstanding my warnings against using examples as guiding principles, my coffee-brewing example effectively demonstrates how processes move from being highly tacit to highly methodological. If you cannot decide the stages of your processes, try matching them to this example.

- *Beware of mirages.* To manage its knowledge effectively, your company must progress to stage 5, 6, or 7. Be wary of using this framework as your only KM metric. Stage 8 on the process knowledge competence framework is a mirage.

- *Cross-functional is fully functional.* Make sure that you have someone from senior management on board, along with a knowledge champion. The knowledge analyst, who plays the integrative part, should be able to elicit both extant and missing knowledge and to analyze the possible categories in which each piece of knowledge or stream of knowledge fits best.

- *Identify, evaluate, and rate critical process knowledge.* Look at all the intangible assets and knowledge assets that exist in your company, including its rituals, processes, structure, communities, and people.

- *Use a consistent framework.* Document the results of the audit in the consistent Capability Framework to allow for comparison over time. Focus on the cells with low scores *and* those that represent critically weak areas.

- *Select your company's niches carefully.* The audit provides a clearer picture of the niches on which a company must focus its KM efforts. You can identify promising processes that stand to gain most (positions B and D in the strategic capability framework).

A preliminary audit provides a good point both for identifying areas and processes that can benefit from KM most and for deciding on the structure of the implementation team. Chapter 14 discusses knowledge metrics that can directly link KM design to business strategy. You might want to glance at the measures there and at the toolkit in Appendix A before you proceed to the next chapter, in which, as the fifth step on our 10-step road map, we will analyze a strategy for building the KM team that will actually develop and implement your company's KM system.

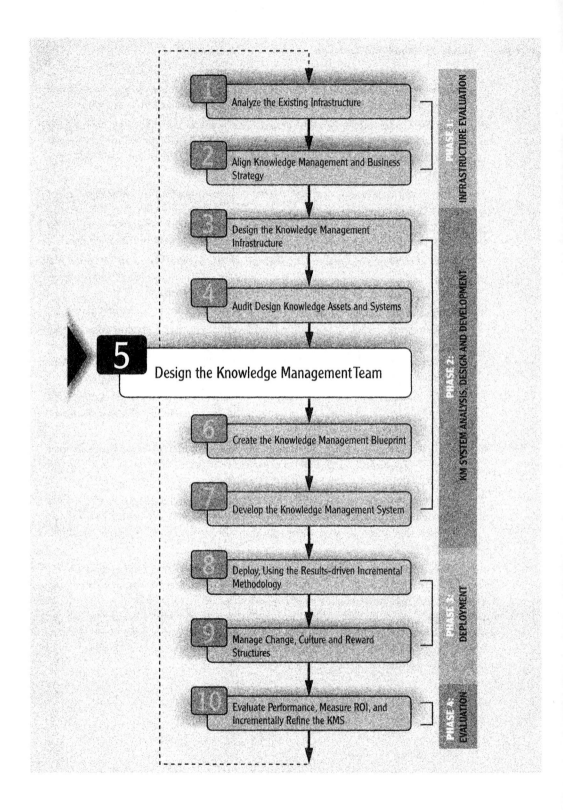

1   Analyze the Existing Infrastructure

2   Align Knowledge Management and Business Strategy

3   Design the Knowledge Management Infrastructure

4   Audit Design Knowledge Assets and Systems

5   Design the Knowledge Management Team

6   Create the Knowledge Management Blueprint

7   Develop the Knowledge Management System

8   Deploy, Using the Results-driven Incremental Methodology

9   Manage Change, Culture and Reward Structures

10   Evaluate Performance, Measure ROI, and Incrementally Refine the KMS

PHASE 1:
INFRASTRUCTURE EVALUATION

PHASE 2:
KM SYSTEM ANALYSIS, DESIGN AND DEVELOPMENT

PHASE 3:
DEPLOYMENT

PHASE 4:
EVALUATION

CHAPTER 9
DESIGNING THE KNOWLEDGE MANAGEMENT TEAM

IN THIS CHAPTER

- ✔ Design the KM team.
- ✔ Identify sources of requisite expertise.
- ✔ Identify critical points of failure: requirements, control, management buy-in, and end user buy-in.
- ✔ Structure the KM team: organizationally, strategically, and technologically.
- ✔ Balance technical and managerial expertise; manage stakeholder expectations.
- ✔ Resolve team-sizing issues.

GOOD JUDGMENT COMES FROM EXPERIENCE, AND EXPERIENCE OFTEN COMES FROM BAD JUDGMENT.
—RITA MAE BROWN

A KM system is built on expertise, skills, and insights of a diverse variety of stakeholders who might have little in common from a functional standpoint. This can be an uneasy partnership for many functional specialists who rarely cross paths with others.[1] Nevertheless, the quality of the collaborative relationship between these stakeholders determines the ultimate success of the system.[2] Bringing together the best of domain experts does not guarantee an effective KM team unless there is collective chemistry. Selecting the right blend of team members to lead the KM project clearly is a critical step.

The fifth step on the KM road map involves design of the KM team that will build, implement, focus, and deploy the KM system. In this chapter, we identify sources of internal and external expertise needed, prioritize stakeholder needs, evaluate member selection criteria, and examine team life span and sizing issues. We identify characteristics of the KM project leader to determine mechanisms to streamline internal dynamics and maximize user participation.

SOURCES OF EXPERTISE

KM teams draw their expertise from several sources:

- Internal, centralized IT departments
- Team-based local experts
- External vendors, contractors, partners, and consultants
- End users and front-line staff

Although we cannot undermine the importance of IT staff that will actually build a system, the most important part of this team member set is the set of local team-based expert(s). The burden of balancing counteracting requirements falls on the shoulders of the KM team (see Figure 9-1). As we discussed in the Chapter 8, drawing participants from a variety of functional groups within and outside your company is essential.[3] If done properly, this approach will become the strength of your KM team and a major contributor to the success of such an endeavor.

LOCAL EXPERTS AND INTRADEPARTMENTAL GURUS

Active end-user involvement throughout the KM project is critical to its success. In most companies, there are the early adopters of technology—the so-called gurus within your company. These are the people who come in early or stay late to play with new tools that become available. Even though many of these folks tend to be nontechnologists, they are the best people to gauge the possible usefulness of each feature that your system has. These local experts are often the first to notice the limitations of existing systems and to think of possible upgrades and changes to meet the evolving needs of their group. Examples of such workers include

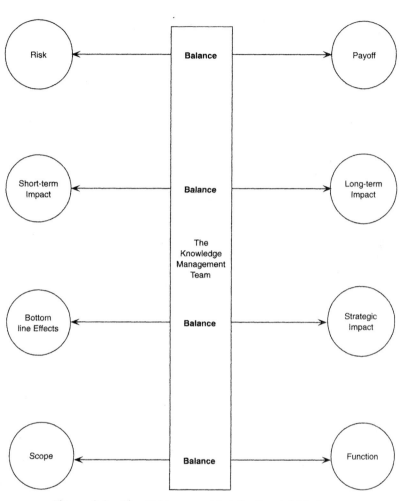

Figure 9-1 The KM team must strike the right balance.

marketing people who realize that existing technology could possibly be used to deliver the latest sales figures and data needed by traveling salespeople in remote locations.

INTERNAL IT DEPARTMENTS

Relying solely on local experts, of course, has its limitations. Even though local experts might possess a fairly high degree of technical knowledge besides knowledge of their own job, they might lack an understanding of the interdependencies between complex systems, networks, and technology that pure technologists such as the IT staff might be able to bring in. Whereas the local experts will bring in the business case and ideas, it is IT staff who will bring in knowledge of:

- Infrastructural capabilities and limitations
- Connectivity and compatibility among the team-based systems and the overall organizational technology infrastructure
- Standardization issues across different platforms, applications, and tools
- Technicalities underlying the adaptation of these tools by various knowledge worker groups within the company

When you are selecting team members from the internal IT department within your company, it is critical that you select personnel with credibility in the eventual user group. This helps ensure that the *relevant* set of stakeholder needs is adequately represented. With increased emphasis on customer service, it is easy for internal customers to outsource their development services to external consultants. Therefore, delegates selected from the IT department must have a more expansive view of who the customer is. Technical skills, of course, are a priority in making these decisions.

LATERALITY

Laterality refers to the ability to cut across functional boundaries and relate to people from different areas.[4] People who exhibit this characteristic are best suited to be on a KM team. Such members can:

- Act as a bridge and as interpreters between people from different backgrounds, skill areas, and specializations
- Learn faster than the average person in your company and are not defensive about their lack of understanding or knowledge in areas other than their own
- Bring value to the overall team synergy because they tend to be confident but not egoistically constrained
- Learn the basic lingo and understand the frameworks to which their collaborators refer
- Have the ability to deal creatively and rationally with individual differences

Groups of such people have also been referred to as *communities of practice;* they are characterized by:

- Multifunctional groups that incorporate diverse viewpoints, training, ages, and roles
- Enacting a common purpose by engaging in real work, building things, solving problems, delivering service, and using real tools

- Developing intellectual property, knowledge, firm culture, internal language, and new skills
- Making lasting changes in the people and the competence that they embody

CONSULTANTS

Even though most of the technical, design, and soft skills needed for the KM project might be available in-house, there might be some areas that are no one's strength within the company. These shortcomings can often be overcome by bringing in external consultants. Internal participants might have slight cultural differences, owing to their differing departmental and functional affiliations, but they are still tied together by a common frame of reference built around the overall company culture, dominant values, and image.[5] However, external consultants do not always fit into this frame of reference. Because external participants often lack this common frame of reference, it is essential that other binding mechanisms, such as their personal characteristics, be strongly matched with those of internal team members.

Nevertheless, this lack of shared culture can often be turned from a liability into an asset. These external participants *can* bring a balanced, unbiased outsider perspective into the entire design process.

In such cases, trust becomes another significant issue. Given the nature of the consulting business, it should come as no surprise if the consultant is developing exactly the same type of system for your competitor a few months down the road. Selecting a consultant should, therefore, be partially based on the extent to which the person (or consulting company) is willing to transfer existing skills to your company's employees. Some of the other issues that must be considered while selecting a consultant include:

- The consultant's reputation for integrity
- The consultant's history that demonstrates the ability to maintain confidentiality about past projects
- Whether the consultant has worked successfully for your own company on earlier projects
- Whether the consultant (or consulting company) is working on a similar project for a competitor
- Whether your internal team trusts and has confidence in the consulting company

In any case, highly specialized and capable consultants are often hard to find. Because KM projects are strategically oriented, the level of confidentiality must be backed up with specific, legal nondisclosure agreements. Where highly confidential material is involved, it might be a better idea to have an employee trained in the deficient area, rather than bring in a consultant. An option that is always open, budgets permitting, is to lure a consultant from the consulting position to a permanent job within your company. However, corporate budgets can often restrict this option.

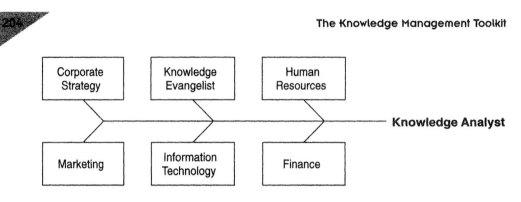

Figure 9-2 KM team structure.

KM stakeholders should typify the group that they represent. For example, the person representing your company's human resources (HR) department should be one who is typical (where the meaning of *typical* is highly subjective) of the HR department and has had a sufficient level of experience within your own company.

As Figure 9-2 and Table 9-1 show, the human resources and knowledge evangelists or senior management provide overall stability to the KM project team.

Table 9-1 Structuring the KM Team

Focus	Shareholder Group	Role in the KM Project	Characteristics Strongly Desired
Teams	User teams Finance Marketing Other functional areas with which the knowledge management initiative is concerned	• Provide functional expertise. • Provide business expertise in their specific area. • Participate in the process design stage. • Help in the implementation stages of the system.	• Must understand work processes in their area. • Must have good interpersonal and team skills. • Must have a certain degree of credibility within other participating groups. • Must be willing to see from other functional viewpoints.
Technology	IT experts/information systems Internal IT staff	• Provide technology expertise.	• Must understand technology in depth. • Must have good interpersonal skills.

Table 9-1 Structuring the Knowledge Management Team (cont.)

Focus	Shareholder Group	Role in the Knowledge Management Project	Characteristics Strongly Desired
Technology (cont.)	External consultants	• Participate in the actual implementation and design. • Represent the internal and internally proficient technologists. • Actually write the code. • Bring in a perspective on functional capabilities and limitations of existing systems.	• Must have strong team skills. • Must be willing to understand the perspectives brought in by other team members and actually incorporate them into the design. • Must be willing to learn. • Must be credible. • Must have an expansive customer orientation.
Organizational	Senior management/sponsors/ knowledge champion(s)/CKO	• Support the legitimacy of the project. • Bring in vision that correlates with the overall company-wide vision. • Serve on steering committees (if needed). • Commit the resources needed.	• Understand the management and strategic processes. • Must be credible. • Must have a strong leadership position that almost everyone on the team accepts. • Must have a clear idea of the bigger picture of where knowledge leveraging should take the company. • Must "eat their own dog food," that is, they must themselves believe what they say. • Need to be thoroughly convinced of the worth of the project.

MANAGERS

The status and influence of senior managers would make one assume that they are the least likely group to be left out of the development process. However, several studies have shown that this exclusion is not only possible but also one that frequently does happen.[6] As teams become too deeply engrossed in the user/developer relationship, senior managers tend to be left out of the loop. Lack of their active involvement can jeopardize the entire project.

TEAM COMPOSITION AND SELECTION CRITERIA

As with most other technologically driven enterprise-wide teams, functional diversity in KM teams should be taken as a given characteristic.[7] Teams need to be designed for effectiveness. Although there is no straightforward formula for designing a good KM team, the team's design has much to do with the nature of the project itself. Functional diversity can lead to only two possible outcomes, depending on how it's handled. The first and common outcome is destructive conflict and tension. The second, more desirable outcome is characterized by synergy, creativity, and innovation. This happens only when laterality among team members is high and there is sufficient room to accommodate different backgrounds, values, skills, perspectives, and assumptions that the members bring into the team. Table 9-2 summarizes the major team design considerations.

TEMPORARY VERSUS PERMANENT TEAM MEMBERS

KM is unlike a typical business restructuring or technology introduction project. Those projects are temporary and depend on temporary teams, whereas a KM project needs at least a small portion of the group to be permanent. A KM project is not over once a KM system is implemented; it must go on and continually improve and change with changing external and internal environments. Although some members might be needed on the team only during the initial stages, others are not as temporary. This book uses the term *core team* to refer to this permanent, essential group. Team members can be dedicated to the project either full time or part time. The size of the core team must be kept to the smallest size possible—the smallest member count that can actually do the work.[8] Temporary team members often belong to specific user groups. The core team should consist of only the following participants:

- Knowledge champion or a senior manager.
- IT staff.
- User delegates representing the core business area that is going to depend on the KM system. This could be engineering staff, in case the KM system is built to support research and development; it could be marketing if the KM system is for sales force enablement, etc.

Table 9-2 Designing the Knowledge Management Project Team

Team Design Element	Characteristics of the KM Team Members Selected	Notes
Defining the knowledge management project leader's role	The leader of the team: • Must be credible. • Must have a sufficient level of authority and resource capability. • Should not change; must be stable. • Must know how to facilitate, consult, and resolve conflicts. • Must take charge of the conventional project management, scheduling, and coordination duties. • Must have direct reporting capability to upper management or should be drawn from within upper middle management. • Must manage the life cycle of the team, as well as selection of the core team members. • Must encourage structured decision making. • Must be experienced in both complex projects and in various roles within the company.	These criteria can be also used for selecting the project leader.
Defining the team composition and selection criteria for team members	Knowledge management project team members must be drawn from different functional areas and departments of the firm. As expected, they will have different areas of specialization and backgrounds. The following common characteristics must be shared by members selected for the team: • Must have specialized expertise. • Must have had sufficient experience within the company or working with the company as an external consultant. • Must have the required competencies that truly represent the concerns of the department or functional area that the team member represents. • Might work full time or part time on this project. • Might be a member of the core team or the temporary startup team. • Must demonstrate laterality. • Must believe in the project and must have a clear vision for what improved knowledge flows can and should do for this unit or department.	All groups that will be affected by the knowledge management project and, conversely, all groups that are expected to use and contribute to this knowledge and knowledge management efforts must be adequately and accurately represented in the team.

The remaining participants, in most cases, should be involved in the startup phases of the project and can be called in later for further input as and when needed.

TEAM LIFE SPAN AND SIZING ISSUES

There are two schools of thought on the future of KM. One school believes that KM will continue to depend on people to manage knowledge throughout the lifetime of the organization; the second and more convincing school believes that KM is a *self-eliminating* initiative. This means that, as a company begins to accept KM practices, they should, over several years, become so second nature to employees as the company evolves that eventually there should be no need for a knowledge manager or CKO to manage knowledge. Knowledge workers themselves should be able to handle all KM tasks, once KM becomes embedded in the company culture and in work practices.

One would argue why the KM team members would, in the first place, do their job so well that it would eliminate their very need! That is a hard question to answer. Though there is a lot of ongoing research to find an answer to this question, there is little other than very strong financial and promotional incentives that can help here. For that matter, team members on the KM team should be promised strong rewards and promotions if the KM initiative truly succeeds. A team whose members set out to work with the fear of losing their jobs by performing too well is bound to be undermotivated, if not unmotivated.[9]

THE PROJECT LEADER

The KM project team leader's role, by its very nature, is different from one occasioned by a typical organizational change or technology implementation project. The leader does not direct: Instead, he or she facilitates. The KM project leader may or may not be the same person as the CKO (or equivalent). Unlike conventional project management, KM projects need leadership that helps create a supportive, unobtrusive, and focused environment within which team members can concentrate on their primary substantive tasks with minimal distraction. The project leader must take on the conventional load of tracking progress, budgets, workloads, and schedules. The KM project leader serves as the visionary for the entire project by helping members on the team understand the project's mission and align their efforts with the project's overall goals and objectives. A project leader must resolve internal dynamics, serve as a translator, and take charge of task delegation, as the following sections describe.

INTERNAL DYNAMICS

The project leader must facilitate the internal functioning of the KM team by helping members objectively resolve differences, using structured decision-making techniques. Although conflict is undesirable on a large scale, a basic level of conflict is essential and inevitable in teams as diverse as KM teams tend to be.[10] Many of the differences that emerge are due to the differing needs and concerns of the stakeholder groups involved. The project leader plays an essential part here by helping team members understand why even trivially straightforward issues and differences seem to be so difficult to resolve. In their facilitating role, project leaders can pose the key questions, clarify differences and their underlying assumptions, then give members of the KM team sufficient room to actually resolve these differences.

TRANSLATION AND DELEGATION

The project leader also needs to be able to act as a translator in the startup stages of the project when the user teams and the IT participants fail to understand each other's viewpoints because of vocabulary differences. What might comprise a good design in the opinion of a technologist might not qualify as a good design in the opinion of a marketing manager, for example. Therefore, the project leader must not try to push or pull the team toward specific directions, design solutions, or technology choices. Instead, he or she must facilitate effective and well-moderated brainstorming within the group. Besides this role, the project leader must brief senior management on the progress and milestones in the project.

To determine the actual issues of concern and to identify the actual knowledge flow problems that exist within the company, the project leader should encourage participants to actually collect relevant data from their own departments through meetings, surveys, interviews, and focus groups. These communications can ensure that the direction the team is taking is not unduly influenced by the ill-placed opinion of specific stakeholders and instead reflects the actual concerns that their departments might have.

USER PARTICIPATION

It is the project manager's role to ensure that the KM project is going in a direction that builds toward a system that users *actually need.* Although the actual requirements might have been elicited in the knowledge audit described in Chapter 8, maintaining the link between the users and the KM group ensures that changing conditions are kept in view. One of the most effective ways of verifying this linkage is to show a preliminary version of the KM system to actual users.

Prototypes: A Stitch in Time Saves Nine

Systems developers have long realized the value of prototypes. A prototype provides both the developers—in this case, the KM team—and the users with an idea of how the system in its final form will function.

By using such a prototype, even if it is incomplete, users can see the possibilities of the KM system under construction, and this improved understanding of the final product can lead to or trigger highly desirable refinement of its features, interface, functionality, and design. Tweaking the system's design based on user feedback in the prototype stages can save your company much headache and unnecessary rework-related expenses at a later date. Other ways the project manager can link to the final user are illustrated in Figure 9-3.

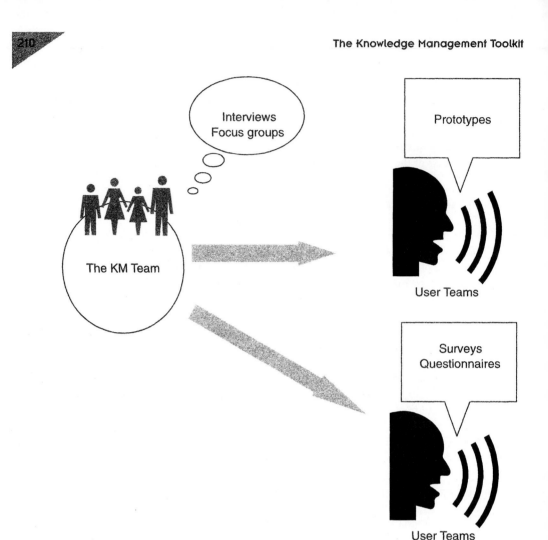

Figure 9-3 Prototyping and other methods of linking the user and the KM project.

THE KM TEAM'S PROJECT SPACE

One of the first tasks that the KM team needs to undertake is that of understanding the project's strategic intent, organizational context, technological constraints, monetary limitations, and short-term as well as long-term goals. Members of your KM team should be able to provide adequate answers to these questions collectively:

1. What is the company's envisioned strategic and performance goal?
2. Where does the KM team fit in the organizational hierarchy?

CASE STUDY: HOW KM WAS IMPLEMENTED AT HEINEKEN NV, HOLLAND

When Heineken NV, the Dutch company that brews a popular brand of beer by the same name, designed a number of scenarios to see whether its corporate office could become more process oriented, it became clear that three questions needed to be answered:

1. What is the added value of the corporate office?
2. What strategic processes does it apply?
3. How can the corporate office be organized around these processes?

The main purpose of the corporate office was defined as providing effective support to the executive board in formulating and realizing the strategy of the company as a whole. The corporate office's role was, therefore, thought of as the creator of strategic and operational knowledge that exists above the business units; that knowledge is easily accessible and adds value, as evidenced by the competitive advantage of Heineken.

The next step was to define the company strategic processes of the corporate office.

- Those directly related to the strategy of the company;
- Those semipermanent in character, changing only when the strategy of the company "as a whole" changes;
- Those making a multifunctional contribution to the entire company that rises above the business units and is divisible into separate strategic processes.

Heineken then created several scenarios:

- Strengthening worldwide market presence
- Stimulating operational excellence
- Optimizing management performance
- Maximizing company financial leverage

In these scenarios, the corporate office was no longer organized by functional disciplines. Instead, many people would be organized in teams around the company's strategic processes. Corporate office professionals could work on several teams, both as team members and team leaders. Thus, one day, a financial controller could work on a team in the acquisition of an Asian brewer and contribute to the strengthening of the worldwide market presence. The next day, the same specialist could work on a team advising on the fiscal plan of a specific operating division. Board members would no longer be responsible for only specific functions. Besides their operational responsibilities, they would each also be responsible for one of the strategic processes, such as corporate process responsibilities. The delivery of this responsibility and, therefore, the added value and accountability would become more explicit and clearly defined.

The teams were eventually connected in what the company described as "smart networks," where workers work together in soft networks of people and knowledge. They are supported by hard networks, forming an electronic performance system with productivity tools, communication tools, etc.

3. Does the KM project fit vertically or horizontally in the value chain?

4. What are the financial and time constraints for the project?

5. What are the technical limitations of existing technology platforms?

6. What are the critical elements in terms of skills, people, and knowledge that are still missing in the team?

7. What are the immediate payoffs? If there are none, when will the payoffs begin to show up? If that is not viable either, how will the value of the project be demonstrated and tested? The discussion on metrics in Chapter 14 can assist in this evaluation.

8. What level of commitment does the team have from the senior management and from the users? If it's poor, what can be done about it? Are there representatives from both these camps on the KM team?

9. What are the cultural blockades that should be expected? Does the company culture actually fit with the knowledge-sharing attitude that is needed to make a KM system work? If not, what changes in reward structure are necessary? Who has the authority to make such changes? Are they willing to make them?

10. Has any competitor or noncompeting firm implemented a project like this? What do we know about it? If it was successful, is there some way to get a key participant to switch jobs?

Judging the *true* value of the project is a critical issue. If the project costs more than the long-term value or options-based flexibility that it adds to the firm, it's probably not worth the investment. Therefore, exploring these initial questions is critical before the next step can be taken. If there are no direct answers, surrogate measures might be adopted. If your KM team cannot collectively answer these questions, revisit its structure and constituents. For example, if the primary objective of the KM project is to improve product quality by managing past and current knowledge about product quality problems, it might be valuable to question quality quantitatively. How much quality and at what cost? Can the customers tell the difference? Will they be willing to pay, say, 7 percent more for the same product if higher quality is guaranteed?

MANAGING STAKEHOLDER EXPECTATIONS

The second task, after the KM team has decided on an initial set of objectives for the KM initiative, is to present this work formally to various stakeholder groups. The biggest advantage of such an interaction is that it can help the team compare the project's objective with stakeholder expectations and perceptions. Resolving differences at this point is a more efficient approach than trying to fix basic design assumptions and errors after the fact—when the project is ready for implementation.

CHEMISTRY

Choice of individuals aside, the features of the team are determined best by considering all of its members taken together. Figure 9-4 illustrates two different types of teams that can be formed simply by choosing a different aggregation of individual members.

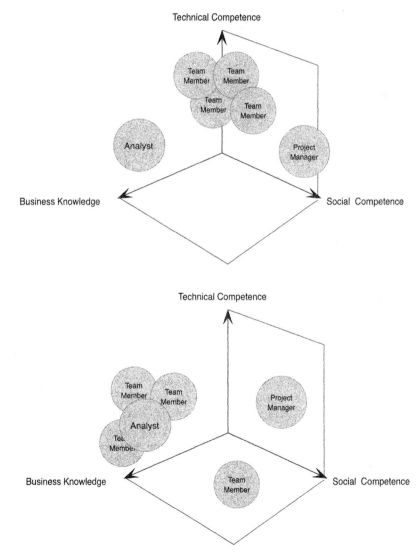

Figure 9-4   Two types of teams based on the chemistry of individual members.

For simplicity's sake, consider that three types of members exist: the project manager, systems analysts, and functional members. The first team clearly is one that's better suited for a project that is technically challenging. The second team is clearly better suited for a project of moderate technical complexity but high conceptual novelty. One must, therefore, consider how well a team's potential members fit together as a whole. Chemistry within a team is an essential but often overlooked consideration.

HIGHWAYS TO FAILURE

Even though information technology represents about half of all business equipment spending in the United States and nearly 5% of the gross domestic product in developed countries, success in notoriously elusive in software projects (www.oecd.org). A survey of 8000 software projects in 400 U.S. firms found that only one in six was successful. Of the remaining, about one third were never completed and over half were over budget, did not finish on time, or failed to deliver the promised functionality. Such failures annually cost U.S. businesses about $78 billion in development costs, and another $22 billion in cost overruns.

THE BREAKPOINT: BUY-IN FAILURE

Lack of an active role of the top management has been identified as the primary reason that many projects fail; the second reason is failure of the users to buy in to the project. If you decide to invest in a KM project and either your top management remains unconvinced of the value of the idea or the users you are building it for fail to see why they need the system, you are venturing into murky waters.

CATEGORIZING RISKS

Figure 9-5 illustrates the four categories in which KM project risks can be classified. This framework describes four quadrants on which project risk can be classified: the levels of risk (high/low) and the levels of control that a project manager has on each category.[11] Customer mandate (shaded quadrant, Figure 9-5) is a high-risk area over which you have little control.

Customer mandate refers to the level of buy-in from the ultimate users, who in effect are your system's customers. Unless they buy in to the whole notion of the KM system that you are building or planning to build, they will not have the inclination to use or support it.

Similarly, initial commitment from the top management is a necessary but insufficient condition for your project's success. This support must be ongoing and active throughout the project. The problems with many of the companies that we have studied often fall into one of these two areas. Once a project has been initiated, the project leader must gauge the level of

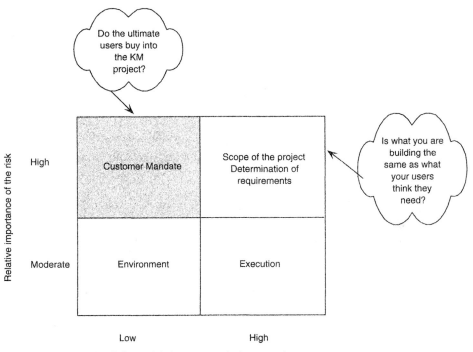

Figure 9-5   Categorizing risks in building the KM system proactively.

commitment from both senior management and the end-user community to avoid being caught in a situation where support for the project suddenly evaporates.[12]

CONTROLLING AND BALANCING REQUIREMENTS

As shown in Figure 9-5, there are some areas where you, as the knowledge champion or KM project manager, have significant control. However, there are some areas in which you have little or no control. Not having control over an area does not, by any stretch of imagination, mean that it will not contribute to the potential failure of your project! Customer or end-user buy-in and the environment in which the KM system will be used are two such factors. The only thing you can do about customer buy-in problems is to try selling the project harder and to gauge end-user needs more appropriately; the operating environment is an entirely different story. That is where the cultural aspects of a KM system and the people around it (discussed in Chapter 13) come into play. Although all these risks must be thought of together rather than independently, a strong focus must be on the risks over which you have little control.

SOLVING USER BUY-IN PROBLEMS

End-user buy-in problems can be tackled effectively by including representatives from the actual would-be end-user community in the KM team. The scope and requirements of the project can be more in line with what the actual would-be users need, and once they are on your side, you have a few more in your group of KM advocates when it comes to facing senior management. Similarly, management must be actively involved for two reasons:

- To ensure that senior managers *actually* buy into the project
- To ensure that the "bigger-picture" that management has in mind is well accommodated and incorporated

Some of these risks cannot be controlled by the KM project champion, leader, or team, but you certainly can influence them. KM initiatives can be trickier than their notoriously political cousin, data warehousing.

LESSONS LEARNED

The fifth step on the KM road map involves designing and building an effective KM implementation team. The ultimate goal, after the KM enabling technology and culture are in place, is to encourage every employee to become a manager of knowledge. Employees shouldn't have to think twice before they contribute, use, validate, update, or apply knowledge explicated within and outside the firm. Keep the following lessons in mind while designing a KM team:

- *Identify a few key core stakeholders.* A KM project must go on and continually improve and change with changing external and internal environments. Select a group of people representing IT, management, and the end-user group that will form a core part of your team on a relatively long-term basis. Other team members can serve temporarily.
- *Identify sources of requisite expertise.* Sources of expertise representing all divisions or departments that will use the KM system are best drawn from those organizational units. Managerial participants with sufficient knowledge of the company and a clear big picture provide strategic direction for the project.
- *Select a visionary and experienced project leader.* The KM project leader helps members of the team understand the project's mission and align their efforts with the company's overall goals and objectives.
- *Identify critical failure points.* There are some high-risk areas where the knowledge champion has little control: those involving end-user and management support.

- *Avoid external consultants if possible. Be* warned that, due to the nature of the consulting business, your competitor might have a system similar to yours a few months down the road.

- *Balance the KM team's managerial and technological structure.* KM is not solely a technical project, so the project team needs to balance both managerial and technical participants.

In the next chapter, we discuss the design and implementation of the technology infrastructure and architecture for KM.

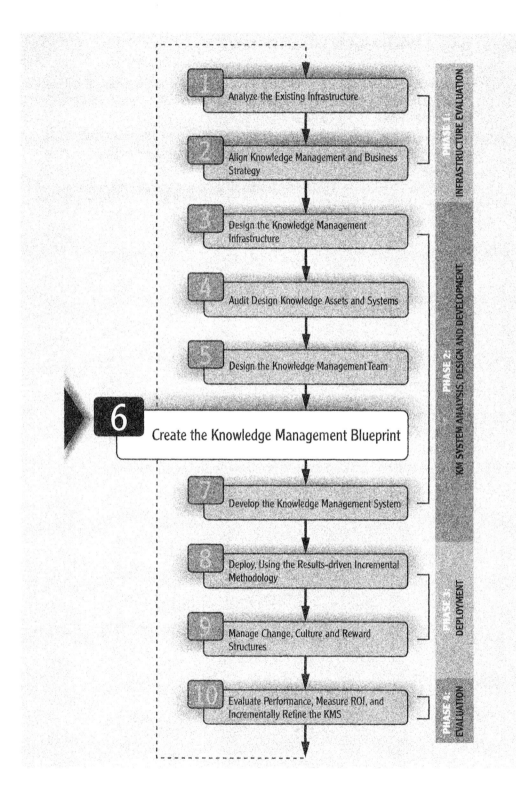

1 Analyze the Existing Infrastructure

2 Align Knowledge Management and Business Strategy

3 Design the Knowledge Management Infrastructure

4 Audit Design Knowledge Assets and Systems

5 Design the Knowledge Management Team

6 Create the Knowledge Management Blueprint

7 Develop the Knowledge Management System

8 Deploy, Using the Results-driven Incremental Methodology

9 Manage Change, Culture and Reward Structures

10 Evaluate Performance, Measure ROI, and Incrementally Refine the KMS

PHASE 1: INFRASTRUCTURE EVALUATION

PHASE 2: KM SYSTEM ANALYSIS, DESIGN AND DEVELOPMENT

PHASE 3: DEPLOYMENT

PHASE 4: EVALUATION

CHAPTER 10

CREATING THE KNOWLEDGE MANAGEMENT SYSTEM BLUEPRINT

IN THIS CHAPTER

✔ Develop the KM architecture.
✔ Understand and select the architectural components.
✔ Optimize for performance, interoperability, and scalability.
✔ Understand repository life cycle management.
✔ Understand and incorporate requisite user interface considerations.
✔ Position and scope the knowledge platform initiative.
✔ Make the build-or-buy decision and understand the tradeoffs.
✔ Future-proof the KM system.

HE THAT WOULD PERFECT HIS WORK MUST FIRST SHARPEN HIS TOOLS.
—CONFUCIUS

To remain sustainably competitive, companies must effectively and efficiently create, locate, capture, and share their organization's knowledge, and bring that knowledge to bear on new problems and opportunities in a timely manner. Many companies have become so complex that their knowledge is fragmented, extremely difficult to locate and share, and therefore inconsistent, redundant, and ignored throughout the decisions that drive the company.[1] This is where a stable KM blueprint fits in.

- To be able to leverage this asset effectively, the KM team identified in Chapter 9 needs to build on a KM blueprint that provides a road map for building and incrementally improving a KM system. This chapter describes Step 6 of the 10-step KM road map—creating the KM blueprint.

- We work toward building a KM architecture, understanding its seven layers specifically in the context of your company, and determining how it can be optimized for performance and scalability, as well as high levels of interoperability. We take a closer look at the tradeoffs involved in deciding to build or buy most of the system so that you can make a well-informed choice, taking your own company into account. We will also decide on the components that are needed right from the start.

- KM repository life cycle management, user interface (UI) considerations, and problem scoping are also described. Finally, we discuss practical design considerations to *future-proof* your KM system.

Although explicit knowledge comprises only a minuscule segment of the firm's total knowledge assets, a good KM blueprint also provides for the explication of invaluable tacit knowledge that exists in the minds of its employees. Although tacit knowledge develops naturally as a by-product of action, it is more easily exchanged, combined, distributed, and managed if it is converted to explicit knowledge. It is toward this end that the KM architecture plays a pivotal role.

THE KNOWLEDGE MANAGEMENT ARCHITECTURE

Information technology is a great enabler for sharing, application, validation, and distribution of explicit knowledge. Its weaknesses become apparent when companies try to use the same techniques and systems to leverage tacit knowledge. As this book has stressed, the fundamental challenge, given constraints on available resources, is that of determining which knowledge should be made explicit and which is best left tacit. Striking the right balance and arranging priorities in the right order are critical for competitive performance. It would be safe to assume that there is little that IT can do to support tacit knowledge in any way, shape, or form. It provides a channel for the exchange of such tacit knowledge. For the most part, this channel is not rich enough to truly transfer tacit knowledge. However, it can expedite the integration of tacit knowledge, especially when organizational or interorganizational boundaries are spanned

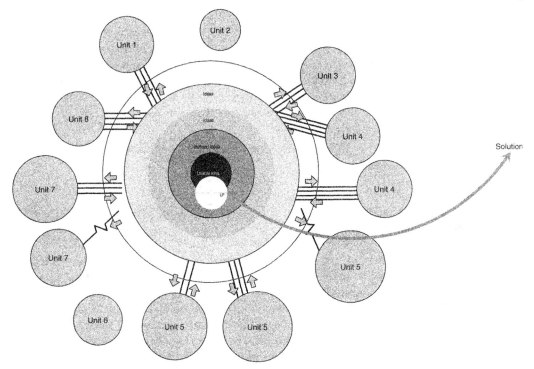

Figure 10-1   Given the appropriate triggers, integration across traditional boundaries rapidly produces innovative new knowledge.

(Figure 10-1). The links between collaborating business units and departments vary from being very strong to very weak, as indicated by different types of lines shown in the figure.

With that in mind, the KM architecture should be seen as an enabler for KM and not a complete solution: a means and not an end in itself. As we analyze KM architecture design, try to relate it to your own company and see which elements seem to fit your case best.

COMPONENTS OF A KNOWLEDGE MANAGEMENT SYSTEM

A KM system, in its initial stages, can be broken into several subcomponents:

1. *Repositories:* Repositories hold explicated formal and informal knowledge, as well as the rules associated with them for accumulation, refining, managing, validating, maintaining, contextualizing, and distributing content.

2. *Collaborative platforms:* Collaborative platforms support distributed work and incorporate pointers, skills databases, expert locators, and informal communications channels.

3. *Networks:* Both digital and social networks support communications and conversation. Digital networks are hard networks such as intranets, extranets, shared spaces, and supply chain networks. Social networks are soft networks such as communities of practice, industry-wide coalitions, and trade associations. We do not discuss networks in depth here because we started with the assumption that your company already has network infrastructure in place.

4. *Culture:* Cultural enablers to encourage sharing and use of the above. This topic is covered in Chapter 13.

THE KNOWLEDGE REPOSITORY

An information repository differs from a knowledge repository in the sense that the context of the knowledge object needs to be stored, along with the content itself. A knowledge platform may consist of several repositories, each with a structure that is appropriate for the particular type of knowledge or content that is stored. Such repositories may be logically linked to form a cohesive, consolidated repository. The content of each will provide the context for interpreting the content of other repositories. However, they can be logically viewed in an integrated manner to provide a composite picture of what is contained within them, along with the associated context. Figure 10-2 illustrates how this association is possible.

Repositories such as these should record the following elements of knowledge content:

- *Declarative knowledge,* such as significant and meaningful concepts, categories, definitions, and assumptions

- *Procedural knowledge,* such as processes, sequences of events and activities, and actions

- *Causal knowledge,* such as rationale for decisions, rationale for rejected decisions or alternatives, eventual outcomes of activities, and associated informal pieces

- *Context* of the decision circumstances, assumptions, results of those assumptions, and informal knowledge, such as video clips, annotations, notes, and conversations

Well-integrated knowledge repositories do not require the user to know in which repository the knowledge resides. In other words, transparency, as perceived by the user, is highly desirable and very much possible. Other companies actually allow the creators or authors of a knowledge content unit to tag an expiration date to the content. This ensures that content that is no longer valid or that content that expires after a certain date is automatically relegated to an *expired* status. If you are making critical decisions based on available information, knowing what is old, outdated, incorrect, or invalid can help you avoid potentially expensive mistakes. Therefore, such tools partially automate maintenance and validation of explicated knowledge within the KM system.

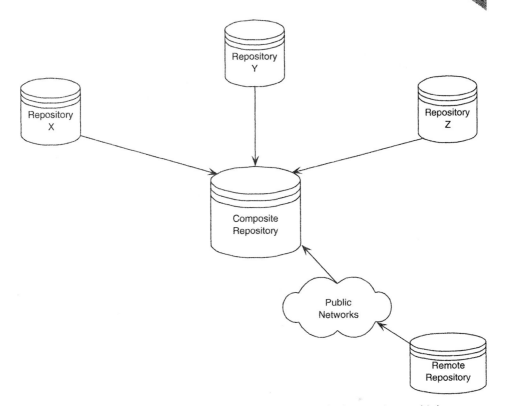

Figure 10-2   Building a composite knowledge repository by integrating multiple knowledge repositories.

The Perils of Integrative Repositories

Although integrative repositories might seem like a good idea to begin with, they can be the victims of their own success. As users begin to add content to multiple repositories, and if there is no clear-cut validation or expiration mechanism, a situation similar to an information overload problem can begin to emerge.

A good example is Accenture's *KnowledgeSpace*. With the extensive use of the Lotus Notes–based repositories, the extant content has grown into almost 3,000 repositories of Notes discussion databases. If this were one integrated repository, maintenance of these could have been managed better and more efficiently. However, centralized administration is not a viable option for a KM system, because content needs to be added and revalidated by the people who actually use it, not by a central "knowledge administrator." There are plenty of other examples of such problems that arise when companies fail to manage the explicated repository life cycle.

Managing content in repositories should not be limited to adding new content but should also include throwing out, if you will, old content. Obsolete content must be regularly deleted; less relevant content must be archived. What is left must be "defragmented" to eliminate redundancies, combine similar contributions, generalize content for smoother reuse, and possibly restructure classification mechanisms and tag handles. Companies that want their KM system to succeed must proactively maintain their knowledge repositories instead of waiting for signs of noticeable decline in quality. Reactivity is of little help if invalid or outright obsolete content influences a critical, irreversible decision.

Centralizing storage is a viable possibility and perhaps the way to go if you are building such a repository from scratch, but you must ensure that the power of content and context management ultimately lies in the hands of its users, not technology maintenance staff. This would also necessitate a capable, high-bandwidth communications network spanning the entire enterprise.

If you already have some repositories to begin with or if the platforms in use are too diverse to physically integrate cost-effectively, you might simply rely on a Web-based front end to integrate existing repositories while building new ones on a centralized base.

Content Centers

When you are trying to integrate multiple function- or department-specific repositories into one central repository, pay close attention to content centers that are typically good candidates for integration. A wide variety of relevant information is publicly available in electronic form. A sample checklist for competitive knowledge, provided below, is an example of a good starting point. Such checklists can be useful for making sure that existing and available sources are tapped.

1. What are others saying about your competition?
   - *Public:* case studies, articles, newspapers, consultants, employee search firms, and consumer groups
   - *Trade and professional organizations:* trade publications, industry news, customers, users, vendors, suppliers, and professional organizations
   - *Investors and government agencies:* securities analysts, industry data, government agencies, and litigation information sources

2. What are your competitors saying about themselves?
   - *Public:* advertising, promotional material, articles, employment advertisements, and press releases
   - *Trade and professional organizations:* licenses, manuals, patents, and trade shows
   - *Investors:* Annual reports, stock issues, and annual meetings

Open and Distributed

The use of open systems ensures that employees can obtain information they need from any place and at any time. Adherence to industry standards ranging from Hypertext Markup Language (HTML), Extended Markup Language (XML), Transmission Control Protocol/Internet Protocol (TCP/IP), and Open Database Connectivity (ODBC) means that you can implement the KM system quickly and easily extend and customize it in the future. Because content might be distributed across multiple platforms, devices, servers, and locations, the ability of the KM system to build on this characteristic is crucial.

In the Search of Meaning: Aggregation and Mining

As anyone who has used a search engine on the Internet can tell you, simple keyword searches often result in a meaninglessly large number of *hits*. To save users from this, a well-designed KM system should include a mechanism to cluster search results appropriately in different prespecified content categories, as discussed in the knowledge map discussed in Chapter 7. The user can drill down into a relevant category without having to learn the subtleties of complex query languages and syntaxes. If clustering is deployed, it should be done using multiple methods. One such method could be content categories; others could be source, date, author, department, and other company-specific taxonomies.

Although information retrieval tools and relevance rankings still fall short of the requirements, a number of commercial tools based on pattern recognition, agent-based retrieval, and thesauri *almost* make the mark. For example, if a user is looking for *KM consulting*, the system should be able to figure out what he or she *means,* rather than report all keyword hits. When using the term *KM consulting*, the user could potentially be looking for information on consultants, KM in consulting practices, reports by consulting companies, or knowledge and management consulting, among others. A simple but effective approach for a KM system, for example, could be to respond with all of these possible choices and ask the user which of those options she *means*. The user should have the ultimate choice of method.

From Skills Databases to Knowledge Directories

Companies such as Microsoft have traditionally relied on skills databases to locate subject matter experts, both within and outside their organizational bounds. Although such a mechanism is useful, it needs to be kept up to date. Due to this extra bit of effort required of users and a lack of incentive to put that effort in, skills databases in most companies have been notoriously unsuccessful. A knowledge directory takes the concept underlying skills databases one step further by linking people to their skills, experiences, know-how, insights, and contributions to discussions and debates within the KM system. Such a knowledge directory can infer what an employee knows, based on the knowledge that he or she shares and contributes. This automation also overcomes the overreliance on manual updates to keep skills databases current and arguably helps match employees with their interests and not just past work experience.

Automated Categorization

As we discussed in Chapter 7, each contribution of knowledge should contain relevant metadata or tags that associate it with the broad category under which it falls. Categorization need not be a manual procedure and often can be accomplished, in part, by knowing the nature of the contribution, such as its context, source, and originator.

Personalized Content Filtering and Push Delivery

Personalized content filtering refers to the process of categorizing items by their content: images, video, sound, text, etc. A user profile defines the content *types* that are relevant to each user. Different tools use different techniques to create such profiles. The tools range from a simple registration process (where a user indicates areas of interest) through the entire spectrum to determine profiling information by clustering bookmarks (which raises some privacy concerns) or browsing habits. These profiles can then be updated through automatic refinement and derivation by statistical learning algorithms that many commercial packages use. Marimba, Netscape, BackWeb, and PointCast offer products in this area.

The limitation of such tools is that most of them need high bandwidth that remote connections, such as dial-up telephone lines, lack. Broadband access might change this scenario to one more viable for the deployment of content push technologies. Much can be learned from Amazon.com (as well as CDNow.com) and the way it keeps track of its customers' interests, based on past purchases. Like anything else, the effectiveness of this mechanism depends on the level of accuracy with which the underlying assumptions work. Amazon.com, for example, assumes that you are buying books that you are interested in (which is often the case). When you visit that site again, it recommends new books that are of a similar nature or fall within a broad category as your previous purchases. When you browse books, the site often makes recommendations such as "Since you are interested in X you might also be interested in Y" or "Other people who bought books by XYZ also bought books by DEF."

A similar method can be emulated in the design of KM systems. Users who look for information on a certain topic can, for example, automatically have that topic added to their profiles.

Another excellent implementation that has a lot to teach is the Ingenta Reveal search service (www.ingenta.com) provided by UnCover Corporation. Although this site is primarily of interest to academics and researchers, its design has a number of useful tips for KM system push delivery design, in general. Subscribers can specify up to 25 searches for an annual fee. The service then automatically searches through new issues of 17,000 different research journals and reports matches to the user periodically by sending an e-mail message. A similar idea could be used in a KM system to report new relevant additions to the company's explicated repository. Variations from delivery time frames and criteria can be easily implemented. Each user can then receive pointers to new content added both to the explicated knowledge repository and to the more tacit sources, such as new employee skills and discussions.

THE COLLABORATIVE PLATFORM

The collaborative platform, along with the communications network services and hardware, provides the pipeline to enable the flow of explicated knowledge, its context, and the medium for conversations. Besides this, the collaborative platform provides a surrogate channel for defining, storing, moving, and linking digital objects, such as conversation threads that correspond to knowledge units. The collaborative platform enables the content of the KM system with a high degree of flexibility so that it is rendered meaningful, useful, and applicable across the many possible contexts of use. Most importantly, the collaborative platform empowers the user. The user can either search for content—the pull approach to content delivery—or subscribe to content, that is, have content pushed to him or her.

Collaborative Filtering

Sharing of knowledge through peer recommendations is a widely used mechanism for distributing information. Collaborative filtering can be built into a KM system by deploying one of two possible mechanisms:

1. *Active filtering:* Users manually define filters and pointers to interesting content and share them across their work group.

2. *Automated filtering:* Statistical algorithms make recommendations based on correlations between the user's personal preferences and content ratings. Content ratings can be generated either automatically (such as those produced by measuring the average time all readers spent on reading the item) or by manually assigning an average rating (aggregated across multiple readers).

Community-Centered Collaborative Filtering

Automated collaborative filtering might seem to be a reasonable approach, but it will not provide the expected benefits or gain a sufficiently high level of commitment from its users if it ignores the community that it is built for. Separation of automated filtering from personal relationships limits its usefulness to a greater degree than one might expect. The network of existing social relationships between employees can be a valuable basis for improving the collaborative filtering process. Although anonymity of contributors is essential, anonymous reviews tend to carry less weight than do signed ones. This is especially true in collaborative communities where people know colleagues by name and reputation. Reputation, trust, and reciprocity come into the picture of collaborative process enhancers when contributions are (optionally) signed.

Meta Knowledge

Meta knowledge implies *knowing what you know.* When a request for information is sent to a computer-based repository or database, the system has no way of determining whether the information is known or present in its memory. For example, if a traditional database is confronted with a request for information on two customers, only one of which exists in the database, the system will have to search exhaustively through all records before it can determine whether a record on the missing customer exists in the database. In the same vein, when a company is faced with an incoming glut of information, confusion often surrounds the determination of the presence or absence of that information. In other words, there is little that the company can do to figure out whether that information represents something truly new or unknown.

New information can often result in strategic redirection of work processes. However, if a company cannot determine this redirection fast enough, as is often the case, it might be too late to act or make relevant changes to work processes.

Creation of meta knowledge is often extremely context dependent and requires the use of pattern recognition or analogical reasoning. Being able to extract meta knowledge from knowledge is a necessary characteristic of an effective KM system.

Accommodating Multiple Degrees of Context

The effective use of IT tools requires that an organization share an interpretive context.[2] The higher the degree to which such a similar background, experience and context is shared by people working together, the more effective is the use of such technology enablers. If this were the requirement for effective sharing of knowledge through such a KM system, most companies should have a reason to panic. Most companies build on cross-functional teams—people with differing backgrounds, areas of expertise, organizational affiliations, and culture to solve problems, make decisions, and develop new products and services. In work groups where context is not well shared, knowledge tends to be primarily tacit in nature. Therefore, the significance of rich communications channels and a high degree of interactivity cannot be overemphasized. If loose social bonding exists between potential users of the system, ensure that rich communications (video conferencing, voice, multimedia support, and informal channels) are built into your KM system as an integrated feature, not as a separate add-on component. In other words, make sure that it is a design feature and not merely an afterthought.

Technology Choices

When choosing a technology or a vendor, it is vital to consider whether that technology or that vendor will be around for the entire life of the system. Many other questions come up, as well:

- Will the vendor's technology capture enough of the market to ensure that ancillary products and services remain available?
- Can the technology deliver the consistency that the application requires?
- Can the technology provide the quality that the market and your customers demand?

Companies have, time and again, floundered in making good decisions when the basis of those decisions, especially technology choice decisions, was solely existing market leadership of those choices. Even the IBM slogan "Nobody gets fired for choosing IBM," begins to fizzle here. The best-in-its-class technologies do no good if the provider loses the standards battle against a competitor, especially when standards differ significantly. The Web, though evolving, seems to be a technology that promises to be around for a while.

INTEGRATIVE AND INTERACTIVE KNOWLEDGE APPLICATIONS

At a high level, a KM application set can be viewed from two angles of functionality. The first view is the *integrative* view and the second is the *interactive* view. Both these viewpoints must be satisfied *simultaneously* to provide a requisite broad set of knowledge processing and management capabilities.

The integrative ability, as illustrated in Figure 10-3, supports the collation of distributed knowledge repositories containing explicated or explicitly captured content. The difference between explicated and explicitly captured content is a subtle yet important one. Explicated content is content that has been codified or formalized for storage in conventional repositories, such as databases. Examples include project time lines, presentation overheads, memos, and code documentation. Explicitly captured content could include a recording of a manager's talk or a product designer's vision of a product. This type of content might have been recorded in a system, but its context might not have been recorded or might be subject to multiple, incompatible interpretations.

Support for interactivity is required to allow the integration and possible capture, analysis, or even explication of tacit knowledge of the system's users (who are sometimes called *knowledge authors*).

We next discuss the integrative and interactive components, then we fit them into place in the overall architecture on which we are basing our blueprint.

INTEGRATIVE APPLICATION SUPPORT

The integrative component of a KM system helps users in critically evaluating, interpreting, and adapting knowledge to new contexts, domains, and applications. Integrative applications, as Figure 10-3 shows, support sequential flow of explicated knowledge in and out of the repository. The integrative application component provides a shared medium for knowledge exchange, where members of the user community (e.g., company employees and partners) share, see, and contribute their knowledge, task experiences, and views. The authors and consumers, therefore, directly interact with this application, rather than with each other. As Figure 10-3 clarifies, this component focuses on the explicit knowledge that can be put into and stored within the repository and not on the tacit knowledge that the authors and consumers possess. The authors are often also the consumers of knowledge, and their positions are often

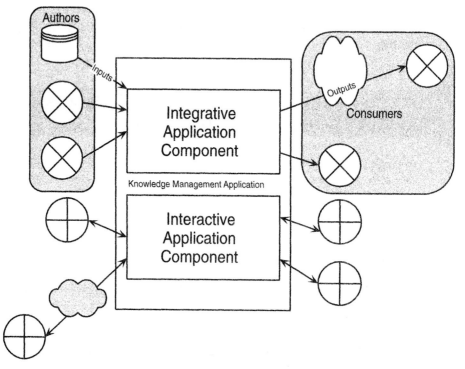

Figure 10-3 A KM application needs both integrative and interactive capabilities to provide the richness of media required for effective knowledge processing.

interchangeable, depending on their current activity and direction of knowledge flows they are engaged in. Integrative functionality in a KM system provides the key centripetal force that pulls together all explicated knowledge assets that a company has.

Knowledge Flow Models: Centripetality and Centrifugality

Let us compare that model with the concepts underlying electronic publishing. Electronic publishing follows a *centrifugal* model unlike KM's *centripetal* model. This conceptual difference is illustrated in Figure 10-4.

In electronic publishing, consumers rarely fall into the same community of practice or work group as the authors. Content, in that case, tends to be relatively stable, and further additions to it are made solely by the knowledge authors. The consumer accepts the content on an as-is basis and, in some cases, might be allowed and able to provide feedback to the knowledge author(s). In this sense, intranets have traditionally been closer to electronic publishing than to KM. Companies have posted reports, files, memos, and directories to intranets in a way that is quite similar to electronic content publishing.

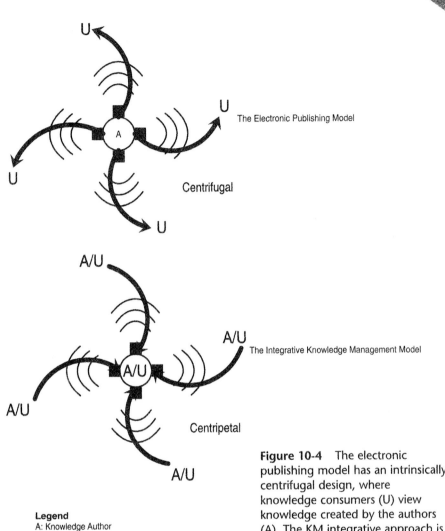

The Electronic Publishing Model

The Integrative Knowledge Management Model

Figure 10-4   The electronic publishing model has an intrinsically centrifugal design, where knowledge consumers (U) view knowledge created by the authors (A). The KM integrative approach is, in contrast, centripetal.

Legend
A: Knowledge Author
U: Knowledge Consumer
A/U: Author and Consumer

THE INTERACTIVE APPLICATION COMPONENT

The integrative components of a KM system primarily support codified and explicitly captured knowledge. However, as we have seen in earlier chapters, the tacit component must be effectively supported if effective knowledge transfer and sharing are to take place and the explicated content is to retain its proper context.

The interactive component, therefore, focuses on enabling interaction among people and providing a basic channel for sharing tacit knowledge. In such a component, building or enhancing the repository is not the primary focus. Development of content within the repository is a (secondary) by-product of the collaborative work that it enables.

Such applications can vary from relatively structured to totally unstructured, depending on the levels of expertise and similarities between the authors and consumers (acting interchangeably). Toward the more structured types of deployments are Web-based forums and specialized discussion groups. Such forums consist of the same group of participants comprising the set of content authors who are also the consumers (see the interactions in the illustrated in Figure 10-5). Moving toward the somewhat totally unstructured type application

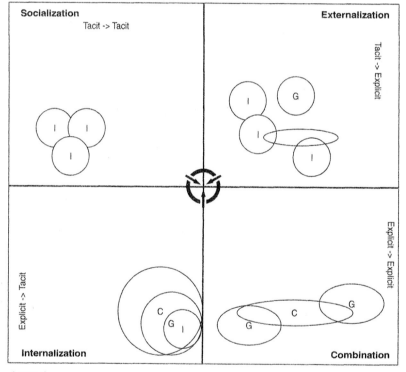

Legend
C: Company's Knowledge
G: Group or Team Knowledge
I: Individual Employee's Knowledge
Based on Nonaka , Reinmoeller , et al. (1998). The ART of Knowledge: Systems to Capitalize on Market Knowledge, *European Management Journal* 16(6), 673-684.

Figure 10-5 Rich media forums that run through high-bandwidth networks often tend to be the most complex knowledge interaction applications, because they span the entire knowledge cycle.

deployments are video conferencing tools and like technologies. Technology elements such as electronic whiteboards fall some where in between. Forums, including live text/video-based ones, are the most complex types of applications because of their high level of interactivity and their inherent characteristic of spanning the entire tacit and explicit knowledge processing cycle.

As interaction complexity rises, your challenge is to make the interactive KM components of a system more social, cognitive, and behavioral, and less technical in focus. We must, therefore, create a flexible KM system blueprint and customize it to make room for future changes.

THE FIT INTO OVERALL ARCHITECTURE

To see how the integrative and interactive components fit into our architecture, let us review the seven layers that were discussed in Chapter 7 (see Figure 10-6) before looking deeper.

Each layer is described in detail in Chapters 11 and 12, and we are already acquainted with the first and third layers (see Chapter 7). For now, let's examine how this architecture meets the requirements set forth in the preceding sections of this chapter.

Figure 10-7 shows the generic system architecture. The KM system deployment initiative assumes that you already have a corporate network in place. The KM applications will go one layer above this existing architecture. The shaded components in Figure 10-7 indicate the components of the system architecture that must be modified to build a KM system.

The middleware architecture is modified to incorporate applications that otherwise might not talk to each other in a tightly integrated system. The repository architecture includes all existing databases.

Figure 10-8 shows how the dimensions of the overall system architecture can be viewed for modification.

As the integrative component of a KM system comes into play, the overall effect on the existing system components is visible in the level of integration that is provided. In this case, the clients can be located anywhere and can connect to the enterprise through a universally initiated network connection (see Figure 10-9). The effects of the interactive components are farther reaching.

BUILD OR BUY?

If you run a for-profit business, in most likelihood, you have both time and resource constraints under which you are expected to run the show. Building a KM system can often be the best, albeit more expensive, way to go, but customizing an off-the-shelf system is usually a faster alternative. When you begin development, your choices are:

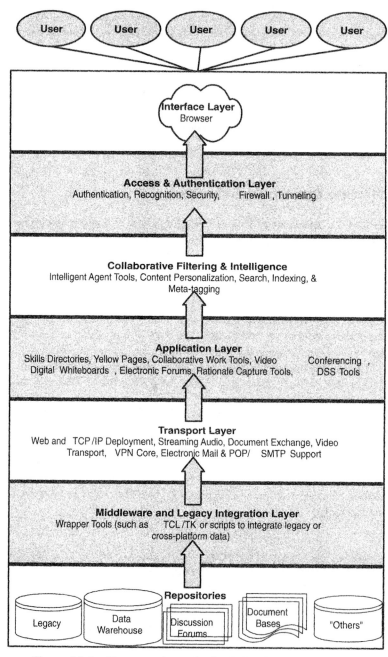

Figure 10-6   The seven layers in the KM architecture revisited.

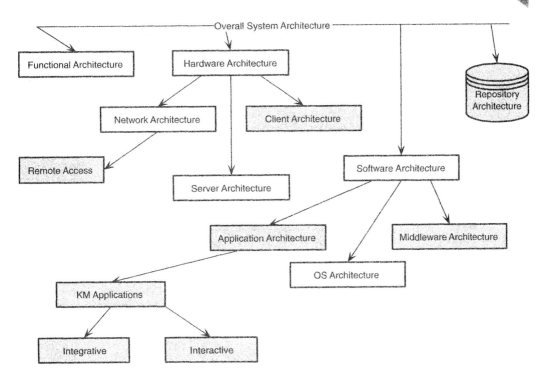

Figure 10-7   Architectural components (shown shaded) to be modified or expanded to integrate the KM system with the existing architecture.

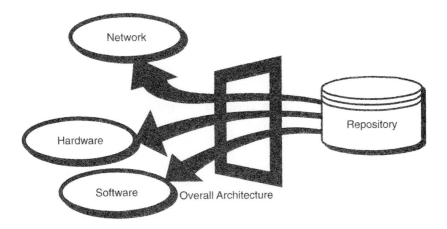

Figure 10-8 Interactions between the architectural components of the overall system architecture.

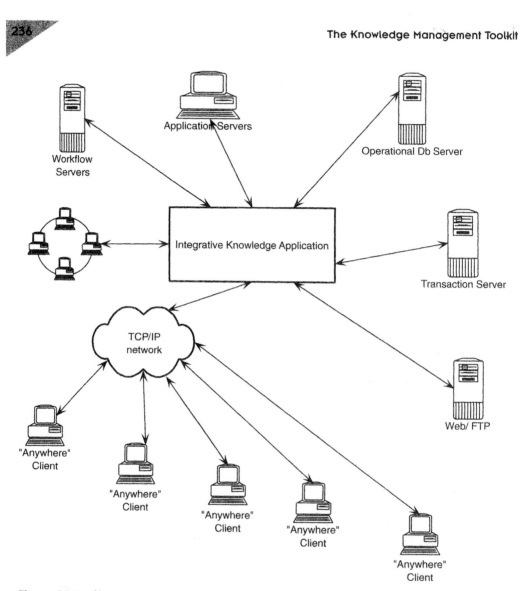

Figure 10-9 The composite enterprise, as viewed after the integrative KM applications are introduced.

- To build a system in-house, using team members from the internal IT department and the end-user community of knowledge workers for whom the system is being built
- To add external consultants to strengthen the weaker expertise areas for the option described above
- To develop the system from scratch (not recommended)

- To buy an off-the-shelf, shrink-wrapped solution and customize it
- To buy an off-the-shelf solution sold by a consulting group and modify it to meet your needs
- To buy and combine an off-the-shelf set of applications and customize it to fit your needs
- To build in part and buy in part
- A combination of the above approaches

Your decision will be influenced by the time, resources, and money at your disposal. The size of the end-user group will also influence the make-or-buy decision. If you are a small company with under a hundred employees, financial considerations might force you to take the off-the-shelf option. However, if there is serious support for the project right from the beginning or if you are a larger company, you should consider doing at least a part of the development in-house and plugging in the rest of the components. With powerful Web development tools that are now available, the development of the intranet-based front end need not be a pain. Table 10-1 compares the options that are available.

PERFORMANCE AND SCALABILITY

Scalability refers to the ability of the KM system to support an increasing number of users and a higher load of transactions. It is essential that a system be scalable well beyond the original level if the number of users is expected to grow as system use becomes more prevalent. This is especially true if you decide to build a KM system from off-the-shelf components. A system that performs well within a work group of limited size might not perform well when it is extended to an enterprise-wide level. An obvious but frequently ignored issue, scalability can make the KM system a victim of its own success if it comes in as an afterthought.

Scalability also affects performance of the system at later stages. Keep the following set of key performance-related factors in mind when you are deciding on the design of a KM system:

1. *Plan and account for additional time delays as usage grows.* Time delays for retrieval of information from a message or transaction database must be kept to a minimum. As the number of users grows, failure on this front might result in unacceptable delays in responses to even the simplest queries.

2. *Keep repository update times in perspective.* Time for updates and inserts of new records into the database or repository must be kept to a minimum.

3. *Keep time delays for navigating between different parts of the interface to a minimum.* For example, it should *not* take a minute for dialog boxes to reappear when a user switches from a messaging application to a bulletin board application. Two to three seconds, as a rule of thumb, is a longest acceptable delay for local applications.

Table 10-1 Making the Build-or-Buy Decision

Option	Upfront Cost	Quality of Solution	Time to Develop	Flexibility	Customizability	Notes
Customized in-house development	High	Depends	High	High	High	Quality can vary. Depends on the expertise available within the company.
Customized in-house development with consulting support	High	Depends; better than above	Medium	High	High	Quality can vary. The skills of the consultant can influence the project. Costs will be higher. There is a risk that the same consultant may develop a similar system for a competitor. Contractual agreements are needed to prevent this.
Customized solution provided by a consulting company	Medium	Average	Low	Medium	Medium	Your competitors might already have the same systems!
Development by the end users themselves	Usually low	Usually low	Depends	High	High	Not recommended.
Standard off-the-shelf and out-of-the-box solution	Low	High	Zero	Low	Low	The only time investment required is the installation time.
Customized off-the-shelf solution	Medium	High	Low	Medium to low	Medium	This should be among your first set of choices.
Off-the-shelf components integrated through an intranet	Low	High	Low	Extremely High	Extremely high	This should be your first choice!

USER INTERFACE DESIGN CONSIDERATIONS

Several design features of the user interface need to be considered. Without an effective user interface, even the best KM system is bound to fail.

- *Functionality:* The idea behind a user interface is to allow users to accomplish their tasks intuitively, effectively, *and without frustration* over the system's usability. The system needs to take the end user's needs and requirements into consideration.

- *Consistency:* Systems that have a consistent interface are often considered easier to use. There should be consistency across all parts of the KM system in the ways in which information is presented, accessed, and used.

- *Visual clarity:* Users need to be able to find information that they need easily. Present all information that relates to the user's task on one screen if possible and hide unrelated information or controls by default. Have sufficient white space on the screen and use lowercase text for textually dense portions of the interface. This not only makes the text easier to read but also decreases search time. Serif fonts look good on paper, but they are more difficult to read on a screen. Use a sans serif font if you use a small point size for screen text. Use hyperlinks to provide further information on a text string to avoid excessive cluttering on a screen. Avoid excessive jargon or abbreviations that can change meaning from one user to another.

- *Navigation and control:* The way in which information is structured has a clear impact on its accessibility. A site map can be *very* useful with a browser-based front end. If there are multiple tools within the KM system, the user should be able to tell which tool he or she is using at a given moment. Avoid using multiple modes of operation, and have one shared interface to all underlying applications, such as messaging, document repository navigation, and discussion forums. Audible cues can be helpful, as long as they are not overused or distracting.

- *Relevance:* Display only the information relevant to the user's task. This might be a tricky scheme to implement, because there will be as many preferences as there are users, so allow users to customize their interface to a certain degree.

- *Feedback:* The system's users should receive feedback from the system so that they know what the system is doing and what is expected (from either the system or the user) next. Audible cues and alerts can be useful, as long as they are not overly intrusive.

Figure 10-10 summarizes these interface design considerations.

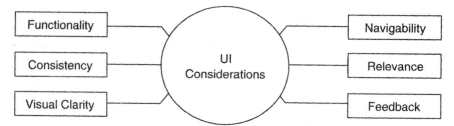

Figure 10-10   User interface considerations.

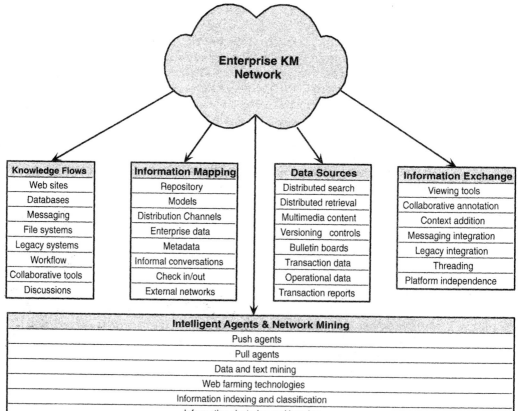

Figure 10-11   A network-oriented view of the KM system.

A NETWORK VIEW OF THE KM ARCHITECTURE

You should also take the time to consider the KM system from a network design perspective. The term *network* should not be confused with the idiosyncratic communications network in the generic sense. An alternative view of the KM system architecture described in Figure 10-6 is provided in Figure 10-11.[3]

The network constitutes both the technological network and the underlying social and organizational network in which the technology operates. As Figure 10-11 shows, the entire KM system can be viewed as a networked whole, comprising data sources, information exchange-enabling networks, knowledge flow channels, static and mobile intelligent agents, and integrative technologies that bind them all together.

Nevertheless, the technical aspects of the knowledge network design should be kept in focus. Optimize network usage by paying close attention to the implementation of technologies that support compression (for large files, teleconferencing, and voice), byte-level differential updating (for document and content versioning/updates), and multithreaded communications (for discussion groups and Web forums). However, those are still just the technical aspects of the design.

Although this view can be used for planning the underlying network requirements, it is too simplistic to base your company's KM architecture on. However, the presence of collaborative tools in almost every element of this knowledge network hierarchy reinforces the importance of enabling rich collaboration through the system, whereby users can add contextual information to the artifacts and elements in the KM system. Examples of such features include the ability to add notes, markings, annotations, and marginal notes on documents, and the ability to track and maintain multiple versions of documents as they are collaboratively exchanged. As business needs evolve, the components within this network might change, but the overall structure of the network should remain relatively stable; it is an indicator of the stability of the infrastructure itself.

If we classified the KM system within the hierarchy of the IT infrastructure, it should broadly fall under the category of shared IT applications and services, as shown in Figure 10-12. These are applications and infrastructural elements that remain relatively stable over time, even as the deployed applications evolve.

FUTURE-PROOFING THE KNOWLEDGE MANAGEMENT SYSTEM

Collaborative KM systems should be able to grow and adapt to changing business needs. Keep the following tips in mind while making the key design decisions on your company's KM system.

1. *Accept the inevitability of change.* One thing companies can count on is that technology will change.[4] What might be state of the art today might be outdated long before you

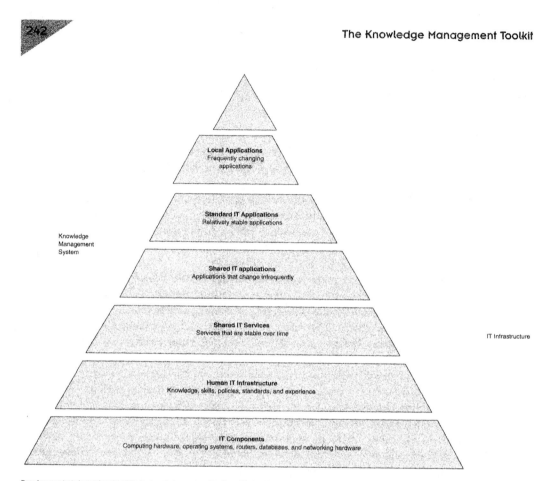

Knowledge
Management
System

Local Applications
Frequently changing
applications

Standard IT Applications
Relatively stable applications

Shared IT applications
Applications that change infrequently

Shared IT Services
Services that are stable over time

IT Infrastructure

Human IT Infrastructure
Knowledge, skills, policies, standards, and experience

IT Components
Computing hardware, operating systems, routers, databases, and networking hardware

Based on an adapted extension of the infrastructure design suggested by Peter Weill and Marianne Broadbent in *Leveraging the New Infrastructure: How Market Leaders Capitalize on Information Technology*, Harvard Business School Press, Boston, Massachusetts, (1998), page 86.

Figure 10-12   The KM system falls in the infrastructural portion of the information technology architecture.

recoup your investment. The standards underlying Internet-based systems inherently have a high degree of modularity and extensibility. Use the Internet/intranet approach where feasible. That way, your KM system will still be in business if the vendor that supplies the proprietary technology you use goes out of business.[a]

---

[a]This approach also allows smooth integration with outside systems that might not be using the same software as you. Use object-oriented techniques for components that you decide to build in-house. First, doing so allows a certain degree of flexibility that might be needed to adapt the system to changes in business structure and processes. Second, the techniques enable reuse of some of the components and processes in other implementations. In addition to object orientation, use a results-driven incremental deployment process to expand the KM system. Chapter 12 describes the RDI methodology.

BUILDING CYC: HAL'S LEGACY OR A SHATTERED DREAM?

Cycorp, Inc., based in Austin, Texas, is the leading supplier of formalized common sense tools. Its Cyc software has been under development since 1984 by artificial intelligence pioneer Doug Lenat. The Cyc product family comprises an immense multicontextual knowledge base, an efficient inference engine, a set of interface tools, and a number of special-purpose application modules running on UNIX, Windows NT, and other platforms. The knowledge base is built on a core of over one million hand-entered assertions or rules designed to capture a large portion of what we normally consider consensus knowledge about the world.

The project originally began with Microcomputer Corporation's (MCC) ambition to create an artificial intelligence tool with general knowledge at the level of an average human being. The idea was to create a program, Cyc, with common sense (see www.cyc.com). The team would "prime the knowledge pump" by handcrafting and spoon-feeding Cyc with a couple of million important facts and rules of thumb. The goal was to give Cyc enough knowledge by 1995 to enable it to learn more by means of natural language conversations and reading, and by 2000, to have it learning on its own by automated-discovery methods guided by minitheories of the real world. After millions of dollars and over 10 years of work by dozens of Ph.D.s, the Cyc project only brought us to the realization that even creating common sense (not intelligence) equaling that of an average human being was close to impossible. Things that you and I simply "know" are things that Cyc had to be taught through complex rules—millions of them. For example, Cyc had to be taught that:

- Once people die, they stop buying things.
- Trees are usually outdoors.
- Glasses containing liquids should be carried right side up.

Details on what is considered one of the most ambitious projects ever carried out by the artificial intelligence community can be found on the spin-off company's Web site at www.cyc.com; it's worth a look. Although the dream of artificial intelligence has not been realized, Cyc has found some interesting applications in the business world. The moral: Tacit knowledge is occasionally best left tacit. Don't get too caught up trying to convert all tacit knowledge into explicit knowledge: It's neither possible nor feasible—even with unlimited resources, time, and money (as Cyc demonstrates). Your blueprint should, therefore, reflect the scope of the KM system that you are trying to build.

2. *Business drivers:* Commercial knowledge is very close in concept to what the French call *bricolage:* the provisional construction of a messy array of rules, tools, heuristics, and guidelines that produce according to the expertise and sensitivity of the *craftsman,* not the empirical accuracy of the rules, tools, and guidelines. This notion implies that the people who use a KM system are the ones who create value out of it or collusively decide to let it die. Focusing on the properties of technology, independent of its identified

needs, is a recipe for failure. Technology design must be driven by business objectives, problems, and opportunities. In other words, keep the design of your KM system *mission focused.*

3. *Common standards:* Stick to standards that have the highest level of industry support. Using a vanilla intranet-based design is a better choice than using a proprietary technology, such as Lotus Notes. This practice also keeps costs down in the long run. It also enables better integration of work tools and prevents the creation of useless *islands of information and technology.*

4. *Users:* Keep your users on the forefront. Make sure that users are actively involved not only in the future refinements of the system, but also in the initial design and prototyping stages. Failure to gain their buy-in can potentially lead to the lack of acceptance and subsequent failure of your entire endeavor.[6]

5. *Intuitive:* Make the KM system intuitive to use. If you have ever tried to reprogram your number header on a personal fax machine and had no clue where to begin, you can empathize with the users who *could* feel the same way when a system is not intuitive to use.[7,]

6. *Metrics and performance:* Measure performance and actively incorporate feedback that you get from your users.

7. *Legacy integration:* Bias your technology choices in favor of software components that integrate well with your company's legacy systems. Even the most difficult integration processes can be accomplished with commercially available tools, such as KQML (Knowledge Query Markup Language) and similar scripting languages.

LESSONS LEARNED

A KM system built without a well-defined architecture will lead only to chaos at later stages. Make sure that the architecture is clearly defined, because this part of the infrastructure can be very expensive to fix at a later stage. Keep in mind these points:

- *Understand the architectural components of the KM system.* Pay close attention to integrative repositories, content centers, knowledge aggregation and mining tools, the collaborative platform, knowledge directories, the user interface options, push delivery mechanisms, and integrative elements.

- *Design for both interactive and integrative content aggregation.* Both these needs must be met simultaneously.

- *Optimize for performance, scalability, and flexibility.* Make sure that your KM system works as well for 600 people as it does for 60.

- *Plan for interoperability.* Plan for high levels of interoperability with existing protocols and implementations.

- *Decide whether to build or buy.* One option is not necessarily better than the other; examine the pros and cons of each option.

- *Pay attention to the user interface and its design.* The user interface provides an excellent opportunity for ensuring buy-in by the user community. A user interface that is built in synchrony with the user community help creates a perception that the KM system is an asset and not a liability that needs to be side-stepped

- *Position and scope the KM system.* In some cases, it is not only difficult, but also foolhardy to try explicating tacit knowledge that your employees possess. Scope the system to support only those categories of knowledge that have the potential for maximizing opportunity and returns.

- *Future-proof your KM system.* Take substantive steps to ensure that your KM system does not become obsolete as technologies or business environments evolve. If the system is well future-proofed, changes should affect only the content in your KM system, not its underlying architecture.

Now, with our blueprint for your KM system, let us proceed to the seventh step in the KM road map: developing the actual system.

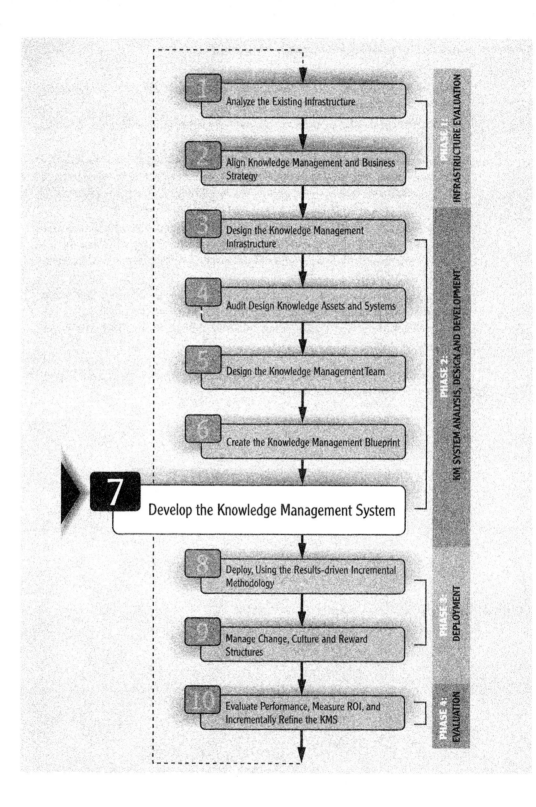

1. Analyze the Existing Infrastructure

2. Align Knowledge Management and Business Strategy

PHASE 1: INFRASTRUCTURE EVALUATION

3. Design the Knowledge Management Infrastructure

4. Audit Design Knowledge Assets and Systems

5. Design the Knowledge Management Team

6. Create the Knowledge Management Blueprint

PHASE 2: KM SYSTEM ANALYSIS, DESIGN AND DEVELOPMENT

7. Develop the Knowledge Management System

8. Deploy, Using the Results-driven Incremental Methodology

9. Manage Change, Culture and Reward Structures

PHASE 3: DEPLOYMENT

10. Evaluate Performance, Measure ROI, and Incrementally Refine the KMS

PHASE 4: EVALUATION

CHAPTER 11
DEVELOPING THE KNOWLEDGE MANAGEMENT SYSTEM

IN THIS CHAPTER

- ✔ Define the capabilities of each layer of the KM system architecture in the context of your company.
- ✔ Create platform independence, leverage the intranet, enable universal authorship, and optimize video.
- ✔ Develop the access and authentication layer: secure data, control access, and distribute control.
- ✔ Develop the collaborative filtering and intelligence layer.
- ✔ Develop and integrate the application layer with the intelligence layer and the transport layer.
- ✔ Leverage the extant transport layer.
- ✔ Develop the middleware and legacy integration layers
- ✔ Integrate and enhance the repository layer.
- ✔ Shift from a client/server to agent computing orientation.

NOW, IF ESTIMATES MADE BEFORE THE BATTLE INDICATE VICTORY, IT IS BECAUSE CAREFUL CALCULATIONS SHOW THAT YOUR CONDITIONS ARE MORE FAVORABLE THAN THOSE OF YOUR ENEMY; IF THEY INDICATE DEFEAT, IT IS BECAUSE CAREFUL CALCULATIONS SHOW THAT FAVORABLE CONDITIONS FOR BATTLE ARE FEWER. WITH MORE CAREFUL CALCULATIONS, ONE CAN WIN; WITH LESS, ONE CANNOT. HOW MUCH LESS CHANCE OF VICTORY HAS ONE WHO MAKES NO CALCULATIONS AT ALL!
—SUN TZU IN *THE ART OF WAR*

Once you have created a blueprint for your KM system, the next step, Step 7, is that of actually putting together a working version of the system. Development of the system begins by defining the seven layers of the KM architecture. Of the many possible interface choices, leveraging the existing intranet is the most feasible and effective approach. In this chapter, we see how to convert the intranet to the front end for your KM system.

We look at the layers from these points of view:

- Interface layer—incorporating platform independence, optimizing content, and enabling universal authorship
- Access and authentication layer—providing a firewall for internal content
- Collaboration layer
- Application, transport, and repository layers—forming a nodding acquaintance with these three layers
- Middleware and legacy integration layers—connecting the KM system to both true legacy data and recent legacy data repositories and databases

We also see how to take advantage of the hardware built around these standards.

THE BUILDING BLOCKS: SEVEN LAYERS

Let's go back to the KM system architecture introduced in Chapter 10 and see how the seven layers are actually built (see Figure 11-1). The seven layers within the KM system architecture provide a guideline for the choice of technology components that enable effective sharing of knowledge across a distributed enterprise. What we have analyzed up to now is the functionality provided by each of these layers. Let us now see how a KM system can actually be built along each layer.

1. Interface layer
2. Access and authentication layer
3. Collaborative filtering and intelligence layer
4. Application layer
5. Transport layer
6. Middleware and legacy integration layer
7. Repository layer

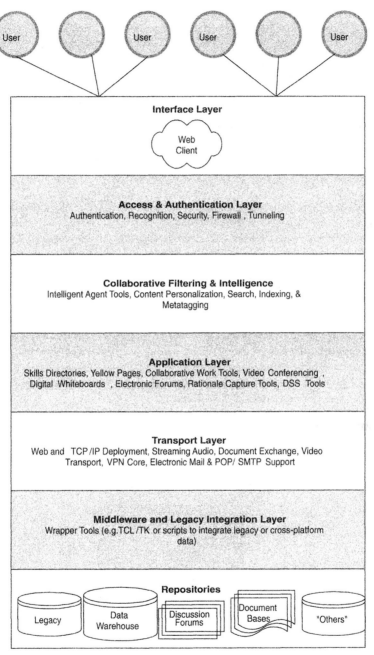

Figure 11-1   The seven layers of the KM system architecture.

THE INTERFACE LAYER

The top layer moves information in and out of the KM system. When this information is relevant, timely, and actionable, it represents knowledge. The top layer, the interface layer, connects to the people who use this IT infrastructure to create, explicate, use, retrieve, and share knowledge.

CHANNELS FOR TACIT AND EXPLICIT KNOWLEDGE

The interface layer is the primary point of contact between the users and KM system content. Technology best supports explicit knowledge; we considered how the inclusion of informal communications channels and a rich medium was critical to the success of a KM system. The interface layer must provide a channel for tacit as well as explicit knowledge flow.

The essential step in tacit knowledge transfer between people is the conversion of tacit knowledge to information and back to tacit knowledge, as Figure 11-2 illustrates.

Whether this transfer happens through formal processes, such as knowledge capture in databases, or through informal mechanisms, such as conversations, this intermediate step is almost always involved. The implication of this intermediacy is that knowledge *can* be transferred through something as complex as an intranet or a discussion database, or through something as straightforward and commonplace as a telephone, fax, or a face-to-face conversation. Technology is not a precursor to knowledge exchange but an enabler in situations that do not allow for face-to-face transfer of knowledge.

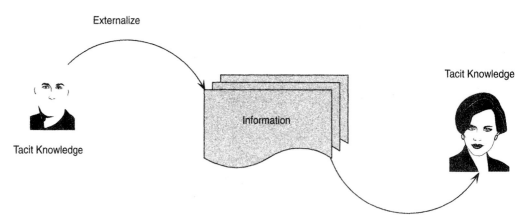

Figure 11-2   Knowledge transfer involves information as an intermediate state.

Contextual Expression at the Interface

The artificial intelligence (AI) community spent years trying to figure out ways to encapsulate knowledge in a repository. The efforts of the AI research community met with failure to accomplish this even with common-sensical knowledge but were not entirely in vain: All the effort that the AI community expended over the past 50 years has brought us to the realization that human intelligence and knowledge cannot be fully codified. With that in mind, let's realize that a KM system should not seek to eliminate the need for direct human interaction. There is a lot of context (such as the tone of conversation or facial expressions) that cannot be represented well in any type of knowledge base or repository.

Electronic mail, a component of communications technology on which most of us overly rely, provides a good case in point: How many of your e-mail messages has some recipient misunderstood or misinterpreted because of your inability to add context or tone? As we saw in Chapter 5, technology helps KM primarily in two respects: storage and communication. Although storage includes databases, repositories, etc., it does not limit communications technology to the connections between such databases. The catch phrase is *rich communications*— communications that can allow people to converse almost as well as they would if they were talking face to face. What does that bring to mind? Video conferencing, chat, live audio applications, the telephone, its Internet spin-offs, and other informal interaction mechanisms.

As Figure 11-3 shows, tacit knowledge can be transferred by purely explicit mechanisms through possible explication; by purely informal mechanisms, such as conversations; or by technological enablers, such as electronic whiteboards that fall somewhere in between these two extremes.[1]

The interface layer is the layer at which users of the KM system interact with the system. The interface layer provides a universal mechanism for accessing all the layers below it. By choosing the Hypertext Transfer Protocol (HTTP) standard underlying the Web, users can

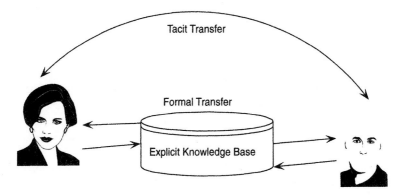

Figure 11-3   Transfer of knowledge can be through informal or formal channels.

access data formats independently of the platform on which data resides. A typical organization has Windows PCs, Macintoshes, Linux, and UNIX machines that store content that is appropriate to the respective platforms. Trying to integrate all this existing content on one single platform would not only be prohibitively expensive but would also require changing—often forcing users to change the environment in which they work. Besides, legacy data that exists on such platforms is extremely difficult to move because of the (often) proprietary mechanisms used to store it.

Using a Web browser as the final interface allows these islands of information to be connected at an external level. Legacy data on UNIX machines can, for example, be read, written, and edited through a Web browser, using scripting languages such as Tool Command Language/Toolkit (TCL/TK) and Knowledge Query Markup Language (KQML) to create *wrappers*.

PLATFORM INDEPENDENCE

The use of a Web browser as a client also enables universal access to the relevant portion of the KM system from any location or computer terminal connected to the Web.[2] Although using an application through a Web browser can be painstakingly slow if the application itself is accessed through a slow dial-up connection, most companies considering KM are expected to have high-speed networks already in place.

Content can further be optimized to move through low-bandwidth networks with the use of cache memory (which is already a part of most Internet browsers) on the client and server side, by minimizing the depth/resolution of graphics, and by using mobile applications written in Java. However, a slow network will impede smooth functioning of the system if multimedia content, such as images, video, and sound, are routinely transmitted over such networks.

LEARNING FROM INTRANETS

All basic ideas underlying the design of an intranet front end apply well to this layer. To be useful, an intranet site must organize information and assemble it in a consistent, logical, and systematic manner. With respect to a KM system, an intranet front end must allow users to get to the information that they need in a painless and fast manner. What you definitely do not want is users lingering over their browsers in frustration. Frustration usually results from the inability to find exactly the information that is needed (and information that probably exists) in real time. This failure relegates that information back to its default status of information that simply exists, rather than elevating it to the status of usable knowledge.

OPTIMIZING VIDEO CONTENT

Many browser plug-ins counter the speed limitations of networks by incorporating a feature called *fast start*. This technique applies to video clips that are stored as a part of aggregated content and allow a video clip to start playing before the clip is fully downloaded. For most video content that is involved in a knowledge-sharing application, video quality is not the primary concern; the concern is the system's ability to deliver video content in real time in the face of network bottlenecks and speed limitations.

The catch is that a clip plays in real time only if the data rate that the network connection can handle either equals or exceeds the movie's data rate. Many Hypertext Markup Language (HTML) editors enable an autoplay function through an HTML tag by default to start playing a clip as soon as it is accessed. This might not be a desirable setting in most intranets; disable it to provide additional control to the end user who wants to bypass the video clip to get to some other piece of linearly arranged information.

The essential point to keep in mind while configuring a server for video delivery is to optimize the video clip file itself for existing network bandwidth. Calculate the data rate considering using the worst-case scenario with a sufficient number of users simultaneously connected to the available channel.

For example, if a typical channel available on an office network has a bandwidth of 100 Mbps and 15 users are connected to that channel, it will be unwise to estimate that streaming video content needs to be optimized for a channel capacity of 100 Mbps. On the other hand, it is unlikely that all users will be sharing an equivalent portion of the available bandwidth at a given time. The correct answer for the channel capacity needed for optimizing video content and resolution lies somewhere in between.

A safe assumption to make as a starting point would be to optimize content for 60 percent of the available bandwidth, then realign it based on actual usage patterns. In any case, it is better to underestimate available bandwidth than to shoot yourself in the foot by overestimating it.

UNIVERSAL AUTHORSHIP

Another benefit of using a Web-based front end is that users working on different platforms can add content to the overall repository, irrespective of their platform.[3]

A LIVE WALKTHROUGH: URBAN MOTORS

See the Urban Motors KM system deployment on the companion CD-ROM. Both a case file (PDF) and a working version of the system are presented on the CD-ROM.

THE ACCESS AND AUTHENTICATION LAYER

The layer immediately below the interface layer is the access and authentication layer. This is the layer that authenticates valid users. Security and restricted access for the remaining layers are maintained at this level. The strength of security provided by this layer has increased, largely because of the increase in company intranets and the resulting rise in vulnerabilities.

Companies are increasingly adopting intranets and extranets to connect workers both within and beyond their organizational boundaries. Intranets and extranets are hybrid information systems built on open Internet protocols, such as HTTP, Transmission Control Protocol/Internet Protocol (TCP/IP), and related Web technologies. They enable business partners to share resources efficiently to accomplish common goals, such as information exchange, collaboration, invoicing, electronic funds transfer, supply chain management, document exchange, and communication. The architecture of extranets is derived from and often integrates both intranets and corporate Web sites.

Extranets not only provide the privacy and security of intranets (which are designed exclusively for internal usage) but also permit restricted access for external users via Internet connections or virtual private networks (VPNs). The majority of extranet development uses the Internet as an access mechanism, due to its low usage cost. Technologies are interchangeable because they use standard Internet protocols. This means the extranet is platform independent and not bound by proprietary protocols or technologies. Tools and services that use open protocols can be introduced with relative ease as features and functionality necessitate change. Because an extranet uses the Internet, data that moves across it goes over the open and exposed information superhighway. Security then becomes a primary concern. This book will not go into depth on security implementation, but there are many books on the subject of Web security.[4]

Some of the issues that must be addressed are:

- *Access privileges*: Assign rights to permit different levels of access to data such as read-only, write, edit, and delete capabilities.
- *Firewalls:* Construct a firewall between the extranet and Internet. Thoroughly test the firewall by mock attacks.
- *Backups:* Create backups, staging areas, and mirror sites. Duplicate information so that, should disaster strike, such as hardware failures, security violations, or undetected viruses, the network and its data can be quickly reconstructed. Online backup services are extremely cost-effective and offer unprecedented safety.

VIRTUAL PRIVATE NETWORKS

The Internet is, in many respects, similar to the interstate highway system. Just as some interstates require the payment of a toll for entry, the Internet requires an online Internet service provider (ISP) for access. However, the ride itself is free.

Penetration of the Internet in most business networks provides multitudinous opportunities to eliminate the expense and gain the speed of high-speed private lines by means of VPN technology. VPNs eliminate the need for fixed point-to-point communication lines. Instead, they operate within a public network, such as the Internet, but with security that is as strong as that of more expensive, leased private lines. Various mechanisms allow this operation; most rely on tunneling that works by running one protocol inside another—in effect, creating a private tunnel. By running the network protocol inside the Internet TCP/IP protocol, proprietary protocol networks connect and communicate over the Internet.

STANDARDS AND PROTOCOLS FOR EXPANSIVE NETWORKS

Many of the cost savings of extranets come from their reliance on nonproprietary solutions for cross-platform, Internet-based applications. Some of the standards that have been put forth and endorsed at the industry level include:

- *LDAP:* Lightweight directory access protocol is a format to store contact and network resource information, register Web clients and application servers, and store certificates in a directory.
- *PPTP:* Point-to-point tunneling protocol is an extension of the Internet point-to-point protocol used in everyday Internet communications. PPTP permits network protocols to be encrypted inside the Internet TCP/IP protocol so that proprietary protocol networks can connect and communicate over the Internet.
- *S/MIME:* Secure Multipurpose Internet Mail Extensions is a standard that lets users send secure e-mail messages using certificate-based encryption and authentication. S/MIME is one part of the RSA Labs Public Key Cryptographic Standard framework. X.509 Certificates is a specification for electronic credentials used for strong authentication and encryption. These certificates provide a secure container of validated and digitally signed information. Operation of digital certificates can be limited to within an intranet or between enterprises with public certificates.
- *vCARD:* Virtual Card is a format for storing and presenting contact or registration information.
- *Signed Objects:* Signed Objects is a format for automating trusted software and document distribution.

BIOMETRICS AND OTHER FORMS OF AUTHENTICATION

Biometrics, voice recognition, and fingerprint recognition are promising technologies that will allow users of a company or enterprise-wide network to get into the system in a rather transparent manner.

For companies that already have an adequate network in place, the access and authentication layer of a KM system does not require extensive work. Most of the components needed here will either already be in place or can easily and inexpensively be put in by the computing support staff.

THE COLLABORATIVE FILTERING AND INTELLIGENCE LAYER

The collaborative filtering and intelligence layer is the one that constitutes intelligence within a KM system. The process of adding tags and metatags to knowledge elements (units of actionable information), either through automated mechanisms or manual procedures, is done at this level. Intelligent agents are perhaps the best thing to happen to artificial intelligence in terms of viable applications to the Web. Collaborative filtering and business intelligence tools are built into this layer and, as we see later, they build very heavily on agent technology.

FROM STATIC TO DYNAMIC STRUCTURES

Figure 11-4 shows how information on the Web is structured. Each document is connected to other documents through hyperlinks. These links are statically contained in each document and refer to other documents, video files, and sound files, by Uniform Resource Locators (URLs). Activating a hyperlink means jumping from one document to another.

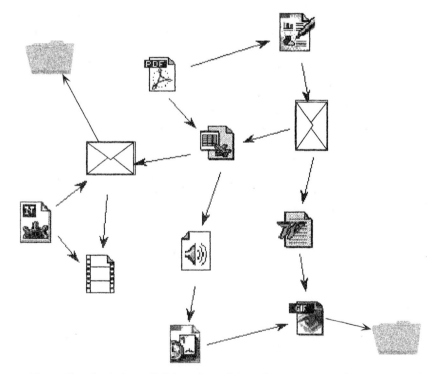

Figure 11-4   The classic hyperlink-based model used to structure information on the Web.

This approach has contributed enormously to the growth of the Web but has created other problems at the same time:

- *Navigational encumbrances:* Navigating large hypertext documents is difficult. As the number of documents and their hyperlinks grows, users find it increasingly hard to get an overview of available information to find the information they are looking for.

- *Extensive collaborative authoring:* Intranet sites almost always require collaboration from a multitude of authors. Problems grounded in link consistency come up here. Deleting a document breaks the links in other documents that point to the document just deleted. This often results in the infamous *Error 404* message.

- *Orphan links:* A document becomes unreachable when the last link pointing to it is removed. These problems compound in a multiple-author environment because the actions of one author (deleting a link or a document) can lead to problems with another author's documents without the other author ever knowing of the existence of the problem. The basic Web model is, therefore, unable to support a mechanism that is well suited for collaborative work.

- *Difficulty in generating complex views:* The simple URL-based navigation mechanism used by hypertext makes it impossible to combine individual documents to self-contained information components that can be reused in different contexts in slightly different ways, known as *customizable views.*

Various commercial tools use the concept of abstract structural elements called *containers.* A container contains a number of other elements, which could be documents or other containers.

Virtual Folders

Commercial software tools allow for the creation of virtual folders on an end user's desktop. Using such a mechanism, users can reach the same information element in multiple ways:

1. *By navigating:* Users can point and click by following hyperlinks.
2. *By searching metadata:* Users can search metatags associated with files and digital content.
3. *By searching content:* Users can search, using keywords that are matched against content within documents.
4. *By subscription:* Users can subscribe to predefined channels or, through the use of intelligent agents, they can receive notifications about new documents that match prespecified criteria.

This concept is also based on the presumption that users will not add content to the corporate repositories if it is too complex for them to do so. The goal is to make it possible to add to the repository with little or no effort on the part of the user. Without such functionality, this work runs the risk of being *perceived* as useless at code check-in/check-out procedures that most programmers unwillingly have to follow.

Automatic Full-Text Indexing

The collaborative filtering layer is responsible for indexing content in a manner that permits fast retrieval through multiple search mechanisms.

Automatic Metatagging

Metatags can be automatically added to documents and other content, using software tools that are readily available. Some tools allow the KM team to add metatags beyond those that the vendor might have already specified, but most do not. Such metatags include information such as:

- Who published the document?
- When was it last modified?
- Who reviewed it?
- Who approved it?
- What is the size of the document?

FROM CLIENT/SERVER TO AGENT COMPUTING

Agents, based on an old metaphor in the field of AI, have suddenly become a part of mainstream computing because of their suitability for open environments such as the Web. Agents can be thought of as active objects with their properties tailored to environments such as the Web and intranets.[5] Agent properties relevant to KM include the ability of agents to perceive, reason, and act in the environments within which they operate. Second, some agents have an ability to learn from past mistakes at an explicit level, something very much in line with what a KM system is intended to support. Because information cannot be understood without the context of its creation or the processes that lead to its consumption, the ability of agents to learn from past failures and to bring that learning to bear on future actions is very relevant.

Agents can be broadly classified into three categories: agents that are static in the client, agents that are static in the server, and agents that are mobile.[6] The primary types of agents that have direct implications for KM systems are mobile agents—ones that can move from one server to another to find the information that they need.[7,a]

The concept of agent mobility grows out of three preceding technologies:

---

[a]Many of the commercial tools mentioned in this book and included on the companion CD already use agents in the background. Besides these tools, IBM Japan also freely distributes an intelligent agent programming language called *ASDK* (Aglets Software Development Kit). ASDK is available for download at http://www.trl.ibm.co.jp/aglets/ free of charge. Documentation is available both in English and Japanese. IBM, however, charges for the most current version of this kit.

- Process migration
- Remote evaluation
- Mobile objects

Of all possible options, Java is the language best suited for implementing mobile agents because it allows the conversion of an agent into a form suitable for electronic transmission and its subsequent reconstruction on the receiving end.

Figure 11-5 shows a comparison between traditional client/server architecture and agent computing models of network operations. In the client/server setup, the network load primarily exists between the client and the server (indicated by more interaction lines between the client and the server). On the other hand, in the agent computing model, this load is shifted to the space between the agent and the server. The overall load on the network, therefore, is dramatically reduced.

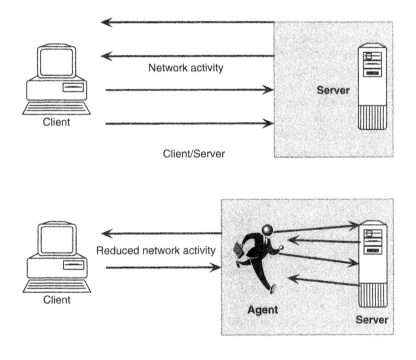

Figure 11-5   Client/server versus agent computing models.

Benefits of Agent Mobility

Although the area of intelligent agents is still being investigated by researchers, a few characteristics of mobile agents show a lot of promise in terms of their application to KM systems. Mobility is an orthogonal property: Not all agents are mobile. Agents that cannot move are often referred to as *stationary agents*. Stationary agents execute only on the system on which they are initially invoked. All communications and interactions with other systems are done with a communications protocol such as *remote procedure call* (RPC).

In sharp contrast, a mobile agent is not bound to the system on which it is executed.[8,9] Such an agent is free to move around the network across multiple hosts. Even though it is created in one execution environment, it can transport its *state*[b] and code with it to the next host within the network, where it continues code execution.

Mobile Agents for Knowledge Management

Why are mobile agents so attractive in designing KM platforms? There are six reasons.

1. *Mobile agents reduce network load:* Distributed systems on which a KM system is based often rely on communication protocols that involve multiple interactions between computers within a network to accomplish a given task. Mobile agents let systems cut down on the number of such interactions and, as a result, reduce the load on the network by a considerable amount. Even if you already have a very fast network in place, the bandwidth freed up by such agents can be used to move bandwidth-intensive content, such as sound and video, over the same network. Mobile agents move the computation to the data, rather than the data to the place of computation. When large volumes of data are present on remote hosts, mobile agents process data locally on the remote host and transfer the results to the local client.

2. *Real-time operations:* Mobile agents help perform transnetwork operations in real time. They can be dispatched from a central host and execute at the destination, thereby overcoming the effects of network latency and transit time that otherwise make real-time operations impossible.

3. *Protocol encapsulation:* Mobile agents can encapsulate various protocols and build a channel for communication between two machines that ordinarily cannot create a mutually interpretable protocol for data exchange. This is a significant enabler for legacy system and data integration.

4. *Asynchronous and autonomous execution:* We saw the need to be able to connect mobile workers and tools, such as personal digital assistants (PDAs), digital notepads, and palmtops, to network nodes. Very often, such wireless connections depend on cellular phone lines, which can be very expensive to operate on a continual basis. Mobile agents can execute independently of both the process and the device that created them. This implies that a PDA user could send out an agent to look for specific information, then disconnect from a network. The agent can then autonomously perform its search task

---

[b]*State* refers to an agent's attribute values that tell it what to do next when it resumes execution at its destination node.

and reconnect to the PDA user to report back what it found. Therefore, the need for continuous connectivity is minimized.

5. *Seamless integration and heterogeneity:* Networks are usually heterogeneous because of the different and often incompatible hardware and software that runs on such hardware. Because mobile agents are generally computer and transport-layer independent and depend only on their execution environments, they can seamlessly integrate devices across such heterogeneous networks.[10]

6. *Mobile agents are fault tolerant:* If a network node such as a server is going down, agents can be warned in good time about an impending nodal crash. They can then continue their operations on another host and save time, as well as their effort.

Agents and Push Models for Knowledge Delivery

Mobile agents embody the push model. Agents can disseminate news, bulletins, warnings, notifications, and automatic software and content updates. This makes mobile agents especially useful for delivery of knowledge in accordance with the push delivery model.

The strength that mobile agents bring to such knowledge-centered applications lies in their *asynchrony.* An agent can monitor information at the source without being dependent on the system from which it originates. Agents can also be dispatched to wait for information matching certain prespecified criteria to become available. A user can, therefore, dispatch an agent using such software, and the agent can either report the results on a periodic basis or report if and when it finds something relevant.

LOOKING FOR IKUJIRO NONAKA WITH MOBILE AGENTS

An example of a knowledge delivery application is CARL UnCover's Reveal service. My own ongoing research is based on a stream of research introduced by a Japanese scholar, Ikujiro Nonaka. Dr. Nonaka is based in Japan (and divides his time between Japan and Berkeley, California), and he publishes in a variety of research-oriented journals in the United States, Japan, and Europe. Considering the fact that there are 17,000 major journals in existence worldwide, it would be impossible to keep track of what he is publishing. Besides, there might be research papers that he has coauthored with other researchers. Mobile agents solve my problem in a perfect manner.

Using Reveal UnCover (http://www.ingenta.com), I can specify a number of loosely structured searches. Agents are assigned to each search. At any given time, I can have up to 25 sets of agents working for me. An agent waits to come across an instance of the search term *Ikujiro Nonaka* all week. If it comes across a match, it reports back to me by sending me an e-mail. It also tells me what the e-mail is about (adds context, without which the information might have no meaning for me). The following is an example e-mail:

```
From: uncover@csi.carl.org
Date: Wed, 17 Mar 2003 14:10:26 -0700 (EST)
To: Amrit_Tiwana@bus.emory.edu
Subject: Reveal Alert: Nonaka
Your Reveal search strategy: N Nonaka which was matched against an
article this week.
JT Prometheus : the journal of issues in technology
DA DEC 01 1998 v 16 n 4
PG 421
AU Nonaka, Ikujiro
AU Ray, Tim
AU Umemoto, Katsuhiro
TI Japanese Organizational Knowledge Creation in Anglo-American
Environments.
Thank you for using REVEAL.
```

THE APPLICATION LAYER

The application layer is the next layer. Applications such as skills directories, yellow pages, collaborative tools (often the back ends of Web-based collaborative tools), video conferencing software and hardware (and integration with the rest of the system), and conventional decision support tools are placed at this level. As shown in Figure 11-1, the Web front end comes above this level, so numerous tools at this level might have a common Web front end integrated with them. Discussion webs and forums for group problem solving and deliberation also exist at this level, even though the actual interface might be a plain Web browser. Actual applications that constitute this layer are specific to the functions and processes supported by the KM system, as discussed in Chapters 7 and 10.

THE TRANSPORT LAYER

Assuming that your company has a network in place, the transport layer already exists. This includes at least the following components to support a KM system:

- TCP/IP connectivity throughout the organization.
- An up-and-running Web server.
- A POP3/SMTP or MAIL server.
- A VPN to support remote communications, access, and connectivity.
- Support for streaming audio and video on the central server(s).

THE MIDDLEWARE AND LEGACY INTEGRATION LAYER

The legacy integration layer provides connections between legacy data and existing and new systems. The term *legacy systems* is often used in the context of mainframes, but for the purpose of building a KM system, we need a broader and more accurate definition incorporating both mainframe systems and other contemporary, retired, custom systems. When you attempt to standardize on one platform for reasons such as cost of training, maintenance, or acquisition, you must make sure that both the data and the critical applications existing on incompatible platforms remain usable. The middleware layer provides connectivity between old and new data formats, often through a Web front end. Although this problem is well documented in the area of systems integration and legacy integration, it needs to be addressed within the context of a KM system. A number of companies have used technologies similar to TCL/TK scripts to integrate data sources such as those on mainframes that were otherwise hard to integrate. Similarly, KQML allows the application of ideas underlying intelligent agents to enable legacy and incompatible data integration.

THE REPOSITORY LAYER

This bottom layer in the KM system architecture is the repository layer. This layer consists of operational databases, discussion databases, Web forum archives, legacy data, digital or digitized document archives, and object repositories. Islands of data—often standalone and distributed—exist in this layer. As we move up the layers in this architecture, these repositories are integrated and combined with contextual information and tacit knowledge. In all likelihood, this layer already exists in your organization if you are thinking of putting together a KM system.

LESSONS LEARNED

The seventh step in the 10-step KM road map involves actually building the system. Keep the following highlights of what we discussed in this chapter in view:

- *The seven-layer KM system architecture.* Understand exactly what purpose each layer serves. A poorly performing layer can marginalize the performance of the entire system and can be an expensive bottleneck to fix at a later date. Several components of this architecture already exist in your company. Analyze which portions of this architecture need to be developed from the ground up, which need to be built further on existing components, and which are already in place in their entirety.

- *The interface layer is what users actually see.* The interface layer is the topmost layer in the KM system architecture. Remember that this layer can be easily built with an intranet development tool, then customized. The interface layer must create platform independence, leverage the intranet, and enable universal authorship. Because a large proportion of content enters and leaves the KM system through this layer, it must be optimized to handle unconventional traffic, such as audio and real-time video.

- *Secure content using the access and authentication layer.* If you have a company-wide network, you already have most security mechanisms in place. Make sure that you extend these mechanisms to secure KM system content and raw data; restrict access to only authorized users, and distribute control.

- *KM system intelligence lies in the collaborative filtering and intelligence layer.* The collaborative filtering and intelligence layer can help advance the system from a client/server to an agent computing orientation. A number of commercially available tools can be used to build this layer without too much groundwork. Intelligent agents can significantly drive this layer. Deploying such agents rarely requires programming from scratch. Be careful about vendor claims while selecting components of this layer, and use qualifying criteria discussed in this chapter to make an informed choice.

- *Integrate applications with the intelligence layer and transport layer.*

- *Leverage the extant transport layer.* The transport layer is built on existing network infrastructure. If you already have a 100-Mbps network in place, you can leave this layer untouched. Remote access through direct connections and dial-up lines must be able to handle rich communications traffic from traveling users and occasional home-office workers.

- *Think beyond the mainframe legacy.* Develop the middleware and legacy integration layer to connect mainframe legacy data, incompatible platforms, inconsistent data formats, and retired systems.

- *Integrate and enhance the repository layer.* Often, repositories need to be supplemented with new ones to be able to handle various types of content, such as discussions in discussion databases.

Part IIC
The Third Phase:
Deployment

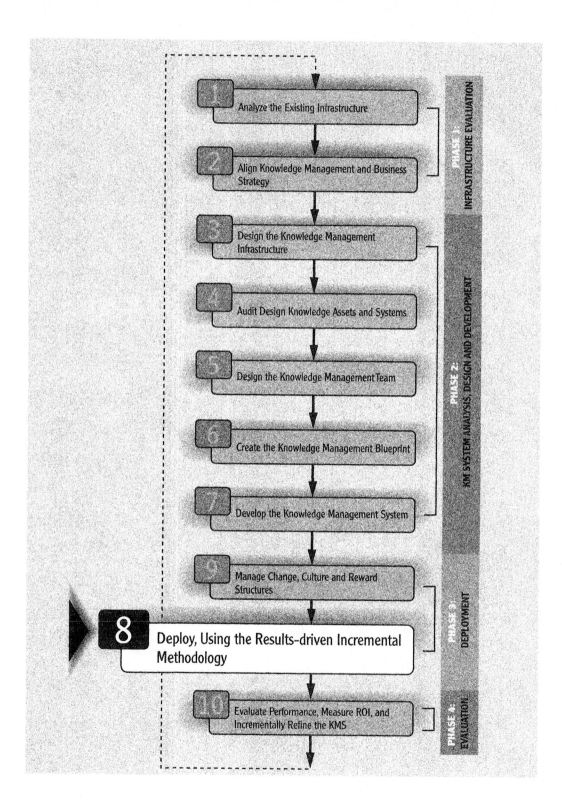

1 Analyze the Existing Infrastructure

2 Align Knowledge Management and Business Strategy

3 Design the Knowledge Management Infrastructure

4 Audit Design Knowledge Assets and Systems

5 Design the Knowledge Management Team

6 Create the Knowledge Management Blueprint

7 Develop the Knowledge Management System

9 Manage Change, Culture and Reward Structures

8 Deploy, Using the Results-driven Incremental Methodology

10 Evaluate Performance, Measure ROI, and Incrementally Refine the KMS

PHASE 1: INFRASTRUCTURE EVALUATION

PHASE 2: KM SYSTEM ANALYSIS, DESIGN AND DEVELOPMENT

PHASE 3: DEPLOYMENT

PHASE 4: EVALUATION

CHAPTER 12

PROTOTYPING AND DEPLOYMENT

CHAPTER OBJECTIVES

✔ Make an informed decision about the need for a pilot KM deployment.

✔ Select the right nontrivial and representative pilot project.

✔ Identify and isolate failure points in pilot projects.

✔ Understand the KM system life cycle.

✔ Understand the scope of KM system deployment.

✔ Identify and avoid the traps in the RDI methodology to maximize payoff.

✔ Use the RDI methodology to deploy the system.

TRY A THING YOU HAVEN'T DONE THREE TIMES.
ONCE, TO GET OVER THE FEAR OF DOING IT. TWICE, TO LEARN HOW TO DO IT.
AND A THIRD TIME, TO FIGURE OUT WHETHER YOU LIKE IT OR NOT.
—VIRGIL THOMSON

The eighth step in the KM implementation road map, the deployment stage, is the point where the differences between what appears to be a seductive technological solution and what's actually needed become apparent. The root of implementation disasters is in the assumption that the intrinsic value of a KM system will lead to its enthusiastic adoption and use. This assumption is too often shot to pieces.

In this chapter, we examine how you decide about the need for a pilot KM deployment, how you select the right pilot project, and how you identify and isolate its likely failure points. We talk about results-driven incrementalism (RDI): how to use it to deploy a pilot KM system project; how to create and maximize release payoffs; and how to avoid implementation pitfalls.

MOVING FROM FIREFIGHTING TO SYSTEMS DEPLOYMENT

Besides training costs, companies almost never budget for nontechnology costs related to deployment and implementation of KM systems. Without such support, implementation of a system resembles ad hoc firefighting more than something that seems as though it has a plan. Deploying any new system is usually a learning experience. The KM team can learn from the users' perceptions about the system, study its functionality and the suitability of the chosen interface, and discover unanticipated changes that must be made.

PROTOTYPING

Prototypes are perhaps the most underused form of *rejection insurance* that a development team can ever purchase. When you are in the midst of building a system, don't wait to finish the product before you put it into a pilot deployment. If all you have at the beginning is the interface, run it by a few users. Their comments could spare your team the agony of reworking the final pilot version. Iteratively improving a system with incremental prototypes lets the users see, touch, and feel a system even before it is completed.[1] By being able to solidify the abstract details that you might have been giving to your potential users, you stand a chance to give your system a thorough test run even before it's ready.

PILOT DEPLOYMENTS

A pilot implementation of the KM system on a small scale can lead to insights that might prove to be invaluable *before* the full-blown system is implemented at an enterprise-wide level. For example, users in a particular group such as marketing might feel that the user-friendly interface that your team designed is not exactly all that user-friendly. Knowing this ahead of time provides a time buffer for appropriate changes.

When such changes are made, they are best implemented in *chunks,* that is, a set of technology modules that functionally fit together and can be implemented *as a whole.* The change implemented within such a chunk should be large enough to enable potential users to accomplish a task in a measurably improved way.

A pilot test reveals significant and often fundamental design flaws early on in the deployment process. At that stage, it is still possible to rework the problematic aspects of the design to meet the needs of the users and suit their preferences without major expense or significant rework.

Selecting a Pilot Project

The pilot project is an important step that helps companies both in evaluating the technology and in learning how it creates or contributes to actual business value. Unfortunately, many companies make the mistake of selecting the wrong project as a pilot project.

To maximize the potential impact of the KM project right from the pilot stage, pick the pilot project with care. Once you have chosen the best possible pilot case for KM, you are better able to judge whether similar projects on an enterprise-wide scale will have a potent enough impact to justify their cost.

Find a project that the team agrees will have significant potential impact. Knowledge-intensive projects that run on a very tight time schedule are often the best place to begin. At the same time, be careful not to force the technology on a stream of work that constitutes the lifeblood of your company's income. Make sure that the team members that you choose for the pilot KM project are those people in your company who truly buy into the value of KM for the business processes that they are considering. User mandate coupled with managerial mandate is critical. If the users for whom you are building the system do not believe that such an infrastructure will truly help them, that is probably the wrong project to choose. Follow these tips for evaluating potential projects and their viability as pilot projects:

- Avoid trivial projects.
- Stay away from your company's lifeblood.
- Favor projects with widespread visibility and noticeable effects.
- Select a problem with which the chosen piece of technology fits well.
- Set tangible deadlines and metrics for success.
- Select a process-intensive application that can be highly impacted by the use of a KM system.

Here is an example of a project in a consulting company. Consider a system to support bidding for potential clients. A pilot for that case is a system that allows a consultant to pull up information (related information and information from past projects) to bid for a consulting project. Such a project is not overly critical if it fails outright. If it does not work, it will still mean that the consultant can continue to bid the way he would have normally. Because such a project is time critical, it will greatly enhance the process if it works. At the same time, such a project will have very visible and tangible outcomes if the KM system helps

> ### BEYOND JAVA
>
> Without sufficient feedback, even the most basic assumptions about your users can fall apart and lead to chaotic failure or rejection of the entire system.* An example of such a failure was obvious on the design of a Java-enabled Web site that was implemented at a major American university. The design team never quite involved any of the 30,000 regular users (mostly students and faculty) in the design process where the interface was completely revamped to work with Java-based menus. Fancy technology and novel design do not always meet the needs of users. In this case, the new interface, although much flashier than the original version, was painstakingly slow when users tried to access it through slow dial-up connections from home, as they often did, resulting in mass dissent and resentment over the usability of the new interface. The end result was that the design team had to re-create a non-Java version of the same system, as well. However, the only way to go to the non-Java version of the site was to go through the Java version and click on the "Non Java version" hyperlink!

the work group manage and access existing knowledge efficiently and effectively. Although this example applies to a consulting firm, projects in the same vein can be easily identified in most other types of businesses, as well. A similar pilot project, for example, can also be implemented in an engineering or contracting firm.

Lessons from Data Warehouses

Data warehouses are the political cousins of KM systems. There is probably a lot to learn from other firms' experiences with data warehousing. Data warehouses, necessarily, are expensive undertakings. At the end of 1999, there were over a thousand vendors specializing in data warehouse solutions, software, and hardware. A typical project cost over $1 million, yet the failure rates exceeded 50 percent.

Most companies pursued investments in data warehouses to improve the quality of information within the organization and to improve access to it (see Figure 12-1). Many companies start with small versions of a data warehouse (akin to pilot projects), usually centered on an application or a data set. Such a *data mart* is often an *independent proof-of-concept* system that can be built in a short time frame at a lower cost (than the entire data warehouse) and can possibly generate a high payoff. Similarly, pilot projects for KM systems can provide such a proof of concept and simultaneously allow you to figure out every *goof of concept* early on.

The danger of implementing and experimenting with such a pilot is that its success can lead to rapid proliferation of data marts that are independent of one another. Creating silos of information often comes with demanding integration problems at later stages. Similarly, KM system pilots, if successful, can rapidly lead to the rise of small, independent, and specialized KM systems (which are not even KM systems in the true sense) that can rapidly create disconnected silos of knowledge.

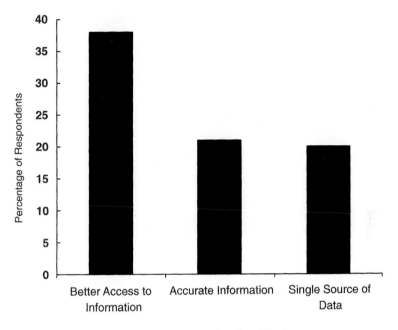

Figure 12-1   Reasons for investing in a data warehouse (numbers based on H. Watson and B. Daley, Datawarehousing: A Framework and Survey of Practice, *Journal of Datawarehousing,* vol. 2, no. 1, 1997, 10-17).

Whereas data warehouses do not lend their intangible payoffs for measurement without pain, KM can use a few proven metrics. The key barrier to further development shows up when management (often) expects to see a return on investment (ROI) analysis on the initial funding proposal itself. Although the usual benefits such as time savings, better decisions, improved processes, and support for strategic business needs can always be listed, some quantitative, hard-dollar figures are often requested.

LEGACY DEPLOYMENT METHODS

The incremental approach to systems development and deployment, illustrated in Figure 12-2, assumes that functions required of a system, such as a KM system, cannot be known completely in the initial stages. This approach suggests that developers implement a part of the system and increment it rapidly, as new requirements surface. This way, the entire system can be implemented in increments, and changes can be made along the way.

LESSONS FROM WAL·MART

Wal-Mart is an excellent example of a company that has structured its work processes around its data warehouse. It collects data from its 2,800 stores in real time to be able continually to maintain its 24-terabyte warehouse. By using such massive amounts of data, it has successfully streamlined its logistics and reduced overheads that allow it to stay healthy while its competitors have been busy closing down their stores or going out of business. The big lesson from Wal-Mart is about transparency. Most employees are perhaps not even aware that every time they scan a product at the checkout counter or on the shelf, they are updating data that is fed to the central data warehouse. Wal-Mart's employees do not have to do an extra thing to contribute to the set of inputs that feed the main system.

UPS's Web-based package tracking system is another close example. A KM system that is truly not considered a pain by its users needs to come close to this level of transparency.

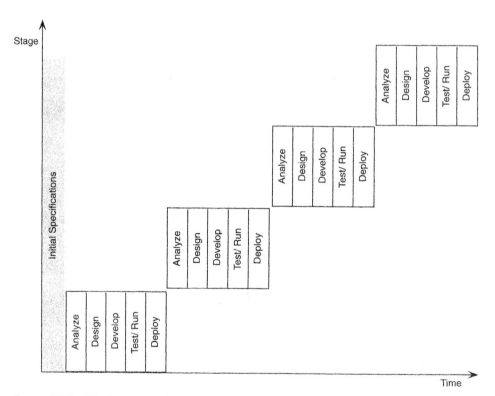

Figure 12-2   The incremental approach embraces a sequential, linear philosophy for systems development.

The waterfall model, the parent of the incremental model for systems development, was the mainstay of the systems development methodologies for years but has recently fallen out of favor. It is called the *waterfall model* because of the shape of the sequential activities that constitute it. The critical points of failure are shaded in Figure 12-3. The requirements determination phase, as shown in Figure 12-3, is the point within the waterfall methodology where many projects start out on the wrong foot. The waterfall method allows little scope for the last phase, the post-deployment review, which was added to the original model at a later stage. In addition, because "clients" often express opinions or preferences much later in the process, not all requirements are captured in the initial phases. Without stable requirements, development activities in parallel can be poor, at best.

The waterfall model is a bad approach to take for implementing complex systems. It not only allows but also encourages implementers to focus on the technology itself, rather than on the changes needed at a company level to actually derive business value from the new functionality that it provides.

If the feedback and learning loop are incorporated into this model and the project is broken down into discrete phases that build on one another, it gives us the incremental

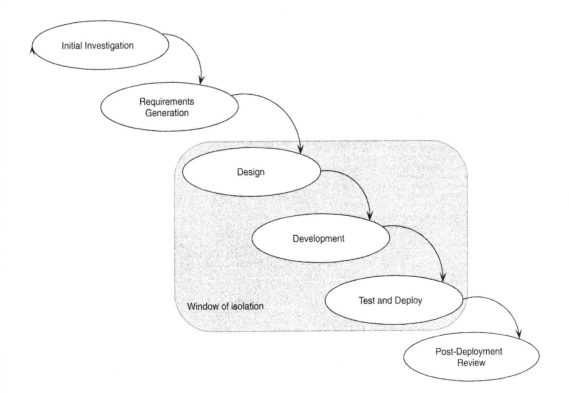

Figure 12-3 The waterfall methodology.

approach model shown in Figure 12-2. However, due to their lack of flexibility and their relative inability to track complex relationships, these two methods provide little support for managing a relatively complex project such as a KM system. An alternative approach is the *spiral model* approach, also called the *learning loop* approach, discussed next.

THE INFORMATION PACKAGING METHODOLOGY

The learning loop or spiral model approach to system deployment is often called the *information packaging methodology* (IPM). The basic processes involved in the IPM approach are shown in Figure 12-4. The first stage involves architecture and system planning. Design and analysis follow this. Next, the actual technology implementation is done. Finally, the system is deployed and evaluated against user reactions and formal alignment metrics, such as balanced scorecards or quality function deployment (QFD). Measurement of the level of strategic alignment level connects phases 1 and 4. This connection distinguishes this methodology from conventional systems development by bringing in the softer (strategic and human issues) factors influencing systems success. The spiral represents the infinite loop between stages 4 and 1 that leads to iterative and incremental improvements in chunks.

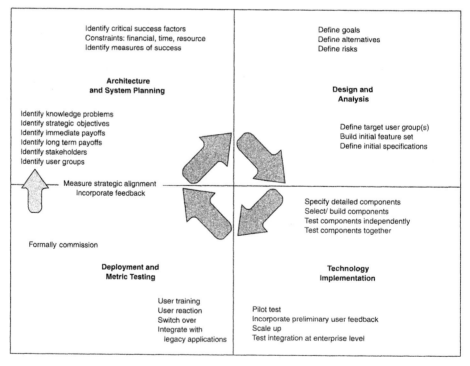

Figure 12-4   The information packaging methodology.

An alternative way that the information packaging spiral methodology can be represented is shown in Figure 12-5.

The information packaging methodology can be scaled up to an enterprise level; however, especially in complex projects such as KM system development that can be very expensive and very instrumental to the firm, the fact remains that even this methodology has its limitations when it comes to large-scale systems.

THE "BIG BANG" APPROACH TO DEPLOYMENT

One of the common misnotions associated with software projects is, in part, the root of frequent adoption of the wrong—"big bang"—approach to systems deployment: *Delivery equals implementation.* That is, develop the software system in its entirety and implement everything at once, after the code is compiled. This approach is in stark contrast to the incremental approach that any complex and encompassing project, such as a KM system, requires.

In the past, software packages seemed to contain more rigid assumptions about organizational structures, processes, and norms. Advanced software is no longer brought in to automate some process that is done manually; it is brought in to make a fundamental shift in the ways in which work is done and policies are run.

Project teams that use the traditional model for systems development have relied on the big bang finish, where a lengthy period of disconnected effort results in a supposedly working product, as characterized in Figure 12-6.

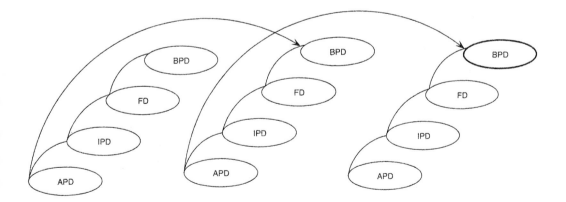

BPD: Business Process Design
FD: Functional Design
IPD: Interface Prototype Design
APD: Application Prototype Design

Figure 12-5   A spiral representation of the information packaging methodology.

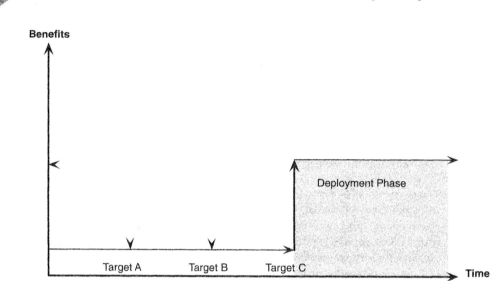

Figure 12-6   The traditional development model relies on the idea of the big bang deliverable.

As Figure 12-6 shows, the deployment team's targets or milestones A, B, and C pass but no benefits are realized by the company until the end of target deadline C. Here, the system goes "live," and the entire set of benefits is realized simultaneously. Although developers always hope that those benefits are truly realized, if something was messed up by the time the team reached target A, it remained so through all successive stages, and successive work was done on a faulty foundation. If something could have been tweaked at stage A to simplify work at stages B and C, it was impossible with the traditional model.

Software deployment has taken on the nature of sometimes evolutionary, sometimes revolutionary technological process innovation. Even when parts of your KM system are purchased off the shelf, you should not assume that the difficulties of writing the system code have already been packaged up or eliminated by the vendor! Installing, configuring, and customizing some of the complex commercial software systems have complexity levels that come close to custom development associated with them. Although this shift from project factors to processes might be the only possible approach that can be applied in situations that do not allow technology pieces to be subdivided into independent modules, divisibility is often the norm in complex applications.

ENTERPRISE INTEGRATION: BOON OR BANE?

Just as the demise of the typewriter changed the focus of our work from dealing with a physical machine to dealing with a software program, the penetration of computers in work-related activities has had exactly the same effect on work processes. The problem lies in the expansive flexibility of software. This has arguably reduced up-front costs of putting a system in place, but there are newer problems that come as a part of the package.

Baan and PeopleSoft, for example, are massive and expensive enterprise-level packages but still cost a fraction of what something similar would cost to develop in-house. This flexibility is a boon because it offers intensively amplified benefits and abundance of functionality. But this boon is also the bane. The excessive flexibility means that you have to tweak it to work for *your* company, and this necessity changes a software introduction initiative into an organizational change initiative. The one of several thousand possible configurations that you choose to use must complement the processes, policies, culture, structure, and metrics specific to your company.

THE RESULTS-DRIVEN INCREMENTAL METHODOLOGY

Implementation of complex pieces of technology such as a KM system need a new approach that can overcome the limitations posed by all deployment strategies discussed earlier. RDI is the most promising methodology for such use. The RDI methodology specifies that the project be broken up into a series of short, fast-paced development cycles coupled with intensive implementation cycles, each of which delivers a *measurable* business benefit.[2,3] The "benefits curve" for such a technique is illustrated in Figure 12-7. Benefits are realized as each discrete

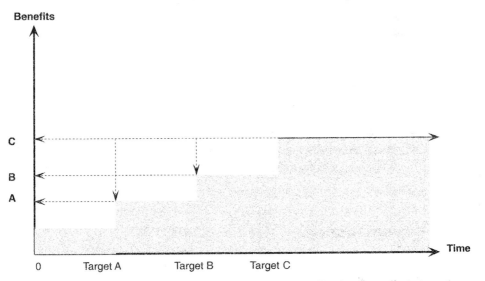

Figure 12-7   Benefits of each RDI stage are realized immediately after completion of each release.

stage is completed (benefits are shown in the shaded area in the figure), as opposed to cumulatively at the end of several stages.

The most obvious benefit of the RDI approach is that business benefits of the KM system can be realized much sooner, compared with a more traditional *big bang* approach. Implementers using this methodology report that the method increases not only the speed of the achievement of some tangible business benefit, but also the overall level of benefits. In addition, it dramatically reduces the overall time required to implement the project. Because every step taken is a concrete one and points of failure are rectified immediately after that step, it is more likely that the project will actually get completed.

STEPS INVOLVED IN THE RDI METHODOLOGY

The steps in the RDI methodology are based on five underlying ideas:

1. *Objective-driven decision support:* Use targeted business results and end objectives to drive decision making at each point throughout the deployment process. For example, each phase of KM system implementation has its desired results (the *whys*) and projected outcomes (the *so whats*) clearly answered before it is initiated.

2. *Incremental but independent results:* Divide the implementation into a series of nonoverlapping increments, each of which enables measurable business benefits and improvements, even if no further increments are implemented.[2]

3. *Software and organizational measures clearly laid out at each stage:* Each increment must implement *everything* required to produce the desired subset of results. This means that software functionality must be accompanied by the necessary changes in policies, processes, and measures that are needed to make it work. The deployment plan should also include appropriate rewards that encourage employees to integrate it into existing work processes.

4. *Intensive implementation schedules:* Each increment must be planned in a way that it can be implemented within a short time frame. Depending on the overall complexity of the KM project, the time for completion of each incremental feature should range from two weeks to three months.

5. *Results-driven follow-ups:* Results of each increment must be the basis for adjusting and fine-tuning potential flaws in subsequent increments.

BUSINESS RELEASES

Incremental segments of an implementation using the RDI methodology are called its *business releases*. The notion of a release comes from the software industry, where the software developer takes several iterations to get the final, polished version of the product to the customer (often over a period of several years). In the meantime, as the new and improved version is being developed, the customer can get an intermediate release and realize some of the final set of benefits and functionality that are expected. Each release constitutes a software-based system, and accompanying organizational measures to make it work. The performance of each release is judged against a few *key performance indicators* (KPIs), which guide the next release.

Business releases must be short and, unlike software releases, must not overlap. Long segments defeat the entire purpose of deploying the RDI methodology by working against the goal of providing isolated, independent, and cumulative episodes of functionality and learning.[a] Each business release should address at least the following questions:

- What is the targeted business result?
- What is the *exact* software functionality required to achieve these results?
- How will the results be measured?
- What complementary changes are needed in policies, incentives, metrics, and procedures?

Without specific answers to these questions, it is too easy to fall into the old trap of non-independent increments that do not deliver actual business benefits. Table 12-1 offers a sample set of questions and answers for a discussions database implementation in a consulting firm.

As you will notice, metrics in this sample business release are largely subjective. Although quantitative metrics are often desirable, it is hard to make accurate judgments about those figures. In such cases, make sure that you have at least clearly defined the basis for defining success. If you can make estimates of benefits (nonrandomly generated) in quantitative terms, add them to the business release. For example, if you can estimate or accurately "guesstimate" that you expect to reduce the average cost per contract by 12 percent or by $7,000, by all means, add it to the information above. However, if you cannot accurately determine these numbers within a reasonable margin of error, it's best not to guess in the dark. Such guesswork might undermine the actually delivered benefits in comparison with some guesstimated number, creating a perception of failure.

The Traps in Selecting the Release Sequence

The important consideration in the use of RDI methodology is the sequence in which business releases are taken up. The ideal sequence should promote multiple objectives for KM deployment.

- *Expected success:* Focus the initial releases on those areas that are most favorable to success. A flopped business release 1.0 is unlikely to retain management support and funding.

---

[a]If segments are long, RDI methodology begins to resemble the big bang notion of all-at-once delivery of tools.

Table 12–1 A Sample Business Release for a Consulting Company, Based on the RDI Methodology

Incremental Business Release	Details
Business release number	23454-11
Start date	05-11-2008
Due date	05-28-2008
Release manager	Leigh Jones
Targeted business result	Improve partners' use of records and code from past ERP implementation in Malaysia to slash costs of new ERP projects in Singapore
Software functionality	An intranet connected to the Singapore office. Access to design documentation on the Malaysia document server must be available. Hyperwave information server and a VPN must be used to enable low-cost access without a dedicated line. The software must support Mac and Windows users. The link must be secured with SSL. Use 128-bit encryption provided by software that is not subject to export restrictions from the United States.
Preliminary metrics and success measures	An improvement in the speed of execution of contracts Lower cost per contract Reduced travel expenses on the Singapore Penang route
Policy changes	Incorporate the following into partner appraisals: • Use of the new system to access information • Timely filing of project data • Cost reduction: travel and project averages
Accessibility	Provide each partner a laptop with a wireless LAN link; alternatively provide each partner a wireless PDA, a wireless connection, a direct access account, and an analog modem.
Other measures and notes	To be added

- *Cumulative:* Begin with an area where learning is most cumulative. This could be something as explicit as the interface or something as hidden as the mechanism for data access. Whatever areas you select, make your choice such that the lessons learned in the initial releases are those that can potentially impact the KM project the most. Using such incremental and cumulative business releases divides both learning and deployment into discrete and more manageable chunks.

- *Highest payoff:* Take up the releases that have the possibility of the maximum payoff early on in the process and those with marginal payoffs toward the end. That way, you will know whether the biggest benefits of KM can be realized with the approach you adopted.

- *Balance the above:* The three tips above are counter-supportive. For example, a business release with the highest expectation of success might not be the one with the highest payoffs. Similarly, one with the highest payoff might not be one that produces cumulative learning. The trick lies in balancing the above three at an optimal point. Determining an optimal point where the payoffs are maximized and the risks minimized is subjective and often depends on your particular situation.

Process Divisibility and RDI Releases

The RDI methodology works best if the technology component of KM itself is divisible, as is usually the case. This means that results and benefits that have accumulated still remain, even if subsequent segments are never implemented. Unlike other traditional approaches to systems deployment, neither the cause nor its benefits are lost if the KM project is scrapped at a later stage.

Divisibility can be viewed from two possible perspectives.[4] The first perspective divides the technology in such a manner that successive increments involve the same software modules but at a deeper level of detail. The alternative is to break the technology deployment into pieces, each of which is implemented at the deepest level of detail in the first round itself. The second approach is more feasible for building a KM system. This prevents the usual excuse that the benefits could not be realized because the implementation process was not completed.

The RDI methodology provides a technique that allows for refinement of the current stock of deployment and process knowledge in ongoing releases. The RDI methodology beats all older techniques by allowing the actual targeted users to become the critical link between the KM system development team and the end users that constitute the actual set of knowledge workers.

RDI's Role in Tool and Task Reinvention

New technologies are almost never perfect when they are initially introduced.[5,6] Users' efforts to apply technologies to their work processes and tasks reveal problems and contingencies that were not apparent before introduction. These problems, in turn, require adaptation of the

> ### MONSANTO'S PILOT PROJECT
>
> Monsanto, a Chicago-based company with over 2,000 employees, is the owner of leading brands of nutrition products, such as NutraSweet and Equal. The employee base consists of sales, marketing, research, manufacturing, and administrative personnel. Monsanto began its KM efforts with a small community of analysts consisting of marketing and business strategy analysts. This effort served as a pilot project for the large-scale deployment of their knowledge-sharing network, based on Plumtree knowledge server. As John Ferrari, the process and technology manager at Monsanto, puts it, "You do not want to focus too much time and energy into solving technology problems; focus on process issues and use off-the-shelf customizable applications where possible."
>
> By using a pilot deployment, Monsanto identified the areas in which expected problems of deploying a large-scale, organization-wide KM system were concentrated. The pilot implementation led them to believe that about 75 percent of the issues were people, process, and culture issues. Technology, the easy part, was the remaining 25 percent.

technologies already in use. Reinvention of the tools, interfaces, and task environments, such as the design or aesthetic fit of the KM system, often goes hand in hand with reinvention of the job itself ("using" the KM system). It would be ideal if the design of the KM system were such that the interface was very similar to the one that existed earlier and the whole process of using the KM system was almost transparent to the user. However, this is rarely possible.

On one hand, you will have a set of technophobic users to deal with. Such users will fear the introduction of a new technology that changes the way they have always worked. On the other hand are the technoliterate users who run the risk of getting so caught up in exploring the features of the new system that they neglect the tasks that they actually need to accomplish using the system. This implies that both these categories of users should be kept in mind while designing the system. The interface itself should be user customizable to a fairly high degree. Appropriate reward structures based on the level of use of the new KM system for accomplishing tasks, shared by both these categories of users will prevent problems with either group.

Cross-Functional Synergy

Synergy refers to the ability of the system to produce a result that is greater than the sum of individual components. In this case, synergy is the ability of the KM system to allow different groups of users, representing different functional departments, to produce results exceeding those that they would produce if working without the support of such a system. Synergy has often been called the *Holy Grail of business strategy*.[7] A successful KM deployment should bring in synergy between knowledge workers from different functional areas and departments. This goal is often pursued but rarely achieved. By bringing the work, documents, pointers, results, people, data, and other artifacts on one common collaborative platform, KM promises to enable such synergy. However, due to the multiplicity of functional areas that are expected to structure their work around a common system, it is critical that the viewpoints that form the basis for improvement, both before and after implementation, are not solely those of one group or department. Sharing resources is a necessary condition for creating synergy, but it is rarely sufficient.[8]

The Complexities of Collaboration

As the complexities of collaboration are unleashed with the use of a KM system, the processes of dealing with this type of complexity must be addressed from both the KM team's perspective and the end user's viewpoint. The critical set of complexities that you need to be concerned about while designing a KM strategy result from the changed face of interaction between people who exchange knowledge to perform their tasks and their inability to decompose tasks and decisions into smaller chunks or segments. The various levels of complexity that must be figured into the design of a KM system include[9-11]:

- *Logistical complexity:* Resulting from a high volume of transactions, projects, categories, and tasks that a typical knowledge worker needs to deal with.
- *Technological complexity:* This is rooted in the inherent nature of the systems and technologies that the user needs to interact with, both at a product and service level and at a process level. Although some of these, such as interaction complexity, are decomposable, others are not.
- *Organizational complexity:* This results from the meshing and collation of multiple organizations and departments into one work group. It may come from the new procedures that employees are expected to adhere to, changed structures of interaction (e.g., an employee needs to report to a team member in another firm but is appraised by his or her boss locally), and similar factors.
- *Environmental complexity:* This comes from the pace of change in markets, regions, and industries that drives adaptation of knowledge and its frequent invalidation (that knowledge you know no longer holds true).

Avoiding Overengineering

Overengineering refers to the act of implementing system functions that may never be used or adding details that are unnecessary for deriving the desired business results. The RDI methodology prevents the common tendency to overengineer technology solutions and maintains implementation focus and momentum. This substantially reduces the risk of failure and expedites the realization of business benefits. Although many managers may preach incrementalism in systems deployment, they rarely practice it. The reasons are twofold:

1. Incrementalism and structured methodologies are viewed as being noncomplementary.

2. The benefits of incrementalism are perceived to be so marginal that it *seems* that it is not worth the effort.

Developing Clear Communication Processes

Develop a clear communication process that explains the expectations and reasoning behind the introduction and integration of the KM system with business processes. This communication leaves no surprises for the users and makes it easier for them to accept a culture where continuous change is a normal part of work life.[12]

Human Barriers in Technology Design

Some technology vendors would wrongly have you believe that technology can capture all tacit knowledge in a database. Not all tacit knowledge can be captured in a database, but a significant proportion of pointers to it can be. However, without an incentive that makes it a part of the natural way in which a person works, it is unlikely that even such pointers will be added to the system.

The key lies in offsetting such human barriers by a combination of appropriate design of technology and complementary incentives. If you asked your employees to keep their skills up to date in a skills database, that task will probably slide down to the bottom of their list of priorities. An immediate reward for an employee can compensate for an immediate effort that can result in a long-term reward for the firm. Linking long-term goals to long-term rewards rarely works.

One Infinite Loop

Apple Computer, Inc.'s address is an interesting one: One Infinite Loop, Cupertino, California. This address also captures the essence of what represents the completion of a KM system implementation in the true sense. However tempting it might be to say that the KM system implementation is complete after Step 10 in the KM road map, we know better. To keep a KM system kicking and alive, it needs iterative improvements as the business environment and accompanying processes evolve over time.

CASE STUDY: CUSTOMER KNOWLEDGE INTEGRATION AT NORTEL

Nortel Corporation sells a suite of design and manufacturing applications in the United States and Europe. The Global Support Group (GSG) provides support to both European and United States customers. There are groups of support personnel in both the United States and Europe. Nortel is required to provide 24-hour support, seven days a week, with limited budgets and restricted head counts of workers.

Issues

Nortel was facing problems with providing support to its customers, primarily because there was no suitable mechanism that allowed a support representative to check whether anyone in the support organization had encountered a certain problem before. This meant that the teams in different offices did not share any of their knowledge related to problem solving and ended up reinventing solutions multiple times. Nortel identified several knowledge-related problems that its support group faced:

- An unclear definition of roles and responsibilities of personnel
- Lack of a formal process and guiding documentation
- Informal service level agreements
- Inconsistent measures of customer satisfaction
- Lack of formal training for support staff
- No centralized collection or repository of predefined solutions
- Excessive rework and reinvention of solutions (no formal mechanism for capturing problems and solutions)
- European and U.S. offices operating as groups of teams, rather than as a single distributed team
- Lack of knowledge sharing between teams based in the two continents

The Three Phases of Organizing Knowledge

The support group KM team at Nortel decided to manage knowledge more effectively, hoping to help the support group perform better, given budget and head-count constraints. They decided to tackle the whole process of managing knowledge in three discrete steps.

- *Phase 1:* Capturing knowledge and processes that were being used by their American and European support offices
- *Phase 2:* Consolidating these processes to provide an environment for cooperative trans-Pacific problem solving
- *Phase 3:* Implementing integrated systems to enable collaborative knowledge-intensive processes

Nortel began by bringing in an external consultant, who interviewed support staff in both Europe and the United States. After receiving positive feedback from these interviewees, the KM team concluded that it had the support of prospective end users. To gain acceptance, the external consultant(s) presented their understanding of the process to key stakeholders and support staff. Following this, feedback from employees was incorporated into the process descriptions that the consulting company had written. The processes identified were then classified into different areas of process ownership. Roles were assigned to each area on the basis of training provided to support employees.

Nortel support staff members were then trained in terms of the new, integrated processes that were synthesized. As a final step, an integrated progress tracking system was implemented that allowed team members to track progress on solving a problem as teams across the globe worked on it. The final step in terms of support technology was the implementation of a centralized database, where all problems and their outcomes were recorded.

Although the implementation done by Nortel seems to be less sophisticated in comparison with some other companies' KM systems, its results were delivered exactly where they were needed most. Remember that esoteric notions of organizational good cannot drive KM until it is helping the company solve critical process problems and eliminating knowledge-related problems that are threatening to bring the company down. Nortel expended more effort on the people side than it did on the technology side—a perfect way to begin when the processes themselves are not clearly understood or explicitly defined. The lesson here is that the problem should define KM technology; technology should not define the problem (or solution).

LESSONS LEARNED

Step 8, the deployment stage, is the point where the KM rubber actually meets the road. Keep the following key points about the deployment stage in mind:

- *Select and test-fire the KM system using a pilot deployment.* Select a pilot project that is representative and that will help identify and isolate failure points in the final deployment stages. Select a project that has high visibility and tangible outcomes.

- *Use prototypes to involve end users.* Many flawed assumptions in the system's design can be corrected inexpensively, using information generated from prototypes so that potential users see, touch, and feel a system even before a system is completed.

- *Focus on the RDI methodology.* Use the RDI methodology to deploy the system. Convert factors to processes. Eliminate information packaging methodology, SDLC (systems development lifecycle) orientation, and traditional big bang methodological variants.

- *Create effective business releases.* Create cumulative, results-driven business releases. Select and initialize releases with the highest payoffs first.

- *Budget for nontechnology costs in RDI business releases.* Besides training costs and work processes integration, budget for costs related to deployment and implementation of your KM system.

- *Develop a clear communication process with users.* Develop a clear communication process that explains the expectations and reasoning behind the introduction and integration of the KM system with business processes.

- *Strive for iterative perfection.* A healthy KM system needs iterative improvements as the business environment and accompanying processes evolve over time. The deployment process should not come to a halt once Step 10 of the KM "methodology" is completed.

Next, let's meet the people who are essential to the long-term success of a KM system and see what's needed to ensure their unequivocal support and the eventual success of the KM platform.

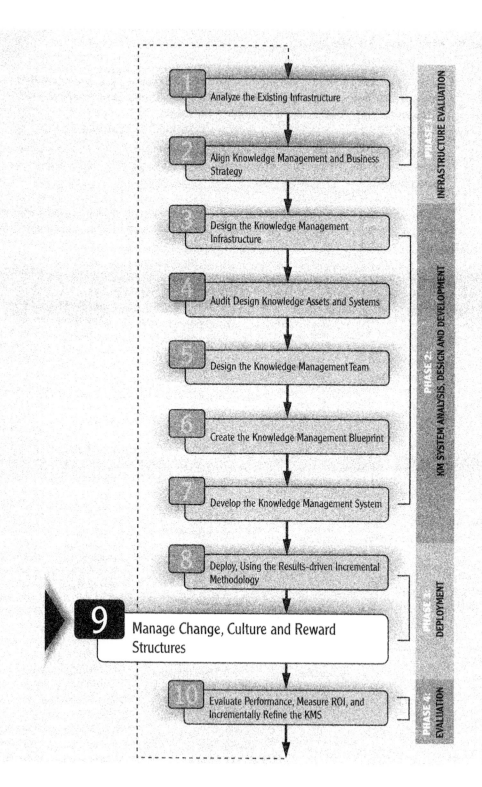

1. Analyze the Existing Infrastructure

2. Align Knowledge Management and Business Strategy

3. Design the Knowledge Management Infrastructure

4. Audit Design Knowledge Assets and Systems

5. Design the Knowledge Management Team

6. Create the Knowledge Management Blueprint

7. Develop the Knowledge Management System

8. Deploy, Using the Results-driven Incremental Methodology

9. Manage Change, Culture and Reward Structures

10. Evaluate Performance, Measure ROI, and Incrementally Refine the KMS

PHASE 1: INFRASTRUCTURE EVALUATION

PHASE 2: KM SYSTEM ANALYSIS, DESIGN AND DEVELOPMENT

PHASE 3: DEPLOYMENT

PHASE 4: EVALUATION

LEADERSHIP AND
REWARD STRUCTURES

THERE IS ONLY ONE WAY UNDER HIGH HEAVEN TO GET ANYBODY
TO DO ANYTHING. AND THAT IS BY MAKING THE OTHER PERSON WANT TO DO IT.
—DALE CARNEGIE

Knowledge sharing cannot be mandated. The whole notion of sharing what an employee knows is diametrically opposite to the way in which reward structures in most companies work. Why would any employee want to share knowledge if that knowledge is what provides the employee's job security?

Successful KM takes cultural change and a change in the reward structures that drive work in most companies. *You have to gain the hearts and the minds of the workers. They are not like troops; they are more like volunteers.*[1]

This chapter discusses the leadership roles of people involved in a KM team. Until now, we have focused on the key participants in the KM team. However, any KM initiative needs a champion, a leader who will take charge of running the show *after* implementation begins. So we look at what Nonaka calls *knowledge activists*[2] and discuss the role of the *Chief Knowledge Officer* (CKO). After examining the technological and organizational roles of the CKO, we evaluate whether your KM project even needs a formal CKO. Finally, we turn to change management processes—new reward structures and process enablers that can be put in place to complement the KM system.

FROM THE CHIEF INFORMATION OFFICER TO THE CHIEF KNOWLEDGE OFFICER

CIOs have distinct responsibilities: IT strategy, development of systems, connectivity, IT support, and general IT management. The CIO need not always be entreprenurially oriented to be successful, but the same is not true for the CKO. The CIO can rarely be both the CIO and the CKO; the characteristics underlying the CKO's role are different.

Whether the individual holds the title of Best Practices Manager, CEO, or Strategic Knowledge Manager, the key role that this individual plays is still the same: to make the KM system and processes an integral part of regular, daily work. Although there is often a CIO where there is a CKO, the reverse is not always true.[3]

KNOWLEDGE MANAGEMENT LEADERSHIP ROLES

The leader of a KM initiative walks in the following role shoes:

- *Championing:* Actively promoting the KM platform, its adoption, and its use.
- *Educating users:* Users not only need to know about the use and value of KM, they also need to be shown what's in it for them. That is, corporate knowledge objectives should be tied to personal rewards, such as compensation and promotion.
- *Educating the management team:* Management support is critical for the long-term success of any strategic KM system, and showing managers the value of KM is a necessary precursor to successful management of knowledge.

- *Measuring the impact of KM:* Metrics, the hardest part of KM, are also the most convincing of all talking points. (Chapter 14 examines metrics in depth).

- *Mapping and defragmenting existing knowledge:* KM must begin with what already exists. Don't try to build new knowledge repositories before you've inventoried the critical parts of explicit and tacit knowledge that already exist.

- *Creating the technology channels:* Technology channels are the sociotechnical networks that help move knowledge around the organization in an efficient manner. The choice of technology channels is largely determined by the CKO's understanding of what would work, user perceptions of what they need, and organizational work culture.

- *Integrating business processes with the technology enablers:* KM systems must be built to support business processes. A high-level manager (CKO or equivalent) is usually in the best position to identify business processes that most affect the bottom line.

INFORMALITY AT XEROX

Anthropologists at the Xerox Palo Alto Research Center observed, for example, that whenever field representatives gathered, they exchanged horror stories about the problems that they had encountered, their bad experiences, and how they resolved them. Xerox initially discouraged these informal get-togethers because it wanted to eliminate employee downtime. But when the company recognized the value of the knowledge exchanged, it equipped the reps with telephone headsets so they could continue their conversations even on the road. The system has since been expanded to include a database that captures information submitted by Xerox's representatives.

The Knowledge Leader's Job Description

The CKO focuses on correcting the knowledge flow and eliminating related deficiencies and inefficiencies that exist within the company. The CKO job description looks like this.

1. *Optimizing process design for KM:* Design processes for creating new knowledge, distributing existing knowledge, and applying or reusing what is already known.

2. *Creating channels:* Create channels for leveraging untapped knowledge and competencies within the firm. This also implies leveraging the latent value of hidden knowledge for the good of business development—a commonly observed deficiency in CKOs researched.

3. *Integrating KM:* Embody KM in the routine tasks and activities of the firm's employees.

4. *Breaking barriers and eliminating impediments:* Break down technical, cultural, and workflow barriers in communication and knowledge exchange processes. The CKO must also break internal funding barriers by making a strong case for KM investments.

5. *Watching the learning loop:* Ensure that the firm is learning from its past mistakes and failures. Although this problem might seem to be ridiculous on first thought, companies in the United States alone spend close to $10 billion on repeating mistakes and solving problems that do not need to be solved again.[a]

6. *Creating financial and competitive value:* Create value out of both the knowledge assets and the KM system. Value need not be solely financial.

7. *Supporting IT and eliminating knowledge flow gaps:* Support the above tasks with IT; bridge knowledge flow gaps.

The Chief Knowledge Officer as Organizational Glue

Not listed in the CKO's job description is a major challenge—convincing two distinct groups about the value of KM. The first group is management, and the second group is the knowledge workers who will actually use KM as a part of their work. Management needs to be convinced that KM will have a financial payback and will not turn into a financial black hole; employees need to be convinced that KM will not be yet another pain in the neck, akin to project charts, fill-in grids, time sheets, or code check-in/check-out procedures. Persuasive arguments required to convince these two groups can often conflict.

The CKO serves the purpose of *organizational glue* that brings these groups together. Figure 13-1 shows some of the people in the management and user community that a CKO needs to unite. On one side, there are the champions who believe in KM and are willing to stand behind it, even if it takes a leap of faith. The CKO might fall into this group.

SELLING FORESIGHT LIKE TRADING OXYGEN

Selling foresight to senior management and potential users of a KM system is like selling oxygen, suggests George Von Krogh,[5,6] of the University of St. Gallen in Switzerland. Oxygen is something that people need but cannot see. The only way of knowing that you got the oxygen that you paid for is to see it on a well-calibrated meter attached to the oxygen cylinder.

With KM, the customer, who might be the sponsor, the employee, the knowledge worker, the end user, or the collaborator, cannot really see *what* he or she is buying. You, the seller in this case, need instruments that are well calibrated to show that you have delivered what you promised in exchange for the money, effort, funding, or resource that was given to you. The internal working of those instruments has to be well understood both by you and the person(s) to whom you are selling the idea of KM.

Besides being understood, the use of metrics and values must also be agreed on.

---

[a]This estimate is based on research from organizational learning. Similar figures reported in software-based reuse research and estimates by consulting groups widely vary.

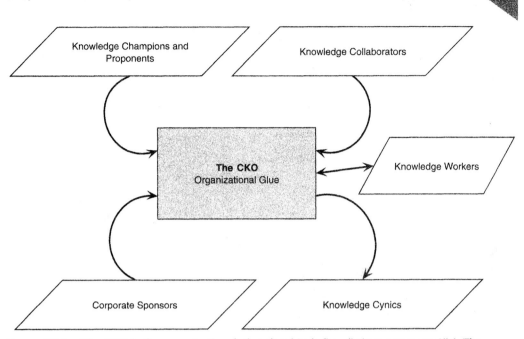

Figure 13-1   The CKO is the organizational glue that binds five distinct groups to KM. The directions of the arrows show support or opposition to KM, in general[4]

Then there is a core group with whom a CKO needs to collaborate. These are the knowledge collaborators that often include IT staff, intranet zealots, human resources managers, and occasionally, department (typically technical) heads. Only rarely do collaborators come from outside the organization. External consultants who have jumped on the KM bandwagon rarely know as much as you might know about managing your own firm's knowledge.

Aside from knowledge champions, corporate sponsors, and adherents are the knowledge cynics who do not agree on the value of KM. Although having a few cynics is perhaps a good thing, too many can hinder the KM initiative. Without bringing all these stakeholders together on common ground, a CKO cannot even begin to put KM policies and processes in place.

Initiatives and the Chief Knowledge Officer

The initiatives that a CKO must take fall into four broad categories, as shown in Figure 13-2.

The primary task of a CKO is to enable, not control, KM. Management initiatives relating to both tacit and explicit knowledge can be subclassified into two groups of tasks for a CKO: the organizational and the technical responsibilities.

On the technological front, a CKO needs to build channels for distribution of explicit knowledge and sharing of tacit knowledge. On the organizational front, these tasks include the following.

Organizational   Technical

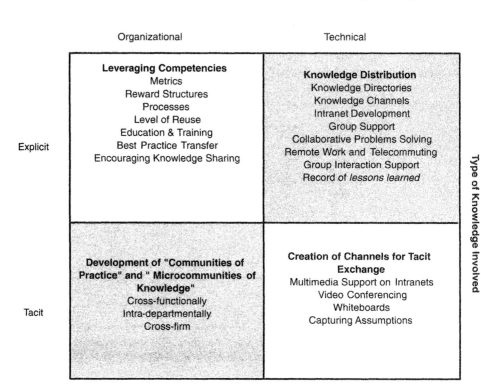

Type of Initiative

Figure 13-2   Four categories of initiatives for which the CKO or equivalent is often responsible.

1. *Identifying knowledge gaps:* Identify knowledge gaps that exist in critical work processes and assess ways and tools to bridge such gaps.

2. *Creating a culture of knowledge sharing:* Change corporate culture from that of defensive knowledge hoarding to a knowledge-sharing one. The basic assumptions that most companies have developed in the Western hemisphere are based on the well-proven notion that retaining knowledge and keeping it to yourself works rather well for job security, respect among peers, and compensation rewards. Breaking organizations out of this mold requires strong incentives and the elimination of related risks. These incentives must provide a compelling response to workers who ask the question, "Why should I ever share the very knowledge that provides me my job security?"

3. *Creating appropriate metrics:* Create metrics for knowledge work (see Chapter 14) and reward schemes for individuals who share their knowledge.

4. *Developing communities of practice:* Communities of practice must extend across the department(s), throughout the firm, and across collaborating firms, customer sites, allies, and partners.

5. *Diffusing best practices:* Enable sharing and transfer of best practices across the board.

6. *Training:* Educate knowledge workers about the value of KM, then train them to use the KM system and related protocols. This includes showing knowledge workers how to ask better and smarter questions of their knowledge resources and repositories.

7. *Structuring processes:* Not only should processes be structured, but the CKO should also promote better understanding of the types of knowledge created and used by them.

8. *Removing knowledge-sharing barriers:* Remove technical and sociocultural barriers to knowledge sharing, transfer, use, and distribution.

9. *Aligning local knowledge:* Align local knowledge creation activities in individual departments and teams with the long-term strategic knowledge vision of the firm.

10. *Creating process triggers:* Improve the level of reuse of existing knowledge by creating *process triggers*[7] and context for reuse. Examples of process triggers could include questions such as:

   • Why is the customer retention level so low for product *X*?

   • Why does the customer want to buy a competing product (at a higher price) after having tried ours?

   • Why is the customer not satisfied with our product?

   • Why do our products fail to drive out competition?

   • Why is our pricing strategy not working?

   • Why does it take us six months to launch a product that took four months to develop?

11. *Making KM a part-and-parcel of routine work:* Some theorists have suggested that a successful CKO is one who integrates KM so tightly with the company's ways and processes that the CKO position is eliminated. This also means that the expectations from a CKO and his or her future role in the company must be clearly articulated.

In trying to gain commitment from top managers, you, as a champion of KM, must realize that many, if not most, managers have been trained to handle industrial companies and not knowledge-based ones. Senior managers are often concerned with the potential impact that investments in KM initiatives might directly have on bottom-line results. These concerns often tend to outweigh the other, less tangible and arguably longer-term results of managing this asset. After all, what good is the world's best KM system when the company is on the verge of bankruptcy? So get real and demonstrate in surrogate measures how the speed and quality of service to your clients will gain from, say, exchanging best practices. Those might be more saleable arguments.

Top management's active support and understanding of the role that knowledge has to play, whether your company is a small business or a multinational business, is critical for its success. Most companies researched by this author seem to view establishing management support as the biggest challenge. How do you convince senior management that money spent on managing the company's knowledge is more important than some other seemingly critical expenses that the company needs to incur? It is an uphill battle to convince top management of the need for such operational KM. They demand dollar values and hard figures, neither of which can be easily provided. *Establish top management sponsorship with ongoing involvement during the design, development, and implementation stages of your KM system.*

This brings us back to the question of metrics and surrogate metrics. Having clear-cut deadlines and projections, even if they are surrogate measures, helps to convince senior management. A major company that this author investigated successfully leveraged the knowledge of sales employees to reap very strong competitive positions for the company in various markets in which it competed. However, the KM project leader demonstrated the entire benefit of the project in terms of savings in package delivery expenditures that resulted from the use of the supporting "intranet" until the senior management bought into his idea that the management of knowledge was actually helping the entire company in a larger way.

DOW CHEMICAL AND MANAGEMENT SUPPORT

Dow Chemical Company, a company that employs approximately 50,000 people across its 115 manufacturing sites located in over 30 countries, sells over $20 billion of products belonging to its 2,400 product families. Upper management began its KM efforts with the firm belief that its intellectual assets needed to be managed as seriously as its hard assets. The company owns approximately 30,000 patents. In a highly research-oriented company such as Dow, typically one of 15 new projects succeeds. The company's senior management formulated a clear-cut vision for its KM project with a definite target: to increase this success rate from 1 in 15 to 1 in 5. This end needed a system that strategically directed existing knowledge into new ventures and projects. With assets such as patents, the intellectual property of the company is well articulated.

In cases like this, it is always better to shoot toward leveraging those assets that are most suited for strategic business purposes before trying to implement a theoretically complete and encompassing effort to manage *all* forms of knowledge.

Similarly, the technological initiatives that a CKO is responsible for include the following:

1. *Building directories:* Create skills and knowledge directories.

2. *Creating channels:* Create channels for exchange of documents and other codified forms of explicated knowledge.

3. *Extending the intranet:* Develop the intranet and include rich multimedia support within it.

4. *Supporting group work:* Support group and collaborative work through technology tools and new policies that promote such work.

5. *Providing tools for collaborative problem solving:* Develop and implement tools for collaborative problem solving.

6. *Supporting remote work:* Provide support for distributed work, remote access, telepresence, and telecommuting.

7. *Building repositories:* Build repositories to store "lessons learned." These can begin with simple Notes databases and later expand to relational databases tightly integrated with the intranet front end.

8. *Infusing external knowledge:* Enable infusion of external task-specific, domain-specific, and competitive knowledge to provide a more stable competitive stand for the firm.

9. *Enabling tacit knowledge application:* Improve knowledge-application using tools, such as video conferencing, whiteboards, mind maps, etc.

10. *Introducing cross-functional tools:* Introduce tools for capturing and exposing assumptions of teams whose members often come from different functional backgrounds.

THE SUCCESSFUL KNOWLEDGE LEADER

Because the CKO often works closely with the technology staff, he or she must have a fairly good understanding of the technology that will be deployed as a part of the KM system. Credible discussions with technology partners are unlikely to happen if a CKO unsure of what an intranet even is.

On the other hand, the CKO also needs the skills of an effective manager and an entrepreneur. A CKO needs to understand the workings of the company inside out to be able to comprehend its vital processes. In a way, a CKO must be successful as a *merchant of foresight.*[8] The job involves radical redesign of performance measurement metrics and employee compensation systems to encourage employees to share what they know effectively. These two qualities go hand in hand for a typical CKO whose primary responsibility is to be able to create and see the *big picture* and, at the same time, translate it into tasks and concrete deliverables.

HISTORY

The CKO needs to have the breadth of understanding of a CEO and the technological understanding level approximating that of a CIO. It comes as no surprise that many CKOs come with a wide variety of experiences in one or more companies, and many have in the past served as CIOs. A formal technical background is not the norm; many CKOs have come from a diverse array of departments, such as human resources, internal consulting, finance, marketing, new product development, and even academia.

Most CKOs are hired internally, simply because there is a stronger likelihood that such a person would have a deeper knowledge of the given firm and a clearer understanding of the big picture. Remember, a formally appointed CKO is *not* always necessary for a KM project, as long as someone is galvanizing and coordinating the KM initiative well (especially in smaller companies, where a senior manager or CEO can handle the task).

CHEVRON'S CASE

Chevron used several tactics to gain support for the CKO's role at both the managerial level and the user level.[9] These include:

1. *Tying KM initiatives to the knowledge vision:* Chevron uses something equivalent to *The Chevron Way*—an integrated value statement that endorses the management and transfer of knowledge and best practices.
2. *Telling success stories of the KM initiatives at each top management meeting:* This keeps the KM program highly visible.
3. *Removing barriers to knowledge sharing:* The not-invented-here syndrome and the lack of motivation to find new ideas to improve processes were two barriers that had to go. Chevron opened communication channels between executives, managers, employees, customers, and suppliers.
4. *Applying and demonstrating:* All stakeholder groups had a chance to see the benefits of such practices and systems.

REWARD STRUCTURES TO ENSURE KNOWLEDGE MANAGEMENT SUCCESS

Employees who will actually use the KM system must have their expectations clearly laid out. Each employee must know why his or her opinion and contribution to the KM system, as a whole, counts. Trust and cooperation are critical factors in the smooth integration of a KM system into the firm's employee base and as a cultural whole.[10] If a knowledge-related role is assigned and results are expected, the CKO must ensure that employees are given the time to contribute to it as a part of their jobs.[11]

It's the CKO's responsibility to motivate employees to use and add value to the KM system and, in turn, the firm. Many companies have successfully established this link. At Buckman Labs, for example, incentive, evaluation, and promotion systems are designed to recognize those who do the best job of knowledge sharing and to penalize those who don't. Similarly, Chaparral Steel has successfully changed its pay structure to reward accumulation of skills in addition to performance.

Pfizer has developed *competence models* for its treasury executives that call for more than basic financial skills. Knowledge building and knowledge sharing are considered critical for management as the company has successfully created knowledge linkages across the organization. For this reason, the contribution to such linkages is strongly linked to employee compensation packages.

The knowledge leader should also consider the relative stability of employees, their jobs, and modes of working. Figure 13-3 illustrates how a KM initiative leader can choose between a learning and a sharing culture, although the two are not mutually exclusive. On one side of the 2 × 2, the extent to which your employee pool is stable is shown. For simplicity, this is shown at two levels, where employees are either stable in their jobs or frequently change jobs. On the other side is the mode of working that your company uses: project-oriented or function-oriented. For example, many software, law, and architecture businesses are project-oriented, whereas many services, utility, and marketing companies are function-oriented. In project-oriented work environments, managers must promote development of "T-shaped skills."[12] Such skills are where individuals possess deep understanding of their own domain and possess sufficient knowledge of their peers' domains so as to be able to comprehend the value that their knowledge brings to their own contributions. Considering both these aspects together can guide managers about what is in the best interests of their company, though not necessarily in the best interests of their employees.

	Stable	Mobile
Project-Oriented	Learning Culture	Sharing Culture
Function-Oriented	Learning Culture (Acquisition-oriented)	Sharing Culture

Figure 13-3   A KM leader can nurture either a learning or a sharing culture.

LESSONS LEARNED

We examined the role and need for a leadership role for continued success of the KM system and the KM strategy. As the ninth step in the 10-step methodology, we discussed how change management must occur and how reward structures must be modified to help the KM system succeed.

Some tips that you should take away with you include:

- *You might or might not need a CKO:* A separate person serving as the CKO might be justified in large companies, but is not always a requirement. The ideal CKO always encompasses the definition of the role and not the person with that title: It can be an existing senior manager, the CEO, or even the CIO. The CKO should have a fairly good understanding of the company's business model and driving technology enablers. Plan for KM success using the CKO as an agent for selling foresight, and select one who can actually make a convincing case for KM in front of knowledge skeptics.

- *Understand a CKO's role exactly:* The CKO serves as organizational glue that binds key stakeholders in a company. Understand how a CKO is related to the CIO, CFO, and CEO, and choose a leader who qualifies. Remember that most successful CKOs come from within the organization and rarely, if ever, from outside.

- *KM is about 30 percent technical:* The hardest part comes after the KM system is built. That part involves the cultural changes needed in the company's work processes to make KM acceptable as a way of work life for both your company's knowledge workers and managers. These challenges dwarf those faced by data warehouses and electronic commerce systems.

- *KM needs strong reward structures:* Knowledge sharing cannot be mandated; it can only be encouraged by complementary reward structures that encourage knowledge sharing and use.

The success of KM in any company, big or small, depends on how well the knowledge champion (whatever you decide to call him or her) brings all stakeholders—management, employees, partners, and sponsors—together in agreement on beliefs and expectations. A KM project *sold* to this stakeholder group is already on its way to success, even before the first line of code is written or an initial strategic change made.

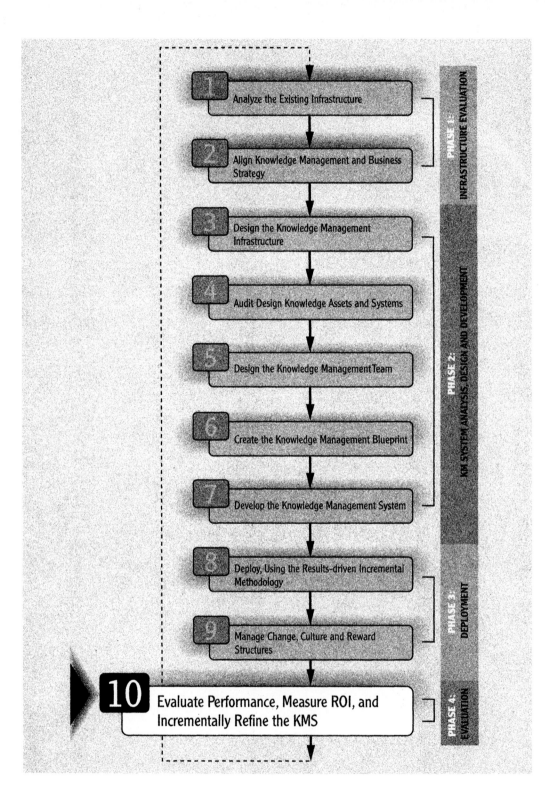

1 Analyze the Existing Infrastructure

2 Align Knowledge Management and Business Strategy

3 Design the Knowledge Management Infrastructure

4 Audit Design Knowledge Assets and Systems

5 Design the Knowledge Management Team

6 Create the Knowledge Management Blueprint

7 Develop the Knowledge Management System

8 Deploy, Using the Results-driven Incremental Methodology

9 Manage Change, Culture and Reward Structures

10 Evaluate Performance, Measure ROI, and Incrementally Refine the KMS

PHASE 1: INFRASTRUCTURE EVALUATION

PHASE 2: KM SYSTEM ANALYSIS, DESIGN AND DEVELOPMENT

PHASE 3: DEPLOYMENT

PHASE 4: EVALUATION

CHAPTER 14

REAL-OPTIONS ANALYSIS FOR KNOWLEDGE VALUATION

VAGUELY RIGHT IS BETTER THAN PRECISELY WRONG
—L. LODISH[1]

Having deployed the KM system and put a KM strategy in place, how do you evaluate its business impact? Although innovative companies, such as Dow Chemical, Skandia, Canon, and Buckman Laboratories, track knowledge growth, I have yet to come across one that has a strong measurement program. With this in mind, in this chapter, the 10th step of the KM road map, we see how traditional metrics (such as ROI and Tobin's q) are incomplete for deducing KM effectiveness. We explore the powerful approach of real-options analysis, a method that garnered its originators a Nobel Prize for economics. Finally, through case studies, we see how successful companies approached metrics, what errors they made, and what we can learn from both their mistakes and successes.

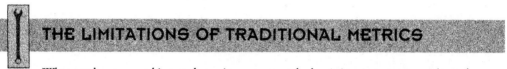

THE LIMITATIONS OF TRADITIONAL METRICS

What can be measured is not always important, and what is important cannot always be measured. It does not take an Einstein to conclude that the value of KM cannot be fully measured in terms of financial ROI.

FINANCIAL RETURN ON INVESTMENT AND TOBIN'S Q

A relatively old measure that has been in use for many years within business and academic circles is Tobin's q. This metric essentially measures the ratio between the firm's market valuation and the cost of replacing its physical assets. Although Tobin's q provides a snapshot of the firm's state of intellectual health at a given point in time, it provides no direction for KM strategy development. It does not tell you what you are doing wrong or what to focus on. What is needed is a more dynamic view of knowledge performance that can help a firm trace both the growth and decline of its knowledge assets and the reasons underlying such changes. Traditional metrics such as Tobin's q do not tell a firm how it can create further value, prevent imitation or substitution,[2] and leverage its knowledge assets to gain a sustainable competitive advantage.

Nevertheless, when it comes to measuring ROI in KM, two conventional approaches are in common use: putting a dollar figure on intellectual assets and determining dollar amounts saved or earned from using existing knowledge.

TOTAL COST OF OWNERSHIP

Current methods of measuring and evaluating information technology investments do little justice to information technology itself. How then, can we expect those methods to be able to give us a clear picture of how our knowledge investments—which stretch far beyond pure technology alone—are faring? Our interviews and studies show that companies do not always

Two Ways to Measure—The Case of KEMA and Platinum

Companies have approached knowledge measures from different perspectives. What is commonly seen is a combination of:

A cost-based approach
- Did it reduce costs?
- Did we accomplish more by spending the same?

A market-value-based approach
- Did it improve our market leadership?
- Did it bring more stability to the company?
- Did we increase our market share?
- Did our company stock rise in value?

An effect-on-income approach
- What effect did it have on expense reduction?
- What effect did it have on customer retention?
- What effect did it have on repeat business?
- What effect did it have on profit margins?
- What effect did it have on the bottom line?

One way to measure the performance of knowledge investments is to put a dollar value on the company's intellectual assets. In doing this, one might examine the firm's patents, proprietary technologies, or products. When we talk about products, we also need to take into account processes. Very often, a company gains an edge because it can perform certain tasks in a better, cost-effective, or quality-enhancing way. Many companies, such as the Swedish financial services group Skandia, have calculated a dollar value for intellectual capital to claim that previously immeasurable productivity gains were overlooked by "old economy" accountants. The Dutch engineering business, KEMA, calculated that its employees are worth more than the profits they make from installing and fixing power supplies. In 1994, KEMA put a price tag of 700 million Dutch guilders (US $400 million) on the intellectual prowess of its 1,200 employees, calculated as a sum of training fees, experience within the company, and the value of university degrees. In 1994, however, KEMA's profits had amounted to just 19.8 million Dutch guilders (US $12 million), representing a rather poor return on the company's knowledge "investment."

When the company realized the actual value, it was rather concerned at the poor return on its knowledge-based investments. This made the future work for the company's management clear—to make more money out of the knowledge assets it had.

Separate work was done on three fronts: Strategic KM (understanding what kinds of intelligence the company would like), operational KM (defining processes to help staff learn), and the valuation of knowledge as an asset.

The second type of measurement mechanism looks at how much money the firm saves or makes if it relies on using knowledge that exists both inside and outside the firm. For example, does using knowledge help the company get a newer version of its products out on the shelves faster? Does it reduce costs? Similarly, processes can be measured on the basis of how much they add to productivity, speed, additional revenues, and customer satisfaction. Yet another way might be to measure cost savings associated with putting a given piece of information online, as opposed to circulating it on paper.

Platinum Technology has successfully used this approach. Platinum rationalized the expense involved in initiating a KM program in terms of the dollar figures they saved in FedEx expenses in the very first year. Instead of using some elusive measure to justify the value of KM to senior management, Platinum's KM champions used something very visible and clearly defined (FedEx savings) to measure cost savings that resulted from using the KM system. The actual benefits, as would be anyone's guess, were much higher than just these cost savings.

Soon, it will become clear why such measurements do not truly reflect the value added by management of a firm's knowledge. There is no perfect way to determine just how much knowledge and its effective management contributed to the outcomes.

demand solid business cases for IT investments but have trouble handling decisions based on *soft* gains and benefits. Maturity of judgment becomes a distinctive inhibiting factor that prevents them from making decisions where limited quantitative data exists.

Many companies have responded by falling back on a *total cost of ownership* (TCO) approach. This methodology identifies and measures components of IT expense beyond the initial cost of implementation. Although TCO can be a useful tool to reduce ongoing costs by improving IT management practices, it does not provide a sound foothold for decision making, for several reasons:

- It leaves out significant cost categories, such as complexity costs.
- It ignores benefits beyond pure costing.
- It neglects strategic factors.
- It provides little or no basis for comparison with other departments and other companies, such as competing firms in the same markets.
- Life cycle costs are difficult to gauge.

Applying TCO blindly can lead to impolitic decisions. For example, the decision to switch vendors to get the lowest prices does not capture the implicit cost of supporting multiple vendors, the cost of dealing with compatibility issues, or the benefits of high-volume purchasing.

LESSONS FROM THE TELEPHONE

Just as a telephone is hard to cost-justify and evaluate, KM is something firms often find difficult to cost-justify in the face of other needed investments but is something they want and should have. Even though middle managers feel the need for a strong KM initiative, convincing senior management to shell out the couple of million dollars for an initiative with intangible results can be a hard sell. However, there are ways and means to measure the short-term gains to demonstrate the need for and the extent of the longer-term *guesstimations* of added value.

THE WORLD THROUGH GREEN GLASSES

A recurring problem in KM is the problem posed by a lack of standard metrics for measuring the impact of KM. Two of the most widely cited research projects relating to KM and organizational learning are the case descriptions provided by DeGeus[3] at Shell Corporation and by Ray Stata[4] at Analog Devices. DeGeus's approach at Shell used scenarios in the strategic planning cycle that encouraged managers to revisit and challenge commonly accepted assumptions. The underlying belief was that learning would not take place unless managers exposed the hidden and embedded assumptions with which they approached new problems.[a]

Similarly, Stata found that focusing on activities, such as improving response time to external changes, and utilizing planning and quality improvement as learning tools, rather than as purely administrative tools, could accelerate learning.

Chaparral Steel, a large U.S. steel producer, similarly found that there was a lot to gain by emphasizing problem solving, constantly integrating internal and external knowledge into daily work-related activities of employees [5,6] and allowing the time and resources needed to make this integration happen. In addition, a good reward structure helped.

COMMON TRAPS IN CHOOSING METRICS

No metric is better than one that is absolutely wrong. A choice of a wrong metric can have more ill effects than positive ones. Metrics, when applied to knowledge work or in general, are vulnerable to seven common traps.

---

[a]This finding is very much in line with some of the research done by some of my own colleagues. For example, see the research work done by Balasubramaniam Ramesh at the J. Mack Robinson College of Business at Georgia State University, Atlanta and at the Naval Postgraduate School, Monterey, California.

Trap 1: Using Too Many Metrics

On the opening page of their book, *The Balanced Scorecard* (Harvard Business School Press) Kaplan and Norton have an interesting discussion between a pilot and a passenger. The pilot says that he needs to work on airspeed, so he ignores the altitude and fuel gauge altogether. "It is not what I am focusing on," he says. Amused at their own interesting analogy, they think that you would not want to fly in his plane, ever! Isn't this very close to what companies do when they focus on a single metric, such as the bottom line or market share? On the other hand, some go to the opposite extreme and try to simultaneously track too many.

A few robust metrics are better than a number of marginal ones. They need to focus on the past, present, and future simultaneously to be able to relate past performance, present processes, and future results.[b] Use 20 as a cutoff rule of thumb number for the few but essential metrics that can be simultaneously tracked.

Trap 2: The Consequences of Delayed Rewards

Rewards that are tied to metrics with a relatively longer term focus should be robust and structured in a manner that allows employees to reap short-term benefits by successfully achieving them. Job mobility is a fact of life. Delayed rewards will only bias employees to work toward metrics that deliver short-term payoffs to them. To keep the long view, select metrics that can be measured today but have impact on future outcomes. Alternatively, the long-term gains of the firm should be tied closely to the compensation of the employees (using, for example, stock options).

Trap 3: Metrics that Are Hard to Control

Companies often make the grave mistake of implementing metrics that are beyond the control of their employees. Phrases such as "build a $7 billion wireless applications market by 2008," "let every hand in America hold a palmtop by 2010," or "put an embedded PC in every bottle of wine" are visionary ideas but almost impossible to control or achieve through systematic efforts. Such statements look good but only on paper

Trap 4: Metrics that Tear People Away from Business Goals

The key idea is that the metrics that you select must encourage individual decisions that also move your company in the same directions as its long-term goals. Common reasons why this does not happen are:

- Individual contributions to a business's long-term goals are not rewarded with short-term payoffs or rewards.

---

[b]The common problem that many measurement programs become victims of is putting too much focus on the past. Knowing the past is good, but it rarely is sufficient to give you a concrete idea about where your present efforts are leading your company. Forget quantity; focus instead on linking measures to strategic capabilities, competitive positioning, customer expectations, and financial indicators.

- Metrics that are too ambiguous or expansive ("increase the competitive positioning of XYZ Corp.") are hard to measure.

Some metrics might seem reasonable, but when they are put into action, they result in counterproductive consequences. Agency theorists have long recognized this tension between what's good for an employee today and what's good for the business down the road.[7] This concept is illustrated in Figure 14-1.

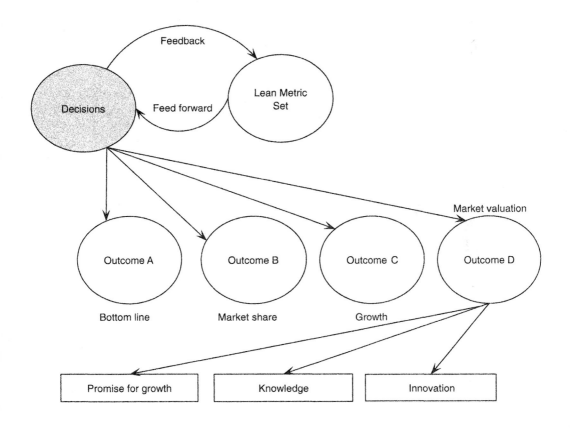

Figure 14-1   With a good set of lean metrics, decisions that improve them are the same decisions that improve the company's desired long-term outcomes.

RIGHT ANSWERS TO WRONG QUESTIONS

An interesting example[8] comes from a services firm that wanted to improve customer satisfaction with its telephone customer support center. Reasonably enough, the firm's managers decided to use the following metrics. On first thought, all of these seemed to make perfect sense. They were:

- Number of rings before the phone was answered
- Average waiting time before a representative came on line
- Number of calls answered per hour per representative
- Number of times a customer was put on hold
- Percentage of each hour that an average representative spent talking to a customer

All of them seemed easy to measure accurately and with little human effort. Very soon, the firm improved on all of these measures, but customers were highly dissatisfied. When the researchers probed a little deeper, they realized how the choice of metrics had created an *exactly opposite* effect of the one the firm had expected. Representatives were rushing their customers through their queries, were hanging up on them, giving them the most convenient answers, refusing to transfer them to more knowledgeable staff, and had become driven by exactly what was being measured—a lot of calls per hour without long holding times!

As Figure 14-2 illustrates, these metrics did not produce an effect that was intended because the ones that mattered most (customer satisfaction and accurate answers) were never measured. Perhaps they were more difficult to measure, and automated telephone monitoring equipment could not be used for the purpose. If such wrong metrics had not been chosen, customer satisfaction levels would not have taken the downward nosedive that they did.

Metrics that trigger agency conflict prove more damaging than helpful. Not all metrics that can be measured easily and cleanly, such as calls answered per hour or sales pitches per week, are necessarily good. Similarly, for knowledge work, measuring aspects such as time spent reading knowledge reports or intranet screens are poor metrics. I could as well be sipping a cappuccino (God forbid a Heineken!) and playing Quake II on my laptop while my desktop is connected to the KM system at work. The number of contributions by employees to a knowledge repository is an equally worthless measure. Employees then try to maximize the *number* of contributions, and the value of those contributions takes second place.[c] There is something to be learned from McKinsey; McKinsey evaluates the number of times its consultants' contributions are accessed by other consultants.

[c]When I tried to judge the level of contribution of the students (forum members) in one of my classes based on the number of contributions, I ran into a similar problem. Members tried to push up the count of their contributions, rather than focus on their relative worth. I tried a more successful approach later on: I counted the number of follow-up comments that their contributions raised and the number of times they responded to other people's posts. Such a policy was arguably more conducive to conversations and problem solving.

AGENCY-AGENT CONFLICTS

A summary of agency-agent conflict theory: A manager or employee will maximize the metrics that are actually measured. If a manager is told that a high market share for a product indicates brand value, he or she will try to maximize the market share of that product, even though quality (not measured) might be equally important. John Hauser and Gerald Katz explain this concept,[8] which is further illustrated in Figure 14-2.

Let A, B, C, Y, and Z be some arbitrary metrics. If all five of these are important, but only three of these—A, B, and X—are actually measured, employees will focus only on those and simply ignore Y and Z, however important they might be. Managers and employees who maximize A, B, and X will be rewarded for their performance, even if Y and Z go to the dogs. Soon, the entire company or department is focused on improving the metrics that are actually measured because they alone provide an indication of the quality of their work. If A, B, and X lead to productive results, the metrics are *considered* effective. If they fail to produce good results, they are considered ineffective. Hauser and Katz suggest that the chosen metrics gain tremendous inertia and that

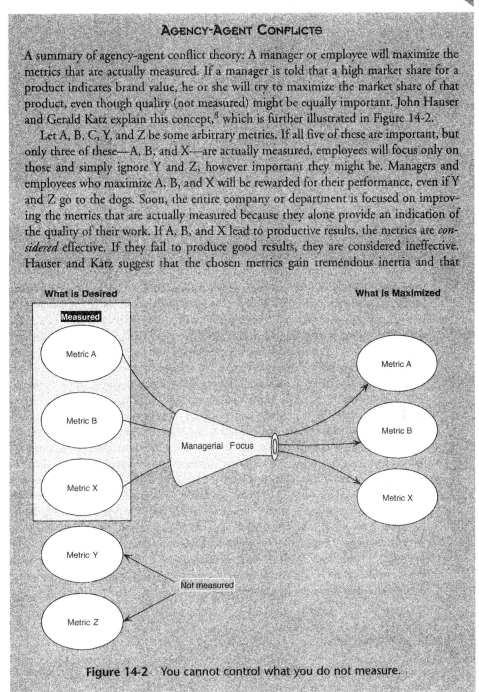

Figure 14-2   You cannot control what you do not measure.

employees who have painfully learned to maximize the chosen metrics fear to change course. The problem begins right there.

Knowledge sharing and creation often tend to be akin to metric Y—ignored and little rewarded. Knowledge-intensive companies, on the other hand, have included knowledge sharing and creation in their repositories of critical metrics. Every employee's compensation is, in part, determined by the amount of knowledge that the employee adds and the frequency with which other employees refer back to that contribution.[d] Choosing the right metrics is, therefore, critical, both to evaluate the performance of your KM strategy and to make it work in the first place.

REAL-OPTIONS ANALYSIS

Any reasonable and sensible manager, when confronted with a request for a few million dollars for managing the intangible asset that knowledge is, will bring up the question about what the expected payoff is. Many business decisions or investments cannot be made solely on the basis of hard data, such as financial numbers. No amount of analysis can eliminate the uncertainty associated with decisions, but real-options analysis can reduce these uncertainties and help quantify expected outcomes and risks. An investment in a KM system is rarely a one-step process.[9] A system, however elaborate, can be thought of as a sequential set of smaller systems, each of which can be pursued further or abandoned, based on the results from the preceding stage. This is especially true if the results-driven incrementalism (RDI) approach is adopted for development and deployment of the system. Each increment can be though of as investing in an option to pursue further opportunities for development and extension. This logic allows us to use real options, an approach derived from financial options theory for which Myron Scholes and Robert Merton were awarded the 1997 Nobel Prize in economics. The strength of options-based analysis lies in its ability to account explicitly for the value of flexibility for which traditional metrics cannot account.[10] This approach befriends uncertainty that other approaches fear. The higher the level of uncertainty (for example, Level 3 or 4 in our discussion in Chapter 6), the higher will be the value of flexibility. This approach also encourages managers to think of every investment in KM as an initial investment against a future possibility, such as an unanticipated shift in markets, change in customer preferences, unexpected innovation, or regulatory change.

THE OPTION SPACE

A KM project results in an initial cost that is fixed and irrecoverable.[11] In addition, each increment adds some variable cost to the picture (Figure 14-3).

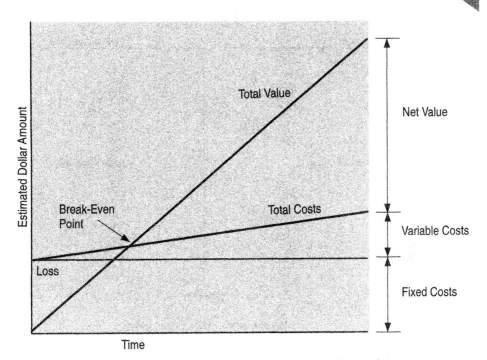

Figure 14-3   Costs and value generated from a specific KM investment.

The ratio of the net value to the sum total of such costs for each independent and decomposable investment is the starting point for options-based analysis. This option-value metric is represented on the X-axis of the option value space shown in Figure 14-4.[12] The Y-axis is the volatility metric. Together, these constitute the *option space*. At the middle of the option space is the Y-axis, with the two axes meeting at 1.00. This is the point where the estimated value equals costs. To the left of this point is the space where this ratio is less than unity, and to the right it exceeds unity. Correspondingly, KM investments that fall into the left side of this space (the negative region) are less likely to be as attractive as those that fall to the right (the positive region).

The option space can further be divided into a half-dozen segments that represent relative differences, compared with the adjacent segments. As we move clockwise from region 1 in Figure 14-5 to region 3, the KM investments that fall in the three regions range from ones that are relatively risk free and highly attractive to those that are fairly promising. As we continue further, the project possibilities that we encounter become decreasingly attractive, as Figure 14-5 illustrates.

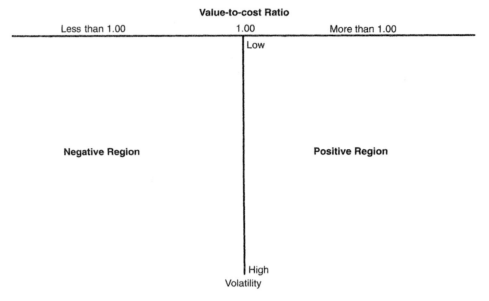

Figure 14-4   The option space.

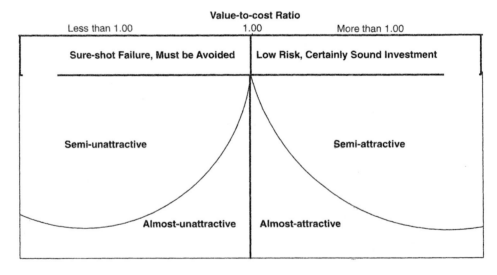

Figure 14-5   Regions of attractiveness in the options space.

KNOWLEDGE MANAGEMENT INVESTMENTS AS A PORTFOLIO OF OPTIONS

A series of investments in a KM initiative can be thought of as a series of options that build toward a portfolio.[13] Each investment might have a different level of risk, strategic intent, and time to fruition, as Figure 14-6 illustrates.

The goal is to nurture and manage a KM initiative as a *portfolio* of well-balanced investments. This requires managers to think in terms of all of the investments taken together, not independently.[14] Managers actively cultivating a portfolio of investments in KM can then attempt to push their KM investments as far to the right as possible before they move to the top region on either side. A comprehensive visual representation of the KM portfolio can be created by locating each investment in the real-options space. Figure 14-7 illustrates this for four hypothetical projects. Remember that adding a new project to the mix might shift the locations of the existing project opportunities. This is largely because of the complementarities[15] among investments: Adding one might make the others more attractive and less risky. The space should, therefore, be redrawn for each additional possibility that is considered.

Real-options analysis can allow managers to think several moves ahead of their present investments. The analytical approach powerfully combines both strategic and financial approaches to investment evaluation.[16] However, putting a dollar amount on the two option-space variables is the harder part. Proxy measures, such as patent counts, process innovation metrics, product development cycle time gains, and defect reduction, are one inelegant way.

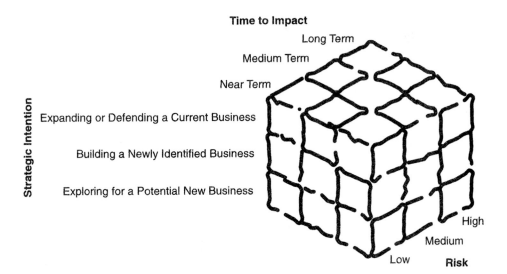

Figure 14-6   Features of a portfolio of KM investments.

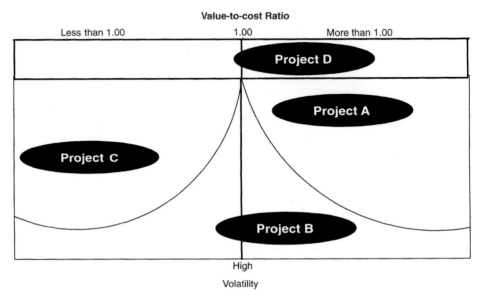

Figure 14-7 A portfolio of KM investments mapped to an options space.

Due to the extensive differences that exist between firms of a similar nature, a measure that might apply to one might not apply well to another. The following sections describe several approaches for calculating the input values for real-options models.

MEASURING INPUTS FOR REAL-OPTIONS MODELS

We met Roger Bohn's *Stages of Knowledge* framework in the preceding chapters. Thanks to its simplicity and ease of use, it provides a more readily usable methodology for measurement of process and technological knowledge. However, the biggest strength of this framework is also its primary weakness. *The Stages of Knowledge* technique is good at providing a 15,000-foot view and a clear *bigger picture*, but it does not let you examine processes and improvements at a lower level. We began with that model, but we will need to progress to some technique that is better suited for a microlevel analysis.

In the following sections, we examine three possible approaches to provide inputs for the foregoing real-options models. The first is a straightforward benchmarking methodology; this can be a good starting point, but in the long term, this technique loses value and flexibility. The second technique is the House of Quality.[17-23] That competes with the third technique, the *Balanced Scorecard* approach. The advantage of the House of Quality methodology is that it has been widely used, and a number of low-cost software tools partially automate its application.

BENCHMARKING

Benchmarking is an undertaking of companies that aim to emulate the ways things are done best anywhere, within or outside their firm, industry, or sector.[24] Many large firms have adopted benchmarking as a significant, systematic technique for measuring the company's performance toward its strategic goals. One argument for benchmarking is that there are existing best practices within different parts of the same company.[25] We begin by identifying those skills and capabilities within our own organizations before we look outside. Texas Instruments, Harris Corporation, AMP, UNISYS, and Rank Xerox have tried this approach and reaped substantial benefits and cost savings.[26] Benchmarking can also provide insights into areas such as:

- Overall productivity of knowledge investments
- Service quality
- Customer satisfaction and operational level of customer service
- Time to market in relation to other competitors
- Costs, profits, margins
- Relationships and relationship management

"The Wise Learn Many Things from Their Enemies"[27]

Even though the term *benchmarking* probably did not exist in 414 B.C., the time of the Aristophanes quote above, he said something very profound about it (Aristophanes could not guess at that time that his ideas would be so applicable to knowledge management)! By benchmarking your own business against your competitor's, you get information on how to tweak your company's performance goals to stay competitive, in relation to your competitors. By using such a relative measure, all companies stand to gain. By knowing where they stand on the intellectual forefront in relation to their competition, companies can focus on improving processes and process knowledge in areas where their scores are below average. Benchmarking, like any other business process, is most likely to produce a payback when strategic business objectives and goals drive it.[26]

Benchmark Targets

Table 14-1 summarizes possible targets against which you can benchmark your company's KM initiatives. You can identify other relevant targets from your own company, from rival firms, from nonrival firms, or from averages representing your industry or sector.[28] Each has its own benefits and down sides; the choice, finally, is one of subjective judgment and weighted costs.

There are companies that represent *the ideal firm* within each industry. Lacking any other options, this is usually the best place to begin. These firms have performance levels that other firms aspire to. In the software industry, arguably every firm aspires to be a Microsoft. In terms of customer loyalty, every firm aspires to be an Apple Computer. Other "role models" are listed in Table 14-2.

Table 14-1 What Do You Benchmark Against?

Benchmark Target	Upsides	Downsides
Other units within your company	This breaks down internal barriers to communication and conversation between various divisions and offices of your company; targets are easily accessible.	Internal policies might come into play; the measures are not indicative of what is considered superior performance in your industry.
Competing firms	Your company is measured against its direct competition; you get a fair understanding of the knowledge assets of your competitors as an aggregate; partners can easily be identified.	Legalities can make this very difficult; if a trusted third party such as a consulting firm is brought in, additional costs are imposed.
Industry	All of the above; this also lets you gauge your company's standing in the overall market	This can be very expensive; privacy issues begin to surface.
Cross-industry	You might be able to gain valuable insights from noncompeting firms and apply them to your own company.	All of the above; this does not let you gauge your company's standing in relation to your competitors; the sample population is not truly representative of your own industry or sector; it is often difficult to persuade companies to participate in such an effort; the cost of such an effort is rarely worth it.

Although benchmarking can be a good starting point, you need to be aware of its limitations. Benchmarking, by itself, cannot be used as a strategy for KM. Many companies, including Xerox, have successfully used it in their *10-step* program, but it is not a sufficient metric for knowledge work in and of itself. However, it can provide useful quantitative inputs for your real-options models.

THE BENCHMARKING PROCESS

On the lines of Xerox's benchmarking program, Spendolini[29] has suggested a five-step procedure for benchmarking efforts. An adapted version of this process applied to knowledge work is shown in Figure 14-8.

The benchmarking process can be used for *self-comparison,* as well. That is, you can use the benchmark to obtain an initial benchmark value before you implement a KM system or

Table 14-2 Prevalent Role Models in the Benchmarking Process

Performance Areas	Commonly Accepted Role Models
Speed of product development	The former Netscape Corporation
KM integration	Buckman Labs
Software development and marketing	Microsoft Corporation
Innovation and new product development	3M
Customer loyalty	Apple Computer
Brand management	Disney
JIT manufacturing	Toyota
Logistics	Wal-Mart
KM measurement efficacy	Skandia
Mail order	Dell, L.L. Bean
Franchising	McDonalds
Quality management	Motorola
Product line recognition	O'Reilly Publishers
Strategic planning	General Electric
Cost-based competition through market demand volume	E-machines Inc., Airtran, Southwest Airlines, Taco Bell

program. You can then, at a later stage, run the same benchmark to see whether anything has improved from last time. For example, you might want to see whether your knowledge-sharing network and customer support repository has had a positive effect on the average level of customer satisfaction. You can benchmark the level of customer satisfaction both before and after the new system is implemented and see whether any changes occurred. Be cautioned, however, that this is a slippery road: If you select the wrong benchmark, you will end up focusing on the wrong set of processes.

BENCHMARK LESSONS

If you consider your company's KM system to be a competitive resource, build into it the four things that benchmarking teaches.[30]

1. *Make it valuable.* Focus on including knowledge that is most valuable, then expand the coverage to less valuable knowledge. The key phrase is "valuable knowledge with relatively short-term payoffs." However, be careful not to ignore the long-term payoffs and investments. Let the types of knowledge (such as customer support knowledge, design

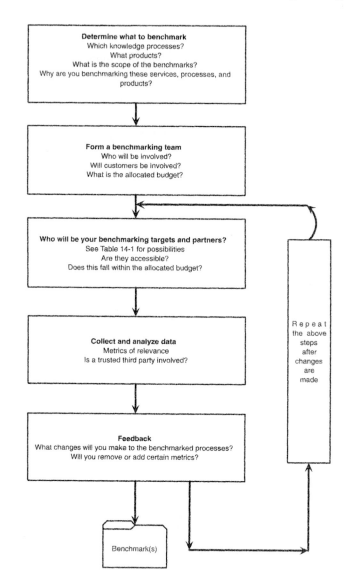

Figure 14-8 The benchmarking process adapted to knowledge work.[28,29]

knowledge, and competitive bid-related knowledge) that have immediate outcomes be the starting point, then expand the benchmark's coverage to other, less compelling or semi-significant areas. Benchmarking will, at the very least, provide information about the areas where you lag behind your competition. Focus on those areas *first*.

Anecdotal evidence suggests that managers do not buy into ideas that strain finances of a company without short-term payoffs for too long. Even though a comprehensive KM strategy might be at work in the background, show your senior management some short-term outcomes.

2. *Make it rare.* Focus on the areas of knowledge that give you an edge over competition. Through benchmarking studies, you can easily figure out the areas in which your competition is not strong. If any of those areas are a possible source of competitive advantage, by all means, support them!

Gateway, for example, is known for its customer service. If you have a problem with a computer you bought from them, you know that you will probably find a knowledgeable customer support representative on the other end. Almost all PC manufacturers have some kind of customer support, but Gateway decided to strengthen this over anything else. Most of Gateway's customers tend to be repeat buyers, simply because of its excellent customer service. Gateway also uses a customer knowledge repository to be able to track all previous problems that a customer might have had in the past.

Some companies build a competitive advantage by taking one of the given metrics to a level that is rare and that customers value. NEC has built on this rarity, as well. NEC's printer division provides an overnight replacement warranty for all its laser printers for two years from the date of purchase. By being able to track customer information through a sophisticated knowledge retrieval system, NEC provides overnight replacements after asking little more than one question (the printer's serial number) on the phone.[e]

3. *Make it hard to copy.* Customer data is an excellent example of a resource that is very hard to copy. Benchmarking can help you figure out the resources that you have and your competition does not. If you focus on resources that can be copied, it will, at best, buy you a temporary competitive advantage. However, if you focus on knowledge areas in which your employees possess skills, you can make it immensely difficult for your competition to copy those without luring away your employees. Consulting companies have known this for a long time, and it's about time you thought of applying the same idea to the knowledge assets within your own company.

4. *Make it hard to substitute.* Whatever categories of knowledge you focus on, make sure that straightforward substitutes do not exist. Companies that thought they had gained an edge by outsourcing a part of their manufacturing operations to firms in Third World countries did not take long to realize that everyone else could do the same. And they did.

Knowledge relating to skills, reputation, and experience cannot be easily substituted with close equivalents. Make sure you focus on such areas when you begin.

---

[e]My own experience with NEC bears this out. When I encountered a problem with my 1-year-old NEC laser printer, after a little more than one question I was told that my replacement printer was on the way and would be in the next day. With such excellent customer service, anyone could guess which laser printer I will buy next time I am in the market for one.

Benchmarking is unlikely to reveal such areas unless a high level of job diversity in the employee pool is involved in the effort.[f]

Benchmarking practices often reveal anecdotal evidence and impressions about competition. It's dangerous to rely on such impressions[28] because they cannot be generalized in any way. Benchmarking is most useful when you know what your expectations and objectives are and when the process itself is closely tied to your firm's knowledge drivers for strategy.

HOUSE OF QUALITY AND QUALITY FUNCTION DEPLOYMENT

The House of Quality approach was developed by Hauser and Clausing in a paper that originally appeared in the *Harvard Business Review*.[17] The use of this technique is commonly referred to as *Quality Function Deployment* (QFD). This methodology has been successfully adapted to link customer needs to business processes and internal decisions. Figure 14-9 shows the basic House of Quality metrics matrix.

House of Quality Metrics Matrix

We begin by listing the desirable outcomes on the left wall of the house. As the QFD method incorporates an increasing number of these desired outcomes, the *outcomes* wall of the *house* begins to build upward.

Be careful to select outcomes that are clearly observable without much delay. Being able to see outcomes clearly does not imply that they must be easily measurable quantitatively. Outcomes can be high level or low level. Examples of such outcomes include:

- Improve knowledge sharing to a level where 20 percent of an average employee's work is based on existing knowledge.
- Speed up problem solving by a factor of 5 percent over the next six months.
- Improve quality such that the rate of failure of product X decreases by 15 percent within the next 12 months.
- Generate more conversations among employees in the Atlanta and Barbados offices (a relatively vague but measurable outcome).
- Increase customer satisfaction levels by 50 percent (as measured by our surveys).

Although these should not exactly be your own goals, the point is that, even though some of the objectives might be high level, the outcomes are observable. On the other hand, objectives such as "create new knowledge" or "dominate the South American coffee markets

---

[f]This is in line with the Ikujiro Nonaka's idea that employees might not be aware of factors contributing to their success because these factors are often deeply embedded in their practices. Diversity in the population implies that participants starting at the upper-management level and going right down to the lay worker are involved.

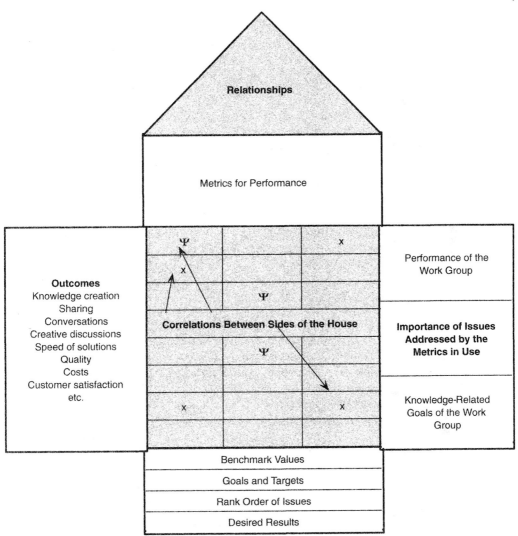

Figure 14-9 The basic metrics matrix used in the implementation of the House of Quality methodology.

(where the coffee market is a vague definition, domination is not articulated, and the extent of what is considered South American is unclear) are too vague. You'll never know when you get there, and when you get there, you'll never know that you are already there!

To designate relative priorities for these objectives, we attach weights to each of them. These weights form the right-hand wall of the house and indicate the importance of the issues in question. The selected objectives are grouped and listed on the left-hand side of the house

INDICATORS AT SKANDIA

Skandia's Intellectual Capital (IC) annual report also provides indicators of some other parameters that can be added to the House of Quality outcomes for analysis of KM effectiveness. Some ideas for such parameters, including some found in Skandia's IC annual report, are the following.

- Competence development expenses per employee in dollars
- Employee satisfaction
- Marketing expense per customer
- Time spent on systematic packaging of know-how for use after a project is completed
- Research and development expense to overhead expense ratios
- Training expenses per employee
- Payback on development activities
- Average development time per new product
- Average expense per dollar earned (for example, in consulting)
- Renewal expense per existing customer
- Level of customer attrition
- Expense of business development (new customers) per dollar spent on overheads
- Training expenses per customer per year in dollars
- Information-gathering expenses per existing customer
- Total competitive intelligence expense per year
- Expense (dollars) of distribution of new sales material and data
- Time spent per unsuccessful business bid
- Total number of patents held
- Number of patents pending
- Average time of approval for pending patents
- Employee attrition rate
- Dollar figure value of losses per employee lost
- Dollar figure value of losses per employee lost to a competing firm
- Expense of reinventing solutions per year
- Success ratio of new products and/or services
- Number of ideas implemented from the "suggestion box"
- Total production capacity or internal production capacity
- Capacity utilization
- Delivery time deviation rate

matrix. The relative weights are assigned to each of these objectives on a scale of 1 to 5. Appropriate performance metrics can then be listed and clustered on the top of the matrix (the ceiling). The matrix itself indicates the levels of correlation between the metrics and the performance outcomes. The decisions and metrics that also improve the outcome are said to have a high level of correlation. The interrelationships between all these parameters are represented on the roof of the house. By looking at the correlations within the body of the matrix, we can accurately focus on those areas of KM that are most likely to affect overall company performance and help us move toward preset goals.

THE BALANCED SCORECARD TECHNIQUE

The third approach that is a viable method for measuring knowledge-centric performance of your organization is the *Balanced Scorecard* approach. Kaplan and Norton originally proposed the Balanced Scorecard in their landmark article published in the *Harvard Business Review*.[31] The Balanced Scorecard provides a technique to "maintain a balance between long-term and short-term objectives, financial and nonfinancial measures, lagging and leading indicators, and between internal and external perspectives." The basic scorecard for translating vision and strategy into actual goals is shown in Figure 14-10.

The Balanced Scorecard can also be used to evaluate the impact of the KM system on four complementary criteria. The four processes involved in using the Balanced Scorecard approach for managing knowledge are described in Figure 14-11. These processes, specifically put in the context of KM, involve the following steps.

1. *Translate the KM vision.* As Figure 14-11 describes, this is the first process in the Balanced Scorecard strategy. At this stage, managers need to reach consensus as to why knowledge is being managed or needs to be managed. What are the firm's visions for the KM investment? The vision needs to be translated into concrete goals and objectives before any actions can be measured. The beauty of the Balanced Scorecard is that it can be used to create short-term, specific goals for individual employees, all of which feed to the organizational vision.

   While we are on the subject of vision, let me make it very clear that the vision rarely comes by copying the mission statement! Mission statements often carry too much fluff or are at too high a level to be actually useful. They need to be brought down to the level where two people can agree on what it says after reading the same document, and that is rarely the case with mission statements that most companies have. That's probably the reason why most mission statements are updated only when the next year's annual reports are due.[31,g]

2. *Communicate and link.* This lets you measure as you go along your objective of selling the idea to your company's employees. You can gauge how well your employees are being trained to use the system as a part of their work. You can also measure how well you have linked rewards to both the effective use and contribution of knowledge. Here, the KM champion must communicate the strategy along the entire rung of employees and demonstrate the links between individual employee goals, and the departmental/organizational goals, in terms of leveraging knowledge.

---

[g] As Kaplan and Norton have suggested, statements such as "number one supplier," "best in class," and "empowered organization" should be kept far away from the Balanced Scorecard.

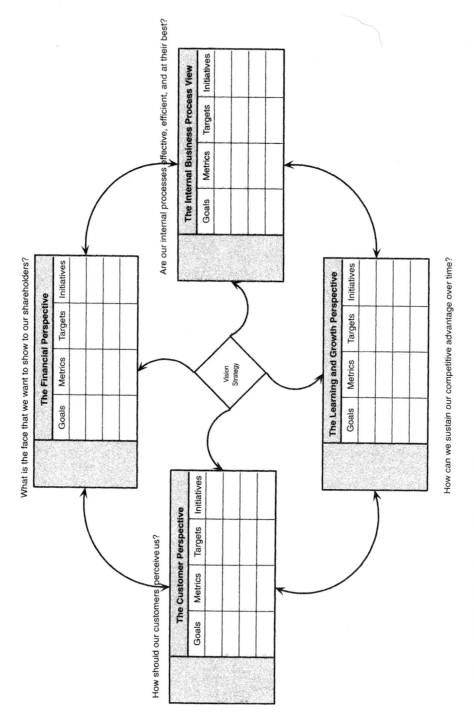

Figure 14-10 The Balanced Scorecard is a useful tool for translating strategy and vision into actual goals and targets.

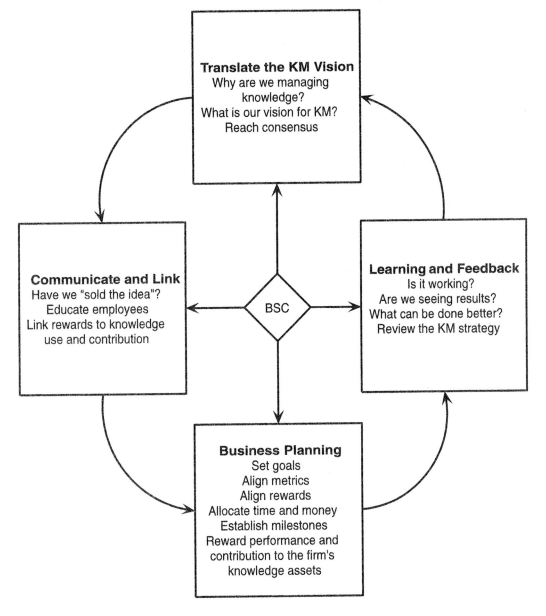

Figure 14-11   The KM Balanced Scorecard.

3. Do a reality check. This part of the Balanced Scorecard strategy determines how well your chosen metrics, explicated goals, targets, and allocated resources align with the initial ideas you had in mind for the KM system.

4. *Incorporate learning and feedback.* The Balanced Scorecard lets you evaluate the goals, metrics, and targets that you have chosen for your KM system, then analyze how well they are actually working.

In summary, the Balanced Scorecard approach lets you track the current health of the KM strategy that you have chosen for your company.

By replacing the original four perspectives with measures successfully used by Skandia, a knowledge-based version of the Balanced Scorecard can be obtained. The underlying implementation and use would be akin to the conventional Balanced Scorecard method, but the measures provided will be those relating to KM. This way, the financial, customer-related, process capability-related and employee performance-related gains coming from the KM system can be simultaneously tracked.

The actual implementation and use of the Balanced Scorecard approach is beyond the intended scope of this chapter. Now you have a starting point for applying the Balanced Scorecard to KM. For implementation level details, I recommend reading *The Balanced Scorecard.*[36]

As Kaplan and Norton state, a Balanced Scorecard need not have just four dimensions. It can have five, six, or seven. The only concern in going beyond seven is that you have too much to keep track of, and a lot of it isn't even *critical.* KPMG, for example, uses five different dimensions for its scorecards (see Table 14-3).

Table 14-3 KPMG's Choice of Dimensions for Its Balanced Scorecard

Balanced Scorecard Dimensions	Questions
Client orientation	What do I want to achieve with my existing clients?
Market orientation	What am I going to do to decrease existing client turnover and find new clients? What am I going to do to strengthen my position in the business?
People orientation	What am I going to do to enable the team that I am managing to function better and to help my employees gain stronger competencies?
Result orientation	How can I attain better results with the same inputs? How can I increase the added value of my teams and myself?
Personal effectiveness	What am I going to do in the coming year to improve weak points and strengthen strong points?
Professionalism	How do I keep abreast of the newest developments? How do I collaborate with my peers more extensively?

Although these choices seem reasonable, I recommend that you try using the dimensions suggested in Figure 14-12 which are based on Skandia's Navigator and which the company has used very effectively. The choice of dimensions is not set in stone. As long as you are sure about what you are measuring and why you are measuring it, that variable has a justifiable place on the Balanced Scorecard that your company adopts.

Advantages of Knowledge Management Balanced Scorecards

The Balanced Scorecard has some characteristics that the other approaches discussed in this chapter do not have. These characteristics make it especially useful as a knowledge metric.

- The ability to provide a snapshot of the intellectual health of your firm at any point in time.
- Built-in cause-and-effect relationships that can help you guide your KM strategy.
- A sufficient (neither too many nor too few) number of performance drivers and metrics.
- Capability to communicate the KM strategy throughout the firm.
- Capability to link individual goals with the overall knowledge strategy of the firm. This implies that each employee can *do his or her own* Balanced Scorecard and continue to contribute toward the goals of the KM system and strategy without even realizing it!
- A direct and often missing link between long-term knowledge and competence goals of the firm and its annual budget.
- Translation of the lofty visions of a firm into more doable, realistic, manageable, and specific performance goals.
- Logical integration into the overall strategy of your business while still making sense.
- Objective measurement of the contribution of knowledge to the more intangible sources of competitive advantage, such as customer satisfaction and employee skills and competencies.
- A direct link to financial measures and your KM system's effect on the company bottom line.

Limitations of Knowledge Management Balanced Scorecards

On the downside, a well-designed Balanced Scorecard is more difficult to develop than a similar quality function deployment (QFD) model. It is rarely possible to adopt directly another firm's Balanced Scorecard because subtle differences exist even between *very* similar firms.

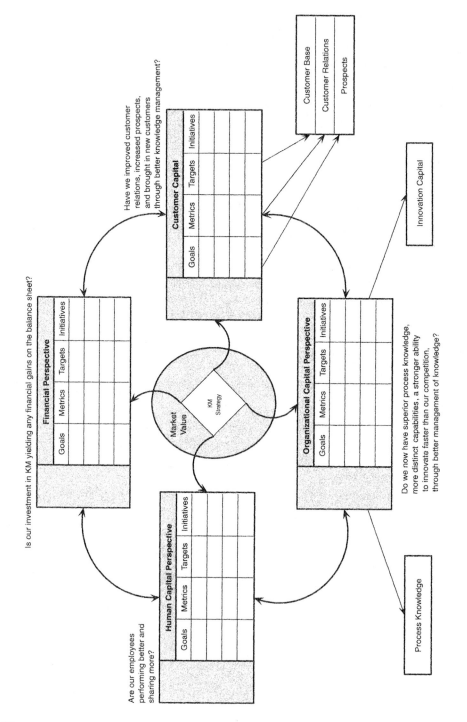

Figure 14-12 A modified KM scorecard.

ALTERNATIVE METRICS

Besides the three methods that we discussed in this chapter, there are two other specific ways to evaluate Returns on Knowledge Investments (RoKIs): the Skandia method, and the FASB method. None of these are mainstream, nor do they lend themselves to easy adaptation by most organizations because of vagueness and company specificity (in the case of Skandia's method) involved; they are mentioned here only for completeness.

The Skandia Method

The method used by the Swedish insurance company Skandia is one of the pioneering attempts at measuring knowledge. Skandia still refuses to call it *knowledge* and calls it *intellectual capital* instead. Skandia uses a number of ratios in which the company not only looks back at the past but also looks at the present and to the future. The objections to this method include the notion that such ratios are easy to influence, and each company can decide for itself which ratios to use and which not to use. Skandia makes its IC reports, which are an addendum to its annual financial report, publicly available over the Web (see www.skandia.se). The IC addendum to the annual report makes very interesting reading and provides insights into the manner in which the pioneering company approached KM metrics.*

The FASB Method

The other method that has been developed in the United States by the Financial Accounting Standards Board (FASB) is the FASB Knowledge Measurement Method, which aims to find an answer to the question of how companies can and should report their knowledge. The proposed method is based on the notion that there should be a division between financial capital and intellectual capital in a company's annual report. If this actually becomes a guideline, companies will be legally required to present and evaluate their knowledge assets in a standard format in their annual reports. That will produce an unprecedented amount of valuable information for the company's shareholders and other interested parties.

---

*Also see the APQC Process Classification Framework, a digital version of which is provided on the CD-ROM accompanying this book.

LESSONS LEARNED

There are no perfect metrics for knowledge work, but this chapter provides you with a good starting point. Measuring the performance of your KM system and its contribution to your company's financial and competence bottom line is absolutely critical. After all, measuring where KM is taking you and demonstrating it well might be critical for the next round of funding that the project will receive from your CFO.

Keep the following tips in mind while devising KM metrics for your company.

- *Metrics define KM success.* Robust metrics help measure the business impact of KM. A few robust metrics with immediate reward ties for knowledge workers are better than many weak ones that cannot be controlled. Focus on knowledge that is valuable, rare, hard to copy, and hard to substitute when you are trying to decide on metric variables. Reward both internal and external knowledge integration through metrics that can be measured today with impact on future outcomes.

- *Use real-options analysis.* The various approaches described in this chapter can provide useful inputs for real-options-based analyses of both existing KM investments and future opportunities. This approach explicitly accounts for the value of flexibility in your business's context—a luxury that no other metric affords.

- *Manage a KM initiative as a portfolio of projects.* The options space model described here allows you to manage a KM project as a collection of smaller subprojects and initiatives. Just as in a financial portfolio, you must diversify; plan on near-term impact with some and longer term impact with some.

- *Do not ignore the soft stuff.* Metrics must take both hard and soft results into account to present a true picture of your firm's intellectual health.

- *Metrics in the rear view mirror appear more significant than they are:* Ask yourself the question, Do we have metrics that can serve as early warning signals for future problems and those that signal future opportunities?

PART III
SIDE ROADS:
APPENDICES

Digital Appendix A

The Knowledge Management Assessment Kit

This appendix brings together lists, questions, evaluation formats, diagnostics instruments, and techniques to help you get started on the KM road. For convenience, these processes are assembled as electronic software-based forms on the companion CD-ROM. Each user-editable (fill-in PDF and Microsoft Word) form can be customized and filled out with details specific to your KM project, then printed.

You follow the phases of the now-familiar 10 steps, beginning with an inventory of existing physical assets and going to the more difficult task of inventorying existing knowledge. Use this tool to gauge the preimplementation rankings on the specified criteria and to track improvement after the introduction of a KM system and KM strategy.

As with most projects, preplanning and thorough grounding in the subject are essential to success. And they take the most time and effort. So take time and whatever effort is needed to work through the forms provided in this Knowledge Management Assessment Kit (KMAK). Edit, circulate, send out for review by colleagues, and revise. Then go through that cycle again. By the end of this process, you'll find that you have agreeable answers to questions that will come up at various stages on the 10-step road map.

The result of this kit is your own, populated road map, which serves as a guide to, as well as a checklist for an effective, valuable, efficient KM system. We provide an example that was built from the preceding chapters.

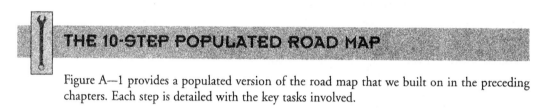

THE 10-STEP POPULATED ROAD MAP

Figure A—1 provides a populated version of the road map that we built on in the preceding chapters. Each step is detailed with the key tasks involved.

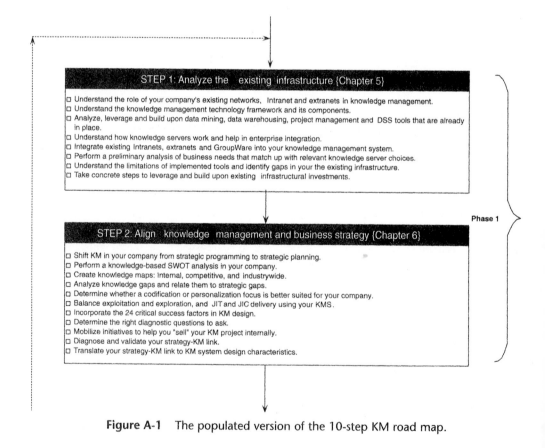

STEP 1: Analyze the existing infrastructure (Chapter 5)

☐ Understand the role of your company's existing networks, Intranet and extranets in knowledge management.
☐ Understand the knowledge management technology framework and its components.
☐ Analyze, leverage and build upon data mining, data warehousing, project management and DSS tools that are already in place.
☐ Understand how knowledge servers work and help in enterprise integration.
☐ Integrate existing Intranets, extranets and GroupWare into your knowledge management system.
☐ Perform a preliminary analysis of business needs that match up with relevant knowledge server choices.
☐ Understand the limitations of implemented tools and identify gaps in your the existing infrastructure.
☐ Take concrete steps to leverage and build upon existing infrastructural investments.

Phase 1

STEP 2: Align knowledge management and business strategy (Chapter 6)

☐ Shift KM in your company from strategic programming to strategic planning.
☐ Perform a knowledge-based SWOT analysis in your company.
☐ Create knowledge maps: Internal, competitive, and industrywide.
☐ Analyze knowledge gaps and relate them to strategic gaps.
☐ Determine whether a codification or personalization focus is better suited for your company.
☐ Balance exploitation and exploration, and JIT and JIC delivery using your KMS.
☐ Incorporate the 24 critical success factors in KM design.
☐ Determine the right diagnostic questions to ask.
☐ Mobilize initiatives to help you "sell" your KM project internally.
☐ Diagnose and validate your strategy-KM link.
☐ Translate your strategy-KM link to KM system design characteristics.

Figure A-1 The populated version of the 10-step KM road map.

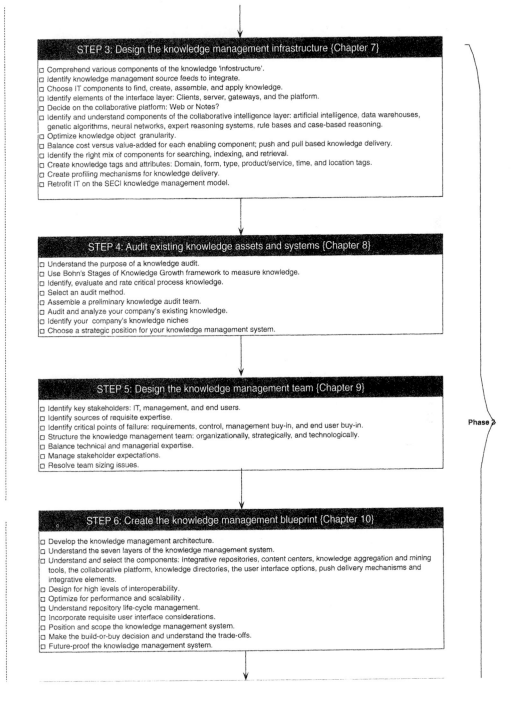

STEP 3: Design the knowledge management infrastructure {Chapter 7}

☐ Comprehend various components of the knowledge 'infostructure'.
☐ Identify knowledge management source feeds to integrate.
☐ Choose IT components to find, create, assemble, and apply knowledge.
☐ Identify elements of the interface layer: Clients, server, gateways, and the platform.
☐ Decide on the collaborative platform: Web or Notes?
☐ Identify and understand components of the collaborative intelligence layer: artificial intelligence, data warehouses, genetic algorithms, neural networks, expert reasoning systems, rule bases and case-based reasoning.
☐ Optimize knowledge object granularity.
☐ Balance cost versus value-added for each enabling component; push and pull based knowledge delivery.
☐ Identify the right mix of components for searching, indexing, and retrieval.
☐ Create knowledge tags and attributes: Domain, form, type, product/service, time, and location tags.
☐ Create profiling mechanisms for knowledge delivery.
☐ Retrofit IT on the SECI knowledge management model.

STEP 4: Audit existing knowledge assets and systems {Chapter 8}

☐ Understand the purpose of a knowledge audit.
☐ Use Bohn's Stages of Knowledge Growth framework to measure knowledge.
☐ Identify, evaluate and rate critical process knowledge.
☐ Select an audit method.
☐ Assemble a preliminary knowledge audit team.
☐ Audit and analyze your company's existing knowledge.
☐ Identify your company's knowledge niches
☐ Choose a strategic position for your knowledge management system.

STEP 5: Design the knowledge management team {Chapter 9}

☐ Identify key stakeholders: IT, management, and end users.
☐ Identify sources of requisite expertise.
☐ Identify critical points of failure: requirements, control, management buy-in, and end user buy-in.
☐ Structure the knowledge management team: organizationally, strategically, and technologically.
☐ Balance technical and managerial expertise.
☐ Manage stakeholder expectations.
☐ Resolve team sizing issues.

STEP 6: Create the knowledge management blueprint {Chapter 10}

☐ Develop the knowledge management architecture.
☐ Understand the seven layers of the knowledge management system.
☐ Understand and select the components: Integrative repositories, content centers, knowledge aggregation and mining tools, the collaborative platform, knowledge directories, the user interface options, push delivery mechanisms and integrative elements.
☐ Design for high levels of interoperability.
☐ Optimize for performance and scalability .
☐ Understand repository life-cycle management.
☐ Incorporate requisite user interface considerations.
☐ Position and scope the knowledge management system.
☐ Make the build-or-buy decision and understand the trade-offs.
☐ Future-proof the knowledge management system.

Phase 2

STEP 7: Develop the knowledge management system {Chapter 11}

- ☐ Define the capabilities of each layer of the seven-layer KMS architecture in the context of your company.
- ☐ Develop the interface layer. Create platform independence, leverage the intranet, enable universal authorship.
- ☐ Develop the access and authentication layer: secure data, control access, and distribute control.
- ☐ Develop the collaborative filtering and intelligence layer.
- ☐ Develop and integrate the application layer with the intelligence layer and the transport layer.
- ☐ Leverage the extant transport layer.
- ☐ Develop the middleware and legacy integration layer to connect mainframe legacy data, incompatible platforms, inconsistent data formats, and retired systems.
- ☐ Integrate and enhance the repository layer.
- ☐ Apply DMA and WebDAV standards to explicit content and documents.
- ☐ Advance the system from a client/server to agent computing orientation.

STEP 8: Deploy using the results driven incremental methodology {Chapter 12}

- ☐ Select a nontrivial and representative pilot project.
- ☐ Identify and isolate failure points in the pilot project.
- ☐ Use prototypes for proof-of-concept evaluation.
- ☐ Understand the knowledge management system life cycle.
- ☐ Understand the scope of knowledge management system deployment.
- ☐ Use the RDI methodology to deploy the system.
- ☐ Convert factors to processes.
- ☐ Create cumulative results-driven business releases.
- ☐ Select and initialize releases with the highest payoffs first.
- ☐ Eliminate Information packaging methodology and SLDC orientation.
- ☐ Identify and avoid the traps in the RDI methodology.

Phase 3

STEP 9: Manage change, culture and reward structures {Chapter 13}

- ☐ Understand how a CKO is related to the CIO, CFO, and CEO.
- ☐ Decide whether you need an actual/formally-appointed CKO.
- ☐ Organize the four broad categories of the CKO's responsibilities.
- ☐ Understand the CKO's technological and organizational functions.
- ☐ Understand the backgrounds the industry's most successful CKOs come from.
- ☐ Enable process triggers for knowledge management system success.
- ☐ Plan for knowledge management success using the CKO as an agent for selling foresight.
- ☐ Manage and implement cultural and process change to make the knowledge management system succeed.
- ☐ Decide what reward structures are needed to complement successful knowledge management and how you can implement them.

STEP 10: Real Options-based ROI and Performance Metrics {Chapter 14}

- ☐ Understand how to measure the business impact of knowledge management.
- ☐ Calculate ROI for knowledge management investments.
- ☐ Decide when to use benchmarking as a comparative knowledge metric.
- ☐ Evaluate knowledge management ROI using the Balanced Scorecard method.
- ☐ Use Quality Function Deployment for creating strategic knowledge metrics.
- ☐ Create a set of lean metrics.
- ☐ Identify what not to measure.
- ☐ Understand alternative metrics such as the Skandia Navigator and the FASB approach.
- ☐ Classify and evaluate processes using the APQC Process Classification framework.
- ☐ Review and select software tools for tracking complex metrics.

Phase 4

A 30-page KM assessment manual (see APPENDIX-A.PDF in the APPENDIX directory) is provided electronically on the CD-ROM, along with the knowledge management toolkit, digital version. The digital version of this appendix discusses the details of each step of the road map and describes how to use specific evaluation forms to assess various aspects of KM in the context of your organization. This will help you ensure that your KM system is strategically integrated with actual business processes relevant to your company.

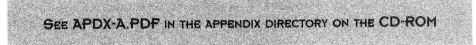

SEE APDX-A.PDF IN THE APPENDIX DIRECTORY ON THE CD-ROM

DIGITAL APPENDIX B

ALTERNATIVE SCHEMES FOR STRUCTURING THE KNOWLEDGE MANAGEMENT PLATFORM FRONT END

Web-based front ends for KM systems, such as intranets, need not be arranged in traditional hierarchical structures. This 11-page digital appendix provides examples of several alternative arrangement schemes both for site contents and maps. Each style is followed by an example and a location URL that you can investigate further. See APPENDIX-B.PDF in the APPENDIX directory on the companion CD-ROM for a complete digitized version of this appendix.

As part of this appendix, the following schemes are described with case examples:

- Alphabetical
- Alphanumerical
- Dewey Decimal Coding
- Public library classification

- Universal Decimal Classification
- ACM Computing Classification
- Library of Congress Classification
- Predicast Revised Event Coding

SEE APPENDIX-B.PDF IN THE APPENDIX DIRECTORY

Digital Appendix C
Software Tools

COMPUTERS MAKE IT EASIER TO DO A LOT OF THINGS, BUT MOST
OF THE THINGS THEY MAKE IT EASIER TO DO DON'T NEED TO BE DONE.
ANDY ROONEY

The digitized, printable version of this appendix is provided on the companion CD-ROM. Look for APPENDIX-C.PDF under the APPENDIX directory. This 25-page digital appendix reviews some software tools that are relevant to the creation of a KM platform. Many of the tools reviewed here are also included on the companion CD-ROM (indicated by 🖫).

SEE APPENDIX-C.PDF IN THE APPENDIX DIRECTORY

ENDNOTES

CHAPTER 1

1. Drucker, P., *Management Challenges for the 21st Century*, Harper Business, New York (1999), p. ix.

2. Klasson, Kirk, Managing Knowledge for Advantage: Content and Collaboration Technologies, *The Cambridge Information Network Journal,* vol. 1, no. 1 (1999), pp. 33–41.

3. See OECD Report, *Investment in Knowledge*, <www.OECD.org>, 2001.

4. Davenport, Thomas H., and Laurence Prusak, *Working Knowledge: How Organizations Manage What They Know,* Harvard Business School Press, Boston, (1998), p. 5.

5. Quintas, Paul, Open University Professor of Knowledge Management, quoted in Open Eye: Head Back to the Business Cafe, *The Independent*, London, February 4, (1999), p. OE9.

6. Ahuja, G., Collaboration Networks, Structural Holes, and Innovation: A Longitudinal Study, *Administrative Science Quarterly,* vol. 45 (2000), pp. 425–455.

7. Drucker, P. N. "The New Workforce," in *The Next Society: A Survey of the Near Future, The Economist*, November 3, 2001, pp. 8–11.

8. Carrillo, J., and Gaimon, C., Improving Manufacturing Performance Through Process Change and Knowledge Creation, *Management Science*, vol. 46, no. 2 (2000), pp. 263–288.

9. See Bair, Jim, Knowledge Management: The Era of Shared Ideas, *Forbes*, September 22, (1997).

10. See Hansen, M., N. Nohria, and T. Tierney, What's Your Strategy for Managing Knowledge? *Harvard Business Review*, March–April (1999), pp. 106–116.

11. Postrell, Virginia, *The Future and Its Enemies*, Touchstone Books, New York, (1998).

12. Iansiti, M., How the Incumbent Can Win: Managing Technological Transitions in the Semiconductor Industry, *Management Science*, vol. 46, no. 2 (2000), pp. 169–185.

13. Abramson, Gary, The Thrill of the Hunt, *CIO Enterprise*, January 15, (1999), pp. 35–42.

14. See Miner, A., Bassoff, P., and Moorman, C., Organizational Improvisation and Learning: A Field Study, *Administrative Science Quarterly*, vol. 46 (2001), pp. 304–337.

15. Khurana, Anil, Managing Complex Production Processes, *Sloan Management Review* (Winter 1999), pp. 85–97.

16. See Fabris, Peter, You Think Tomaytoes, I Think Tomahtoes, *CIO* (April 1 1999), pp. 46–52 for a detailed account of how Bay Networks ended up saving $10 million a year through KM.

17. Iansiti, Marco, and MacCormack, Alan, Developing Products on Internet Time, *Harvard Business Review* (September–October 1997), pp. 108–117.

18. Alavi, M, Knowledge Management and Knowledge Management Systems: Conceptual Foundations and Research Issues, *MIS Quarterly*, vol. 25, no. 1 (2001), pp. 107–136.

19. Christensen, C., Suarez, F., and Utterback, J., Strategies for Survival in Fast-Changing Industries, *Management Science*, vol. 45, no.12 (1998), pp. 207–220.

20. Dempsey, Michael, Buzzword Has Already Made a Lot of Enemies: The Role of the Chief Knowledge Officer, *Financial Times*, London (April 28, 1999), p. 2.

21. Lapre, M., and Wassenhove, L., Creating and Transferring Knowledge for Productivity Improvement in Factories, *Management Science*, vol. 47, no. 10 (2001), pp. 1311–1325.

22. Krochmal, Mo, Tech Guru: People Are Key to Knowledge Management, *New York Times*, (June 9, 1999), quoting Laurence Prusak, Executive Director of KM at IBM.

23. MacCormack, A., Verganti, R., and Iansiti, M., Developing Products on Internet Time: The Anatomy of a Flexible Development Process, *Management Science*, vol. 47, no. 1 (2001), pp. 133–150.

24. Yourdon, E., *Managing High-Intensity Internet Projects*, Yourdon Press/Prentice Hall, Upper Saddle River (2002).

25. Zack, Michael H., Developing a Knowledge Strategy, *California Management Review*, vol. 41, no. 3 (Spring 1999), pp. 125–145.

26. Also see Drucker, P., *Management Challenges for the 21st Century*, Harper Business, New York (1999), p. 33.

27. Shenhar, A., One Size Does Not Fit All Projects: Exploring Classical Contingency Domains, *Management Science,* vol. 47 no. 3 (2001), pp. 393–414.

28. Also see Zmud, R. W., An Examination of "Push-Pull" Theory Applied to Process Innovation in Knowledge Work, *Management Science,* vol. 30, no. 6 (1984), pp. 727–738.

CHAPTER 2

1. Ford Motor Company home page <http://www.ford.com>.

2. Sharp Electronics Corp. home page <http://www.sharp-usa.com>.

3. Leifer et al., presentation at Stanford Center for Design and Manufacturing Research, Palo Alto, CA, March 1990.

4. See Davenport, Thomas, Jarvenpaa, and Beers, Michael, Improving Knowledge Work Processes, *Sloan Management Review* (Summer 1996), pp. 53–65; Davenport, Thomas, DeLong, David, and Beers, Michael, Successful Knowledge Management Projects, *Sloan Management Review,* vol. 39, no. 2 (1998), pp. 43–57.

5. Dhar, Vasant, and Stein, Roger, *Seven Methods for Transforming Corporate Data into Business Intelligence,* Prentice Hall, Upper Saddle River, NJ (1997).

6. Yli-Renko, H., Autio, E., and Sapienza, H., Social Capital, Knowledge Acquisition, and Knowledge Exploitation in Technology-based Firms, *Strategic Management Journal,* vol. 22 (2001), pp. 587–613.

7. See Tiwana, A., and McLean, E., Managing the Unexpected, *Communications of the ACM* (2002–forthcoming) and Alavi, M., and Tiwana, A. Knowledge Integration in Virtual Teams: The Potential Role of Knowledge Management Systems, *Journal of the American Society for Information Science and Technology* (2002–forthcoming).

8. Nonaka, I., and Konno, N., The Concept of "Ba": Building a Foundation for Knowledge Creation, *California Management Review,* vol. 40, no. 3 (1998), pp. 40–55.

9. Davenport, Thomas, DeLong, Davis, and Michael Beers, Successful Knowledge Management Projects, *Sloan Management Review,* vol. 39, no. 2 (1998), pp. 43–57.

10. Song, Michael, and Montoya-Weiss, Mitzi, Critical Development Activities for Really New versus Incremental Products, *Journal of Product Innovation Management,* vol. 15 (1998), pp. 124–135.

11. Grudin, J., Evaluating Opportunities for Design Capture, in M. Carroll (Ed.), *Design Rationale: Concepts, Techniques and Use,* Lawrence Erlbaum Associates, Mahwah, NJ (1996).

12. Teece, David, Research Directions for Knowledge Management, *California Management Review,* vol. 40, no. 3 (1998), pp. 289–292.

13. See Asea Brown Boveri's Web site at <www.abb.com>.

14. Drucker, P., *Management Challenges for the 21st Century*, Harper Business, New York (1999).

15. Nonaka, I., A Dynamic Theory of Organizational Knowledge Creation, *Organization Science*, vol. 5 (1994), pp. 14–37.

16. Jones, Malcolm M., and McLean, Ephraim R., Management Problems in Large-Scale Software Development Projects, *Industrial Management Review*, vol. 11 (Spring 1970), pp. 1–15.

17. Pisano, G., "Knowledge, Integration, and the Locus of Learning: An Empirical Analysis of Process Development," *Strategic Management Journal 15* (1994) pp. 85–100.

18. Basili, V., and Caldiera, G., Improve Software Quality by Reusing Knowledge and Experience, *Sloan Management Review* (Fall 1995) pp. 55–64.

CHAPTER 3

1. Davenport, Thomas H., and Prusak, Laurence, *Working Knowledge: How Organizations Manage What They Know*, Harvard Business School Press, Boston (1998).

2. Tversky, A., and Kahneman, D., The Framing of Decisions and the Psychology of Choice, *Science,* vol. 211 (1981), pp. 453–458.

3. Rowe, G., and Wright, G., The Delphi Technique as a Forecasting Tool: Issues and Analysis, *International Journal of Forecasting*, vol. 15 (1999),pp. 353–375.

4. Baerentsen, K. B., and Slavensky, H., A Contribution to the Design Process, *Communications of the ACM*, vol. 42, no. 5 (1999), p. 72.

5. Buckley, P., and Carter, M., Knowledge Management in Global Technology Markets: Applying Theory to Practice, *Long Range Planning*, vol. 33 (2000) pp. 55–71.

6. See Davenport, Thomas H., Jarvenpaa, Sirkka, and Beers, Michael, Improving Knowledge Work Processes, *Sloan Management Review* (Summer 1996), pp. 53–65.

7. Davenport, Thomas H., *Process Innovation: Reengineering Work through Information Technology*, Harvard Business School Press, Boston (1993).

8. Ramesh, Balasubramaniam, and Sengupta, Kishore, Multimedia in a Design Rationale Decision Support System, *Decision Support Systems*, vol. 15 (1995), pp. 181–196.

9. Nonaka, Ikujiro, The Knowledge Creating Company, *Harvard Business Review* (November–December 1991), pp. 2–9.

10. Nonaka, Ikujiro, and Konno, Noboru, The Concept of "Ba": Building a Foundation for Knowledge Creation, *California Management Review*, vol. 40, no. 3 (1998), pp. 40–55.

11. See Dhar, Vasant, and Stein, Roger, *Seven Methods for Transforming Corporate Data into Business Intelligence*, Prentice Hall, Upper Saddle River, NJ (1997).

12. Eureka, William E., and Ryan, Nancy E., *Quality Up, Costs Down: A Manager's Guide to Taguchi Methods and QFD*, ASI Press, Burr Ridge, IL (1995).

13. Fahey, Liam, and Prusak Laurence, The Eleven Deadliest Sins of Knowledge Management, *California Management Review*, vol. 40, no. 3 (1998), pp. 265–276.

14. Davenport, Thomas H., and Prusak, Laurence, *Working Knowledge: How Organizations Manage What They Know*, Harvard Business School Press, Boston (1998).

15. See Ramesh B., Tiwana A., Supporting Collaborative Process Knowledge Management in New Product Development Teams, *Decision Support Systems*, vol. 27 no. 1–2 (1999) pp. 213–235.

16. MacCormack, A., Verganti, R., and Iansiti, M. Developing Products on Internet Time: The Anatomy of a Flexible Development Process, *Management Science*, vol. 47 no. 1 (2001), pp. 133–150.

17. Simon, Herbert A., Bounded Rationality and Organizational Learning, *Organization Science*, vol. 2, no. 1 (1991), pp. 125–134

18. Travic, Robert, Information Aspects of New Organizational Designs: Exploring the Non-Traditional Organization, *Journal of the American Society for Information Science*, vol. 49, no.13 (November 1998), pp. 1224–1244.

19. Quinn, James B., *Intelligent Enterprise: A Knowledge and Service Based Paradigm for Industry*, Free Press, New York (1992).

20. Quinn, James B., Anderson, Philip, and Finkelstein, Sydney, Managing Professional Intellect: Making the Most of the Best, *Harvard Business Review* (1996), pp. 71–80.

21. Iansiti, Marco, and MacCormack, Alan, Developing Products on Internet Time, *Harvard Business Review*, (September–October 1997), pp. 108–117.

22. Larsson, R., Lars, B., Henriksson, K., and Sparks, J., The Inter-Organizational Learning Dilemma: Collective Knowledge Development in Strategic Alliances, *Organization Science*, vol. 9, no. 3 (1998), pp. 285–305.

23. Nevis, E., DiBella, A., and Gould, J., Understanding Organizations as Learning Systems, *Sloan Management Review*, Winter (1995) pp. 73-85.

CHAPTER 5

1. Tapscott, D., Ticoll, D., and Lowy, A., *Digital Capital: Harnessing the Power of Business Webs*, Harvard Business School Press, Boston (2000).

2. Yoffie, D. B., and Cusumano, M. A., Building a Company on Internet Time: Lessons from Netscape, *California Management Review*, vol. 41, no. 3 (1999), p. 8.

3. Buur, J., and Bagger, K., Replacing Usability Testing with User Dialogue, *Communications of the ACM*, vol. 42, no. 5 (1999), p. 63.

4. Nonaka, I., and Konno, N., The Concept of "Ba": Building a Foundation for Knowledge Creation, *California Management Review*, vol. 40, no. 3 (1998), pp. 40–55.

5. Tiwana, A., and Ramesh, B., Integrating Knowledge on the Web, *IEEE Internet Computing* (May–June 2001), pp. 2–9.

6. Tiwana, A., Affinity to Infinity: Peer-to-Peer Knowledge Platforms, *Communications of the ACM*, in press.

7. Davenport, T., and Prusak, L., *Working Knowledge*, Harvard Business School Press, Boston (1998).

8. Tiwana, A., and Ramesh, B., Integrating Knowledge on the Web, *IEEE Internet Computing* (May–June 2001), pp. 2–9.

9. Schilling, M., Toward a General Modular Systems Theory and Its Application to Interfirm Product Modularity, *Academy of Management Review*, vol. 25, no. 2 (2000), pp. 312–334.

10. Baldwin, C., and Clark, K., Managing in an Age of Modularity, *Harvard Business Review* (September–October 1997), pp. 84–93.

Chapter 6

1. Fahey, Liam, and Prusak, Laurence, The Eleven Deadliest Sins of Knowledge Management, *California Management Review*, vol. 40, no. 3 (1998), pp. 265–276.

2. Courtney, H., Kirkland, J., and Vigueire, P., Strategy Under Uncertainty. *Harvard Business Review* (November–December 1997), pp. 67–79.

3. Volberda, H., Toward the Flexible Form: How to Remain Vital in Hypercompetitive Environments. *Organization Science,* vol. 7, no. 3 (1996), pp. 359–374.

4. See Leonard-Barton, Dorothy, and Sensiper, Sylvia, The Role of Tacit Knowledge in Group Innovation, *California Management Review*, vol. 40, no. 3 (1998), pp. 112–131.

5. Barton, Jeff, presentation given at the Empower'98 conference, October, Chicago, IL.

6. The idea of using these three categories for creating a knowledge map was first suggested by Michael Zack. See Developing a Knowledge Strategy, *California Management Review*, vol. 41, no. 3 (Spring 1999), pp. 125–145.

7. Zack, Michael H., Developing a Knowledge Strategy, *California Management Review*, vol. 41, no. 3 (Spring 1999), pp. 125–145.

8. Adapted from Zack, Michael H., Developing a Knowledge Strategy, *California Management Review*, vol. 41, no. 3 (Spring 1999), pp. 125–145, 130.

9. Also see Kim, W. Chan, and Mauborgne, Renée, Strategy, Value Innovation, and the Knowledge Economy, *Sloan Management Review* (Spring 1999), pp. 41–54.

10. Based on Weill, Peter, and Broadbent, Marianne, *Leveraging the New Infrastructure: How Market Leaders Capitalize on Information Technology*, Harvard Business School Press, Boston (1998), p. 41.

11. Fisher, G., Lemke, A., McCall, R., and March, A., Making Argumentation Serve Design, *Human Computer Interaction*, vol. 6 (1991), pp. 393–420.

12. Also see Fisher, G., Lemke, A., McCall, R., Ostwald, J., Reeves, B., and Shipman, F., Supporting Indirect Collaborative Design with Integrated Knowledge Based Design Environments, *Human Computer Interaction*, vol. 7 (1992), pp. 281–314.

CHAPTER 7

1. See Zack, M., Managing Codified Knowledge, *Sloan Management Review* (Summer, 1999) pp. 45–58.

2. See Davenport, T., Jarvenpaa, S., and Beers, M., Improving Knowledge Work Processes, *Sloan Management Review* (Summer 1996), pp. 53–65.

3. Tiwana, A., and Ramesh, B.. Integrating Knowledge on the Web, *IEEE Internet Computing* (May–June 2001), pp. 2–9.

4. Also see Claudio Ciborra and Gerardo's GroupWare and Team Work in New Product Development: The Case of Consumer Goods Multinationals in *GroupWare and Teamwork*, John Wiley & Sons, New York (1996), pp. 121–137.

5. Based on an adaptation from Li Calantone, The Impact of Market Knowledge Competence on New Product Development: Conceptualization and Empirical Examination, *Journal of Marketing*, vol. 62 (October 1998), pp. 13–29.

6. Noted in Davenport, Thomas, and Prusak, Laurence, *Working Knowledge: How Organizations Manage What They Know*, Harvard Business School Press, Boston (1998).

7. Dhar, V., and Stein, R., *Intelligent Decision Support Methods: The Science of Knowledge Work*, Prentice Hall, Upper Saddle River, NJ (1997).

8. For a comprehensive technological treatment of neural networks, see Anderson, J. A., and Rosenfeld, E., *Talking Nets: An Oral History of Neural Networks*, MIT Press, Cambridge, MA (1998).

9. Arbib, M., *The Metaphorical Brain 2: Neural Networks and Beyond*, John Wiley & Sons, New York (1989).

10. Applications in the domain of financial planning are discussed in Beltratti, A., and Margarita, S., *Neural Networks for Economic and Financial Modeling*, International Thomson Computer Press, Boston (1996).

11. Levine, D. S., and Aparicio, M., *Neural Networks for Knowledge Representation and Inference*, Lawrence Erlbaum Associates, Hillsdale, NJ (1994).

12. This example is chosen for its ease of comprehensibility and similarity to Wiig's discussion of urology knowledge in Wiig, Karl, *Knowledge Management Foundations—Thinking about Thinking—How People and Organizations Create, Represent and Use Knowledge*, Schema Press, Arlington, TX (1993).

13. These attributes are identified on the basis of extensive research on knowledge usage and reported in Heijst, Spek, et al., The Lessons Learned Cycle in U. Borghoff and R. Pareschi (Eds.), *Information Technology for Knowledge Management*, Springer-Verlag, Berlin (1998) pp. 17–34.

14. Purvis, R. L., Sambamurthy, V., and Zmud, R. W., The Assimilation of Knowledge Platforms in Organizations: An Empirical Investigation. *Organization Science*, vol. 12, no. 2 (2001), pp. 117–135.

15. Alavi, M., Knowledge Management and Knowledge Management Systems: Conceptual Foundations and Research Issues, *MIS Quarterly*, vol. 25, no. 1 (2001), pp. 107–136.

16. Nonaka, I., and Nishiguchi, T., Social, Technical, and Evolutionary Dimensions of Knowledge Creation, in I. Nonaka and T. Nishiguchi (Eds.), *Knowledge Emergence: Social, Technical, and Evolutionary Dimensions of Knowledge Creation*, Oxford University Press, New York (2001), pp. 286–289.

17. This section is adapted from Tiwana, A., Affinity to Infinity: Peer-to-Peer Knowledge Platforms. *Communications of the ACM*, in press (2002).

18. Rushkoff, D., *Cyberia: Life in the Trenches*, HarperCollins, New York (1994).

19. Granovetter, M., The Strength of Weak Ties, *American Journal of Sociology*, vol. 78 (1973), pp. 1360–1380.

20. Hansen, M., The Search-Transfer Problem: The Role of Weak Ties in Sharing Knowledge across Organizational Subunits, *Administrative Science Quarterly*, vol. 44 (1999), pp. 83–111.

21. The ART (action-reflex-trigger) concept along with the SECI model were proposed in I. Nonaka and J. Reinmoeller, The ART of Knowledge: Systems to Capitalize on Market Knowledge, *European Management Journal*, vol. 16, no. 6 (1998), pp. 673–684. This figure is an extension of those ideas.

CHAPTER 8

1. Teece, D., Capturing Value from Knowledge Assets: The New Economy, Markets for Know-How, and Intangible Assets. *California Management Review*, vol. 40, no. 3 (1998), pp. 55–79.

2. See also Hall, R., and Andriani, P., Analyzing Intangible Resources and Managing Knowledge in a Supply Chain Context, *European Journal of Management*, vol. 16, no. 6 (1998), pp. 685–697, for a first-hand account of intangible asset management.

3. See Porter's work on sustainable competitiveness in Montgomery, Cynthia A., and Porter, Michael E., *Strategy: Seeking and Securing Competitive Advantage*, Harvard Business School Press, Boston (1991).

4. For a critical assessment of its weaknesses, see Zack, Michael H., Developing a Knowledge Strategy, *California Management Review*, vol. 41, no. 3 (Spring 1999), pp. 125–145.

5. See Novins Armstrong, Choosing Your Spots for Knowledge, *Ernst and Young Journal* (1998), pp. 45–52, for a further discussion on this.

6. See Hansen, M., Nohria, N., and Tierney, T., What is Your Strategy for Managing Knowledge? *Harvard Business Review* (March-April 1999), pp. 106–116.

7. Ramesh B., Tiwana A., Supporting Collaborative Process Knowledge Management in New Product Development Teams, *Decision Support Systems*, vol. 27, no. 1–2 (1999) pp. 213-235.

8. Mintzberg, Henry, Quinn, James B., and Voyer, John, *The Strategy Process*, Prentice Hall, Englewood Cliffs, NJ (1995) provides an outline of some of the other strategic issues that might be important in such a situation.

9. Albert, Steven, and Bradley, Keith, *Managing Knowledge: Experts, Agencies and Organizations*, Cambridge University Press, New York (1997).

CHAPTER 9

1. Sethi, R., Smith, D., and Park, W., Cross-Functional Product Development Teams, Creativity, and the Innovativeness of New Consumer Products. *Journal of Marketing Research*, vol. 38 (Feb. 2001), pp. 73–85.

2. Tiwana, A., and McLean, E., Managing the Unexpected. *Communications of the ACM*, in press.

3. Ancona, D. G., and Caldwell, D. F., Bridging the Boundary: External Activity and Performance in Organizational Teams, *Administrative Science Quarterly*, vol. 37, no. 4 (1992), pp. 634–665.

4. Mankin, D., Cohen, S., and Bikson, T., *Teams and Technology* (1st ed.), Harvard Business School Press, Boston (1996).

5. Sackmann, S., Culture and Subcultures: An Analysis of Organizational Knowledge, *Administrative Science Quarterly*, vol. 37, pp. 140–161.

6. Armstrong, C., and Sambamurthy, V., Information Technology Assimilation in Firms: The Influence of Senior Leadership and IT Infrastructures, *Information Systems Research*, vol. 10, no. 4 (1999), pp. 304–327.

7. Ashby, W. R., Requisite Variety and Its Implications for the Control of Complex Systems, in G. Klir (Ed.), *Facets of Systems Science*, Plenum Press, New York (1991), pp. 405–417.

8. Tiwana, A., and McLean, E., Managing the Unexpected, *Communications of the ACM* (2002), in press.

9. Osterloh, M., and Frey, B., Motivation, Knowledge Transfer, and Organizational Forms, *Organization Science,* vol. 11, no. 5 (2000), pp. 538–550.

10. Heiskanen, A., Newman, M., and Similä, J., The Social Dynamics of Software Development, *Accounting, Management and Information Technologies,* vol. 10, no. 1 (2000), pp. 922–959.

11. Keil, M., Cule, P. E., Lyytinen, K., and Schmidt, R.C., A Framework for Identifying Software Project Risks, *Communications of the ACM,* vol. 41, no. 11 (1998), pp. 76–83.

12. Keil, M., Tiwana, A., and Bush, A., Reconciling User and Project Manager Perceptions of IT Project Risk: A Delphi Study, *Information Systems Journal,* vol. 12 (2002), pp. 103–119.

CHAPTER 10

1. Zack, M., Managing Codified Knowledge, *Sloan Management Review* (Summer 1999), pp. 45–58.

2. Cramton, C., The Mutual Knowledge Problem and Its Consequences for Dispersed Collaboration, *Organization Science,* vol. 12, no. 3 (2001), pp. 346–371.

3. Alavi, M., and Tiwana, A., Knowledge Integration in Virtual Teams: The Potential Role of Knowledge Management Systems, *Journal of the American Society for Information Science and Technology,* in press.

4. Tiwana, A., and Ramesh, B., Integrating Knowledge on the Web, *IEEE Internet Computing* (May–June 2001), pp. 32–39.

5. Mankin, D., Cohen, S., and Bikson, T., *Teams and Technology,* 1st ed., Harvard Business School Press, Boston (1996).

6. Keil, M., Tiwana, A., and Bush, A., Reconciling User and Project Manager Perceptions of IT Project Risk: A Delphi Study, *Information Systems Journal,* in press.

7. See Lynch, P., Horton, S., *Web Style Guide: Basic Design Principles for Creating Web Sites,* Yale University Press, New Haven, CT (1999).

CHAPTER 11

1. See also Nonaka, I., and Nishiguchi, T., Social, Technical, and Evolutionary Dimensions of Knowledge Creation, in I. Nonaka and T. Nishiguchi (Eds.), *Knowledge Emergence: Social, Technical, and Evolutionary Dimensions of Knowledge Creation,* Oxford University Press, New York (2001), pp. 286–289.

2. Tiwana, A., and Ramesh, B., Integrating Knowledge on the Web, *IEEE Internet Computing* (May–June 2001), pp. 32–39.

3. Tiwana, A., and Ramesh, B., A Design Knowledge Management System to Support Collaborative Information Product Evolution. *Decision Support Systems,* vol. 31 (2001), pp. 241–262.

4. Tiwana, A., *Web Security*, Butterworth-Heinemann/Digital Press, Boston (1999).

5. Krulwich, B., Automating the Internet: Agents as User Surrogates, *IEEE Internet Computing,* vol. 1, no. 4 (1997), pp. 34–38.

6. Knapik, M., and Johnson, J., *Developing Intelligent Agents for Distributed Systems: Exploring Architecture, Technologies, and Applications*, McGraw-Hill, New York (1998).

7. See also Müller, J. P., *The Design of Intelligent Agents: A Layered Approach*, Springer, Berlin (1996).

8. Nwana, H.S., and Azarmi, N., *Software Agents and Soft Computing: Toward Enhancing Machine Intelligence: Concepts and Applications*, Springer, Berlin (1997).

9. See also Riecken, D., Intelligent Agents. *Communications of the ACM* (July 1994), pp. 18–21.

10. Maes, P., Guttman, R., and Moukas, A., Agents That Buy and Sell, *Communications of the ACM,* vol. 42, no. 3 (1999), pp. 81–91.

CHAPTER 12

1. Bate, P., Khan, R., and Pye, A., Towards a Culturally Sensitive Approach to Organization Structuring: Where Organization Design Meets Organization Development, *Organization Science,* vol. 11, no. 2 (2000), pp. 197–211.

2. Fichman, R., and Moses, S., An Incremental Process for Software Implementation, *Sloan Management Review* (Winter 1999), pp. 39–52.

3. Also see Khurana, A., Managing Complex Production Processes, *Sloan Management Review* (Winter 1999), pp. 85–97.

4. Schilling, M., Toward a General Modular Systems Theory and Its Application to Interfirm Product Modularity, *Academy of Management Review,* vol. 25, no. 2 (2000), pp. 312–334.

5. Orlikowski, W. J., Improvising Organizational Transformation over Time: A Situated Change Perspective, *Information Systems Research,* vol. 7, no. 1 (1996), pp. 63–92.

6. Also see Orlikowski, W. J., Learning from Notes: Organizational Issues in Groupware Implementation, *The Information Society,* vol. 9, no. 2 (1993), pp. 237–250.

7. Sabherwal, R., Hirschheim, R., and Goles, T., The Dynamics of Alignment: Insights from a Punctuated Equilibrium Model, *Organization Science,* vol. 12, no. 2 (2001), pp. 179–197.

8. Gruca, T., Nath, D., and Mehra, A., Exploiting Synergy for Competitive Advantage. *Long Range Planning,* vol. 30, no. 4 (1997), pp. 605–611.

9. Banker, R. D., and Slaughter, S. A., The Moderating Effects of Structure on Volatility and Complexity in Software Enhancement, *Information Systems Research,* vol. 11, no. 3 (2000), pp. 219–240

10. Morel, B., and Ramanujam, R., Through the Looking Glass of Complexity: The Dynamics of Organizations as Adaptive and Evolving Systems, *Organization Science,* vol. 10, no. 3 (1999), pp. 278–293.

11. Stacey, R., Management and the Science of Complexity: If Organizational Life is Nonlinear, Can Business Strategies Prevail? *Research Technology Management* (May–June 1996), pp. 8–10.

12. Tiwana, A., and McLean, E., Managing the Unexpected, *Communications of the ACM* (2002), forthcoming.

CHAPTER 13

1. Anonymous.

2. Nonaka, Ikujiro, and Konno, Noboru, The Concept of "Ba": Building a Foundation for Knowledge Creation, *California Management Review,* vol. 40, no. 3 (1998), pp. 40–55.

3. Earl, M., and Scott, I., What Is a Chief Knowledge Officer, *Sloan Management Review* (Winter 1999), pp. 29–38.

4. Based on an extension of Earl, M., and Scott, I., What Is a Chief Knowledge Officer, *Sloan Management Review,* Winter (1999), pp. 29–38.

5. See Lorange, Peter, *Implementing Strategic Processes: Change, Learning, and Co-operation,* Blackwell Business, Oxford, Cambridge (1993)

6. Also see Von Krogh, George, and Roos, Johan, *Managing Knowledge: Perspectives on Cooperation and Competition,* Sage Publications, Thousand Oaks, CA (1996).

7. Von Krogh, G., Nonaka, I., and Ichijo, K., Develop Knowledge Activists! *European Management Journal,* vol. 15, no. 5 (1997), pp. 475–483.

8. Von Krogh, G., Nonaka, I., and Ichijo, K., Develop Knowledge Activists! *European Management Journal,* vol. 15, no. 5 (1997), p. 477.

9. O'Dell, Carla, and Grayson, C.J., If Only We Knew What We Know: Identification and Transfer of Internal Best Practices, *California Management Review,* vol. 40, no. 3 (1998), pp. 154–173.

10. Hargadon, A., Firms and Knowledge Brokers: Lessons in Pursuing Continuous Innovation, *California Management Review,* vol. 40, no. 3 (1998), pp. 209–227.

11. Davenport, Thomas H., and Prusak, Laurence, *Working Knowledge: How Organizations Manage What They Know,* Harvard Business School Press, Boston (1998).

12. Hansen, M., The Search-Transfer Problem: The Role of Weak Ties in Sharing Knowledge across Organizational Subunits, *Administrative Science Quarterly,* vol. 44 (1999), pp. 83–111.

Chapter 14

1. Originally from Vaguely Right Approach to Sales Force Automation, *Harvard Business Review*, vol. 5 pp. 2, 119–124, as quoted by J. M. Keynes, *Forbes* online edition at *www.forbes.com* (accessed January, 25 1999).

2. See, for example, Barney, J., Types of Competition and the Theory of Strategy: Towards an Integrative Framework, *Academy of Management Review*, vol. 11, no. 4 (1991), pp. 791–800.

3. DeGeus, A., Planning as Learning, *Harvard Business Review* (March-April 1988), pp. 70–74.

4. Stata, Ray, Organizational Learning—the Key to Management Innovation, *Sloan Management Review* (Spring 1989), pp. 63–73.

5. See Leonard-Barton, Dorothy, and Sensiper, Sylvia, The Role of Tacit Knowledge in Group Innovation, *California Management Review*, vol. 40, no. 3 (1998), pp. 112–131

6. Leonard-Barton, D. *Wellsprings of Knowledge*, Harvard Business School Press, Boston, 1995.

7. For a review, see Eisenhardt, K., Agency Theory: An Assessment and Review, *Academy of Management Review,* vol. 14, no. 1 (1989), pp. 57–74.

8. This example is actually a collection of anecdotes across multiple firms reported by Hauser, J., and Gerald, K., Metrics: You Are What You Measure! *European Management Journal*, vol. 16, no. 5 (1998), pp. 517–528.

9. McGrath, R., Failing Forward: Real Options Reasoning and Entrepreneurial Failure, *Academy of Management Review,* vol. 24, no. 1 (1999), pp. 13–30.

10. Kulatilaka, N., and Marks, S., The Strategic Value of Flexibility: Reducing the Ability to Compromise, *American Economic Review* (June 1998) pp. 574–580.

11. Pindyck, R., Irreversible Investment, Capacity Choice, and Value of the Firm, *American Economic Review*, vol. 78, no. 5 (1988), pp. 969–985.

12. Luehrman, T., Strategy as a Portfolio of Real Options, *Harvard Business Review* (September–October 1998), pp. 89–99.

13. Kulatilaka, N., and Perotti, E., Strategic Growth Options, *Management Science*, vol. 44, no. 8 (1998), pp. 1021–1031.

14. Benaroch, M., and Kauffman, R. J., A Case for Using Real Options Pricing Analysis to Evaluate Information Technology Project Investments, *Information Systems Research*, vol. 10, no. 1 (1999), pp. 70–86.

15. Milgrom, P., and Roberts, J., Complementarities and Fit: Strategy, Structure, and Organizational Change in Manufacturing, *Journal of Accounting and Economics*, vol. 19, no. 2/3 (1995), pp. 179–208.

16. Merton, Robert C., Applications of Option-Pricing Theory: Twenty-Five Years Later, *The American Economic Review*, vol. 88, no. 3 (June 1998), pp. 323–349.

17. Hauser, J. and Clausing, D., The House of Quality, *Harvard Business Review*, vol. 3 (1988), pp. 63–73.

18. Bicknell, Barbara A., and Bicknell, Kris D., *The Road Map to Repeatable Success Using QFD to Implement Change*, CRC Press, Boca Raton, FL (1995).

19. Bossert, James L., *QFD, A Practitioner's Approach*, ASQC Quality Press, Milwaukee, WI (1990).

20. Cohen, Lou, *Quality Function Deployment: How to Make QFD Work For You*, Addison-Wesley, Reading, MA (1995).

21. Daetz, Doug, Barnard, William and Norman, Rick, *Customer Integration: The Quality Function Deployment (QFD) Leader's Guide for Decision Making*, John Wiley & Sons, New York (1995).

22. For customer-driven design using QFDs, see Terninko, John, *Step-by-step QFD: Customer-Driven Product Design*, St. Lucie Press, Boca Raton, FL (1997).

23. Zairi, Mohamed, *Quality Function Deployment: A Modern Competitive Tool*, Technical Communications, Letchworth, Hertfordshire, England (1993).

24. Camp, R., *Benchmarking: The Search for Best Practices that Lead to Superior Performance*, ASQC Quality Press, Milwaukee, WI (1989).

25. For an excellent discussion on benchmarking, see O'Dell, Carla S., APQC International Benchmarking Clearinghouse, and American Productivity & Quality Center, *Knowledge Management: Consortium Benchmarking Study: Final Report*, American Productivity & Quality Center, Houston, TX (123 N. Post Oak Lane, 3rd Floor, Houston, TX 77024) (1996) Details of this report are available online at www.apqc.org.

26. O'Dell, Carla, and Grayson, C., If Only We Knew What We Know: Identification and Transfer of Internal Best Practices, *California Management Review*, vol. 40, no. 3 (1998), pp. 154–173.

27. Aristophanes: *Birds*, 414 B.C., as cited at http://www.aphorismsgalore.com. (accessed April 2, 2002).

28. See Drew, S., From Knowledge to Action: The Impact of Benchmarking on Organizational Performance, *Long Range Planning*, vol. 30, no. 3 (1997), pp. 427–441.

29. See Spendolini, M. J., *The Benchmarking Book*, AMACOM, New York (1992).

30. See also Barney, J., Firm Resources and Sustained Competitive Advantage, *Journal of Management*, vol. 17, no. 1 (1991), pp. 99–119.

31. For a detailed discussion, see Kaplan, R., and Norton, D., *Translating Strategy into Action: The Balanced Scorecard*, Harvard Business School Press, Boston (1996).

BIBLIOGRAPHIC
REFERENCES
AND FURTHER READING

Abernathy, W., & Clark, K. (1985). Innovation: Mapping the Winds of Creative Destruction. *Research Policy, 14*(1), 3–22.

Adler, P. S. (2001). Market, Hierarchy, and Trust: The Knowledge Economy and the Future of Capitalism. *Organization Science, 12*(2), 215–234.

Adler, P. S., Goldoftas, B., & Levine, D. I. (1999). Flexibility versus Efficiency? A Case Study of Model Changeovers in the Toyota Production System. *Organization Science, 10*(1), 43–68.

Ahuja, G. (2000). Collaboration Networks, Structural Holes, and Innovation: A Longitudinal Study. *Administrative Science Quarterly, 45*, 425–455.

Alavi, M. (2001). Knowledge Management and Knowledge Management Systems: Conceptual Foundations and Research Issues. *MIS Quarterly, 25*(1), 107–136.

Alavi, M., & Tiwana, A. (2002). Knowledge Integration in Virtual Teams: The Potential Role of Knowledge Management Systems. *Journal of the American Society for Information Science and Technology*, forthcoming.

Alchian, A., & Demsetz, H. (1972). Production Information Costs, and Economic Organization. *The American Economic Review, 62*, 777–795.

Andreu, R., & Ciborra, C. (1996). Organizational Learning and Core Capability Development: The Role of IT. *Strategic Information Systems, 5*, 111–127.

Aoki, M. (1986). Horizontal vs. Vertical Information Structure of the Firm. *American Economic Review, 76*(5), 971–983.

Argote, L., Guruenfeld, D., & Naquin, C. (2001). Group Learning in Organizations. In M. Turner (Ed.), *Groups at Work: Theory and Research* (pp. 369–411). Mahwah, NJ: Lawrence Erlbaum.

Argote, L., & Ingram, P. (2000). Knowledge Transfer: A Basis for Competitive Advantage in Firms. *Organizational Behavior and Human Decision Processes, 82*(1), 150–169.

Arrow, K. (1974). The Limits of Organization. New York: Norton.

Arrow, K. (1994). Methodological Individualism and Social Knowledge. *American Economic Review*, 84(2), 1–9.

Aupperle, K. E. (1996). Spontaneous Organizational Reconfiguration: A Historical Example Based on Xenophon's Anabasis. *Organization Science, 7*(4), 445–460.

Baum, J. A. C., & Ingram, P. (1998). Survival Enhancing Learning in the Manhattan Hotel Industry, 1898–1980. *Management Science, 44*(7), 996–1016.

Berger, P., & Luckmann. (1966). *The Social Construction of Reality: A Treatise in the Sociology of Knowledge*. New York: Anchor Doubleday Books.

Bogner, W. C., & Barr, P. S. (2000). Making Sense in Hypercompetitive Environments: A Cognitive Explanation for the Persistence of High Velocity Competition. *Organization Science, 11*(2), 212–226.

Boisot, M., & Child, J. (1999). Organizations as Adaptive Systems in Complex Environments: The Case of China. *Organization Science, 10*(3), 237–252.

Boland, R. J., Tenkasi, R. V., & Teeni, D. (1994). Designing Information Technology to Support Distributed Cognition. *Organization Science, 5*(3), 456–475.

Bordetsky, A., & Mark, G. (2000). Memory-Based Feedback Controls to Support Groupware Coordination. *Information Systems Research, 11*(4), 366–385.

Brown, C. V., & Magill, S. L. (1998). Reconceptualizing the Context-Design Issue for the Information Systems Function. *Organization Science, 9*(2), 176–194.

Brown, J. S., & Duguid, P. (2001). Knowledge and Organization: A Social-Practice Perspective. *Organization Science, 12*(2), 198–213.

Brown, S. L., & Eisenhardt, K. M. (1997). The Art of Continuous Change: Linking Complexity Theory and Time-Paced Evolution in Relentlessly Shifting Organizations. *Administrative Science Quarterly, 42*(1), 1–34.

Burt, R. (1997). The Contingent Value of Social Capital. *Administrative Science Quarterly, 42*, 339–365.

Ciborra, C. U. (1996). The Platform Organization: Recombining Strategies, Structures, and Surprises. *Organization Science, 7*(2), 103–118.

Cohen, W., & Levinthal, D. (1990). Absorptive Capacity: A New Perspective on Learning and Innovation. *Administrative Science Quarterly, 35*, 128–152.

Conner, K., & Prahalad, C. (1996). A Resource-Based Theory of the Firm: Knowledge versus Opportunism. *Organization Science, 7*(5), 477–501.

Cook, K., & Emerson, R. (1978). Power, Equity, and Commitment in Exchange Networks. *American Sociological Review, 43,* 712–739.

Cool, K. O., Dierickx, I., & Szulanski, G. (1997). Diffusion of Innovations Within Organizations: Electronic Switching in the Bell System, 1971–1982. *Organization Science, 8*(5), 543–559.

Cramton, C. (2001). The Mutual Knowledge Problem and Its Consequences for Dispersed Collaboration. *Organization Science, 12*(3), 346–371.

David, P. (1990). The Dynamo and the Computer: A Historical Perspective on the Modern Productivity Paradox. *American Economic Review, 80*(4).

DeFillippi, R. (2001). Project-Based Learning, Reflective Practices, and Learning Outcomes. *Management Learning, 32*(1), 5–10.

Dijksterhuis, M. S., Van den Bosch, F. A. J., & Volberda, H. W. (1999). Where Do New Organizational Forms Come From? Management Logics as a Source of Coevolution. *Organization Science, 10*(5), 569–582.

DiMaggio, P., & Powell, W. (1983). The Iron Cage Revisited: Institutional Isomorphism and Collective Organizational Rationality in Organizational Fields. *American Sociological Review, 48,* 147–160.

Dixon, N. (2000). *Common Knowledge.* Boston: Harvard Business School Press.

Donaldson, L. (1992). The Weick Stuff—Managing Beyond Games. *Organization Science, 3*(4), 461–466.

Dossantos, B. L., & Peffers, K. (1995). Rewards to Investors in Innovative Information Technology Applications—First Movers and Early Followers in Arms. *Organization Science, 6*(3), 241–259.

Dougherty, D. (1992a). Interpretive Barriers to Successful Product Innovation in Large Firms. *Organization Science, 3*(2), 179–202.

Eisenhardt, K., & Tabrizi, B. (1995). Accelerating Adaptive Processes: Product Innovation in the Global Computing Industry. *Administrative Science Quarterly, 40,* 84–110.

Ekstedt, E., Lundin, R., Soderholm, A., & Wirdenius, H. (1999). *Neo-Industrial Organizing: Renewal by Action and Knowledge Formation in a Project-Intensive Economy.* London: Routledge.

Fahey, L., & Prusak, L. (1998). The Eleven Deadliest Sins of Knowledge Management. *California Management Review, 40*(3), 265–279.

Fairtlough, G. (1994). Organizing for Innovation: Compartments, Competences and Networks. *Long Range Planning, 27*(3), 88–97.

Foss, N. (1996a). Knowledge-Based Theory of the Firm: Some Critical Comments. *Organization Science, 7*(5), 470–476.

Foss, N. (1996b). More Critical Comments on Knowledge-Based Theories of the Firm. *Organization Science, 7*(5), 519–523.

Fransman, M. (1998). Information, Knowledge, Vision, and Theories of the Firm. In G. Dosi & D. Teece & J. Chytry (Eds.), *Technology, Organization, and Competitiveness* (pp. 147–191). London: Oxford University Press.

Galunic, D., & Rodan, S. (1998). Resource Recombinations in the Firm: Knowledge Structures and the Potential for Schumpeterian Innovation. *Strategic Management Journal, 19*, 1193–1201.

Goodman, P., & Darr, E. (1998). Computer-Aided Systems and Communities: Mechanisms for Organizational Learning in Distributed Environments. *MIS Quarterly, 22*(4), 417–440.

Grant, R. (1996a). Prospering in Dynamically-competitive Environments: Organizational Capability as Knowledge Integration. *Organization Science, 7*(4), 375–387.

Grant, R. (1996b). Toward a Knowledge-Based Theory of the Firm. *Strategic Management Journal, 17*(Winter), 109–122.

Gulati, R., & Singh, H. (1998). The Architecture of Cooperation: Managing Coordination costs and Appropriation Concerns in Strategic Alliances. *Administrative Science Quarterly, 43*, 781–814.

Hansen, M. (1999). The Search-Transfer Problem: The Role of Weak Ties in Sharing Knowledge Across Organizational Subunits. *Administrative Science Quarterly, 44*, 83–111.

Hargadon, A., & Sutton, R. (1997). Technology Brokering and Innovation in a Product Development Firm. *Administrative Science Quarterly, 42*, 716–749.

Harmsen, H., Grunert, K., & Bove, K. (2000). Company Competencies as a Network: The Role of Product Development. *Journal of Product Innovation Management, 17*, 194–207.

Hayek, F. (1945). The Use of Knowledge in Society. *American Economic Review, 35*(September), 1–18.

Hedberg, B. L. T., Nystrom, Paul C. and Starbuck, William H. (1976). Camping on Seesaws: Prescriptions for a Self-Designing Organization. *Administrative Science Quarterly, 21*, 41–65.

Helfat, C., & Raubitschek, R. (2000). Product Sequencing: Co-evolution of Knowledge, Capabilities, and Products. *Strategic Management Journal, 21*, 961–979.

Henderson, R., & Clark, K. (1990). Architectural Innovation: The Reconfiguration of Existing Product Technologies and the Failure of Established Firms. *Administrative Science Quarterly, 35*, 9–30.

Hoopes, D., & Postrel, S. (1999). Shared Knowledge, "Glitches," and Product Development Performance. *Strategic Management Journal, 20*, 837–865.

Hurlbert, J., Haines, V., & Beggs, J. (2000). Core Networks and Tie Activation: What Kinds of Routine Networks Allocate Resources in Nonroutine Situations. *American Sociological Review, 65*(August), 598–618.

Iansiti, M., & MacCormack, A. (1997). Developing Products on Internet Time. *Harvard Business Review,* (September-October), 108–117.

Inkpen, A. (1996). Creating Knowledge Through Collaboration. *California Management Review, 39*(1), 123–140.

Jensen, M., & Meckling, W. (1995). Specific and General Knowledge and Organizational Structure. *Journal of Applied Corporate Finance, 8*(2), 4–18.

Johnsson, S. (2000). Innovation in the Networked Firm: The Need to Develop New Types of Interface Competence. In J. Birkinshaw & P. Hagstrom (Eds.), *The Flexible Firm: Capability Management in Networked Organizations* (pp. 106–127). Oxford: Oxford University Press.

Kale, P., Singh, H., & Perlmutter, H. (2000). Learning and Protection of Proprietary Assets in Strategic Alliances: Building Relational Capital. *Strategic Management Journal, 21,* 217–237.

Keil, M., Tiwana, A., & Bush, A. (2001). Reconciling User and Project Manager Perceptions of IT Project Risk: A Delphi Study. *Information Systems Journal,* forthcoming.

Kessler, E. H., & Chakrabarti, A. K. (1996). Innovation Speed: A Conceptual Model of Context, Antecedents, and Outcomes. *Academy of Management Review, 21*(4), 1143–1191.

Kimberly, J. R., & Bouchikhi, H. (1995). The Dynamics of Organizational-Development and Change—How the Past Shapes the Present and Constrains the Future. *Organization Science, 6*(1), 9–18.

Kogut, B. (2000). The Network as Knowledge: Generative Rules and the Emergence of Structure. *Strategic Management Journal, 21,* 405–425.

Kogut, B., & Zander, U. (1993). Knowledge of the Firm and Evolutionary Theory of the Multinational Corporation. *Journal of International Business Studies, 93*(4), 625–645.

Kogut, B., & Zander, U. (1996). What Firms Do? Coordination, Identity, and Learning. *Organization Science, 7*(5), 502–518.

Kuwada, K. (1998). Strategic Learning: The Continuous Side of Discontinuous Strategic Change. *Organization Science, 9*(6), 719–736.

Lado, A., & Zhang, M. (1998). Expert Systems, Knowledge Development and Utilization, and Sustained Competitive Advantage: A Resource-Based Model. *Journal of Management, 24*(4), 489–509.

Lampel, J., Lant, T., & Shamsie, J. (2000). Balancing Act: Learning from Organizing Practices in Cultural Industries. *Organization Science, 11*(3), 263–269.

Leavitt, H. (1996). The Old Days, Hot Groups, and Managers' Lib. *Administrative Science Quarterly, 41,* 288–300.

Levitt, B., & March, J. (1988). Organizational Learning. *Annual Review of Sociology, 14,* 319–340.

Liebeskind, J. P., Oliver, A. L., Zucker, L., & Brewer, M. (1996). Social Networks, Learning, and Flexibility: Sourcing Scientific Knowledge in New Biotechnology Firms. *Organization Science, 7*(4), 428–443.

MacCormack, A., Verganti, R., & Iansiti, M. (2001). Developing Products on Internet Time: The Anatomy of a Flexible Development Process. *Management Science, 47*(1), 133–150.

March, J. (1991). Exploration and Exploitation in Organizational Learning. *Organization Science, 2*(1), 71–87.

Matusik, S., & Hill, C. (1998). The Utilization of Contingent Work, Knowledge Creation, and Competitive Advantage. *Academy of Management Review, 23*(4), 680–697.

McEvily, S., Das, S., & McNabe, K. (2000). Avoiding Competence Substitution through Knowledge Sharing. *Academy of Management Review, 25*(2), 294–311.

Milgrom, P., & Roberts, J. (1990). The Economics of Modern Manufacturing. *American Economic Review, 80,* 511–528.

Miner, A., Bassoff, P., & Moorman, C. (2001). Organizational Improvisation and Learning: A Field Study. *Administrative Science Quarterly, 46,* 304–337.

Miner, A., & Mezias, S. (1996). Ugly Duckling No More: Pasts and Futures of Organizational Learning Research. *Organization Science, 7*(1), 88–99.

Monge, P. R., Cozzens, M. D., & Contractor, N. S. (1992). Communication and Motivational Predictors of the Dynamics of Organizational Innovation. *Organization Science, 3*(2), 250–274.

Morgan, S., & Sorenson, A. (1999). Theory, Measurement, and Specification Issues in Models of Network Effects on Learning. *American Sociological Review, 64*(October), 694–700.

Murnighan, J., & Conlon, E. (1991). The Dynamics of Intense Work Groups: A Study of British String Quartets. *Administrative Science Quarterly, 36,* 165–186.

Nelson, R., & Winter, S. (1977). In Search of a Useful Theory of Innovation. *Research Policy, 6*(1), 36–77.

Nonaka, I. (1994). A Dynamic Theory of Organizational Knowledge Creation. *Organization Science, 5,* 14–37.

Nonaka, I., & Nishiguchi, T. (2001). Social, Technical, and Evolutionary Dimensions of Knowledge Creation. In I. Nonaka & T. Nishiguchi (Eds.), *Knowledge Emergence: Social, Technical, and Evolutionary Dimensions of Knowledge Creation* (pp. 286–289). New York: Oxford University Press.

Osterloh, M., & Frey, B. S. (2000). Motivation, Knowledge Transfer, and Organizational Forms. *Organization Science, 11*(5), 538–550.

Penrose, E. (1955). Limits to the Growth and Size of Firms. *American Economic Review, 45*(2), 531–543.

Pfeffer, J., & Sutton, R. (1999). Knowing "What" to Do is Not Enough: Turning Knowledge into Action. *California Management Review, 42*(1), 83–108.

Pisano, G. P. (1990). The R&D Boundaries of the Firm: An Empirical Analysis. *Administrative Science Quarterly, 35*, 153–176.

Porac, J. F., Thomas, H., Wilson, F., Paton, D., & Kanfer, A. (1995). Rivalry and the Industry Model of Scottish Knitwear Producers. *Administrative Science Quarterly, 40*(2), 203–227.

Powell, W., Koput, K., & Smith-Doerr, L. (1996). Interorganizational Collaboration and the Locus of Innovation: Networks of Learning in Biotechnology. *Administrative Science Quarterly, 41*, 116–145.

Purvis, R. L., Sambamurthy, V., & Zmud, R. W. (2001). The Assimilation of Knowledge Platforms in Organizations: An Empirical Investigation. *Organization Science, 12*(2), 117–135.

Raelin, J. A. (1997). A Model of Work-Based Learning. *Organization Science, 8*(6), 563–578.

Ramesh, B., & Tiwana, A. (1999). Supporting Collaborative Process Knowledge Management in New Product Development Teams. *Decision Support Systems, 27*(1–2), 213–235.

Robey, D., Boudreau, M.-C., & Rose, G. M. (2000). Information Technology and Organizational Learning: A Review and Assessment of Research. *Accounting, Management and Information Technologies, 10*(2).

Sackmann, S. (1992). Culture and Subcultures: An Analysis of Organizational Knowledge. *Administrative Science Quarterly, 37*, 140–161.

Sambamurthy, V., & Zmud, R. W. (2000). Research Commentary: The Organizing Logic for an Enterprise's IT Activities in the Digital Era—A Prognosis of Practice and a Call for Research. *Information Systems Research, 11*(2), 105–114.

Sanchez, R., & Mahoney, J. (1996). Modularity, Flexibility, and Knowledge Management in Product Organization and Design. *Strategic Management Journal, 17*(1), 63–76.

Saviotti, P. (1998). On the Dynamics of Appropriability of Tacit and of Codified Knowledge. *Research Policy, 26*, 843–856.

Simon, H. (1978). Rationality as Process and as Product of Thought. *American Economic Review, 68*(2), 1–16.

Simon, H. (1991). Bounded Rationality and Organizational Learning. *Organization Science, 2*(1), 125–134.

Simonin, B. (1999). Ambiguity and the Process of Knowledge Transfer in Strategic Alliances. *Strategic Management Journal, 20*, 595–623.

Skvoretz, J., & Willer, D. (1993). Exclusion and Power: A Test of Four Theories of Power in Exchange Networks. *American Sociological Review, 58*, 801–818.

Smith, T., & Stevens, G. (1999). The Architectures of Small Networks: Strong Interactions and Dynamic Organization in Small Social Systems. *American Sociological Review, 64*(June), 403–420.

Star, S. L., & Ruhleder, K. (1996). Steps Toward an Ecology of Infrastructure: Design and Access for Large Information Spaces. *Information Systems Research, 7*(1), 111–134.

Starbuck, W. (1992). Learning by Knowledge-Intensive Firms. *The Journal of Management Studies, 29*, 713–740.

Stein, E. W., & Zwass, V. (1995). Actualizing Organizational Memory with Information Systems. *Information Systems Research, 6*(2), 85–117.

Swanson, E. B., & Ramiller, N. C. (1997). The Organizing Vision in Information Systems Innovation. *Organization Science, 8*(5), 458–474.

Teece, D. (1998). Capturing Value from Knowledge Assets: The New Economy, Markets for Know-How, and Intangible Assets. *California Management Review, 40*(3), 55–79.

Tiwana, A. (1998). Interdependency Factors Influencing the World Wide Web as a Channel of Interactive Marketing. *Journal of Retailing and Consumer Services, 5*(4), 245–253.

Tiwana, A. (1999a). *The Contribution of Process Knowledge Management on Efficacy of Collaboration Within Information Product Development Teams.* Paper presented at the 2nd Annual Conference of the Southern Association for Information Systems, Atlanta, Georgia.

Tiwana, A. (1999b). Custom KM: Implementing the Right Knowledge Management Strategy for Your Organization. *Cutter IT Journal (formerly American Programmer)* Reprinted in Yourdon, Ed, *Knowledge Management Strategies,* Cutter Consortium, Arlington, MA, 2000, pp. 11–20, *12*(11), 6–14.

Tiwana, A. (2000a). Knowledge-Enabled Customer Relationship Management: Beyond "Word of Mouse". *Cutter IT Journal (formerly American Programmer), 13*(10), 17–25.

Tiwana, A. (2000b). Managing Micro- and Macro-Level Design Process Knowledge Across Emergent Internet Information System Families. In R. Rajkumar (Ed.), *Industrial Knowledge Management—A Micro Level Approach* (pp. 213–231). London: Springer U.K.

Tiwana, A. (2001). *Knowledge Management: E-Business and Customer Relationship Management Applications.* Upper Saddle River, NJ: Prentice Hall.

Tiwana, A. (2002). Affinity to Infinity: Peer-to-Peer Knowledge Platforms. *Communications of the ACM,* forthcoming.

Tiwana, A., & Bush, A. (2000). *Peer-to-Peer Valuation as a Mechanism for Reinforcing Active Learning in Virtual Communities: An Application of Social Exchange Theory.* Paper presented at the HICSS-33, Maui, Hawaii.

Tiwana, A., & Bush, A. (2001). A Social Exchange Architecture for Distributed Web Communities. *Journal of Knowledge Management, 5*(3), 242–248.

Tiwana, A., & McLean, E. R. (2001a). Effects of Knowledge Integration On Execution Success in Zero-History Software Project Teams. *Emory University (Goizueta Business School) Working Paper.*

Tiwana, A., & McLean, E. R. (2001b). Expertise, Integration, and Responsive Creativity in Innovation-Intensive Software Projects. *Emory University (Goizueta Business School) Working Paper.*

Tiwana, A., & McLean, E. R. (2001c). In Search of Alchemy: Knowledge Integration in Temporary Organizations. *Emory University (Goizueta Business School) Working Paper.*

Tiwana, A., & McLean, E. R. (2001d). Managing the Unexpected. *Communications of the ACM* (forthcoming).

Tiwana, A., & McLean , E. R. (2001e). *Recombinant Knowledge Structures and Model of E-Business Innovation: An Empirical Investigation.* Paper presented at the 9th European Conference on Information Systems, Bled, Slovenia.

Tiwana, A., & McLean , E. R. (2001f). *Towards a Theory of Architectural Knowledge Integration Capability: A Test of an Empirical Model in E-business Project Teams.* Paper presented at the 9th European Conference on Information Systems, Bled, Slovenia.

Tiwana, A., & Ramesh, B. (1999). *Toward a Composite Metric for Electronic Commerce ROI: An Extension of the Balanced Scorecard.* Paper presented at the International Conference of Electronic Commerce Measurement, Singapore, Singapore.

Tiwana, A., & Ramesh, B. (2000). *From Intuition to Institution: Supporting Collaborative Diagnoses in Telemedicine Teams.* Paper presented at the HICSS-33, Maui, Hawaii.

Tiwana, A., & Ramesh, B. (2001a). A Design Knowledge Management System to Support Collaborative Information Product Evolution. *Decision Support Systems, 31,* 241–262.

Tiwana, A., & Ramesh, B. (2001b). Integrating Knowledge on the Web. *IEEE Internet Computing,* (May-June), 32–39.

Tsoukas, H. (1996). The Firm as a Distributed Knowledge System: A Constructionist Approach. *Strategic Management Journal, 17*(Winter Special Issue), 11–25.

Tushman, M., & Anderson, P. (1986). Technological Discontinuities and Organizational Environments. *Administrative Science Quarterly, 31,* 439–465.

Van den Bosch, F., Volberda, H., & Boer, M. (1999). Coevolution of Firm Absorptive Capacity and Knowledge Environment: Organizational Forms and Combinative Capabilities. *Organization Science, 10*(5), 551–568.

Varian, H. (1980). Differential Prices and Efficiency. *American Economic Review,* (70), 651–659.

Volberda, H. (1996). Toward the Flexible Form: How to Remain Vital in Hypercompetitive Environments. *Organization Science, 7*(3), 359–374.

von Hippel, E. (1990). Task Partitioning: An Innovation Process Variable. *Research Policy,* 407–418.

Weick, K. E. (1993). The Collapse of Sense Making in Organizations: The Mann Gulch Disaster. *Administrative Science Quarterly, 38*(4), 628–652.

Weick, K. E. (1998). Improvisation as a Mindset for Organizational Analysis. *Organization Science, 9*(5), 543–555.

Weick, K. E., & Westley, F. (1996). Organizational Learning: Affirming an Oxymoron. In S. F. Clegg & C. Hardy & W. R. Nord (Eds.), *The Handbook of Organization Studies*.: Sage Publications.

West, J., & Dedrick, J. (2000). Innovation and Control in Standards Architectures: The Rise and Fall of Japan's PC-98. *Information Systems Research, 11*(2), 197–216.

Winter, S. (2000). The Satisficing Principle in Capability Learning. *Strategic Management Journal, 21*, 981–996.

Yli-Renko, H., Autio, E., & Sapienza, H. (2001). Social Capital, Knowledge Acquisition, and Knowledge Exploitation in Technology-Based Firms. *Strategic Management Journal, 22*, 587–613.

Zack, M. H. (1999). Developing a Knowledge Strategy. *California Management Review, 41*(3), 125–145.

Zenger, T. R., & Hesterly, W. S. (1997). The Disaggregation of Corporations: Selective Intervention, High-Powered Incentives, and Molecular Units. *Organization Science, 8*(3), 209–222.

Zmud, R. W. (1984). An Examination of "Push-Pull" Theory Applied to Process Innovation in Knowledge Work. *Management Science, 30*(6), 727–738.

GLOSSARY

This section describes common terms relating to knowledge, knowledge management, collaborative work, strategy, methodologies, organizational learning, networks and process management, that have been used throughout the book. Other terms that are explained at depth where they occur, are not included here.

Wrappers Scripts and connection modules that allow personal computers and modern networks to access legacy data.

Strategic positions These represent the knowledge niches on which a company must focus its knowledge management efforts. Based on how the audit process populates the Strategic Capability Framework (see Chapter 8), you can identify promising processes that stand to gain the most through knowledge management.

Synergy The ability of the system to produce a result that is greater than the sum of individual components. In the context of knowledge management, synergy refers to the ability of the knowledge management system to allow different groups of users, representing different functional departments, to produce results exceeding those that they would produce working without the support of such a system.

Analytical Applications Analytical Applications help analyze information. These include fishbone diagrams, cash cow analysis using BCG grids, mind maps, critical path analysis tools, decision trees, force-field analysis, Strengths, Weaknesses, Opportunities, system thinking tools, etc.

Artificial Intelligence   The use of human models for cognition and perception to create computer systems to solve human-like problems.

Business Process Reengineering   BPR focuses on detecting the core processes which make up the business and then reassembling them more efficiently in a way which is free of functional divides and which reduces complexity by reengineering operational and customer directed activities into processes.

Business Value Orientation   Determines where a company principally derives value from.

Chief Knowledge Officer (CKO)   Along with other senior management members, the chief knowledge officer is responsible for creating the vision of what is possible and designing the framework for realizing the results.

Communication Processes   Information Technology and cultural processes that enable people to share information in an efficient and effective manner. Remember that the term *process* does not describe just the technical process underlying message delivery, but the whole act of communicating. If I were to describe it as a purely technical process, I would be straying too far away from knowledge management, where the human and cultural side is as important, if not more, than the technological side.

Content Directors   Executive management levels that design, set and execute strategies on issues for which they provide focus regarding the process of knowledge sharing.

Content Organizers   The organizational unit (usually the corporate office of a company) that coordinates, controls and communicates knowledge by combining and connecting strategy to operations.

Control Processes   Control Processes enable a company to create and maintain stability within business performance and legal and financial systems.

Coordination Processes   Coordination Processes are activities that link strategic and operational processes in an efficient, effective, financially acceptable, timely, and value-adding manner.

Core Competencies   A company's unique combination of available knowledge capabilities that represent its key strength. Core Competencies reflect key strengths of companies to such an extent that they allow the company to sustain its competitive advantage in order to add value to customers. Core competencies are often considered semi-permanent in nature i.e. sustainable over a period of time.

Corporate Processes   Corporate processes are coordination, control and communication processes that allow companies to link strategic processes to operational processes and vice versa.

Customer Capital   The value of an organization's relationships with its customers.

Data Mining   A technique to analyze data in very large databases with the goal of revealing trends and patterns.

Data   Raw transactional representations and outputs without inherent meaning.

Expertise   The ability to take information and apply it to a particular situation.

Firewall   Device that protects a private network from the public domain. A computer that monitors traffic between an Internet site and the Internet. It's designed to prevent unauthorized people from tampering with a computer system thereby increasing security.

Functional Alignment   Remember that companies are not in the business of building knowledge but in the business of creating value, functional disciplines are increasingly redesigned to become more business- and process-oriented. By ensuring functional alignment, functional expertise has a clearer and more direct impact on strategic and operational performance.

Genetic Computing   Genetic Computing uses DNA-strings to perform computations. Its four basic materials adenine, guanine, thymine and cytosine are combined to form strings of information. A closely related concept is that of genetic algorithms. The strength of this emerging technique for arriving at the best fitting solutions comes from the notion of Darwin's theory of natural selection: A test tube of one billion DNA strings has a capacity of one billion parallel computations per second.

Human Capital   The knowledge, skills, and competencies of people in an organization.

Integrated Knowledge Environment   Information technology that supports the flow of knowledge throughout the enterprise.

Intellectual Capital   Intangibles such as information, knowledge, and skills that can be leveraged by an organization to produce an asset of equal or greater importance than land, labor and capital.

Knowledge Integration   Synthesizing the tacit knowledge of different individuals to create new group-level knowledge. Integration involves minimally essential knowledge transfer, and is therefore more efficient.

Knowledge Repository   A collection of information or knowledge, usually centered on specific issues of interest to the company and accessible through technologies such as Intranets and browsers.

Knowledge Segment   Everything a company's professionals and systems know about a specific domain.

Knowledge   A fluid mix of framed experience, values, contextual information, expert insight and grounded intuition that provides an environment and framework for evaluating and incorporating new experiences and information. It originates and is applied in the minds of knowers. In organizations, it often becomes embedded not only in documents or repositories but also in organizational routines, processes, practices, and norms. See Chapters 2 and 3.

Knowledge Management   Management of organizational knowledge for creating business value and generating a competitive advantage.

Lessons Learned and Best Practices   Data bases in which examples of previous experiences are stored, the reasons why they worked best or failed miserably and the lessons that were learned from them.

Operational Processes   Logically-grouped support activities that, together, form a core operational process.

Process Team   Process Team is a group of professionals responsible for a company's operational, corporate and/or strategic processes.

RDI Methodology   A results driven incremental methodology suited for complex projects such as knowledge management system deployment. The key idea is that each phase incrementally builds upon a learning experience gained from the preceding phase.

Reflecting The act of playing back and thinking about the lessons learned each day. This is also called action replay or rationale reconstruction, in some software engineering circles

Sensing   The ability to observe and perceive without passing judgment.

Smart Networks   Smart Networks combine Hard and Soft Networks, as described elsewhere in this glossary. This resulting in effective linking of smart business strategies to every employee throughout the company. Smart Organizations are entirely process- and team-based and use knowledge as their primary asset and are characterized by such Smart Networks.

Soft Networks   The process of establishing a community of practice and collating a number of people who can be called upon when expertise is required.

Strategic Holding   A corporate office acts as a strategic holding when its core purpose is not to direct operational processes but to prepare, design and implement a long-term business strategy.

Strategic Knowledge Management   Strategic Knowledge Management links the building of a company's knowledge to a business strategy.

Structural Capital   The processes, structures and systems that a firm owns less its people. Skandia reported its structural capital in its 1996 annual report intellectual asset supplement.

Team Synergy   The process of working together as a team that creates synergy by combining each member's unique knowledge. The combination is capable of producing results exceeding those possible if each member's capabilities and productivity measures were summed up.

The Process Organization   A process organization is characterized by its horizontal flow of information and communication and its decentralized authority over decisions.

Virtual Competence Center   A virtual team of people organized around a specific knowledge domain.

INDEX

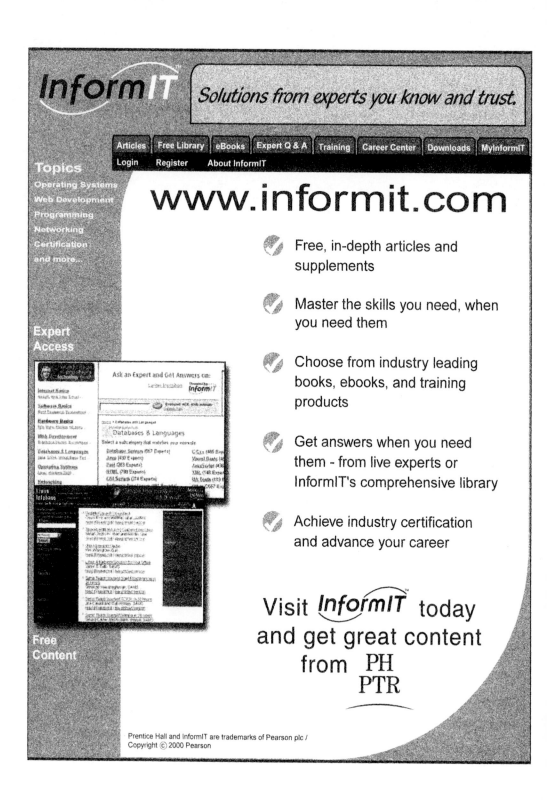

LICENSE AGREEMENT AND LIMITED WARRANTY

READ THE FOLLOWING TERMS AND CONDITIONS CAREFULLY BEFORE OPEN-ING THIS DISK PACKAGE. THIS LEGAL DOCUMENT IS AN AGREEMENT BETWEEN YOU AND PRENTICE-HALL, INC. (THE "COMPANY"). BY OPENING THIS SEALED DISK PACKAGE, YOU ARE AGREEING TO BE BOUND BY THESE TERMS AND CONDITIONS. IF YOU DO NOT AGREE WITH THESE TERMS AND CONDITIONS, DO NOT OPEN THE DISK PACKAGE. PROMPTLY RETURN THE UNOPENED DISK PACKAGE AND ALL ACCOMPANYING ITEMS TO THE PLACE YOU OBTAINED THEM FOR A FULL REFUND OF ANY SUMS YOU HAVE PAID.

1. **GRANT OF LICENSE:** In consideration of your payment of the license fee, which is part of the price you paid for this product, and your agreement to abide by the terms and conditions of this Agreement, the Company grants to you a nonexclusive right to use and display the copy of the enclosed software program (hereinafter the "SOFTWARE") on a single computer (i.e., with a single CPU) at a single location so long as you comply with the terms of this Agreement. The Company reserves all rights not expressly granted to you under this Agreement.

2. **OWNERSHIP OF SOFTWARE:** You own only the magnetic or physical media (the enclosed disks) on which the SOFTWARE is recorded or fixed, but the Company retains all the rights, title, and ownership to the SOFTWARE recorded on the original disk copy(ies) and all subsequent copies of the SOFTWARE, regardless of the form or media on which the original or other copies may exist. This license is not a sale of the original SOFTWARE or any copy to you.

3. **COPY RESTRICTIONS:** This SOFTWARE and the accompanying printed materials and user manual (the "Documentation") are the subject of copyright. You may not copy the Documentation or the SOFTWARE, except that you may make a single copy of the SOFTWARE for backup or archival purposes only. You may be held legally responsible for any copying or copyright infringement which is caused or encouraged by your failure to abide by the terms of this restriction.

4. **USE RESTRICTIONS:** You may not network the SOFTWARE or otherwise use it on more than one computer or computer terminal at the same time. You may physically transfer the SOFT-WARE from one computer to another provided that the SOFTWARE is used on only one computer at a time. You may not distribute copies of the SOFTWARE or Documentation to others. You may not reverse engineer, disassemble, decompile, modify, adapt, translate, or create derivative works based on the SOFTWARE or the Documentation without the prior written consent of the Company.

5. **TRANSFER RESTRICTIONS:** The enclosed SOFTWARE is licensed only to you and may not be transferred to any one else without the prior written consent of the Company. Any unauthorized transfer of the SOFTWARE shall result in the immediate termination of this Agreement.

6. **TERMINATION:** This license is effective until terminated. This license will terminate auto-matically without notice from the Company and become null and void if you fail to comply with any provisions or limitations of this license. Upon termination, you shall destroy the Documentation and all copies of the SOFTWARE. All provisions of this Agreement as to warranties, limitation of liability, remedies or damages, and our ownership rights shall survive termination.

7. **MISCELLANEOUS:** This Agreement shall be construed in accordance with the laws of the United States of America and the State of New York and shall benefit the Company, its affiliates, and assignees.

8. **LIMITED WARRANTY AND DISCLAIMER OF WARRANTY:** The Company warrants that the SOFTWARE, when properly used in accordance with the Documentation, will operate in sub-stantial conformity with the description of the SOFTWARE set forth in the Documentation. The

Company does not warrant that the SOFTWARE will meet your requirements or that the operation of the SOFTWARE will be uninterrupted or error-free. The Company warrants that the media on which the SOFTWARE is delivered shall be free from defects in materials and workmanship under normal use for a period of thirty (30) days from the date of your purchase. Your only remedy and the Company's only obligation under these limited warranties is, at the Company's option, return of the warranted item for a refund of any amounts paid by you or replacement of the item. Any replacement of SOFTWARE or media under the warranties shall not extend the original warranty period. The limited warranty set forth above shall not apply to any SOFTWARE which the Company determines in good faith has been subject to misuse, neglect, improper installation, repair, alteration, or damage by you. EXCEPT FOR THE EXPRESSED WARRANTIES SET FORTH ABOVE, THE COMPANY DISCLAIMS ALL WARRANTIES, EXPRESS OR IMPLIED, INCLUDING WITHOUT LIMITATION, THE IMPLIED WARRANTIES OF MERCHANTABILITY AND FITNESS FOR A PARTICULAR PURPOSE. EXCEPT FOR THE EXPRESS WARRANTY SET FORTH ABOVE, THE COMPANY DOES NOT WARRANT, GUARANTEE, OR MAKE ANY REPRESENTATION REGARDING THE USE OR THE RESULTS OF THE USE OF THE SOFTWARE IN TERMS OF ITS COR-RECTNESS, ACCURACY, RELIABILITY, CURRENTNESS, OR OTHERWISE.

IN NO EVENT, SHALL THE COMPANY OR ITS EMPLOYEES, AGENTS, SUPPLIERS, OR CONTRACTORS BE LIABLE FOR ANY INCIDENTAL, INDIRECT, SPECIAL, OR CON-SEQUENTIAL DAMAGES ARISING OUT OF OR IN CONNECTION WITH THE LICENSE GRANTED UNDER THIS AGREEMENT, OR FOR LOSS OF USE, LOSS OF DATA, LOSS OF INCOME OR PROFIT, OR OTHER LOSSES, SUSTAINED AS A RESULT OF INJURY TO ANY PERSON, OR LOSS OF OR DAMAGE TO PROPERTY, OR CLAIMS OF THIRD PARTIES, EVEN IF THE COMPANY OR AN AUTHORIZED REPRESENTATIVE OF THE COMPANY HAS BEEN ADVISED OF THE POSSIBILITY OF SUCH DAMAGES. IN NO EVENT SHALL LIABILITY OF THE COMPANY FOR DAMAGES WITH RESPECT TO THE SOFTWARE EXCEED THE AMOUNTS ACTUALLY PAID BY YOU, IF ANY, FOR THE SOFTWARE.

SOME JURISDICTIONS DO NOT ALLOW THE LIMITATION OF IMPLIED WAR-RANTIES OR LIABILITY FOR INCIDENTAL, INDIRECT, SPECIAL, OR CONSEQUENTIAL DAMAGES, SO THE ABOVE LIMITATIONS MAY NOT ALWAYS APPLY. THE WARRANTIES IN THIS AGREEMENT GIVE YOU SPECIFIC LEGAL RIGHTS AND YOU MAY ALSO HAVE OTHER RIGHTS WHICH VARY IN ACCORDANCE WITH LOCAL LAW.

ACKNOWLEDGMENT

YOU ACKNOWLEDGE THAT YOU HAVE READ THIS AGREEMENT, UNDERSTAND IT, AND AGREE TO BE BOUND BY ITS TERMS AND CONDITIONS. YOU ALSO AGREE THAT THIS AGREEMENT IS THE COMPLETE AND EXCLUSIVE STATEMENT OF THE AGREEMENT BETWEEN YOU AND THE COMPANY AND SUPERSEDES ALL PROPOSALS OR PRIOR AGREEMENTS, ORAL, OR WRITTEN, AND ANY OTHER COMMUNICATIONS BETWEEN YOU AND THE COMPANY OR ANY REPRESENTATIVE OF THE COMPANY RELATING TO THE SUBJECT MATTER OF THIS AGREEMENT.

Should you have any questions concerning this Agreement or if you wish to contact the Company for any reason, please contact in writing at the address below.

Robin Short
Prentice Hall PTR
One Lake Street
Upper Saddle River, New Jersey 07458

ABOUT THE CD-ROM

The CD-ROM included with *The Knowledge Management Toolkit, Second Edition,* contains the following (restricted versions unless otherwise noted):

The Knowledge Management Toolkit (full version)
> Contains an interactive 10-step roadmap, customizable electronic versions of all KM evaluation forms in PDF and Word for Windows format. Also included is a 30 page KM assessment manual (a digital version of appendix A)

Digital appendices (including the KM Toolkit manual)

Electronic figures
> All figures from the book in electronic format (for royalty-free classroom use with citation; written permission is needed for reproduction in print or electronic form for any other purpose including but not limited to books, Websites, CDs, and documents)

KM platform deployment exemplar
> Fully functional KM platform deployment exemplar with an accompanying Urban Motors case study.

Complete bibliography in electronic form

Software Tools (See Appendix C for details on each of the tools listed below)
AlphaCONNECT Suite
Austin Hayne
BrainForest for the PalmPilot
Ferret Software Suite
HyperWave Information Server
Intranetics 2.0 Demo version
KeyFlow
Mindmanager Personal (full version)
MIS-AG DeltaMiner suite
Opentext LiveLink Intranet
Performance Now
SmartDraw
APQC Process Classification Framework
Ygnius mindmapping software by Gael

The CD-ROM can be used on Microsoft Windows® 95/98/NT/ME/XP®

License Agreement

Use of the software accompanying *The Knowledge Management Toolkit, Second Edition,* is subject to the terms of the License Agreement and Limited Warranty, found on the previous two pages.

Technical Support
Prentice Hall does not offer technical support for any of the programs on the CD-ROM. However, if the CD-ROM is damaged, you may obtain a replacement copy by sending an email that describes the problem to: disc_exchange@prenhall.com.